A·N·N·U·A·L EDITIONS

Criminal Justice

Twenty-Seventh Edition

03/04

EDITOR

Joseph L. Victor

Mercy College, Dobbs Ferry

Joseph L. Victor is professor and chairman of the Department of Law, Criminal Justice, and Safety Administration at Mercy College. Professor Victor has extensive field experience in criminal justice agencies, counseling, and administering human service programs. He earned his B.A. and M.A. at Seton Hall University and his Doctorate of Education at Fairleigh Dickinson University.

Joanne Naughton

Mercy College, Dobbs Ferry

Joanne Naughton is assistant professor of Criminal Justice at Mercy College. Professor Naughton is a former member of the New York City Police Department, where she encountered most aspects of police work as a police officer, detective, sergeant, and lieutenant. She is also a former staff attorney with The Legal Aid Society. She received her B.A. and J.D. at Fordham University.

McGraw-Hill/Dushkin

530 Old Whitfield Street, Guilford, Connecticut 06437

Visit us on the Internet
http://www.dushkin.com

Credits

1. **Crime and Justice in America**
   Unit photo—Courtesy of McGraw-Hill/Dushkin.
2. **Victimology**
   Unit photo—United Nations photo.
3. **The Police**
   Unit photo—United Nations photo.
4. **The Judicial System**
   Unit photo—© 2003 by PhotoDisc, Inc.
5. **Juvenile Justice**
   Unit photo—© 2003 by Cleo Freelance Photography.
6. **Punishment and Corrections**
   Unit photo—© 2003 by Cleo Freelance Photography.

Copyright

Cataloging in Publication Data
Main entry under title: Annual Editions: Criminal Justice. 2003/2004.
1. Criminal Justice—Periodicals. I. Victor, Joseph L. 2. Joanne Naughton, *comp*. II. Title: Criminal Justice.
ISBN 0–07–283827–2   658'.05   ISSN 0272–3816

Twenty-Seventh Edition

Cover image © 2003 PhotoDisc, Inc.
Printed in the United States of America   4567890BAHBAH54   Printed on Recycled Paper

Editors/Advisory Board

Members of the Advisory Board are instrumental in the final selection of articles for each edition of ANNUAL EDITIONS. Their review of articles for content, level, currentness, and appropriateness provides critical direction to the editor and staff. We think that you will find their careful consideration well reflected in this volume.

EDITORS

Joseph L. Victor
Mercy College

Joanne Naughton
Mercy College

ADVISORY BOARD

Harry N. Babb
SUNY at Farmingdale

Peter D. Chimbos
Brescia College - Univ. of Western Ontario

Bernard Cohen
Queens College

Dick DeLung
Wayland Baptist University

Joel Fort
California State University - Sacramento

Arnett Gaston
University of Maryland

Sarah E. Goodman
Mira Costa College

Helen E. Taylor Greene
Old Dominion University

Kenneth Haas
University of Delaware

Raymond A. Helgemoe
University of New Hampshire

Michael K. Hooper
Sonoma State University

Paul Lang, Jr.
Northern Michigan University

Michael A. Langer
Loyola University - Water Tower Campus

Matthew C. Leone
University of Nevada

Celia Lo
University of Alabama

Robert J. McCormack
College of New Jersey

Bonnie O. Neher
Harrisburg Area Community College

George E. Rush
California State University, Long Beach

Leslie Samuelson
University of Saskatchewan

Linda Stabile
Prince George's Community College

David R. Struckhoff
Loyola University - Water Tower Campus

Kenneth Venters
University of Tennessee

Staff

Jeffrey L. Hahn, Vice President/Publisher

EDITORIAL STAFF

Theodore Knight, Ph.D., Managing Editor
Roberta Monaco, Managing Developmental Editor
Dorothy Fink, Associate Developmental Editor
Addie Raucci, Senior Administrative Editor
Robin Zarnetske, Permissions Editor
Marie Lazauskas, Permissions Assistant
Lisa Holmes-Doebrick, Senior Program Coordinator

TECHNOLOGY STAFF

Richard Tietjen, Senior Publishing Technologist
Jonathan Stowe, Executive Director of eContent
Marcuss Oslander, Sponsoring Editor of eContent
Christopher Santos, Senior eContent Developer
Janice Ward, Software Support Analyst
Angela Mule, eContent Developer
Michael McConnel, eContent Developer
Ciro Parente, Editorial Assistant
Joe Offredi, Technology Developmental Editor

PRODUCTION STAFF

Brenda S. Filley, Director of Production
Charles Vitelli, Designer
Mike Campbell, Production Coordinator
Eldis Lima, Graphics
Juliana Arbo, Typesetting Supervisor
Julie Marsh, Project Editor
Jocelyn Proto, Typesetter
Cynthia Powers, Typesetter

To the Reader

In publishing ANNUAL EDITIONS we recognize the enormous role played by the magazines, newspapers, and journals of the public press in providing current, first-rate educational information in a broad spectrum of interest areas. Many of these articles are appropriate for students, researchers, and professionals seeking accurate, current material to help bridge the gap between principles and theories and the real world. These articles, however, become more useful for study when those of lasting value are carefully collected, organized, indexed, and reproduced in a low-cost format, which provides easy and permanent access when the material is needed. That is the role played by ANNUAL EDITIONS.

During the 1970s, criminal justice emerged as an appealing, vital, and unique academic discipline. It emphasizes the professional development of students who plan careers in the field and attracts those who want to know more about a complex social problem and how this country deals with it. Criminal justice incorporates a vast range of knowledge from a number of specialties, including law, history, and the behavioral and social sciences. Each specialty contributes to our fuller understanding of criminal behavior and of society's attitudes toward deviance.

In view of the fact that the criminal justice system is in a constant state of flux, and because the study of criminal justice covers such a broad spectrum, today's students must be aware of a variety of subjects and topics. Standard textbooks and traditional anthologies cannot keep pace with the changes as quickly as they occur. In fact, many such sources are already out of date the day they are published. *Annual Editions: Criminal Justice 03/04* strives to maintain currency in matters of concern by providing up-to-date commentaries, articles, reports, and statistics from the most recent literature in the criminal justice field.

This volume contains units concerning crime and justice in America, victimology, the police, the judicial system, juvenile justice, and punishment and corrections. The articles in these units were selected because they are informative as well as provocative. The selections are timely and useful in their treatment of ethics, punishment, juveniles, courts, and other related topics.

Included in this volume are a number of features designed to be useful to students, researchers, and professionals in the criminal justice field. These include the *table of contents*, which summarizes each article and features key concepts in bold italics; a *topic guide* for locating articles on specific subjects; a list of relevant *World Wide Web* sites; a comprehensive section on crime statistics; a *glossary*; and an *index*. In addition, each unit is preceded by an *overview* that provides a background for informed reading of the articles, emphasizes critical issues, and presents key points to consider.

We would like to know what you think of the selections contained in this edition of *Annual Editions: Criminal Justice*. Please fill out the postage-paid *article rating form* on the last page and let us know your opinions. We change or retain many of the articles based on the comments we receive from you, the reader. Help us to improve this anthology—annually.

Joseph L. Victor

Joseph L. Victor
Editor

Joanne Naughton

Joanne Naughton
Editor

Contents

To the Reader   iv

Topic Guide   x

Selected World Wide Web Sites   xii

UNIT 1
Crime and Justice in America

Eight selections focus on the overall structure of the criminal justice system in the United States. The current scope of crime in America is reviewed and topics such as criminal behavior, cyber-crime, and terrorism are discussed.

Unit Overview   xiv

1. **What Is the Sequence of Events in the Criminal Justice System?,** *Report to the Nation on Crime and Justice,* Bureau of Justice Statistics, January 1998
   This report reveals that the response to **crime** is a complex process, involving citizens as well as many agencies, levels, and branches of government.   2

2. **The Road to September 11,** Evan Thomas, *Newsweek,* October 1, 2001
   For a decade, America has been fighting a losing war against **terrorism.** This article chronicles the missed clues and missteps in a manhunt that is far from over.   8

3. **Crime Without Punishment,** Eli Lehrer, *The Weekly Standard,* May 27, 2002
   Crime has hit record highs in **Europe** and **Canada,** while American streets have become safer. The simple explanation is that the American **justice system** does a better job because of its reliance on **local police** departments. Almost all of the **law enforcement** in nearly all of the other industrialized countries is provided by massive regional or national agencies.   16

4. **Cyber-Crimes,** Brian Hansen, *CQ Researcher,* April 12, 2002
   Hackers and virus writers regularly cause problems in **cyberspace.** Brian Hansen warns that one of the most prevalent and insidious **Internet**-assisted scams is **identity theft;** some merchants have their customers' credit card data just sitting on servers, waiting to be hacked.   19

5. **Making Computer Crime Count,** Marc Goodman, *FBI Law Enforcement Bulletin,* August 2001
   To combat **computer crime,** law enforcement must build an internal capacity to define, track, and analyze these criminal offenses, claims Marc Goodman.   28

6. **Enough Is Enough,** Clifton Leaf, *Fortune,* March 18, 2002
   Of all the factors that lead to **corporate crime,** none comes close to the role of top management in tolerating and even shaping a culture that allows for it. **Accounting fraud** often starts this way, and **prosecutors** can make these **crimes** too complicated. According to Clifton Leaf, they can be boiled down to basic lying, cheating, and stealing.   34

7. **Trust and Confidence in Criminal Justice,** Lawrence W. Sherman, *National Institute of Justice Journal,* Number 248, 2002
   The **criminal justice** system is a paradox of progress. It is less corrupt, brutal, and **racially** unfair than it has been in the past. It has also become more effective, with greater diversity in its staffing. Yet Americans today have less confidence in the criminal justice system than in many other institutions.   42

The concepts in bold italics are developed in the article. For further expansion, please refer to the Topic Guide and the Index.

8. **So You Want to Be a Serial-Murderer Profiler ...,** John Randolph Fuller, *The Chronicle of Higher Education,* December 7, 2001
John Randolph Fuller helps to guide his students by sketching out the various **career options** that are available in **criminal justice**. While it may sound exciting, being a serial-murderer profiler is not a realistic option for most students.   50

UNIT 2
Victimology

Six articles discuss the impact of crime on the victim. Topics include the rights of crime victims, the consequences of family violence, and how to respond to acts of terrorism

Unit Overview   52

9. **What Is a Life Worth?,** Amanda Ripley, *Time,* February 11, 2002
Until the **terrorist** attacks of **September 11, 2001,** resulted in the government's need to establish an unprecedented fund to compensate the surviving families, the mathematics of loss was a little-known science. Now the process is on display as the government attempts to deal with wrenching decisions.   54

10. **Coping After Terrorism,** *OVC Handbook for Coping After Terrorism: A Guide to Healing and Recovery,* September 2001
The terrorist attacks of **September 11, 2001,** have deeply shaken our sense of safety, security, and emotional well-being. The information in this handbook is intended to help people understand their reactions to an act of **terrorism** or mass **violence.**   58

11. **Telling the Truth About Damned Lies and Statistics,** Joel Best, *The Chronicle of Higher Education,* May 4, 2001
We should not ignore all **statistics** or assume that every number is false. Some statistics are bad, but others are useful. Joel Best thinks that we need good statistics to talk sensibly about **social problems.**   63

12. **Violence and the Remaking of a Self,** Susan J. Brison, *The Chronicle of Higher Education,* January 18, 2002
The horror and **violence** associated with the crime of **rape** is clearly evident in the words of Susan Brison as she describes her **victimization,** attempts at coping with the aftereffects, and the eventual remaking of herself into a survivor of this terrible **crime.**   66

13. **Prosecutors, Kids, and Domestic Violence Cases,** Debra Whitcomb, *National Institute of Justice Journal,* Number 248, 2002
The results of new research strongly suggest that **prosecutors** can bring together people with disparate views and hammer out ways to overcome distrust and conflict toward a common goal: protection of **battered women** and their **children.**   70

14. **Strengthening Antistalking Statutes,** *OVC Legal Series,* January 2002
Stalking is a **crime** of intimidation. Stalkers harass and even **terrorize** through conduct that causes fear and substantial emotional distress in their **victims.** Work must be done in the future to better protect stalking victims by strengthening antistalking laws, according to this U.S. Department of Justice report.   76

The concepts in bold italics are developed in the article. For further expansion, please refer to the Topic Guide and the Index.

UNIT 3
The Police

Six selections examine the role and concerns of the police officer. Some of the topics include the stress of police work, multicultural changes, ethical policing, and community policing.

Unit Overview   **82**

15. **The Changing Roles and Strategies of the Police in Time of Terror,** Melchor C. de Guzman, *Academy of Criminal Justice Sciences (ACJS) Today,* September/October 2002

    Melchor deGuzman, in a speech on the changing role of the police in the wake of the *terrorist* attacks on the United States, argues that *crime analysis* and police strategies need to be changed, with a view toward coordination, focus, and education.   **84**

16. **Racial Profiling and Its Apologists,** Tim Wise, *Z Magazine,* March 2002

    Racial profiling cannot be justified on the basis of general crime rate data. But, according to Tim Wise, "unless and until the stereotypes that underlie [it] are attacked and exposed as a fraud, the practice will likely continue...." The fact remains that the typical offender in violent crime categories is white.   **91**

17. **Early Warning Systems: Responding to the Problem Police Officer,** Samuel Walker, Geoffrey P. Alpert, and Dennis J. Kenney, *National Institute of Justice Journal,* July 2001

    Problem *police officers* are well known to their peers, their supervisors, and the public, but little is done about them. A study shows that an early-warning system may have a dramatic effect on reducing *citizen complaints.*   **95**

18. **Crime Story: The Digital Age,** John D. Cohen, Adam Gelb, and Robert Wasserman, *Blueprint,* Winter 2001

    This article explores how new digital technologies have helped to improve *community policing.*   **102**

19. **Ethics and Criminal Justice: Some Observations on Police Misconduct,** Bryan Byers, *Academy of Criminal Justice Sciences (ACJS) Today,* September/October 2000

    Bryan Byers discusses *police misconduct* in terms of *ethical violations* as well as *police departments' responses* to such behavior.   **106**

20. **Spirituality and Police Suicide: A Double-Edged Sword,** Joseph J. D'Angelo, *FBI Behavioral Science Unit,* 2001

    Numerous studies have been conducted to try to learn the extent and the causes of *police suicides.* The author discusses the stigma associated with the subject and argues that an authentic spiritual perspective may help officers who might be at risk.   **110**

UNIT 4
The Judicial System

Five selections discuss the process by which the accused are moving through the judicial system. The courts, the jury process, and judicial ethics are reviewed.

Unit Overview   **114**

21. **Jury Consulting on Trial,** D. W. Miller, *The Chronicle of Higher Education,* November 23, 2001

    The notion of "scientific *jury* selection" took hold in the early 1970s; since then, however, scholars have found little evidence that *social science* makes a big difference in jury selection. Furthermore, even if research offered lawyers a wealth of predictive information, they would not always be able to use it as they do not have complete control over jury selection.   **116**

The concepts in bold italics are developed in the article. For further expansion, please refer to the Topic Guide and the Index.

22. **Opting in to Mental Health Courts,** Anne M. Hasselbrack, *Corrections Compendium,* Sample Issue
Mental health courts are alternatives to traditional courts for offenders whose illnesses are thought to have contributed to their crimes and who could benefit from a proactive approach, involving assessment, medication, counseling, housing, training, and employment, over a strictly punitive approach. **120**

23. **Anatomy of a Verdict,** D. Graham Burnett, *New York Times Magazine,* August 26, 2001
The author describes his experience as a *jury* foreman in a Manhattan murder *trial.* He found that justice does not merely happen; justice is done, made, and manufactured by imperfect, wrangling, venal, and virtuous human beings using whatever means they have. In the example described in this article, when one juror's heavily regulated prescription drug had run out during deliberations, it spelled trouble for the rest of the panel. **123**

24. **Looking Askance at Eyewitness Testimony,** D. W. Miller, *The Chronicle of Higher Education,* February 25, 2000
Eyewitness identification often leads to the *conviction* of *innocent* people. In this article, psychologists offer advice on how to handle such *evidence.* **132**

25. **The Creeping Expansion of DNA Data Banking,** Barry Steinhardt, *Government, Law and Policy Journal,* Spring 2000
Is the increase of *DNA* collection something we should worry about? Barry Steinhardt argues that a DNA sample is far more intrusive than a *fingerprint* because it can reveal much more information. **136**

UNIT 5
Juvenile Justice

Five selections review the juvenile justice system. The topics include effective ways of responding to violent juvenile crime and juvenile detention.

Unit Overview **140**

26. **Sentencing Guidelines and the Transformation of Juvenile Justice in the 21st Century,** Daniel P. Mears, *Journal of Contemporary Criminal Justice,* February 2002
The past decade witnessed dramatic changes to *juvenile justice* in America, changes that have altered the focus and administration of juvenile justice in the twenty-first century. **142**

27. **Hard-Time Kids,** Sasha Abramsky, *The American Prospect,* August 27, 2001
Sasha Abramsky points out in this article that handing down adult prison sentences to *juvenile criminals* is not solving their problems—or ours. **149**

28. **Gangs in Middle America: Are They a Threat?,** David M. Allender, *FBI Law Enforcement Bulletin,* December 2001
No city, town, or neighborhood is totally immune from the threat of *gangs.* Prevention requires that communities provide young people with options that will lead them away from a gang lifestyle. **153**

29. **Trouble With the Law,** Tina Susman, *Newsday,* August 22, 2002
In this article, Tina Susman demonstrates that parents and civic groups decry a system that treats *juveniles* as adults. **160**

30. **Doubting the System,** Tina Susman, *Newsday,* August 21, 2002
Laws on *juveniles* stir debate over punishment and *racism,* according to author Tina Susman in this news piece. **165**

The concepts in bold italics are developed in the article. For further expansion, please refer to the Topic Guide and the Index.

UNIT 6
Punishment and Corrections

Four selections focus on the current state of America's penal system and the effects of sentencing, probation, and capital punishment on criminals.

Unit Overview   **170**

31. Kicking Out the Demons by Humanizing the Experience—An Interview With Anthony Papa, Preston Peet, *Drugwar.com,* May 1, 2002

Anthony Papa is an artist and activist who uses his art to promote **prison** and drug-war reform. He was arrested in a **drug** sting operation in 1985 and served 12 years in Sing Sing prison for his first offense, under the Rockefeller drug laws, before being granted clemency.   **172**

32. Trends in State Parole, Timothy A. Hughes, Doris James Wilson, and Alan J. Beck, *Perspectives,* Summer 2002

According to the authors, the more things change, the more they stay the same in parole issues.   **179**

33. Inmate Reentry and Post-Release Supervision: The Case of Massachusetts, Anne Morrison Piehl, *Perspectives,* Fall 2002

As this Massachusetts analysis shows, those most in need of **parole** supervision are the least likely to receive it. Mandatory **sentencing** laws and restrictions on community placement are some of the reforms that are responsibile for this circumstance.   **187**

34. Rethinking the Death Penalty, Kenneth Jost, *CQ Researcher,* November 16, 2001

While polls still show that a solid majority of Americans favor the use of the **death penalty,** critics have made headway with arguments about the fairness and reliability of the system for meting out death sentences.   **195**

Appendix I. Charts and Graphs   **203**

Appendix II. Crime Clock and Crime in the United States, 2001 Statistics   **204**

Glossary   **215**
Index   **221**
Test Your Knowledge Form   **224**
Article Rating Form   **225**

The concepts in bold italics are developed in the article. For further expansion, please refer to the Topic Guide and the Index.

Topic Guide

This topic guide suggests how the selections in this book relate to the subjects covered in your course. You may want to use the topics listed on these pages to search the Web more easily.

On the following pages a number of Web sites have been gathered specifically for this book. They are arranged to reflect the units of this *Annual Edition.* You can link to these sites by going to the DUSHKIN ONLINE support site at *http://www.dushkin.com/online/*.

ALL THE ARTICLES THAT RELATE TO EACH TOPIC ARE LISTED BELOW THE BOLD-FACED TERM.

Adolescence
  27. Hard-Time Kids
  28. Gangs in Middle America: Are They a Threat?
  29. Trouble With the Law
  30. Doubting the System

Capital punishment
  34. Rethinking the Death Penalty

Career
  8. So You Want to Be a Serial-Murderer Profiler ...

Community policing
  18. Crime Story: The Digital Age

Computer crime
  5. Making Computer Crime Count

Corporate crime
  6. Enough Is Enough

Corrections system
  31. Kicking Out the Demons by Humanizing the Experience—An Interview With Anthony Papa
  32. Trends in State Parole
  33. Inmate Reentry and Post-Release Supervision: The Case of Massachusetts
  34. Rethinking the Death Penalty

Court system
  18. Crime Story: The Digital Age
  22. Opting in to Mental Health Courts
  24. Looking Askance at Eyewitness Testimony
  25. The Creeping Expansion of DNA Data Banking

Crime
  1. What Is the Sequence of Events in the Criminal Justice System?
  2. The Road to September 11
  3. Crime Without Punishment
  5. Making Computer Crime Count
  6. Enough Is Enough
  12. Violence and the Remaking of a Self
  14. Strengthening Antistalking Statutes
  24. Looking Askance at Eyewitness Testimony

Crime in Canada
  3. Crime Without Punishment

Crime in Europe
  3. Crime Without Punishment

Crime statistics
  11. Telling the Truth About Damned Lies and Statistics

Criminal justice
  1. What Is the Sequence of Events in the Criminal Justice System?

  2. The Road to September 11
  3. Crime Without Punishment
  5. Making Computer Crime Count
  7. Trust and Confidence in Criminal Justice
  19. Ethics and Criminal Justice: Some Observations on Police Misconduct
  25. The Creeping Expansion of DNA Data Banking

Cyberspace
  4. Cyber-Crimes

Death penalty
  34. Rethinking the Death Penalty

Discretion
  1. What Is the Sequence of Events in the Criminal Justice System?

DNA
  25. The Creeping Expansion of DNA Data Banking

Drug war
  31. Kicking Out the Demons by Humanizing the Experience—An Interview With Anthony Papa

Ethics
  6. Enough Is Enough
  19. Ethics and Criminal Justice: Some Observations on Police Misconduct

Evidence
  24. Looking Askance at Eyewitness Testimony
  25. The Creeping Expansion of DNA Data Banking

Executive pay
  6. Enough Is Enough

Eyewitnesses
  24. Looking Askance at Eyewitness Testimony

Gangs
  28. Gangs in Middle America: Are They a Threat?

Hackers
  4. Cyber-Crimes

Identity theft
  4. Cyber-Crimes

Internet
  4. Cyber-Crimes

Jury
  21. Jury Consulting on Trial
  23. Anatomy of a Verdict

Juveniles
26. Sentencing Guidelines and the Transformation of Juvenile Justice in the 21st Century
27. Hard-Time Kids
28. Gangs in Middle America: Are They a Threat?
29. Trouble With the Law
30. Doubting the System

Law enforcement
3. Crime Without Punishment
5. Making Computer Crime Count

Mental health
22. Opting in to Mental Health Courts

Organizational misconduct
6. Enough Is Enough

Parole
32. Trends in State Parole
33. Inmate Reentry and Post-Release Supervision: The Case of Massachusetts

Police
3. Crime Without Punishment
15. The Changing Roles and Strategies of the Police in Time of Terror
16. Racial Profiling and Its Apologists
17. Early Warning Systems: Responding to the Problem Police Officer
18. Crime Story: The Digital Age
19. Ethics and Criminal Justice: Some Observations on Police Misconduct
20. Spirituality and Police Suicide: A Double-Edged Sword

Prison
31. Kicking Out the Demons by Humanizing the Experience—An Interview With Anthony Papa
33. Inmate Reentry and Post-Release Supervision: The Case of Massachusetts

Prosecutors
6. Enough Is Enough
13. Prosecutors, Kids, and Domestic Violence Cases

Race
7. Trust and Confidence in Criminal Justice
16. Racial Profiling and Its Apologists
30. Doubting the System

Rape
12. Violence and the Remaking of a Self

Sentencing
33. Inmate Reentry and Post-Release Supervision: The Case of Massachusetts

September 11th attacks, U.S.
2. The Road to September 11
9. What Is a Life Worth?
10. Coping After Terrorism

Social problems
11. Telling the Truth About Damned Lies and Statistics

Social science
21. Jury Consulting on Trial

Stalking
14. Strengthening Antistalking Statutes

Stress
2. The Road to September 11
10. Coping After Terrorism

Suicide
20. Spirituality and Police Suicide: A Double-Edged Sword

Technology
5. Making Computer Crime Count
18. Crime Story: The Digital Age

Terrorism
2. The Road to September 11
9. What Is a Life Worth?
10. Coping After Terrorism
14. Strengthening Antistalking Statutes
15. The Changing Roles and Strategies of the Police in Time of Terror

Trial
23. Anatomy of a Verdict

Victimology
9. What Is a Life Worth?
10. Coping After Terrorism
11. Telling the Truth About Damned Lies and Statistics
12. Violence and the Remaking of a Self
13. Prosecutors, Kids, and Domestic Violence Cases
14. Strengthening Antistalking Statutes

Violence
2. The Road to September 11
10. Coping After Terrorism
12. Violence and the Remaking of a Self
13. Prosecutors, Kids, and Domestic Violence Cases

Women
12. Violence and the Remaking of a Self
13. Prosecutors, Kids, and Domestic Violence Cases

World Wide Web Sites

The following World Wide Web sites have been carefully researched and selected to support the articles found in this reader. The easiest way to access these selected sites is to go to our DUSHKIN ONLINE support site at *http://www.dushkin.com/online/*.

AE: Criminal Justice 03/04

The following sites were available at the time of publication. Visit our Web site—we update DUSHKIN ONLINE regularly to reflect any changes.

General Sources

American Society of Criminology
http://www.bsos.umd.edu/asc/four.html

This is an excellent starting place for study of all aspects of criminology and criminal justice, with links to international criminal justice, juvenile justice, court information, police, governments, and so on.

Federal Bureau of Investigation
http://www.fbi.gov

The main page of the FBI Web site leads to lists of the most wanted criminals, uniform crime reports, FBI case reports, major investigations, and more.

National Archive of Criminal Justice Data
http://www.icpsr.umich.edu/NACJD/index.html

NACJD holds more than 500 data collections relating to criminal justice; this site provides browsing and downloading access to most of these data and documentation. NACJD's central mission is to facilitate and encourage research in the field of criminal justice.

Social Science Information Gateway
http://sosig.esrc.bris.ac.uk

This is an online catalog of thousands of Internet resources relevant to social science education and research. Every resource is selected and described by a librarian or subject specialist. Enter "criminal justice" under Search for an excellent annotated list of sources.

University of Pennsylvania Library: Criminology
http://www.library.upenn.edu/resources/subject/social/criminology/criminology.html

An excellent list of criminology and criminal justice resources is provided here.

UNIT 1: Crime and Justice in America

Campaign for Equity-Restorative Justice
http://www.cerj.org

This is the home page of CERJ, which sees monumental problems in justice systems and the need for reform. Examine this site and its links for information about the restorative justice movement.

Crime Times
http://www.crime-times.org/

This interesting site, listing research reviews and other information regarding biological causes of criminal, violent, and psychopathic behavior, consists of many articles that are listed by title. It is provided by the Wacker Foundation, publisher of *Crime Times*.

Ray Jones
http://blue.temple.edu/~eastern/jones.html

In this article, subtitled "A Review of Empirical Research in Corporate Crime," Ray Jones explores what happens when business violates the law. An extensive interpretive section and a bibliography are provided.

Sourcebook of Criminal Justice Statistics Online
http://www.albany.edu/sourcebook/

Data about all aspects of criminal justice in the United States are available at this site, which includes more than 600 tables from dozens of sources. A search mechanism is available.

UNIT 2: Victimology

Connecticut Sexual Assault Crisis Services, Inc.
http://www.connsacs.org

This site has links that provide information about women's responses to sexual assault and related issues. It includes extensive links to sexual violence–related Web pages.

National Crime Victim's Research and Treatment Center (NCVC)
http://www.musc.edu/cvc/

At this site, find out about the work of NCVC at the Medical University of South Carolina, and click on Related Resources for an excellent listing of additional Web sources.

Office for Victims of Crime (OVC)
http://www.ojp.usdoj.gov/ovc

Established by the 1984 Victims of Crime Act, the OVC oversees diverse programs that benefit the victims of crime. From this site you can download a great deal of pertinent information.

UNIT 3: The Police

ACLU Criminal Justice Home Page
http://www.aclu.org/CriminalJustice/CriminalJusticeMain.cfm

This "Criminal Justice" page of the American Civil Liberties Union Web site highlights recent events in criminal justice, addresses police issues, lists important resources, and contains a search mechanism.

Introduction to American Justice
http://www.uaa.alaska.edu/just/just110/home.html

Prepared by Darryl Wood of the Justice Center at the University of Alaska at Anchorage, this site provides an excellent outline of the causes of crime, including major theories. An introduction to crime, law, and the criminal justice system as well as data on police and policing, the court system, corrections, and more are available here.

Law Enforcement Guide to the World Wide Web
http://leolinks.com/

This page is dedicated to excellence in law enforcement. It contains links to every possible related category: community policing, computer crime, forensics, gangs, and wanted persons are just a few.

www.dushkin.com/online/

National Institute of Justice (NIJ)
http://www.ojp.usdoj.gov/nij/lawedocs.htm

The NIJ sponsors projects and conveys research findings to practitioners in the field of criminal justice. Through this site, you can access the initiatives of the 1994 Violent Crime Control and Law Enforcement Act, apply for grants, monitor international criminal activity, learn the latest about policing techniques and issues, and more.

Violent Criminal Apprehension Program (VICAP)
http://www.state.ma.us/msp/unitpage/vicap.htm

VICAP's mission is to facilitate cooperation, communication, and coordination among law enforcement agencies and provide support in their efforts to investigate, identify, track, apprehend, and prosecute violent serial offenders. Access VICAP's data information center resources here.

UNIT 4: The Judicial System

Center for Rational Correctional Policy
http://www.correctionalpolicy.com

This is an excellent site on courts and sentencing, with many additional links to a variety of criminal justice sources.

Justice Information Center (JIC)
http://www.ncjrs.org

Provided by the National Criminal Justice Reference Service, this JIC site connects to information about corrections, courts, crime prevention, criminal justice, statistics, drugs and crime, law enforcement, and victims.

National Center for Policy Analysis (NCPA)
http://www.public-policy.org/~ncpa/pd/law/index3.html

Through the NCPA's "Idea House," you can click onto links to an array of topics that are of major interest in the study of the American judicial system.

U.S. Department of Justice (DOJ)
http://www.usdoj.gov

The DOJ represents the American people in enforcing the law in the public interest. Open its main page to find information about the U.S. judicial system. This site provides links to federal government Web servers, topics of interest related to the justice system, documents and resources, and a topical index.

UNIT 5: Juvenile Justice

Gang Land: The Jerry Capeci Page
http://www.ganglandnews.com

Although this site particularly addresses organized-crime gangs, its insights into gang lifestyle—including gang families and their influence—are useful for those interested in exploring issues related to juvenile justice.

Institute for Intergovernmental Research (IIR)
http://www.iir.com

The IIR is a research organization that specializes in law enforcement, juvenile justice, and criminal justice issues. Explore the projects, links, and search engines from this home page. Topics addressed include youth gangs and white collar crime.

National Criminal Justice Reference Service (NCJRS)
http://virlib.ncjrs.org/JuvenileJustice.asp

NCJRS, a federally sponsored information clearinghouse for people involved with research, policy, and practice related to criminal and juvenile justice and drug control, provides this site of links to full-text juvenile justice publications.

National Network for Family Resiliency
http://www.nnfr.org

This organization's CYFERNET (Children, Youth, and Families Education and Research Network) page will lead to a number of resource areas of interest in learning about resiliency, including Program and Curriculum for Family Resiliency .

Partnership Against Violence Network
http://www.pavnet.org

The Partnership Against Violence Network is a virtual library of information about violence and youths at risk, representing data from seven different federal agencies—a one-stop searchable information resource.

UNIT 6: Punishment and Corrections

American Probation and Parole Association (APPA)
http://www.appa-net.org

Open this APPA site to find information and resources related to probation and parole issues, position papers, the APPA code of ethics, and research and training programs and opportunities.

The Corrections Connection
http://www.corrections.com

This site is an online network for corrections professionals.

Critical Criminology Division of the ASC
http://www.critcrim.org/

Here you will find basic criminology resources and related government resources, provided by the American Society of Criminology, as well as other useful links. The death penalty is also discussed.

David Willshire's Forensic Psychology & Psychiatry Links
http://members.optushome.com.au/dwillsh/index.html

This site offers an enormous number of links to professional journals and associations. It is a valuable resource for study into possible connections between violence and mental disorders. Topics include serial killers, sex offenders, and trauma.

Oregon Department of Corrections
http://www.doc.state.or.us/links/welcome.htm

Open this site for resources in such areas as crime and law enforcement and for links to U.S. state corrections departments.

We highly recommend that you review our Web site for expanded information and our other product lines. We are continually updating and adding links to our Web site in order to offer you the most usable and useful information that will support and expand the value of your Annual Editions. You can reach us at: *http://www.dushkin.com/annualeditions/*.

UNIT 1

Crime and Justice in America

Unit Selections

1. **What Is the Sequence of Events in the Criminal Justice System?** *Report to the Nation on Crime and Justice,* Bureau of Justice Statistics
2. **The Road to September 11**, Evan Thomas
3. **Crime Without Punishment**, Eli Lehrer
4. **Cyber-Crimes**, Brian Hansen
5. **Making Computer Crime Count**, Marc Goodman
6. **Enough Is Enough**, Clifton Leaf
7. **Trust and Confidence in Criminal Justice**, Lawrence W. Sherman
8. **So You Want to Be a Serial-Murderer Profiler ...**, John Randolph Fuller

Key Points to Consider

- Do you worry when paying bills and making purchases online that someone may be stealing your identity?

- Is the American criminal justice system up to the task of fighting corporate crime?

- With the advantage of 20-20 hindsight, what steps do you think could have been taken prior to September 11, 2001, that might have prevented the attacks?

 **Links: www.dushkin.com/online/**
These sites are annotated in the World Wide Web pages.

Campaign for Equity-Restorative Justice
http://www.cerj.org

Crime Times
http://www.crime-times.org/

Ray Jones
http://blue.temple.edu/~eastern/jones.html

Sourcebook of Criminal Justice Statistics Online
http://www.albany.edu/sourcebook/

Crime continues to be a major problem in the United States. Court dockets are full, our prisons are overcrowded, probation and parole caseloads are overwhelming, our police are being urged to do more, and the bulging prison population places a heavy strain on the economy of the country. Clearly crime is a complex problem that defies simple explanations or solutions. While the more familiar crimes of murder, rape, assault, and drug law violations are still with us, international terrorism has become a pressing concern. The debate also still continues about how best to handle juvenile offenders, sex offenders, and those who commit acts of domestic violence. Crimes using computers and the Internet also demand attention from the criminal justice system.

Annual Editions: Criminal Justice 03/04 focuses directly upon crime in America and the three traditional components of the criminal justice system: the police, the courts, and corrections. It also gives special attention to crime victims in the victimology unit and to juveniles in the juvenile justice unit. The articles presented in this section are intended to serve as a foundation for the materials presented in subsequent sections.

The unit begins with "What Is the Sequence of Events in the Criminal Justice System?" an article that reveals that the response to crime is a complex process, involving citizens as well as many agencies, levels, and branches of government. Then, in "The Road to September 11," Evan Thomas chronicles the missed clues and missteps in a manhunt that is far from over. In "Crime Without Punishment," Eli Lehrer proposes the idea that the American system of local police departments, as opposed to massive regional or national agencies, may be the reason behind the fact that our streets are safer than those of some European and Canadian cities. The problems caused in cyberspace by hackers and virus writers is discussed in "Cyber-Crimes." Then, the steps that law enforcement must take to fight computer crime are described in "Making Computer Crime Count." The role of top management in tolerating corporate crime and the tendency of prosecutors to overcomplicate it are looked at in "Enough Is Enough." Although law enforcement has made great progress regarding corruption, brutality, and racism, Americans do not seem to have noticed, according to Lawrence Sherman in "Trust and Confidence in Criminal Justice." Then, in "So You Want to Be a Serial Murderer Profiler... " John Fuller relates how he helps his students to decide what they might do with the rest of their lives.

What is the sequence of events in the criminal justice system?

The private sector initiates the response to crime

This first response may come from individuals, families, neighborhood associations, business, industry, agriculture, educational institutions, the news media, or any other private service to the public.

It involves crime prevention as well as participation in the criminal justice process once a crime has been committed. Private crime prevention is more than providing private security or burglar alarms or participating in neighborhood watch. It also includes a commitment to stop criminal behavior by not engaging in it or condoning it when it is committed by others.

Citizens take part directly in the criminal justice process by reporting crime to the police, by being a reliable participant (for example, a witness or a juror) in a criminal proceeding and by accepting the disposition of the system as just or reasonable. As voters and taxpayers, citizens also participate in criminal justice through the policymaking process that affects how the criminal justice process operates, the resources available to it, and its goals and objectives. At every stage of the process from the original formulation of objectives to the decision about where to locate jails and prisons to the reintegration of inmates into society, the private sector has a role to play. Without such involvement, the crim-

inal justice process cannot serve the citizens it is intended to protect.

The response to crime and public safety involves many agencies and services

Many of the services needed to prevent crime and make neighborhoods safe are supplied by noncriminal justice agencies, including agencies with primary concern for public health, education, welfare, public works, and housing. Individual citizens as well as public and private sector organizations have joined with criminal justice agencies to prevent crime and make neighborhoods safe.

Criminal cases are brought by the government through the criminal justice system

We apprehend, try, and punish offenders by means of a loose confederation of agencies at all levels of government. Our American system of justice has evolved from the English common law into a complex series of procedures and decisions. Founded on the concept that crimes against an individual are crimes against the State, our justice system prosecutes individuals as though they victimized all of society. However, crime victims are involved throughout the process and many justice

agencies have programs which focus on helping victims.

There is no single criminal justice system in this country. We have many similar systems that are individually unique. Criminal cases may be handled differently in different jurisdictions, but court decisions based on the due process guarantees of the U.S. Constitution require that specific steps be taken in the administration of criminal justice so that the individual will be protected from undue intervention from the State.

The description of the criminal and juvenile justice systems that follows portrays the most common sequence of events in response to serious criminal behavior.

Entry into the system

The justice system does not respond to most crime because so much crime is not discovered or reported to the police. Law enforcement agencies learn about crime from the reports of victims or other citizens, from discovery by a police officer in the field, from informants, or from investigative and intelligence work.

Once a law enforcement agency has established that a crime has been committed, a suspect must be identified and apprehended for the case to proceed through the system. Sometimes, a suspect is apprehended at the scene; however, identification of a suspect sometimes requires an extensive investigation. Often, no one is identified or apprehended. In some instances, a suspect is arrested and later the police determine that no crime was committed and the suspect is released.

Prosecution and pretrial services

After an arrest, law enforcement agencies present information about the case and about the accused to the prosecutor, who will decide if formal charges will be filed with the court. If no charges are filed, the accused must be released. The prosecutor can also drop charges after making efforts to prosecute (*nolle prosequi*).

A suspect charged with a crime must be taken before a judge or magistrate without unnecessary delay. At the initial appearance, the judge or magistrate informs the accused of the charges and decides whether there is probable cause to detain the accused person. If the offense is not very serious, the determination of guilt and assessment of a penalty may also occur at this stage.

Often, the defense counsel is also assigned at the initial appearance. All suspects prosecuted for serious crimes have a right to be represented by an attorney. If the court determines the suspect is indigent and cannot afford such representation, the court will assign counsel at the public's expense.

A pretrial-release decision may be made at the initial appearance, but may occur at other hearings or may be changed at another time during the process. Pretrial release and bail were traditionally intended to ensure appearance at trial. However, many jurisdictions permit pretrial detention of defendants accused of serious offenses and deemed to be dangerous to prevent them from committing crimes prior to trial.

The court often bases its pretrial decision on information about the defendant's drug use, as well as residence, employment, and family ties. The court may decide to release the accused on his/her own recognizance or into the custody of a third party after the posting of a financial bond or on the promise of satisfying certain conditions such as taking periodic drug tests to ensure drug abstinence.

In many jurisdictions, the initial appearance may be followed by a preliminary hearing. The main function of this hearing is to discover if there is probable cause to believe that the accused committed a known crime within the jurisdiction of the court. If the judge does not find probable cause, the case is dismissed; however, if the judge or magistrate finds probable cause for such a belief, or the accused waives his or her right to a preliminary hearing, the case may be bound over to a grand jury.

A grand jury hears evidence against the accused presented by the prosecutor and decides if there is sufficient evidence to cause the accused to be brought to trial. If the grand jury finds sufficient evidence, it submits to the court an indictment, a written statement of the essential facts of the offense charged against the accused.

Where the grand jury system is used, the grand jury may also investigate criminal activity generally and issue indictments called grand jury originals that initiate criminal cases. These investigations and indictments are often used in drug and conspiracy cases that involve complex organizations. After such an indictment, law enforcement tries to apprehend and arrest the suspects named in the indictment.

Misdemeanor cases and some felony cases proceed by the issuance of an information, a formal, written accusation submitted to the court by a prosecutor. In some jurisdictions, indictments may be required in felony cases. However, the accused may choose to waive a grand jury indictment and, instead, accept service of an information for the crime.

In some jurisdictions, defendants, often those without prior criminal records, may be eligible for diversion from prosecution subject to the completion of specific conditions such as drug treatment. Successful completion of the conditions may result in the dropping of charges or the expunging of the criminal record where the defendant is required to plead guilty prior to the diversion.

Adjudication

Once an indictment or information has been filed with the trial court, the accused is scheduled for arraignment. At the arraignment, the accused is informed of the charges, advised of the rights of criminal defendants, and asked to enter a plea to the charges. Sometimes, a plea of guilty is the result of negotiations between the prosecutor and the defendant.

If the accused pleads guilty or pleads *nolo contendere* (accepts penalty without admitting guilt), the judge may accept or reject the plea. If the plea is accepted, no trial is held and the offender is sentenced at this proceeding or at a later date. The plea may be rejected and proceed to trial if, for example, the judge believes that the accused may have been coerced.

If the accused pleads not guilty or not guilty by reason of insanity, a date is set for the trial. A person accused of a serious crime is guaranteed a trial by jury. However, the accused may ask for a bench trial where the judge, rather than a jury, serves as the finder of fact. In both instances the prosecution and defense present evidence by questioning witnesses while the judge decides on issues of law. The trial results in acquittal or conviction on the original charges or on lesser included offenses.

After the trial a defendant may request appellate review of the conviction or sentence. In some cases, appeals of convictions are a matter of right; all States with the death penalty provide for automatic appeal of cases involving a death sentence. Appeals may be subject to the discretion of the appelate court and may be granted only on acceptance of a defendant's petition for a *writ of certiorari*. Prisoners may also appeal their sentences through civil rights petitions and *writs of habeas corpus* where they claim unlawful detention.

Sentencing and sanctions

After a conviction, sentence is imposed. In most cases the judge decides on the sentence, but in some jurisdictions the sentence is decided by the jury, particularly for capital offenses.

In arriving at an appropriate sentence, a sentencing hearing may be held at which evidence of aggravating or mitigating circumstances is considered. In assessing the circumstances surrounding a convicted person's criminal behavior, courts often rely on presentence investigations by probation agencies or other designated authorities. Courts may also consider victim impact statements.

The sentencing choices that may be available to judges and juries include one or more of the following:

- the death penalty
- incarceration in a prison, jail, or other confinement facility
- probation—allowing the convicted person to remain at liberty but subject

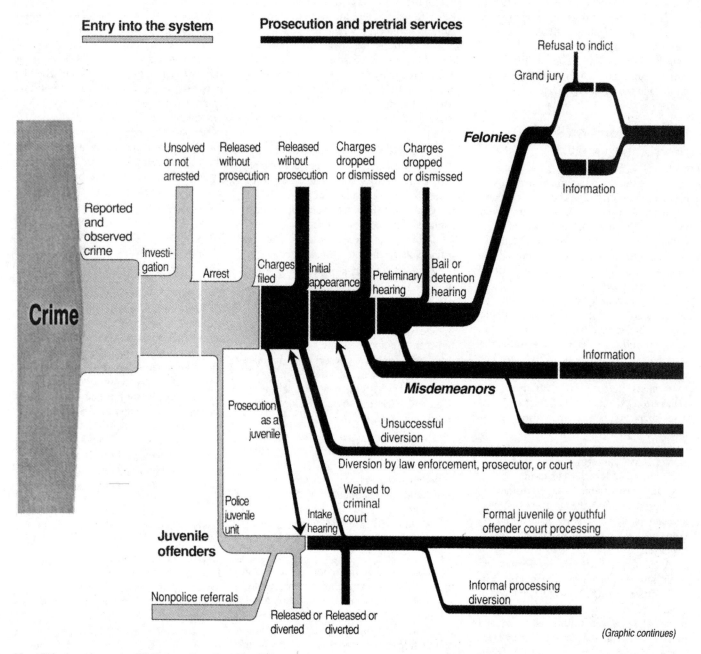

Entry into the system

Prosecution and pretrial services

Note: This chart gives a simplified view of caseflow through the criminal justice system. Procedures vary among jurisdictions. The weights of the lines are not intended to show the actual size of caseloads.

(Graphic continues)

to certain conditions and restrictions such as drug testing or drug restrictions such as drug testing or drug treatment

• fines—primarily applied as penalties in minor offenses

• restitution—requiring the offender to pay compensation to the victim. In some jurisdictions, offenders may be sentenced to alternatives to incarceration that are considered more severe than straight probation but less severe

than a prison term. Examples of such sanctions include boot camps, intense supervision often with drug treatment and testing, house arrest and electronic monitoring, denial of Federal benefits, and community service.

In many jurisdictions, the law mandates that persons convicted of certain types of offenses serve a prison term. Most jurisdictions permit the judge to set the sentence length within certain limits, but some have determinate sentencing laws that stipulate

a specific sentence length that must be served and cannot be altered by a parole board.

Corrections

Offenders sentenced to incarceration usually serve time in a local jail or a State prison. Offenders sentenced to less than 1 year generally go to jail; those sentenced to more than 1 year go to prison. Persons admitted to the Federal system or a State prison system may be held in prison with

Article 1. What is the sequence of events in the criminal justice system?

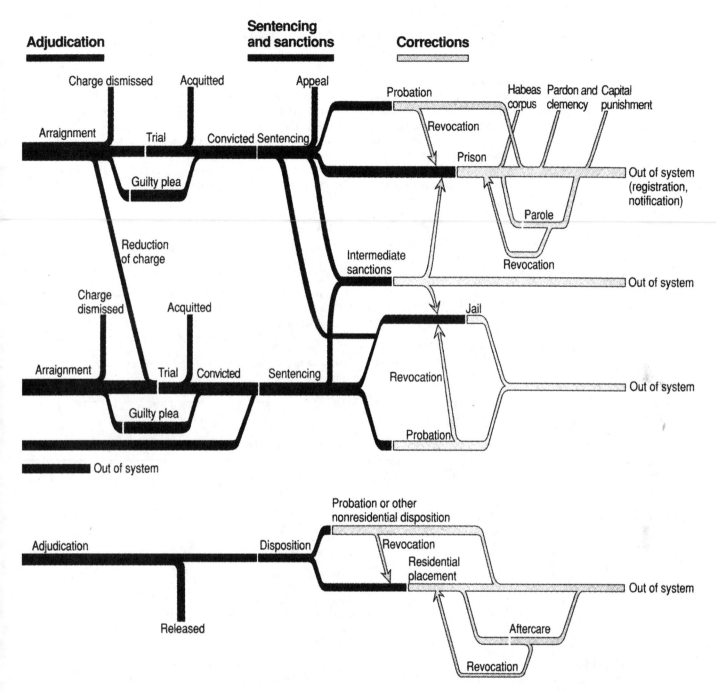

Adjudication

Sentencing and sanctions

Corrections

Source: Adapted from *The challenge of crime in a free society*. President's Commission on Law Enforcement and Administration of Justice, 1967. This revision, a result of the Symposium on the 30th Anniversary of the President's Commission, was prepared by the Bureau of Justice Statistics in 1997.

varying levels of custody or in a community correctional facility.

A prisoner may become eligible for parole after serving a specific part of his or her sentence. Parole is the conditional release of a prisoner before the prisoner's full sentence has been served. The decision to grant parole is made by an authority such as a parole board, which has power to grant or revoke parole or to discharge a parolee altogether. The way pa-

role decisions are made varies widely among jurisdictions.

Offenders may also be required to serve out their full sentences prior to release (expiration of term). Those sentenced under determinate sentencing laws can be released only after they have served their full sentence (mandatory release) less any "goodtime" received while in prison. Inmates get goodtime credits against their sentences automatically or

by earning them through participation in programs.

If released by a parole board decision or by mandatory release, the releasee will be under the supervision of a parole officer in the community for the balance of his or her unexpired sentence. This supervision is governed by specific conditions of release, and the releasee may be returned to prison for violations of such conditions.

5

Discretion is exercised throughout the criminal justice system

Discretion is "an authority conferred by law to act in certain conditions or situations in accordance with an official's or an official agency's own considered judgment and conscience."[1] Discretion is exercised throughout the government. It is a part of decisionmaking in all government systems from mental health to education, as well as criminal justice. The limits of discretion vary from jurisdiction to jurisdiction.

Concerning crime and justice, legislative bodies have recognized that they cannot anticipate the range of circumstances surrounding each crime, anticipate local mores, and enact laws that clearly encompass all conduct that is criminal and all that is not.[2]

Therefore, persons charged with the day-to-day response to crime are expected to exercise their own judgment within limits set by law. Basically, they must decide—

- whether to take action
- where the situation fits in the scheme of law, rules, and precedent
- which official response is appropriate.[3]

To ensure that discretion is exercised responsibly, government authority is often delegated to professionals. Professionalism requires a minimum

level of training and orientation, which guide officials in making decisions. The professionalism of policing is due largely to the desire to ensure the proper exercise of police discretion.

The limits of discretion vary from State to State and locality to locality. For example, some State judges have wide discretion in the type of sentence they may impose. In recent years, other states have sought to limit the judge's discretion in sentencing by passing mandatory sentencing laws that require prison sentences for certain offenses.

Notes

1. Roscoe Pound, "Discretion, dispensation and mitigation: The problem of the individual special case," *New York University Law Review* (1960) 35:925, 926.
2. Wayne R. LaFave, *Arrest: The decision to take a suspect into custody* (Boston: Little, Brown & Co., 1964), p. 63–184.
3. Memorandum of June 21, 1977, from Mark Moore to James Vorenberg, "Some abstract notes on the issue of discretion."

Bureau of Justice Statistics (*www.ojp.usdoj.gov/bjs/*). January 1998. NCJ 167894. To order: 1-800-732-3277.

Who exercises discretion?

These criminal justice officials...	must often decide whether or not or how to—
Police	Enforce specific laws Investigate specific crimes; Search people
Prosecutors	File charges or petitions for adjudication Seek indictments Drop cases Reduce charges
Judges or magistrates	Set bail or conditions for release Accept pleas Determine delinquency Dismiss charges Impose sentence Revoke probation
Correctional officials	Assign to type of correctional facility Award privileges Punish for disciplinary infractions
Paroling authorities	Determine date and conditions of parole Revoke parole

Recidivism

Once the suspects, defendants, or offenders are released from the jurisdiction of a criminal justice agency, they may be processed through the criminal justice system again for a new crime. Long term studies show that many suspects who are arrested have prior criminal histories and

those with a greater number of prior arrests were more likely to be arrested again. As the courts take prior criminal history into account at sentencing, most prison inmates have a prior criminal history and many have been incarcerated before. Nationally, about half the inmates released from State prison will return to prison.

The juvenile justice system

Juvenile courts usually have jurisdiction over matters concerning children, including delinquency, neglect, and adoption. They also handle "status offenses" such as truancy and running away, which are not applicable to adults. State statutes define which persons are under the original jurisdiction of the juvenile court. The upper age of juvenile court jurisdiction in delinquency matters is 17 in most States.

The processing of juvenile offenders is not entirely dissimilar to adult criminal processing, but there are crucial differences. Many juveniles are referred to juvenile courts by law enforcement officers, but many others are referred by school officials, social services agencies, neighbors, and even parents, for behavior or conditions that are determined to require intervention by the formal system for social control.

At arrest, a decision is made either to send the matter further into the justice system or to divert the case out of the system, often to alternative programs. Examples of alternative programs include drug treatment, individual or group counseling, or referral to educational and recreational programs.

When juveniles are referred to the juvenile courts, the court's intake department or the prosecuting attorney determines whether sufficient grounds exist to warrant filing a petition that requests an adjudictory hearing or a request to transfer jurisdiction to criminal court. At this point, many juveniles are released or diverted to alternative programs.

All States allow juveniles to be tried as adults in criminal court under certain circumstances. In many States, the legislature *statutorily excludes* certain (usually serious) offenses from the jurisdiction of the juvenile court regardless of the age of the accused. In some States and at the Federal level under certain circumstances, prosecutors have the *discretion* to either file criminal charges against juveniles directly in criminal courts or proceed through the juvenile justice process. The juvenile court's intake department or the prosecutor may petition the juvenile court to *waive* jurisdiction to criminal court. The juvenile court also may order *referral* to criminal court for trial as adults. In some jurisdic-

tions, juveniles processed as adults may upon conviction be sentenced to either an adult or a juvenile facility.

In those cases where the juvenile court retains jurisdiction, the case may be handled formally by filing a delinquency petition or informally by diverting the juvenile to other agencies or programs in lieu of further court processing.

If a petition for an adjudicatory hearing is accepted, the juvenile may be brought before a court quite unlike the court with jurisdiction over adult offenders. Despite the considerable discretion associated with juvenile court proceedings, juveniles are afforded many of the due-process safeguards associated with adult criminal trials. Several States permit the use of juries in juvenile courts; however, in light of the U.S. Supreme Court holding that juries are not essential to juvenile hearings, most States do not make provisions for juries in juvenile courts.

In disposing of cases, juvenile courts usually have far more discretion that adult courts. In addition to such options as probation, commitment to a residential facility, restitution, or fines, State laws grant juvenile courts the power to order removal of children from their homes to foster homes or treatment facilities. Juvenile courts also may order participation in special programs aimed at shoplifting prevention, drug counseling, or driver education.

Once a juvenile is under juvenile court disposition, the court may retain jurisdiction until the juvenile legally becomes an adult (at age 21 in most States). In some jurisdictions, juvenile offenders may be classified as youthful offenders which can lead to extended sentences.

Following release from an institution, juveniles are often ordered to a period of aftercare which is similar to parole supervision for adult offenders. Juvenile offenders who violate the conditions of aftercare may have their aftercare revoked, resulting

in being recommitted to a facility. Juveniles who are classified as youthful offenders and violate the conditions of aftercare may be subject to adult sanctions.

The governmental response to crime is founded in the intergovernmental structure of the United States

Under our form of government, each State and the Federal Government has its own criminal justice system. All systems must respect the rights of individuals set forth in court interpretation of the U.S. Constitution and defined in case law.

State constitutions and laws define the criminal justice system within each State and delegate the authority and responsibility for criminal justice to various jurisdictions, officials, and institutions. State laws also define criminal behavior and groups of children or acts under jurisdiction of the juvenile courts.

Municipalities and counties further define their criminal justice systems through local ordinances that proscribe the local agencies responsible for criminal justice processing that were not established by the State.

Congress has also established a criminal justice system at the Federal level to respond to Federal crimes such as bank robbery, kidnaping, and transporting stolen goods across State lines.

The response to crime is mainly a State and local function

Very few crimes are under exclusive Federal jurisdiction. The responsibility to respond to most crime rests with State and local governments. Police protection is primarily a function of cities and towns. Corrections is primarily a function of State governments. Most justice personnel are employed at the local level.

From the *Report to the Nation on Crime and Justice*, January 1998. © 1998 by the U.S. Department of Justice, Office of Justice Programs, Bureau of Justice Statistics. Reprinted by permission.

The Road to September 11

It was a long time coming. For a decade, America's been fighting a losing secret war against terror. A NEWSWEEK investigation into the missed clues and missteps in a manhunt that is far from over.

He was more than a little suspicious. At the Airman Flight School in Norman, Okla., the stocky aspiring pilot with the heavy French accent acted oddly. He was abrupt and argumentative, refusing to pay the whole $4,995 fee upfront (he shelled out $2,500 in cash instead). He had been dodgy in his e-mails. "E is not secure," explained Zacarias Moussaoui, 33, who preferred to use his Internet alias, "zuluman tangotango." A poor flier, he suddenly quit in mid-May, before showing up at another flight school in Eagan, Minn. At Pan Am Flying Academy, he acknowledged that the biggest plane he'd ever flown was a single-engine Cessna. But he asked to be trained on a 747 flight simulator. He wanted to concentrate only on the midair turns, not the takeoffs and landings. It was all too fishy to one of the instructors, who tipped off the Feds. Incarcerated because his visa had expired, Moussaoui was sitting in the Sherburne County Jail when some other pilot trainees drove their hijacked airliners into the World Trade Center and the Pentagon.

It's not that the U.S. government was asleep. America's open borders make tracking terrorists a daunting exercise. NEWSWEEK has learned that the FBI has privately estimated that more than 1,000 individuals—most of them foreign nationals—with suspected terrorist ties are currently living in the United States. "The American people would be surprised to learn how many of these people there are," says a top U.S. official. Moussaoui almost exactly fits the profile of the suicide hijackers, but he may or may not have been part of the plot. After Moussaoui's arrest on Aug. 17, U.S. immigration authorities dutifully notified the French (he was a passport holder), who responded 10 days later that Moussaoui was a suspected terrorist who had allegedly traveled to Osama bin Laden's training camps in Afghanistan. Ten days may seem like a leisurely pace for investigators racing against time to foil terrorist plots, but in the real world of international cooperation, 10 days, "c'est rapide," a French official told NEWSWEEK. Fast but, in the new age of terror, not fast enough.

As officials at the CIA and FBI sift through intelligence reports, they are berating themselves for missing warning signs on the road to Sept. 11. Those reports include intercepted messages with phrases like "There is a big thing coming," "They're going to pay the price" and "We're ready to go." Unfortunately, many of those messages, intercepted before the attack, did not reach the desks of intelligence analysts until afterward. In the bureaucracy of spying, 24-hour or 48-hour time lags are not unusual. None of the intercepted traffic mentioned the Pentagon or the World Trade Center. Some hinted at a target somewhere on the Pacific Rim. Nonetheless, an intelligence official told NEWSWEEK: "A lot of people feel guilty and think of what they could have done."

ALL ACROSS THE WORLD LAST WEEK, intelligence services were scrambling to catch the terrorists before they struck again. The scale of the roundup was breathtaking: in Yemen, a viper's nest of terror, authorities hauled in "dozens" of suspected bin Laden followers. In Germany, police were searching for a pair of men believed to be directly involved in the hijacking plot. In France, more than half a dozen were being held for questioning, while in Britain, Belgium and the Netherlands—and Peru and Paraguay—police raided suspected terror hideouts. In the United States, where the FBI has launched the greatest manhunt in history, authorities detained about 90 people. Most of them were being held for minor immigration charges, but investigators were looking for mass murderers. The gumshoes swept up pieces of chilling evidence, like two box cutters stuffed into the seat of a Sept. 11 flight out of Boston—another hijacking target? Boston was jittery over threats of an attack last Saturday. An Arab in a bar was overheard to say that blood would flow in Boston on Sept. 22, and U.S. intelligence intercepted a conversation between Algerian diplomats talking about "the upcoming Boston tea party on Sept. 22." It turned out that some women really were holding a tea party that day. Some federal officials were spooked when manuals describing crop-duster equipment—to spray deadly germs?—were found among Moussaoui's possessions. But a top U.S. official told NEWSWEEK, "I'm not getting into the bunker and putting on a gas mask. We're used to seeing these threats." (Nonetheless, crop-dusters were barred from flying near cities.)

The vast dragnet was heartening, unless one considers that after two American embassies were bombed in 1998, a similar crackdown swept up a hundred potential suspects from Europe to the Middle East to Latin America—and bin Laden's men were still able to regroup to launch far more devastating attacks. Catching foot soldiers and lieutenants will not be enough to stop even greater cataclysms. Last week the authorities were searching for a single man who might have triggered the assault on Washington and New York. In past attacks by bin Laden's Qaeda organization, "sleeper" agents have burrowed into the target country to await their orders. FBI officials now believe that the mastermind was Mohamed Atta, the intense Egyptian who apparently piloted the first plane, American Airlines Flight 11, into the North Tower of the World Trade Center. ("Did he ever learn to fly?" Atta's father, Mohamed al-Amir Atta, said to NEWS-WEEK. "Never. He never even had a kite. My daughter, who is a doctor, used to get

him medicine before every journey, to make him combat the cramps and vomiting he feels every time he gets on a plane.") Though intelligence officials believe they have spotted the operation's paymaster, identified to NEWSWEEK as Mustafa Ahmed, in the United Arab Emirates, Atta was the one hijacker who appeared to have the most contacts with conspirators on other aircraft prior to the attacks, and he was the one who left a last testament. According to a top government source, it included this prayer: "Be prepared to meet your God. Be ready for this moment." Atta's role "doesn't fit the usual pattern," said one official. "It looks like the ringleader went down with the plane."

> ## You could date the arrival of the international jihad in America to the rainy night of Nov. 5, 1990, when a terrorist walked into a Marriott and killed Meir Kahane. The cops bungled the case.

The ultimate ringleader may be somewhere in the mountains of Afghanistan, hiding from U.S. bombs and commandos—but also no doubt plotting his next atrocity. In history's long list of villains, bin Laden will find a special place. He has no throne, no armies, not even any real territory, aside from the rocky wastes of Afghanistan. But he has the power to make men willingly go to their deaths for the sole purpose of indiscriminately killing Americans—men, women and children. He is an unusual combination in the annals of hate, at once mystical and fanatical—and deliberate and efficient. Now he has stirred America's wrath and may soon see America's vengeance. But the slow business of mopping up the poison spread by bin Laden through the Islamic world was almost pitifully underscored after the attack by a plea from FBI Director Robert Mueller. The nation's top G-man said the FBI was looking for more Arabic speakers. A reasonable request, but perhaps a

little late in the game. It's hard to know your enemy when you can't even speak his language.

For most Americans, life was instantly and forever changed on Sept. 11, 2001. But the terror war that led up to the attack had been simmering, and sometimes boiling over, for more than 10 years. It can be recalled as a tedious bureaucratic struggle—all those reports on "Homeland Defense" piling up unread on the shelves of congressmen, droning government officials trying to fatten their budgets with scare stories relegated to the back pages of the newspaper. Or it can be relived—as it truly was—as a race to the Gates of Hell. Before the world finds out what horrors lie beyond, it's worthwhile retracing a decade-long trail of terror to see how America stumbled. The enemy has clearly learned from experience. In December 1994, the Armed Islamic Group (GIA), an Algerian-based terrorist band that would go on to play a prominent role in bin Laden's global army, hijacked an Air France Airbus with 171 passengers aboard. The plan: to plunge into the Eiffel Tower. The problem: none of the hijackers could fly. The Air France pilot landed instead in Marseilles, where French police stormed the plane. It was not too long afterward that the first terrorists began quietly enrolling in flight schools in Florida.

THE UNITED STATES HAS BEEN A LIT-TLE slower on the uptake. Money has not really been the obstacle. The counterterrorism budget jumped from $2 billion to $12 billion over a decade. The United States spends $30 billion a year gathering intelligence. Nor has bin Laden been in any way ignored. For the past five years, analysts have been working through the night in a chamber, deep in the bowels of CIA headquarters, known as the Bin Laden Room. Some experts argued that the CIA was too focused on bin Laden—that, in an effort to put a face on faceless terror, the gaunt guerrilla fighter had been elevated to the role of international bogeyman, to the neglect of shadowy others who did the real killing. Now, as the Washington blame game escalates—along with the cries for revenge—intelligence officials are cautioning that terror cells, clannish and secretive, are extremely difficult to penetrate; that for every snake beheaded two more will crawl out of the swamp; that swamps can never be drained in land that drips with the blood of martyrs; that even the most persuasive interrogations may not crack a suspect who is willing to die.

All true. But the inability of the government to even guess that 19 suicidal terrorists might turn four jetliners into guided missiles aimed at national icons was more than a failure of intelligence. It was a failure of imagination. The United States is so strong, the American people seemed so secure, that the concept of Homeland Defense seemed abstract, almost foreign, the sort of thing tiny island nations worried about. Terrorists were regarded by most people as criminals, wicked and frightening, but not as mortal enemies of the state. There was a kind of collective denial, an unwillingness to see how monstrous the threat of Islamic extremism could be.

In part, that may be because the government of the United States helped create it. In the 1980s, the CIA secretly backed the mujahedin, the Islamic freedom fighters rebelling against the Soviet occupation of Afghanistan. Arming and training the "Mooj" was one of the most successful covert actions ever mounted by the CIA. It turned the tide against the Soviet invaders. But there is a word used by old CIA hands to describe covert actions that backfire: "blowback." In the coming weeks, if and when American Special Forces helicopters try to land in the mountains of Afghanistan to flush out bin Laden, they risk being shot down by Stinger surface-to-air missiles provided to the Afghan rebels by the CIA. Such an awful case of blowback would be a mere coda to a long and twisted tragedy of unanticipated consequences. The tale begins more than 10 years ago, when the veterans of the Mooj's holy war against the Soviets began arriving in the United States—many with passports arranged by the CIA.

Bonded by combat, full of religious zeal, the diaspora of young Arab men willing to die for Allah congregated at the Al-Kifah Refugee Center in Brooklyn, N.Y., a dreary inner-city building that doubled as a recruiting post for the CIA seeking to steer fresh troops to the mujahedin. The dominant figures at the center in the late '80s were a gloomy New York City engineer named El Sayyid Nosair, who took Prozac for his blues, and his sidekick, Mahmud Abouhalima, who had been a human minesweeper in the Afghan war (his only tool was a thin reed, which he used as a crude probe). The new immigrants were filled not with gratitude toward their new nation, but by implacable hatred toward America, symbol of West-

ern modernity that threatened to engulf Muslim fundamentalism in a tide of blue jeans and Hollywood videos. Half a world away, people who understood the ferocity of Islamic extremism could see the coming storm. In the late '80s, Pakistan's then head of state, Benazir Bhutto, told the first President George Bush, "You are creating a Frankenstein." But the warnings never quite filtered down to the cops and G-men on the streets of New York.

The international jihad arrived in America on the rainy night of Nov. 5, 1990, when Nosair walked into a crowded ballroom at the New York Marriott on 49th Street and shot and killed Rabbi Meir Kahane, a mindless hater who wanted to rid Israel of "Arab dogs" ("Every Jew a .22" was a Kahane slogan). The escape plan was amateur hour: Nosair's buddy Abouhalima was supposed to drive the getaway car, a taxicab, but the overexcited Nosair jumped in the wrong cab and was apprehended.

In the mid-'90s Ramzi Yousef took flying lessons and talked of crashing a plane into the CIA or a nuclear facility. At the time the FBI thought the plans grandiose. Now they look like blueprints.

With a room full of witnesses and a smoking gun, the case against Nosair should have been a lay-down. But the New York police bungled the evidence, and Nosair got off with a gun rap. At that moment, Nosair and Abouhalima may have had an epiphany: back home in Egypt, suspected terrorists are dragged in and tortured. In America, they can hire a good lawyer and beat the system. The New York City police hardly noticed any grander scheme. A search of Nosair's apartment turned up instructions for building bombs and photos of targets—including the Empire State Building and the World Trade Center. The police never bothered to inventory most of the evidence, nor were the documents translated—that is, until a van with a 1,500-

pound bomb blew up in the underground garage of the World Trade Center on Feb. 26, 1993. The (first) World Trade Center bombing, which killed six people and injured more than 1,000, might have been a powerful warning, especially when investigators discovered that the plotters had meant to topple the towers and packed the truck bomb with cyanide (in an effort to create a crude chemical weapon). But the cyanide was harmlessly burned up in the blast, the buildings didn't fall and the bombers seemed to be hapless. One of them went back to get his security deposit from the truck rental.

The plotters were quickly exposed as disciples of Sheik Omar Abdel-Rahman, the "Blind Sheik" who ranted against the infidels from a run-down mosque in Jersey City. The Blind Sheik's shady past should have been of great interest to the Feds—he had been linked to the plot to assassinate Egyptian President Anwar Sadat in 1981. But the sheik had slipped into the United States with the protection of the CIA, which saw the revered cleric as a valuable recruiting agent for the Mooj. Investigators trying to track down the Blind Sheik "had zero cooperation from the intelligence community, zero," recalled a federal investigator in New York.

ONE WORLD TRADE CENTER PLOTTER who did attract attention from the Feds was Ramzi Yousef. Operating under a dozen aliases, Yousef was a frightening new figure, seemingly stateless and sinister, a global avenging angel. Though he talked to Iraqi intelligence and stayed in a safe house that was later linked to bin Laden, Yousef at the time appeared to be a kind of terror freelancer. Yousef's luck ran out when the apartment of an old childhood friend, Abdul Hakim Murad, burst into flames. Plotting with Yousef, Murad had been at work making bombs to assassinate the pope and blow up no fewer than 11 U.S. airliners. Murad's arrest in January 1995 led investigators to capture Yousef in Pakistan, where he was hiding out. Murad and Yousef were a duo sent by the Devil: Murad had taken pilot lessons, and the two talked about flying a plane filled with explosives into the CIA headquarters or a nuclear facility. At the time, FBI officials thought the plans were grandiose and farfetched. Now they look like blueprints.

The capture of Yousef was regarded as a stirring victory in the war against terrorism, which was just then gearing up in Washington. But Yousef's arrest illustrates the difficulties of cracking terrorism even when a prize suspect is caught. At his sentencing, Yousef declared, "Yes, I am a terrorist, and I am proud of it." He has never cooperated with authorities. Instead, he spent his days chatting about movies with his fellow inmates in a federal maximum-security prison, Unabomber Ted Kaczynski and, until he was executed, the Oklahoma City bomber Timothy McVeigh.

By the mid-'90s, counterterror experts at the FBI and CIA had begun to focus on Osama bin Laden, the son of a Saudi billionaire who had joined the Mooj in Afghanistan and become a hero as a battlefield commander. Bin Laden was said to be bitter because the Saudi royal family had rebuffed his offer to rally freedom fighters to protect the kingdom against the threat of Saddam Hussein after the Iraqi strongman invaded Kuwait in 1990. Instead, the Saudi rulers chose to be defended by the armed forces of the United States. To bin Laden, corrupt princes were welcoming infidels to desecrate holy ground. Bin Laden devoted himself to expelling America, not just from Saudi Arabia, but—as his messianic madness grew—from Islam, indeed all the world.

Tony Lake, President Bill Clinton's national-security adviser, does not recall one single defining moment when bin Laden became Public Enemy No. 1. It was increasingly clear to intelligence analysts that extremists all over the Middle East viewed bin Laden as a modern-day Saladin, the Islamic warrior who drove out the Crusaders a millennium ago. Setting up a sort of Terror Central of spiritual, financial and logistical support—Al Qaeda (the Base)—bin Laden went public, in 1996 telling every Muslim that their duty was to kill Americans (at first the *fatwa* was limited to U.S. soldiers, then broadened in 1998 to all Americans). From his home in Sudan, bin Laden seemed to be inspiring and helping to fund a broad if shadowy network of terrorist cells. On the rationale that no nation should be allowed to harbor terrorists, the State Department in the mid-'90s pressured the government of Sudan to kick out bin Laden. In retrospect, that may have been a mistake. At least in Sudan, it was easier to keep an eye on bin Laden's activities. Instead, he vanished into the mountains of Afghanistan, where he would be welcomed by extremist Taliban rulers and enabled to set up training bases for terrorists. These camps—crude collections of mud huts—appear to have provided a sort of Iron John bonding experience for thou-

sands of aspiring martyrs who came for a course of brainwashing and bombmaking.

With the cold war over, the Mafia in retreat and the drug war unwinnable, the CIA and FBI were eager to have a new foe to fight. The two agencies established a Counter Terrorism Center in a bland, windowless warren of offices on the ground floor of CIA headquarters at Langley, Va. Historical rivals, the spies and G-men were finally learning to work together. But they didn't necessarily share secrets with the alphabet soup of other enforcement and intelligence agencies, like Customs and the Immigration and Naturalization Service, and they remained aloof from the Pentagon. And no amount of good will or money could bridge a fundamental divide between intelligence and law enforcement. Spies prefer to watch and wait; cops want to get their man. At the White House, a bright national-security staffer, Richard Clarke, tried to play counterterror coordinator, but he was given about as much real clout as the toothless "czars" sent out to fight the war on drugs. There was no central figure high in the administration to knock heads, demand performance and make sure everyone was on the same page. Lake now regrets that he did not try harder to create one. At the time, Clinton's national-security adviser was too preoccupied with U.S. involvement in Bosnia to do battle with fiefdoms in the intelligence community. "Bosnia was easier than changing the bureaucracy," Lake told NEWSWEEK.

Bitter after the Saudis allied themselves with the American infidels against Saddam, bin Laden, his messianic madness growing, devoted himself to destroying the United States.

AN EMPIRE BUILDER WITH A MESSIANIC streak OF his own, FBI Director Louis Freeh was eager to throw G-men at the terrorist threat all over the world. When a truck bomb blew up the Khobar Towers, a U.S. military barracks in Saudi Arabia,

Freeh made a personal quest of bringing the bombers to justice. As Freeh left office last summer, a grand jury in New York was about to indict several conspirators behind the bombing. But, safely secluded in Iran, the suspects will probably never stand trial. The Khobar Towers investigation shows the limits of treating terrorism as a crime. It also reveals some of the difficulties of working with foreign intelligence services that don't share the same values (or rules) as Americans. Freeh's gumshoes got a feel for Saudi justice when they asked to interview some suspects seized in an earlier bombing attack against a U.S.-run military compound in Riyadh. Before the FBI could ask any questions, the suspects were beheaded. An attempt by the FBI to play the role of Good Cop to the Saudis' Bad Cop was thwarted by American sensitivities. After the bombing, FBI agents managed to corner Hani al-Sayegh, a key suspect in Canada. Cooperate with us, the gumshoes threatened, or we'll send you back to Saudi Arabia, where a sword awaits. No fool, the suspect hired an American lawyer. The State Department was convinced that sending the man back to Saudi Arabia would violate international laws banning torture. Their leverage gone, the Feds were unable to make the suspect talk.

The CIA did have some luck in working with foreign security services to roll up terror networks. In 1997 and 1998, the agency collaborated with the Egyptians—whose security service is particularly ruthless—to root out cells of bin Laden's men from their hiding places in Albania. But just as the spooks were congratulating themselves, another bin Laden cell struck in a carefully coordinated, long-planned attack. Within minutes of each other, truck bombs blew up the U.S. embassies in Tanzania and Kenya, killing more than 220. The failure of intelligence in the August 1998 embassy bombings is a case study in the difficulty of penetrating bin Laden's network.

For some of the time that bin Laden's men were plotting to blow up the two embassies, U.S. intelligence was tapping their phones. According to Justice Department documents, the spooks tapped five telephone numbers used by bin Laden's men living in Kenya in 1996 and '97. But the plotters did not give themselves away. Bin Laden uses couriers to communicate with his agents face to face. His Qaeda organization is also technologically sophisticated, sometimes embedding coded messages in innocuous-seeming Web sites. Intelligence experts have worried for some time that the supersecret-code breakers at the National Security Agency are going deaf, overwhelmed by the sheer volume of telecommunications and encryption software that any consumer can buy at a computer store.

If high-tech espionage won't do the job, say the experts, then the CIA needs more human spies. It has become rote to say that in order to crack secretive terrorist cells the CIA needs to hire more Arabic-speaking case officers who can in turn recruit deep-penetration agents—HUMINT (human intelligence) in spy jargon. Actually, the CIA had a sometime informer among the embassy bombers. Ali Mohamed was a former Egyptian Army officer who enlisted in the U.S. Army and was sent to Fort Bragg, N.C., in the early 1980s to lecture U.S. Special Forces on Islamic terrorism. In his free time, he was a double agent. On the weekends he visited the Al-Kifah Refugee Center in Brooklyn, where he stayed with none other than El Sayyid Nosair, the man who struck the first blow in the holy war by murdering Rabbi Kahane. Ali Mohamed went to Afghanistan to fight with the Mooj, but after the 1993 World Trade Center bombing, he flipped back, telling the Feds about bin Laden's connection to some of the bombers. He described how the Islamic terrorist used "sleepers" who live normal lives for years and then are activated for operations. What he did not tell the spooks was that he was helping plan to bomb the U.S. embassies in Africa. Only after he had pleaded guilty to conspiracy in 1999 did he disclose that he had personally met with bin Laden about the plot. He described how bin Laden, looking at a photo of the U.S. Embassy in Nairobi, "pointed to where the truck could go as a suicide bomber."

The story of Ali Mohamed suggests that the calls by some politicians for more and better informants may be easier to preach than practice. The CIA's skills in the dark arts of running agents have atrophied over the years. The agency was purged of some of its best spy handlers after the 1975 Church Committee investigation exposed some harebrained agency plots, like hiring the Mafia to poison Fidel Castro. During the Reagan years, the agency was beefed up, but a series of scandals in the late '80s and the '90s once more sapped its esprit. America's spies were once proud to engage in "morally hazardous duty," said Carleton Swift, the CIA's Baghdad station chief in the late 1950s. "Now the CIA has become a standard government bureaucracy instead of a bunch of special guys."

A number of lawmakers are calling to, in effect, unleash the CIA. They want to do away with rules that restrict the agency from hiring agents and informers with a record of crimes or abusing human rights. Actually, case officers in the field can still hire sleazy or dangerous characters by asking permission from their bosses in Langley. "We almost never turn them down," said one high-ranking official. But that answer may gloss over a more significant point—that case officers, made cautious by scandal, no longer dare to launch operations that could get them hauled before a congressional inquisition.

THE WEAKNESSES OF THE CIA'S DIRECtorate of Operations, once called "the Department of Dirty Tricks," can be overstated. When the CIA suspected that the Sudanese government was helping bin Laden obtain chemical weapons, a CIA agent was able to obtain soil samples outside the Al Shifa pharmaceutical plant that showed traces of EMPTA—a precursor chemical used in deadly VX gas. The evidence was used to justify a cruise-missile attack on the factory in retaliation for the embassy bombings. At the same time, 70 cruise missiles rained down on a bin Laden training camp in Afghanistan.

The Clinton administration was later mocked for this showy but meaningless response. Clinton's credibility was not high: he was accused of trying to divert attention from the Monica Lewinsky scandal. In classic American fashion, the owner of the pharmaceutical plant in Sudan hired a top Washington lobbying firm to heap scorn on the notion that his plant was being used for chemical weapons. But Clinton's national-security adviser at the time, Sandy Berger, still "swears by" the evidence, and insists that the cruise missiles aimed at bin Laden's training camps missed bin Laden and his top advisers by only a few hours.

The Clinton administration never stopped trying to kill bin Laden. Although a 1976 executive order bans assassinations of foreign leaders, there is no prohibition on killing terrorists—or, for that matter, from killing a head of state in time of war. In 1998, President Clinton signed a "lethal finding," in effect holding the CIA harmless if bin Laden was killed in a covert operation. The agency tried for at least two years to hunt down bin Laden, working with Afghan rebels opposed to the Taliban regime. These rebels once fired a bazooka at bin Laden's convoy but hit the wrong

vehicle. "There were a few points when the pulse quickened, when we thought we were close," recalled Berger.

By the final year of the Clinton administration, top officials were very worried about the terrorist threat. Berger says he lay awake at night, wondering if his phone would ring with news of another attack. Administration officials were routinely trooping up to Capitol Hill to sound warnings. CIA Director George Tenet raised the specter of bin Laden so many times that some lawmakers suspected he was just trying to scare them into coughing up more money for intelligence. The Clinton Cassandras emphasized the growing risk that terrorists would obtain weapons of mass destruction—chemical, biological or nuclear. But the threat was not deemed to be imminent. Bin Laden was generally believed to be aiming at "soft" targets in the Middle East and Europe, like another embassy. The experts said that a few bin Laden lieutenants were probably operating in the United States, but no one seriously expected a major attack, at least right away.

The millennium plots should have been a wakeup call. Shortly before the 2000 New Year, an obscure Algerian refugee named Ahmed Ressam was caught by a wary U.S. Customs inspector trying to slip into the United States from Canada with the makings of a bomb. Ressam was a storm trooper in what may have been a much bigger plot to attack the Los Angeles airport and possibly other targets with a high symbolic value. A petty criminal who lived by credit-card fraud and stealing laptop computers, Ressam was part of a dangerous terrorist organization—GIA, the same group that hijacked the Air France jet in 1994 and tried, but failed, to plunge it into the Eiffel Tower. A particularly vicious group that staged a series of rush-hour subway bombings in Paris in the mid-'90s, GIA is a planet in Al Qaeda's solar system. Ressam later told investigators that he had just returned from one of bin Laden's Afghan training camps, where he learned such skills as feeding poison gas through the air vents of office buildings. Some of Ressam's confederates in the millennium plots were never picked up and are still at large. The Canadian Security Intelligence Service is believed to have fat files on the GIA, but like many secret services, the CSIS does not share its secrets readily with other services, at home or abroad. Some U.S. investigators believe that bin Laden was using Canada as a safe base for assaults on the United States. U.S.

border authorities now believe that several of the suicide hijackers came across the border via a ferry from Nova Scotia in the days before the attack on the World Trade Center.

In hindsight, the Ressam case offered clues to another bin Laden trademark: the ability of Al Qaeda-trained operatives to hide their tracks. While renting buildings in Vancouver, Ressam and his confederates frequently changed the names on the leases, apparently to lay a confusing paper trail. A kind of terrorist's how-to manual ("Military Studies in the Jihad Against the Tyrants") found at the home of a bin Laden associate in England last year instructs operatives to deflect suspicion by shaving beards, avoiding mosques and refraining from traditional Islamic greetings. Intelligence officials now suspect that bin Laden used all manner of feints and bluffs to throw investigators off the trail of the suicide hijackers. Decoy terrorist teams and disinformation kept the CIA frantically guessing about an attack somewhere in the Middle East, Asia or Europe all last summer. Embassies were shuttered, warships were sent to sea, troops were put on the highest state of alert in the Persian Gulf. The Threat Committee of national-security specialists that meets twice a week in the White House complex to monitor alerts sent out so many warnings that they began to blur together. One plot seemed particularly concrete and menacing. At the end of July, authorities picked up an alleged bin Laden lieutenant named Djamel Begal in Dubai. He began singing—a little too fast, perhaps—about a plan to bomb the American Embassy in Paris. Was the threat real—or a diversion?

The United States is heavily dependent on foreign intelligence services to roll up terror networks in their own countries. But typically, intelligence services prefer to keep an eye on suspected terrorists rather than prosecute them.

To persuade a foreign government to turn over information on a terrorist suspect, much less arrest him, requires heavy doses of diplomacy. The task is not made easier if different branches of the American government squabble with each other. Last October, the USS Cole, a destroyer making a refueling stop in the Yemeni port of Aden, was nearly sunk by suicide bombers in a small boat. (An earlier attempt, against a different American warship docking in Yemen, fizzled when the suicide boat, overloaded with explosives, sank as it was leaving the dock. Bin Laden,

nothing if not persistent, apparently ordered his hit men to try again.) FBI investigators immediately rushed to the scene, where they were coolly received by the Yemeni government. The G-men became apprehensive about their own security and demanded that they be allowed to carry assault rifles. The U.S. ambassador, Barbara Bodine, who regarded the FBI men as heavy-handed and undiplomatic, refused. After an awkward standoff between the G-men and embassy security officials in the embassy compound, the entire FBI team left the country—for three months. They did not return until just recently.

It now appears that the same men who masterminded the Cole bombing may be tied to the devastating Sept. 11 assault on the United States. Since January 2000 the CIA has been aware of a man named Tawfiq bin Atash, better known in terrorist circles by his nom de guerre "Khallad." A Yemeni-born former freedom fighter in Afghanistan, Khallad assumed control of bin Laden's bodyguards and became a kind of capo in Al Qaeda. According to intelligence sources, Khallad helped coordinate the attack on the Cole. These same sources tell NEWSWEEK that in December 1999, Khallad was photographed by the Malaysian security service (which was working with the CIA to track terrorists) at a hotel in Kuala Lumpur. There, Khallad met with several bin Laden operatives. One was Fahad al-Quso, who, it later turned out, was assigned to videotape the suicide attack on the Cole (not all of Al Qaeda's men are James Bond: al-Quso botched the job when he overslept). Another was Khalid al-Midhar, who was traveling with an associate, Nawaf al-Hazmi, on a trip arranged by an organization known to U.S. intelligence as a "logistical center" and "base of support" for Al Qaeda.

American intelligence agencies intercepted a number of messages pointing to an imminent terrorist assault. But none was analyzed until after the deadly September 11 attacks.

Those two names—al-Midhar and al-Hazmi—would resonate with intelligence officials on Sept. 11. Both men were listed among the hijackers of American Airlines Flight 77, the airliner that dive-bombed the Pentagon. Indeed, when one intelligence official saw the names on the list of suspects, he uttered an expletive. Just three weeks earlier, on Aug. 21, the CIA asked the INS to keep a watch out for al-Midhar. The INS reported that the man was already in the country; his only declared address was "Marriott Hotel" in New York. The CIA sent the FBI to find al-Midhar and his associate. The gumshoes were still looking on Sept. 11.

AT LEAST ONE OTHER NAME FROM THE list of hijackers had shown up in the files of Western intelligence services: Mohamed Atta. He is an intriguing figure, both because of his role as the apparent senior man among the suicide hijackers, and because his background offers some disturbing clues about the high quality of bin Laden's recruits. The stereotype of an Islamic suicide bomber is that of a young man or teenage boy who has no job, no education, no prospects and no hope. He has been gulled into believing that if he straps a few sticks of dynamite around his waist and presses a button, he will stroll through the Gates of Paradise, where he will be bedded by virgins. Atta in no way matches that pathetic creature. He did not come from a poor or desperate fundamentalist family. His father, Mohamed, described himself to NEWSWEEK as "one of the most important lawyers in Cairo." The Atta family has a vacation home on the Mediterranean coast. Their Cairo apartment, with a sweeping view of downtown, is filled with ornate furniture and decorated with paintings of flamingos and women in head scarves.

If anything, Atta seemed like a prodigy of Western modernism. His two sisters are university professors with Ph.D.s. Atta won a bachelor's degree in Cairo in 1990 and went to Germany for graduate work in urban studies.

His thesis adviser in Hamburg, where he studied at the Technical University, called Atta "a dear human being." Only in retrospect does it appear ominous that in his thesis dedication he wrote "my life and my death belong to Allah, master of all worlds." Atta went to bars and rented videos ("Ace Ventura," "Storm of the Century"), but he also grew a beard and began to dress more in Islamic style. He spoke often of Egypt's "humiliation" by the West.

While polite, he also could be haughty. He scorned women, refusing to shake their hands.

That was the only worry of Atta's proud father. "I started reminding him to get married," Atta senior recounted to NEWSWEEK, as he chain-smoked cigarettes ("American blend"). "Many times I asked him to marry a woman of any nationality— Turkish, German, Syrian—because he did not have a girlfriend like his colleagues. But he insisted he would marry an Egyptian. He was never touching woman, so how can he live?" In October 1999, "we found him a bride who was nice and delicate, the daughter of a former ambassador," said Atta senior. But Atta junior said he had to go back to Germany to finish his Ph.D. Actually, he was going to Florida to enroll in flight school.

During his years as a student in Hamburg, Atta would disappear for long periods of time—possibly, to meet with his handlers. U.S. intelligence believes that Atta met in Europe this year with a midlevel Iraqi intelligence official. The report immediately raised the question of Saddam Hussein's possible role in the Sept. 11 atrocity, but intelligence officials cautioned against reading too much into the link. Atta was in close communication with his superiors. On Sept. 4, one week before the bombing, he sent a package from a Kinko's in Hollywood, Fla., to a man named Mustafa Ahmed in the United Arab Emirates. "We don't know for sure what was in the package," said a senior U.S. official. "But Mustafa could be the key to bin Laden's finances. We're taking a hard look at him." (Several of the hijackers also wired money to Ahmed.) There are indications that Atta prepared very carefully for the attack, casing the airport in Boston and flying coast to coast on airliners. He may have had a backup plan: NEWSWEEK has learned that Atta had round-trip reservations between Baltimore and San Francisco in mid-October.

Atta's father refuses to accept his son's role as a suicide bomber. "It's impossible my son would participate in this attack," he said, claiming that he was a victim of a plot by Israeli intelligence to provoke the United States against Islam. "The Mossad kidnapped my son," said Atta. "He is the easiest person to kidnap, very surrendering, no physical power, no money for bodyguards. They used his name and identity… Then they killed him. This was done by the Mossad, using American pilots." Atta's rant was wild and sad—yet it was matched by the vituperations of the virulently anti-American Egyptian press, which spun fantastic plots featuring Mossad agents as the villains.

Atta appears to have been inseparable from another hijacker, Marwan al-Shehhi, up to the moment they parted ways at Logan airport on the morning of Sept. 11. The FBI believes that al-Shehhi piloted the second jetliner, United Airlines Flight 173, into the South Tower of the World Trade Center. Al-Shehhi and Atta roomed together in Florida and were tossed out of Jones Flying Service School for unprofessional behavior. (Instructors complained about their "attitude.") They signed up together for a one-month membership at a gym, the Delray Beach Health Club. They went to Las Vegas, where the FBI believes that several hijackers kept girlfriends. They ate American, but told the employees at Hungry Howie's to hold the ham when they ordered their favorite pizza, a pie with all the toppings called "The Works."

As investigators piece together the lives of the hijackers, details that once seemed innocuous now loom large. Ziad Samir Jarrahi, a Lebanese man, took martial-arts lessons at a Dania, Fla., gym. "What he wanted to study was street-fighting tactics—how to gain control over somebody with your hands, how to incapacitate someone with your hands," gym owner Bert Rodriguez told NEWSWEEK. Did Jarrahi use those tactics in the last, desperate struggle in the cockpit of Flight 93, which crashed in a field outside Pittsburgh? Top law-enforcement officials reported that the voice recorder from Flight 93 picked up sounds of Arab and American voices shouting as the plane went down. Some very brave passengers stormed the cockpit in a last-ditch effort to seize control of the plane. Did they encounter Jarrahi and his newly honed fighting skills?

T HE AVAILABLE EVIDENCE SUGGESTS A death match. When the hijackers struck, at about 9:35 a.m., air-traffic controllers listening in on the frequency between the cockpit and the control center in Cleveland could hear screams, then a gap of 40 seconds with no sound, then more screams. Then, sources say, a nearly unintelligible voice said something like "Bomb onboard." The controllers tried to raise the captain but received no response. Then radar showed the plane turning sharply—toward Washington, D.C. A voice in thickly accented English said, "This is your captain. There is a bomb onboard. We are returning to the airport."

In the passenger cabin, there was bloodshed and fear. At least one passenger was dead, probably with his throat slashed. In the back of the plane, however, five men, all burly athletes, were plotting a rush at the hijackers. "We're going to do something," Todd Beamer told a GTE operator over the air phone. "I know I'm not going to get out of this." He asked the operator to say the Lord's Prayer with him. "Are you ready, guys?" he asked. "Let's roll." The cockpit voice recorder picked up someone, apparently a hijacker, screaming "Get out of here! Get out of here!" Then grunting, screaming and scuffling. Then silence.

Such stories of heroic struggle will be—and should be—told and retold in the years to come. But now investigators are groping with uncertainty, asking: Who else is still out there? And will they strike again? A congressional delegation to CIA headquarters last week reported that mattresses were strewn on the floors. The race is still on, round the clock. Some investigators were trying to follow the money. They learned that in the week before the Sept. 11 attack, the hijackers began sending small amounts of money back to their paymasters in the Middle East. "They were sending in their change," an intelligence source told NEWSWEEK. "They were going to a place where they wouldn't need money." The hijackers apparently didn't need all that much to begin with: law enforcement estimates that the entire plot, flight lessons and all, cost as little as $200,000. That is 10 times more than was spent on the first World Trade Center bombing, but still a low-enough sum so the money could be moved in small denominations among trusted agents. Still, Al Qaeda is reputed to be expert at money laundering. Last week the pressure was on banks all over the world to open up their books (and on the banking lobby in the United States to drop its opposition to new laws that would make it easier for investigators to follow the money). The trail is likely to lead in some diplomatically awkward directions. Moderate Arab regimes are said to try to buy off terrorists. Much of bin Laden's money has come from wealthy Saudis who ostensibly give to Islamic charities. Some of those charities resemble the "widows and orphans" funds the Irish Republican Army uses to finance its bombmaking.

The money trail led investigators last week to a suspect whose background and motives could be the stuff of nightmares. Nabil al-Marabh, a former Boston taxi driver of Kuwaiti descent, is suspected of funneling thousands of dollars in wire transfer through Fleet Bank to the Middle East. The money was allegedly sent to a former Boston cabby implicated in a terrorist plot in Jordan that was foiled at the time of the millennium celebrations. At the same time, investigators say, al-Marabh may have exchanged phone calls with at least two of the Sept. 11 hijackers. Al-Marabh, who like a number of terrorists seems to have used Canada as a sometime sanctuary, was hard to track down. Canadian authorities first informed U.S. Customs about al-Marabh in July, and investigators opened a money-laundering probe. Last week the FBI raided an apartment in Detroit, where al-Marabh had been living. They found instead three men who had once worked as caterers at the Detroit airport (and kept their airport ID badges). In the apartment was a diagram of an airport runway and a day planner filled with notations in Arabic about "the American base in Turkey," the "American foreign minister" and the name of an airport in Jordan. The FBI arrested the men, but al-Marabh was at the time getting a duplicate driver's license at the state department of motor vehicles.

Not just any license. Al-Marabh's license would permit him to drive an 18-wheel truck containing hazardous materials. As it turned out, two of his housemates had also been going to school to learn how to drive large trucks. Carrying what, exactly? And heading where?

This story was written by EVAN THOMAS *with reporting from* MARK HOSENBALL, MICHAEL ISIKOFF, ELEANOR CLIFT *and* DANIEL KLAIDMAN *in Washington*, PEG TYRE *in New York*, CHRISTOPHER DICKEY *in Paris*, ANDREW MURR, JOSEPH CONTRERAS *and* JOHN LANTINGUA *in Florida*, KAREN BRESLAU *in San Francisco*, SARAH DOWNEY *in Minneapolis*, STEFAN THEIL *in Hamburg*, TOM MASLAND *in Dubai and* ALAN ZARENBO *in Cairo*

Crime Without Punishment

As American streets get safer, crime in Europe soars.

by Eli Lehrer

AFTER HE BEAT an 80-year-old grandmother, took a mother with a stroller hostage, and robbed 11 London banks in broad daylight, Michael Wheatley was finally nabbed by British police late last month. Dubbed the Skull Cracker for his habit of pistol-whipping victims, Wheatley had transfixed the London tabloid press with a series of dramatic, violent crimes. Scared Londoners, however, had more to worry about than just the Skull Cracker: In April alone, one gang used a battering ram to steal $14,500 of merchandise from a jewelry store near the city's commercial center, another took to ramming cars into storefronts, and teenage thugs robbed pedestrians of their mobile phones all over the city. Last year, London saw more serious assaults, armed robberies, and car thefts than New York; 2002 could see London's murder rate exceed the Big Apple's.

The same pattern can be seen throughout Europe—indeed, in much of the developed world. Crime has recently hit record highs in Paris, Madrid, Stockholm, Amsterdam, Toronto, and a host of other major cities. In a 2001 study, the British Home Office (the equivalent of the U.S. Department of Justice) found violent and property crime increased in the late 1990s in every wealthy country except the United States. American property crime rates have been lower than those in Britain, Canada, and France since the early 1990s, and violent crime rates throughout the E.U., Australia, and Canada have recently begun to equal and even surpass those in the United States. Even Sweden, once the epitome of cosmopolitan socialist prosperity, now has a crime victimization rate 20 percent higher than the United States.

Americans, on the other hand, have become much safer. Preliminary 2001 crime statistics from the FBI show America's tenth consecutive year of declines in crime. While our homicide rate is still substantially higher than most in Europe, it has sunk to levels unseen here since the early 1960s. And overall crime rates in this country are now 40 percent below the all-time highs of the early 1970s. In 1973, nearly 60 percent of American households fell victim to property crimes. In 2000 (the most recent data available), only about 20 percent did. Among the economically powerful democracies in the Group of Seven, only the Japanese now have a lower victimization rate than the United States.

So why have America's streets become safer even as crime has exploded in Europe? Many commonly cited explanations don't hold water: America's falling population of males in their teens and early 20s helped reduce crime in the early 1990s, but crime continued to fall even as youth populations began to swell later in the decade. While the American Enterprise Institute's John Lott has shown that greater gun ownership reduces crime, this deterrent effect can't explain more than a small part of America's recent success. It's now easier to carry concealed weapons in some parts of the country, but Lott acknowledges that gun ownership levels are about the same as they were when crime hit its all-time highs in America 30 years ago. Third-world immigration, the bugbear of the European right, may drive crime rates up, but violence and theft have also spiked in countries that let in few immigrants.

There is, in fact, a simple explanation for America's success against crime: The American justice system now does a better job of catching criminals and locking them up. But why are America's police agencies performing better than their counterparts elsewhere in the developed world?

Local control may be a critical difference. America has local police departments—think Sheriff Andy Griffith and Deputy Barney Fife—while massive regional or national agencies provide almost all of the law enforcement in nearly all of the other industrialized countries. With about 16,500 police agencies—over 2,000 of which employ only one officer—America's policing system might seem disorganized and amateurish at first glance. All of England has only 39 local police departments, and the Royal Canadian Mounted Police run most of Canada's police agencies. France and a bevy of other nations have unified national police agencies. But when it comes to learning from mistakes and adapting to new circumstances, small organizations have their advantages.

While smart police chiefs have always tried to adapt styles of policing to the particularities of their communities, well-intentioned reform efforts during the American crime explosion led police agencies to discourage officers from making too much contact with citizens and community groups. This eventually sparked a backlash in the form of the "community policing" movement of the late 1980s, which began to encourage police officers and citizens to form crime-fighting partnerships. While some of those efforts were better at producing press releases than arrests, the movement overall has to be counted a success.

Today, styles and philosophies of policing can differ enormously in two suburbs of the same city that would share the same police department almost anywhere else in the developed world. In Simi Valley, a sleepy Ventura County suburb full of Los Angeles police officers and Ronald Reagan memorabilia (his library is there), police scatter kids who hang out in front of movie theaters and reprimand pedestrians who spit on the sidewalk. A jaunt down the 405 freeway in Long Beach, a sometimes chaotic, diverse city full of immigrants, police encourage so-called "positive loitering" by handing out stickers to well-behaved juveniles around parks, movie theaters, and schools. Spitting goes unnoticed. Both approaches work: Long Beach and Simi Valley have each reduced crime over a third since the mid-1990s.

American police departments can adapt more easily to their communities than their counterparts in the E.U. and elsewhere not only because they are smaller but because they need to respond to local elected leaders and voters. Police represent the largest or second largest spending program in nearly every city and town budget. Mayors, city council members, and voters keep close tabs on local police. As representatives of municipal government rather than agencies of a distant provincial council or the national government, successful American police chiefs shape their agencies to fit the desires and demands of local constituencies rather than distant bureaucrats.

In their quest to adapt to the needs of their communities, the best American police departments have created a culture of innovation. While a handful of larger police departments (New York, Chicago, and San Diego most prominently) do provide many new techniques and practices, at least as many successful innovations come from small and mid-sized police agencies, which centralization has eliminated in the rest of the developed world. Moreno Valley, Calif., police have developed a national model for fighting graffiti through rapid-response police-community partnerships; Minneapolis police have built the world's best computer system to monitor pawn shops for stolen goods; and Jacksonville, Fla., police could teach other agencies a few things about neighborhood renewal.

Relatively small American police departments also put more cops on the street. While conventional management theory suggests that administrative savings come from consolidation, larger departments tend to have more blue-uniformed bureaucrats and fewer crime fighters. Only about a third of France's 130,000 police officers, for example, work on the streets. As agencies get smaller, however, they send a greater percentage of their staff to work the streets: In Garden Grove, Calif.—which has one of the lowest police officer-citizen ratios of any American city—85 percent of officers work the streets in one way or another.

Larger agencies (including American ones) face an almost irresistible temptation to move the best officers onto specialized teams directed at particular types of crime or feel-good community involvement programs. While all police departments need some specialists—a green academy graduate can't substitute for a veteran homicide investigator—the most successful agencies keep such special assignments to a minimum. Lowell, Mass., the city with the largest crime decreases in the United States during the 1990s, eliminated nearly all of its special units. And other highly successful departments have followed suit, eliminating or restructuring their special task forces in order to assign more officers to patrol duty and answering citizens' calls.

SUPERIOR POLICING does little good without a commitment from the justice system to keep violent thugs off the streets. The United States has the longest prison sentences in the Western world. According to the Bureau of Justice Statistics and its counterparts in other countries, a convicted armed robber can expect to serve about four and a half years behind bars in the United States, a little over two years in Great Britain, a bit less in Germany, and less than 18 months in France. The United States imprisons nearly 700 out of 100,000 citizens as compared to about 125 in the U.K. and Canada, 100 in Germany, and about 60 in most of Scandinavia. Some of these countries may actually have fewer thugs than the United States, but those left unpunished do enormous damage.

While building and staffing prisons costs a great deal, letting criminals roam free costs even more. One violent criminal can do over a million dollars worth of damage in the space of a year. A single armed robbery costs society more than $50,000, and a hardened thug can commit a hundred such crimes in a year. The European elite still seems to regard Americans' desire to lock up violent criminals as an index of barbarism and America as a nation gripped by violence and infatuated with rough, frontier justice. With violence and theft exploding all over the developed world, however, one has to ask which type of society is barbaric—one that punishes criminals, or one that lets them prey on law-abiding citizens?

Not surprisingly, overwhelming evidence demonstrates that keeping criminals locked up reduces crime. British academic Donald E. Lewis's comprehensive 1986 examination of studies on the correlation between sentence length and crime rates (published in the British Journal of Criminology) concludes that doubling the length of the sentence for a crime will cut the likelihood that criminals will commit that crime by a little less than 50 percent. In a comprehensive comparison of crime rates in the United States and Great Britain, a Bureau of Justice Statistics researcher and the head of Cambridge University's Criminology Institute hit on the key fact: Crime rates fell in the United States as punishment increased and rose in Britain as punishment decreased. As James Q. Wilson has observed, "co-incident with rising prison population there began in 1979–80 a steep reduction in the crime rate as reported by the victimization surveys."

America's criminal justice system has plenty of flaws. While nearly every other developed country has too few local police agencies, the United States has too many: More law enforcement agencies patrol Washington, D.C., (population 572,000) than all of the United Kingdom (population 59.6 million). And the crime picture isn't entirely copacetic: Although murder rates have fallen sharply in the United States even as they rise elsewhere, ours still remains second only to South Africa's among wealthy nations. While most murder victims have some connection to the drug trade or other organized crime, Americans also kill each other at high rates in their homes and streets. American law enforcers could learn a good deal from foreign police agencies when it comes to cracking down on the drug gangs that commit most murders, and should probably provide more funding for domestic abuse awareness programs and battered women's shelters. While keeping thugs locked up helps society, prison conditions remain abysmal: Black and white supremacist gangs run many correctional facilities, guards receive too little training, and male inmates face a constant threat of rape. Efforts to reintegrate prisoners into mainstream society, likewise, border on negligent. Per-inmate funding for rehabilitation has fallen steadily even as more people have gone to prison.

But there is still a lot that the rest of the world can learn from our experience, as problems that European sophisticates still view as uniquely American take root elsewhere. Even as the United States has replaced many of its worst housing projects with mixed-income townhouse developments, multi-family estates on the outskirts of London, Paris, and other European capitals have become at least as dangerous as their American counterparts were during the 1970s and 1980s. As welfare reform and a strong social message that crime does not pay push many former members of the American underclass into the workforce, an entrenched welfare culture grows in many European countries. Writing in the Fall 2001 *Public Interest*, Charles Murray noted that his predictions of a decade earlier about the emergence of a British underclass had come true. By the late 1990s, British levels of unemployment, family breakdown, and violent crime among the welfare underclass were the same or higher than were America's in the 1960s and 1970s.

Americans should not take too much satisfaction in our becoming a safer nation. While crime in America has declined rather spectacularly, it still stands well above the level of civic peace our grandparents enjoyed. But America has moved in the right direction while Europe has moved in the wrong one. The combination of engaged, community-oriented police and ample investment in incarceration is turning the United States into the safest large Western country. Europeans may want to emulate American policies—God forbid!—if they hope to win their own wars against crime.

Eli Lehrer is a senior editor at the American Enterprise and co-author with Edwin Meese of a forthcoming book, "Revolution in Blue: Seven Principles of Community Policing."

Cyber-Crimes

Should penalties be tougher?

Brian Hansen

Cyber-crime has reached epidemic proportions. More than 90 percent of the corporations and government agencies responding to a recent survey reported computer-security breaches in 2001. Disgruntled employees and hackers commit many cyber-crimes, and others are committed by con artists using the web to perpetrate auction fraud, identity theft and other scams. Credit-card users are only liable for the first $50 of fraudulent charges, but financial institutions get hit hard. Identity thefts cost them $2.4 billion in losses and expenses in 2000. Some policymakers, wary of Internet-facilitated terrorist attacks, call for tough, new laws to prevent computer crimes. Others fear that such initiatives will trample on civil liberties. Still others want legislation to make Microsoft and other computer-software companies liable for damages caused by their software-security failures.

THE ISSUES

Carlos Salgado Jr. walked into San Francisco International Airport carrying a tote bag containing an ordinary CD-ROM disk and Mario Puzo's popular Mafia novel *The Last Don*. He passed through security without incident and strolled down the concourse to a passenger lounge near Gate 67. But Salgado, 36, wasn't there to catch a plane.

The freelance computer technician had stolen more than 100,000 credit-card numbers by hacking into several e-commerce databases on the Internet. It was an easy heist for Salgado, who simply used a ready-made computer-intrusion program that he found on the Web. Using a pirated e-mail account to conceal his identity, Salgado arranged to sell the information to an online fence for $260,000. The exchange was set for May 21, 1997.

As a precaution, Salgado put the stolen data on a CD-ROM, but with Hollywood-like flair he encoded the information based on a passage in Puzo's novel. Salgado's story, too, would someday make good reading: He was about to pull off one of the largest cyber-crimes in the Internet's short history. All told, the bank data that Salgado had electronically liberated from the Internet had a combined credit line of more than $1 billion.

Unfortunately for Salgado, he was walking into an FBI sting operation. The bureau had started monitoring Salgado's online machinations after being tipped off by an alert technician at one of the companies Salgado had pilfered. Initially, the FBI knew Salgado only as "SMACK," his on-line "handle." But when he handed over the encrypted CD to an under-cover agent, the feds finally had their man. Salgado pleaded guilty to breaking into a computer network and trafficking in stolen credit cards. He was sentenced to two and a half years in prison.

Few cyber-attacks are as serious as Salgado's. Nonetheless, experts say unauthorized incursions into government and private computer systems are part of a larger—and growing—cyber-crime trend.

"This is the 21st-century equivalent of the armored-car robbery," says Computer Security Institute (CSI) Editorial Director Richard Power. "Why should the bad guys bother dealing with armored cars and police with machine guns when they can knock off a [network] server and get tens of thousands of live credit cards? This is happening all the time now. The Salgado case was just the beginning."

Riptech, Inc., an Internet security firm in Alexandria, Va., verified 128,678 cyber-attacks on just 300 of the companies it serves in the last six months of 2001.[1] To be sure, only a small fraction of these attacks suc-

How to Avoid Internet Scams

Con artists have been quick to seize upon the Internet for new ways to separate consumers from their money. According to the Federal Trade Commission (FTC), the nation's chief consumer-protection agency, the best way to avoid getting taken is to buy with a credit card from a reputable Web site, and to use common sense. The following list of the most popular scams is based on more than 285,000 fraud complaints filed last year on a centralized database utilized by hundreds of law-enforcement agencies. To report Internet scams to the FTC, call 1-877-FTC-HELP (1-877-382-4357), or use the online complaint form at www.ftc.gov/ftc/consumer.htm.

The Scam	The Bait	The Catch	The Safety Net
Internet Auctions	Shop in a "virtual marketplace" that offers a huge selection of products at great deals.	You receive an item that is less valuable than promised, or, worse yet, you receive nothing at all.	When bidding through an Internet auction, particularly for a valuable item, check out the comments about the seller and insist on paying with a credit card or through a reliable payment service such as PayPal or BillPoint.
Internet Access Services	Free money, simply for cashing a check.	You get trapped into long-term contracts for Internet access or another Web service, with big penalties for cancellation or early termination.	If a check arrives at your home or business, read both sides carefully for the conditions you're agreeing to if you cash the check. Monitor your phone bill for unexpected or unauthorized charges.
Credit-Card Fraud	View adult images online for free, just for providing your credit-card number to prove you're over 18.	Fraudulent promoters make charges using your credit-card number, or sell your card number to other online hucksters.	Share credit-card information only with a company you trust. Dispute unauthorized charges on your credit-card bill by complaining to the bank that issued the card. Federal law limits your liability to $50 in charges if your card is misused.
Modem Hijacking	Get free access to adult material and pornography by downloading a "viewer" or "dialer" computer program.	The program you download surreptitiously disconnects your computer's modem from your local Internet Service Provider and reconnects you to a high-priced service overseas. You don't find out until you get a huge phone bill in the mail.	Don't download any program in order to access so-called "free" service without reading all the disclosures carefully for cost information. Just as important, read your phone bill carefully, and challenge any charges you didn't authorize or don't understand.
Web Cramming	Get a free, custom-designed Web site for a 30-day trial period, with no obligation to continue.	Charges appear on your telephone bill, or you receive a separate invoice, even if you never accepted the offer or agreed to continue the service after the trial period.	Review your telephone bills, and challenge any charges you don't recognize.
Multilevel Marketing Plans/ Pyramid Schemes	Make money through the products and services you sell as well as those sold by the people you recruit into the program.	After paying to join the program and purchase inventory, you learn that your "customers" are other distributors, not the general public. Some multilevel marketing programs are actually illegal pyramid schemes. When products or services are sold only to distributors like yourself, there's no way to make money.	Avoid plans that require you to recruit distributors, buy expensive inventory or commit to a minimum sales volume.
Travel and Vacation Scams	Get a luxurious trip with lots of "extras" at a bargain-basement price.	You get lower-quality accommodations and services than advertised, or no trip at all. Or, you get hit with hidden charges or additional requirements after you've paid.	Get references on any travel company you're planning to do business with. Then, get details of the trip in writing, including the cancellation policy, before signing on.
Bogus Business Opportunities	Be your own boss and earn big bucks.	You get scammed in any number of ways. The bottom line: If it looks too good to be true, it probably is.	Talk to other people who started businesses through the same company, get all the promises in writing, and study the proposed contract carefully before signing. Get an attorney or an accountant to look at it, too.

(continued on next page)

How to Avoid Internet Scams *(continued from previous page)*

Online Investment Scams	Make an initial investment in a day-trading system or service, and you'll quickly realize huge returns.	Big profits always mean big risk. Consumers have lost money to programs that claim to be able to predict the market with "100 percent accuracy."	Check out the promoter with state and federal securities and commodities regulators, and talk to other people who invested through the program to find out what level of risk you're assuming.
Health-Care Products/ Services	Items sold over the Internet or through other non-traditional suppliers that are "proven" to cure serious and even fatal health problems.	You put your hopes—and your money—on a marketing company's "miracle" product instead of getting the health care you really need.	Consult a health-care professional before buying any "cure-all" product that claims to treat a wide range of ailments or offers quick cures and easy solutions to serious illnesses.

Source: Federal Trade Commission

cessfully breached the organizations' front-line security measures. Still, 41 percent of Riptech's clients had to patch holes in their computer-security systems after "critical" attacks. And nearly one in eight suffered at least one "emergency" attack requiring some form of data-recovery procedure. (*See graph, "Many Firms Suffered Attacks."*)

"Our findings strongly suggest that once companies connect their systems to the Internet, they are virtually guaranteed to suffer some form of attack activity," Riptech recently reported. "The Internet security threat is real, pervasive and perhaps more severe than previously anticipated."[2]

An annual survey conducted by the FBI and CSI confirms the explosion of cyber-crime to epidemic proportions. More than 91 percent of the corporations and U.S. government agencies that responded reported a computer-security breach in 2001, and 64 percent acknowledged financial losses because of the attacks.[3]

Some cyber-crimes, like Salgado's caper, are committed primarily for money. Others are "inside" jobs perpetrated by disgruntled employees like Timothy Lloyd, a revenge-minded network administrator in New Jersey. After being demoted and reprimanded in 1996, he wrote six lines of malicious computer code that caused $10 million in financial losses for the Omega Engineering Corp.

Lloyd was convicted of sabotaging the company's computer network and last February was sentenced to 41 months in prison and ordered to pay more than $2 million in restitution. At Lloyd's trial, an Omega executive said the firm "will never recover" from the attack.[4]

Many computer attacks are essentially online vandalism. Hackers have defaced countless Web pages, greatly embarrassing major corporations and government agencies. Hackers sometimes act to advance social or political views. Last year, Chinese hackers defaced a host of U.S. government Web sites after a Chinese pilot died in a collision with an American spy plane over the South China Sea. American hackers retaliated by defacing 2,500 Chinese sites. Similar cyber-warfare broke out between American and Middle Eastern hackers after the Sept. 11 terrorist attacks.

To be sure, not all hackers are viewed as criminals. So-called ethical or white-hat hackers who try to break into computer systems at the behest of security-conscious companies are often lauded for advancing the state of computer technology. But "black-hat" hackers, or "crackers," seek to wreak havoc or illegally profit from their cyberspace forays.

"Gray-hat" hackers occupy a shadowy niche somewhere in between these two extremes. While they have no qualms about illegally breaking into computer systems, gray hats generally don't pilfer or damage assets but inform their victims about the security flaws they discover.

Many hackers embrace a controversial philosophy: They show the general public how they compromised particular computer systems by posting their hacking codes, or "scripts," to public areas of the Internet. The hackers say this forces careless companies and slipshod software manufacturers to take computer security more seriously.

Not surprisingly, many organizations don't like having their vulnerabilities publicized in this manner. Law-enforcement agencies typically don't endorse the philosophy, either.

"Thanking hackers who violate the privacy of networks or network users [by] pointing out our vulnerabilities is a little bit like sending thank-you notes to burglars for pointing out the infirmity of our physical alarms," said Martha Stansell-Gamm, chief of the Department of Justice's Computer Crime and Intellectual Property division.[5]

Many of the hacker-crafted scripts that circulate in cyberspace are viruses or worms—programs that can corrupt computer files and spread themselves across the Internet. Novice hackers known as "script kiddies" unleash thousands of viruses and worms every year, often without realizing the potential impact of their actions. Onel de Guzman, the 23-year-old Filipino hacker who has been tied to the "Love Bug," claimed he had no idea the worm would be so devastating. It caused an estimated $10 billion in damage worldwide in May 2000.[6]

Con artists, meanwhile, are using the Web to perpetrate various types of fraud schemes in record numbers, according to law-enforcement officials. "The number of [fraud] complaints has increased steadily over the last two or three years," says Timothy Healy, director of the Internet Fraud Complaint Center (IFCC), operated by the FBI and the National White Collar Crime Center.

Internet auction fraud was the most frequently reported type of complaint handled by the IFCC last year, according to Healy. Fraudsters can rig Internet auctions in a number of ways, such as using shills to drive up the bidding process. Con men also use the Internet to perpetrate a wide variety of investment scams, bogus e-commerce opportunities and confidence rackets. "It's amazing what's out there," Healy says.

One of the most prevalent and insidious Internet-assisted scams is identity theft—stealing credit card and Social Security numbers and other personal information. Some identity thieves hack into e-commerce Web sites to pilfer such data. Others set up bogus Internet sites of their own to dupe unwitting consumers into revealing their credit-card numbers.

Armed with stolen identities, thieves can perpetrate a variety of crimes, from opening bogus bank accounts and writing bad checks to taking out car loans and mortgages in their victims' names.

Under federal law, consumers who use credit cards are liable only for the first $50 of fraudulent charges made on their accounts, and many credit-card companies even waive that amount. Still, identity-theft victims typically incur more than $1,000 in out-of-pocket expenses trying to restore their mangled credit ratings, according to the Federal Trade Commission. (Debit-card purchases do not receive automatic fraud protection.)[7]

Lenders are hit even harder. Identity theft cost financial institutions some $2.4 billion in direct losses and related mopping-up expenses in 2000, according to Celent Communications, a Boston consulting firm.[8]

Controversies abound over how best to deal with Internet hucksters, hackers and virus writers. Some pol-

icymakers, wary of Internet-facilitated terrorist attacks, are calling for tough new laws to prevent computer crimes—including life sentences for some offenses. Others fear that such initiatives will trample on civil liberties. Still others want legislation to make software companies such as Microsoft liable for damages caused by computer-security failures.

As the debate rages, here is a closer look at some of the key questions being asked:

Is it safe for consumers and merchants to do business online?

Only about 40 percent of all adult Internet users in the United States use the Web to shop or pay bills, according to the Census Bureau.[9] Many Americans eschew online shopping, banking and other types of Internet commerce because they fear having their credit card or Social Security numbers stolen, numerous studies have found. For example, 85 percent of the Internet users polled recently by Washington-based SWR Worldwide cited security as the biggest deterrent to e-commerce. A poll by GartnerG2, a Stamford, Conn., firm, put the number worried about security at 60 percent.[10]

According to Gartner, U.S. e-commerce fraud losses in 2001 exceeded $700 million, constituting about 1.14 percent of the $61.8 billion in total online sales. That ratio was 19 times higher than the fraud rate for traditional in-store transactions, which hovered at less than one-tenth of 1 percent during the same time period, Gartner said. Since the e-commerce era began in the mid-1990s, Gartner estimates that one in every six online consumers has been victimized by credit-card fraud, and one in 12 has been hit with identity theft.

"We're not going to see low fraud rates like we have in the brick-and-mortar world until we make some serious changes in the way that online business is conducted," says Avivah Litan, Gartner's vice presi-

dent for research. "There are some big issues to deal with."

For merchants, the Internet is a double-edged sword. While they can broaden their customer bases and increase their revenues by going online, merchants also expose themselves to cyber-criminals.

Some law-enforcement officials concede that they can't keep pace with the number of e-commerce fraud scams already on the Internet. "There's no way that we can police the entire Web with the small staff that we have at this agency," says an official at the FTC, which investigates Internet fraud. "We go after things that are particularly egregious or pernicious, but we really have to strategically target our limited resources."

Other experts downplay the risks associated with online commerce. "I think we're doing quite well in terms of protecting buyers and sellers in the virtual marketplace," says Emily Hackett, executive director of the Internet Alliance, a Washington-based trade group. "The vast majority of online transactions are carried out without any problems at all."

Consumers can protect themselves when shopping online (as well as in traditional brick-and-mortar stores) by using a credit card. Under federal law, consumers are liable for only the first $50 of fraudulent charges made on their credit-card accounts, and many card issuers waive that amount. Users of debit cards, checks or other payment methods are not necessarily protected. Consequently, more than 95 percent of all e-commerce transactions are made with credit cards, Gartner says.

Credit-card companies are liable for fraudulent in-store transactions accompanied by signed (albeit forged) receipts. However, merchants are typically on the hook for any transactions they process without validating the purchaser's signature—which is rarely done over the Internet. Consequently, merchants—not consumers or credit-card companies—bear most of the costs of e-commerce fraud.

Internet Fraud Complaints

Auction and communications fraud and non-delivery of merchandise are the most common fraud complaints reported to the Internet Fraud Complaint Center (IFCC). Losses were especially high with identity theft and investment fraud.

Complaint Type	% of Complainants Who Reported Dollar Loss	Average (median) $ Loss per Typical Complaint
Auction fraud	78.4%	$230
Non-delivery (of purchases or payment)	73.8	225
Credit card/debit card fraud	58.3	207
Confidence fraud	63.1	339
Nigerian letter scam	01.1	3,000
Investment fraud	69.1	469
Check fraud	56.4	194
Business fraud	55.8	192
Identity theft	14.4	520
Communications fraud	78.7	145

Source: "IFCC Annual Internet `Fraud Report,'" National White Collar Crime Center and FBI

Most Internet merchants utilize a fraud-prevention program. But programs very widely in effectiveness and customer convenience. Many small merchants screen their online orders manually, flagging those with unusually high dollar volumes, suspicious billing information or other indicators of fraud. Large merchants often use sophisticated computer software programs to identify potentially fraudulent transactions. Best Buy Co., a consumer electronics retailer, can program its system to red-flag or automatically reject any online orders that originate from countries with high fraud rates.

Many Internet merchants also protect their online sales through the Secure Socket Layer protocol, or SSL. This technology encrypts consumers' credit-card numbers and other personal information so that it can be safely transmitted to merchants' databases. But while SSL allows consumers and merchants to exchange payment information through a secure "electronic pipe," the technology does not protect the database. And since all merchants don't encrypt their customers' data, they provide juicy targets for ill-inten-

tioned hackers. Meredith Outwater, an e-commerce fraud expert at Celent Communications, says fraud-minded hackers constantly surf the Internet looking for these kinds of opportunities.

"Merchants aren't securing their servers enough," Outwater says. "There are merchants who have their [customers'] credit-card data just sitting on servers, waiting to be hacked. That happens more often than data getting intercepted in transmission."

Nonetheless, Kenneth Kerr, a senior analyst at Gartner, does not consider e-commerce to be riskier than shopping in traditional brick-and-mortar stores. "It takes a sophisticated thief to hack into a Web server," Kerr said. "It is a lot simpler to steal identity information in a physical environment like a restaurant."[11]

Many computer-security experts say that consumers should avoid doing business with small e-commerce merchants. "Stay away from the mom-and-pop e-tailers, because they typically don't have the resources to implement a comprehensive, layered approach to security,"

says Victor Keong, a Toronto-based business consultant at Deloitte & Touche. "Merchants that rely only on one layer of security are very vulnerable."

Alfred Hunger, vice president of engineering at SecurityFocus, in San Mateo, Calif., agrees that there is a wide range of security among Internet merchants. "The publicly held e-tailers take [security] much more seriously than the mom-and-pop shops," Hunger says. "The small shops still represent a significant risk."

Should computer network security problems be publicly disclosed?

Hackers and virus writers regularly cause problems in cyberspace by exploiting flaws, or "bugs," in software programs. The computer-security community has long debated the wisdom of informing the general public about these vulnerabilities. Some experts argue that software security bugs should be publicly disclosed as soon as they are detected. Advocates of "full disclosure" say that by publicizing software vulnerabilities immediately, computer users can protect themselves against hackers and cyber-criminals who will inevitably discover and exploit the flaws. Full disclosure also compels vendors to promptly engineer and disseminate software "patches" to fix computer-security problems engendered by their flawed products, these advocates say.

"I'm very big on disclosure because it advances the security posture of everyone," Keong says. "The earlier that [software vendors] get the patches out there, the better."

Salt Lake City-based BugNet is one of several firms that hunts for software flaws and posts warnings about vulnerable systems on its Web site. Eric Bowden, BugNet's general manager, says that such disclosures get software companies to address computer security problems. Bowden denies that his bug hunters are out to embarrass, vilify or extort money from software giants such as Microsoft, as some critics contend.

"BugNet is very solutions-oriented," Bowden says. "We're not in it to point fingers or play the blame-game with [software] developers as much as we're trying to find solutions to serious problems."

Unlike other bug-hunting organizations, BugNet does not immediately publicize detailed information about every software vulnerability it finds. Depending on the type of the bug at hand, BugNet may or may not give a vendor time to engineer a patch before posting a vulnerability warning, Bowden says. Bugs that pose only minor problems usually get posted immediately, he concedes. However, BugNet typically delays publicizing serious security flaws if vendors agree to develop workable patches, he says.

"It's important to get [vulnerability] information out there early, but I also believe in giving vendors enough time to develop some kind of work-around for security bugs," Bowden says. "You can cause a lot of damage by calling attention to a security bug before a patch is available."

Moreover, unlike some other bug-hunting organizations, BugNet does not publish "exploit scripts"—step-by-step instructions that hackers can use to exploit security vulnerabilities. Indeed, novice hackers known as "script kiddies" often download these ready-made scripts and run them without realizing the consequences of their actions, Bowden notes.

"There are millions of script kiddies out there, and I don't want to arm them with the tools to do all kinds of destructive things," Bowden says.

Microsoft couldn't agree more. Scott Culp, manager of Microsoft's security response center, blasted the full-disclosure policy in an essay published last October.

"It's simply indefensible for the security community to continue arming cyber-criminals," Culp wrote. "We can and should discuss security vulnerabilities, but we should be smart, prudent and responsible in the way we do it."[12]

Microsoft advocates a policy of full disclosure but not full exposure. "Our policy on disclosure of security problems is intended to keep our customers safe," a spokesperson says. "If we were to publicize a problem without being able to offer a solution, that would make potential attackers aware of the hole but not give our customers a way to protect themselves."

Last fall, in a controversial move, Microsoft formed an alliance with several bug-hunting firms in an effort to curtail the publication of software-security flaws. At Microsoft's request, the firms agreed to wait at least 30 days before publicizing detailed information about any security-related bugs they discover.

"We want to create an atmosphere where people are more responsible with the disclosure of vulnerability information," said Eddie Schwartz, an analyst at Guardent Inc., a Waltham, Mass., firm that joined the alliance. "Right now, it is way too ad hoc."[13]

Other security experts are less enthusiastic about the alliance's efforts.

"I think the 30-day grace period is just another way for Microsoft and others to once again remove themselves from their responsibility for developing quality software before it hits the streets," said John Cowan Jr., of Louisville, Ky.-based Caldwell Industries Inc.[14]

Bruce Schneier, chief technology officer at Counterpane Internet Security Inc., in Cupertino, Calif., agrees.

"Microsoft's motives in promoting bug secrecy are obvious: It's a whole lot easier to squelch security information than it is to fix problems or design products securely in the first place," Schneier said. "Disclosure doesn't create security vulnerabilities—programmers create them, and they remain until other programmers find and remove them."[15]

Should software companies be liable for Internet security breaches?

Hackers and virus writers frequently launch attacks over the Internet by exploiting security flaws in commercial software. The Boston consulting company @Stake found that 70 percent of the security gaps that plagued its customers' computer networks last year were due to software bugs.[16]

Many computer-security experts say that software manufacturers know about most of these flaws before they put their products on the market. Mark Minasi, an investigative journalist who specializes in technology issues, claims that 90 percent of the bugs that consumers report to software vendors were already known to the vendors at the time of release.[17] Yet, many studies have found that businesses and government agencies that have been attacked via these types of software security gaps have incurred billions of dollars in damages.[18]

There are no laws requiring software vendors to manufacture hack-proof or virus-resistant products. Likewise, no software company has

Many Firms Suffered Attacks

Although most of the cyber-attacks against the clients of Riptech, a computer-security firm in Alexandria, Va., were harmless, more than 40 percent of the firms suffered at least one critical or emergency attack last year, meaning an actual security breach was imminent.

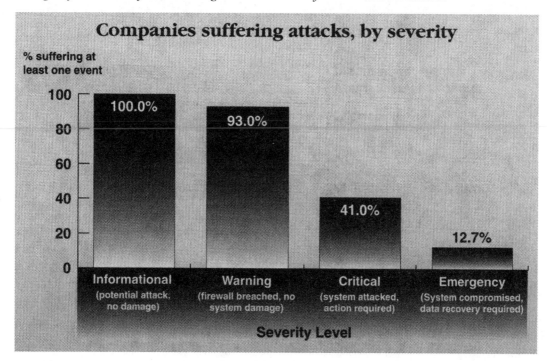

Companies suffering attacks, by severity

% suffering at least one event

Informational (potential attack, no damage)	Warning (firewall breached, no system damage)	Critical (system attacked, action required)	Emergency (System compromised, data recovery required)
100.0%	93.0%	41.0%	12.7%

Severity Level

Source: "Riptech Internet Security Threats Report." January 2002

ever been held responsible for damages stemming from a known security flaw in a product. Software vendors have long avoided this type of liability by inserting disclaimers in the so-called end-user licensing agreements (EULAs) that customers must consent to before using a product. In general, EULAs require users to assume all risks associated with the product. The EULA for Microsoft's Windows 2000 operating system is typical of this type of liability waiver. It states, in part:

"In no event shall Microsoft or its suppliers be liable for any damages whatsoever… arising out of the use of or inability to use the software product, even if Microsoft has been advised of the possibility of such damages."[19]

Given the crucial role that software plays in the modern world, many computer-security experts say it's high time that software compa-

nies take responsibility for producing hack-prone products.

"Software is deployed in places where it's absolutely critical for safety, like in much of our infrastructure," says Hunger of SecurityFocus. "It's totally unreasonable to give software vendors immunity from liability when every other industry— the Fords and the Boeings of the world—are held to a much, much higher standard."

Some legal experts predict that consumers will use the courts to force software vendors to accept liability for unsafe products, as occurred with the tobacco industry. "I think where you're going to see reform come is through lawsuits," said Jeffrey Hunker, dean of the H. John Heinz III School of Public Policy and Management at Carnegie Mellon University in Pittsburgh. "So much of our economic structure depends on computers that it's unsustainable

to hold software companies blameless."[20]

Michael Erbschloe, vice president for research at Computer Economics, in Carlsbad, Calif., says the modern world "doesn't have any choice economically" not to require secure software. "People are getting very tired of the hack attacks and the lax security," Erbschloe adds. "The economic consequences of this run very high, and go to many levels."

Since 1995, computer viruses and worms have caused more than $54 billion in economic damages, Erbschloe estimates. That figure, he notes, does not include the damages inflicted by other types of cyber-crimes, such as computer-facilitated credit-card theft.[21]

A recent National Academy of Sciences report declares that the state of the nation's cyber-security is "far worse than what known best practices" could provide. The report

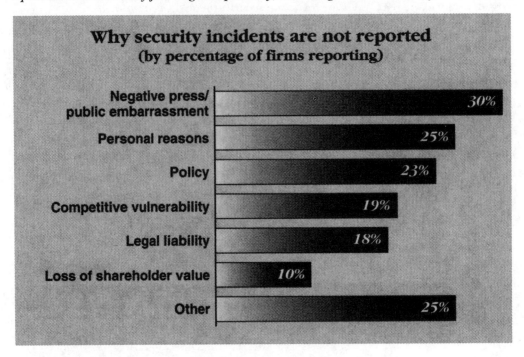

Many Firms Keep Mum About Attacks

A significant percentage of the firms and organizations that suffer security incidents don't report them because they fear negative publicity, according to a recent survey.

Why security incidents are not reported
(by percentage of firms reporting)

Negative press/public embarrassment	30%
Personal reasons	25%
Policy	23%
Competitive vulnerability	19%
Legal liability	18%
Loss of shareholder value	10%
Other	25%

Note: Includes multiple responses; 4,500 security professionals were polled.

Source: InformationWeek, *"Global Information Security Survey, 2001." September 2001*

says that "market incentives" have failed to push software companies and other private-sector interests toward creating a secure computing climate. Consequently, the report recommends that policymakers consider "legislative responses" to improving cyber-security, including making vendors liable for security breaches.[22]

But Mark Bohannon, general counsel and vice president for government affairs at the Software and Information Industry Association, says it would be impossible to hold software vendors responsible for security breaches, because software programs must interact with myriad other computer network systems.

"The notion of holding software vendors liable for security breaches when their products must interoperate with other things that they don't even control just boggles my mind," Bohannon says. "The people who are making these proposals really

need to carefully examine how the industry really works."

Microsoft continues to oppose efforts to make software vendors liable for security breaches. However, CEO Bill Gates says security is now the company's highest priority. In a Jan. 15 e-mail to all Microsoft employees, Gates launched the company's "trustworthy computing" initiative, which he described as "more important than any other part of our work. Our products should emphasize security right out of the box, and we must constantly refine and improve that security as threats evolve. Eventually, our software should be so fundamentally secure that customers never even worry about it."[23]

Gates acknowledged that in the past, Microsoft's biggest priority was adding new features and "functionality" to its products. That can no longer be the case, Gates wrote. "All those great features won't matter un-

less customers trust our software," he declared. "So now, when we face a choice between adding features and resolving security issues, we need to choose security."[24]

To that end, Microsoft sent every one of its more than 9,000 software developers through advanced security-training courses earlier this year. But many security experts question whether Microsoft will follow through.

"Issuing a statement doesn't solve any problems," said Schneier of Counterpane Internet Security. "Microsoft is notorious for treating security as a public-relations problem. Gates said all the right words. If he does that, it will be a sea change. I'd like to believe him, but I need proof."[25]

BugNet's Bowden offered a similar assessment. "It may or may not be lip service," Bowden said. "But it's obvious that they have been bloodied up enough by critics who claimed that their products were too insecure."

Notes

1. "Internet Security Threat Report," *Riptech, Inc.,* February 2002. For related coverage, see Brian Hansen, "Cyber-Predators," *The CQ Researcher,* March 1, 2002, pp. 169–192, and Ellen Perlman, "Digital Nightmare," *Governing,* April 2002, pp. 20–24.

2. *Ibid.*

3. "Computer Crime and Security Survey 2001," Computer Security Institute (CSI) and Federal Bureau of Investigation (FBI), January 2002.

4. Quoted in Sharon Gaudin, "Computer Sabotage Case Back in Court," *Network World Fusion,* April 4, 2001.

5. Quoted in Linden MacIntyre, "Hackers," PBS "Frontline," Feb. 13, 2001.

6. For background, see Richard Power, *Tangled Web: Tales of Digital Crime from the Shadows of Cyberspace* (2000), pp. 150–151.

7. Top 10 Consumer Fraud Complaints of 2001, Federal Trade Commission, Jan. 23, 2002.

8. "Identity Theft and its Effect on the Financial Services Industry," Celent Communications, September 2001.

9. U.S. Census Bureau, *Current Population Survey,* September 2001.

10. GartnerG2, "Privacy and Security: The Hidden Growth Strategy," August 2000.

11. Quoted in Mark W. Vigoroso, "Online Mugging a Threat, but no Showstopper," *E-Commerce Times,* Feb. 1, 2002.

12. Scott Culp, "It's Time to End Information Anarchy," Microsoft Security Response Center white paper, October 2001.

13. Jaikumar Vijayan, "Vendors Lead Effort to Delay Reporting of Security Vulnerabilities," *Computerworld,* Nov. 19, 2001.

14. *Ibid.*

15. Bruce Schneier, "Is Disclosing Vulnerabilities a Security Risk in Itself?" *Internetweek,* Nov. 19, 2001.

16. From "The Injustice of Insecure Software," @Stake white paper, February 2002.

17. Mark Minasi, *The Software Conspiracy: Why Companies Put Out Faulty Software, How They Can Hurt You and What You Can Do About It* (1999).

18. See, for example, CSI and FBI, *op. cit.,* and "Security Review 2002," Computer Economics Inc., 2002.

19. From "End-User License Agreement for Microsoft Software," as posted on Microsoft's Web site.

20. Quoted in Dennis Fisher, "Software Liability Gaining Attention," *Eweek,* Jan. 14, 2002.

21. Computer Economics, *op. cit.*

22. From "Cybersecurity Today and Tomorrow: Pay Now or Pay Later," The Computer Science and Telecommunications Board of the National Research Council (a branch of the National Academy of Sciences), January 2002.

23. Bill Gates, "Trustworthy Computing" memo, Jan. 15, 2002, as posted on Microsoft's Web site.

24. *Ibid.*

25. Quoted in Kristi Helm and Elise Ackerman, "Gates Makes Security Top Focus," *The San Jose Mercury News,* Jan. 17, 2002.

Brian Hansen joined *The CQ Researcher* after reporting for the *Colorado Daily* in Boulder and the Environment News Service in Washington. His awards include the Scripps Howard Foundation Award for Public Service Reporting. His recent *Researcher* reports include "Cyber-Predators," "Intelligence Reforms" and "Distance Learning." He holds a B.A. in political science and an M.A. in education from the University of Colorado.

Making Computer Crime Count

By MARC GOODMAN

Does computer crime pose a serious threat to America's national security? Recent highly publicized computer virus attacks have shown that computer crime has become an increasing problem. Unfortunately, the absence of a standard definition for computer crime, a lack of reliable criminal statistics on the problem, and significant underreporting of the threat pose vexing challenges for police agencies.

Sensational headlines, such as "Nation Faces Grave Danger of Electronic Pearl Harbor,"[1] "Internet Paralyzed by Hackers,"[2] "Computer Crime Costs Billions,"[3] have become common. Law enforcement organizations cannot determine exactly how many computer crimes occur each year. No agreed-upon national or international definition of terms, such as computer crime, high-tech crime, or information technology crime, exists. Thus, as a class of criminal activities, computer crime is unique in its position as a crime without a definition, which prevents police organizations from accurately assessing the nature and scope of the problem.

Internationally, legislative bodies define criminal offenses in penal codes. Crimes, such as murder, rape, and aggravated assault, all suggest similar meanings to law enforcement professionals around the world. But what constitutes a computer crime? The term covers a wide range of offenses. For example, if a commercial burglary occurs and a thief steals a computer, does this indicate a computer crime or merely another burglary? Does copying a friend's program disks constitute a computer crime? The answer to each of these questions may depend on various jurisdictions.[4]

The United States Department of Justice (DOJ) has defined computer crime as "any violation of criminal law that involved the knowledge of computer technology for its perpetration, investigation, or prosecution."[5] Some experts have suggested that DOJ's definition could encompass a series of crimes that have nothing to do with computers. For example, if an auto theft investigation required a detective to use "knowledge of computer technology" to investigate a vehicle's identification number (VIN) in a state's department of motor vehicle database, under DOJ guidelines, auto theft could be classified as a computer crime. While the example may stretch the boundaries of logic, it demonstrates the difficulties inherent in attempting to describe and classify computer criminality.

Over the past 15 years, several international organizations, such as the United Nations, the Organization of Economic Cooperation and Development (OECD), the Council of Europe, the G-8,[6] and Interpol, all have worked to combat the problem of computer crime.[7] These organizations have provided guidance in understanding this problem. Yet, despite their efforts, no single definition of computer crime has emerged that the majority of criminal justice professionals use. Although many state and federal laws define terms, such as "unauthorized access to a computer system" and "computer sabotage," neither Title 18 nor any of the state penal codes provide a definition for the term computer crime.

Defining criminal phenomena is important because it allows police officers, detectives, prosecutors, and judges to speak intelligently about a given criminal offense. Furthermore, generally accepted definitions facilitate the aggregation of statistics, which law enforcement can analyze to reveal previously undiscovered criminal threats and patterns.

Benefits of Reporting Computer Crime Statistics

Crime statistics serve an important role in law enforcement. First, they allow for the appropriate allocation of very limited resources. For example, if a community suffered a 73 percent increase in the number of sexual assaults, police administrators immediately would take steps to address the problem by adding more rape investigators, extra patrol in the specific area, and increased community awareness projects. The aggregation of crime data allows police to formulate a response to a problem. Anecdotal evidence suggests that computer crime presents a growing problem for the public, police, and governments, all who rely on crime statistics for the development of their criminal justice policies and the allocation of extremely limited resources. For police to respond successfully to these crimes in the future, they

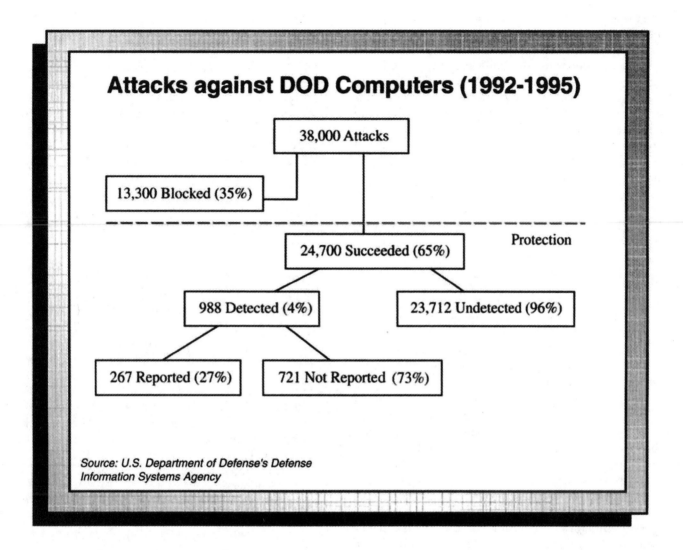

Attacks against DOD Computers (1992-1995)

38,000 Attacks

13,300 Blocked (35%)

Protection

24,700 Succeeded (65%)

988 Detected (4%)

23,712 Undetected (96%)

267 Reported (27%)

721 Not Reported (73%)

Source: U.S. Department of Defense's Defense Information Systems Agency

must increase the resources their departments currently dedicate to the problem—a difficult task.

Agencies must justify training, equipment, and personnel costs necessary to create a computer-competent police force. How can law enforcement managers justify these costs to community leaders without appropriate data to substantiate their claims? Police must document the problem with factual data not information based on media sensationalism or a few notorious attacks.

Second, accurate statistics on computer crime are important for public safety reasons. Computer crimes not only affect corporations but hospitals, airports, and emergency dispatch systems as well. Furthermore, surveys have indicated that many individuals fear for their safety in the on-line world and worry about criminal victimization.[8]

Businesses and individuals rely on law enforcement crime statistics when making important decisions about their safety. Many citizens contact a local police station prior to the purchase of a home in a particular neighborhood to inquire about the number of burglaries and violent crimes in the area. Just as these data provide important information for communities in the "real world," the same is true in cyberspace. For individuals and organizations to intelligently assess their level of risk, agencies must provide accurate data about criminal threats. Access to reliable and timely computer crime statistics allows individuals to determine their own probability of victimization and the threat level they face and helps them begin to estimate probable recovery costs.[9] Law enforcement organizations traditionally have taken a leading role in providing crime data and crime prevention education to the public, which now should be updated to include duties in cyberspace.

Crime statistics facilitate benchmarking and analysis of crime trends. Crime analysts use criminal statistics to spot emerging trends and unique modi operandi. Patrol officers and detectives use this data to prevent future crimes and to apprehend offenders. Therefore, to count computer crime, a general agreement on what constitutes a computer crime must exist.

In many police departments, detectives often compile and report crime data. Thus, homicide detectives count the number of murders, sexual assault investigators examine the number of rapes, and auto detectives count car thefts. Computer crime, on the other hand, comprises such an ill-defined list of offenses that various units within a police department usually keep the related data separately, if they keep them at all. For example, the child abuse unit likely would maintain child pornography arrest data and identify the crime as the sexual exploitation of a minor. A police department's economic crimes unit might recap an Internet fraud scam as a simple fraud, and an agency's assault unit might count an on-line stalking case as a criminal threat. Because most police organizations do not have a cohesive entity that measures offenses where criminals either criminally target a computer or use one to perpetrate a crime, accurate statistics remain difficult to obtain.

The Underreporting Problem

Generally, crime statistics can provide approximations for criminal activity. Usually, people accurately report serious crimes, such as homicide, armed robbery, vehicle theft, and major assaults. Many other criminal offenses, however, remain significantly underreported.

Police always have dealt with some underreporting of crime. But, new evidence suggests that computer crime may be the most underreported form of criminal behavior because the victim of a computer crime often remains unaware that an offense has even taken place. Sophisticated technologies, the immense size and storage capacities of computer networks, and the often global distribution of an organization's information assets increase the difficulty of detecting computer crime. Thus, the vast majority of individuals and organizations do not realize when they have suffered a computer intrusion or related loss at the hands of a criminal hacker.

The U.S. Department of Defense's (DoD) Defense Information Systems Agency (DISA) has completed in-depth research on computer crime. From 1992 to 1995, DISA attacked their own DoD computer systems using software available on the Internet. System administrators did not detect the majority of attacks against DoD computers. Of the 38,000 attacks perpetrated, 96 percent of the successful attacks went undetected. Furthermore, of the detected attacks, only 27 percent were reported. Thus, approximately 1 in 140 attacks were both detected and reported, representing only 0.7 percent of the total. If the detection and reporting of computer crime is less than 1 percent in the nation's military systems, how often might these crimes go unreported when the intended victim is an individual or a small business owner?

Convincing victims who have suffered a loss to report the crime to police constitutes another hurdle facing law enforcement agencies. Surprisingly, many individuals, network administrators, and corporate managers do not realize that attacks against their networks constitute a crime. Worse, many victims who understand that a crime

has taken place may deliberately keep these facts from the police. Victims may have serious doubts about the capacity of the police to handle computer crime incidents in an efficient, timely, and confidential manner.[10] These concerns are true particularly among large corporations who fear damage to their reputation or, worse, their bottom line. In banking and financial sectors, reputation is everything. Information that a criminal has infiltrated a bank's computers and accounts potentially could drive thousands of customers to its competitors.

" . . . accurate statistics on computer crime are important for public safety reasons."

Businesses suffer a variety of losses, both tangible and intangible when hackers attack them. They can lose hundreds of millions of dollars of value, brand equity, and corporate reputation when a business falls prey to a hacker.[11] Most of the companies that suffer Web attacks see their stock prices fall.[12] Furthermore, in recent denial of service attacks, for example, the Yankee Research Group estimated that direct revenue losses due to blocked online transactions and the need for security infrastructure upgrades exceed $1 billion.[13] Because of the high price of victimization, most companies would not want to involve law enforcement and risk a very public arrest or trial attesting to the organization's security and business failings.

The difficulties in computer crime detection and the challenges posed by the reluctance of businesses to admit victimization might demonstrate the underestimation of all statistics related to cybercrimes. However, some less reputable computer security consulting companies may overestimate computer crime and security problems to scare business leaders who, they hope, will turn to these organizations for consulting services and support.

An annual report compiled by the Computer Security Institute in San Francisco, California, and the FBI provides a variety of statistics on computer crime by surveying computer security practitioners in both the private and public sectors.[14] The anonymity offered to survey respondents may contribute to the accuracy of their data. However, the report does not directly poll law enforcement organizations about the number of computer crimes reported to police. Many experts believe that such a task should be carried out by the government, but to date, no single governmental body maintains responsibility for asking police forces about the prevalence of computer crimes reported and investigated.

The Development of a Definition

The development of a simple, widely agreed-upon definition of computer crime among law enforcement may form the first step in counting computer crimes. This definition would help police to communicate more effectively about these offenses and begin to accurately assess the prevalence of criminal victimization.

The earliest work in computer security provides a good foundation upon which police can build such a definition. Traditionally, all computer security efforts have sought to protect the confidentiality, integrity, and availability of information systems.[15]

Confidentiality in computer systems prevents the disclosure of information to unauthorized persons. Individuals who trespass into another person's computer system or exceed their own authority in accessing certain information, violate the legitimate owner's right to keep private information secret. Crimes that violate the confidentiality of computer systems include "unauthorized access crimes" as defined by Title 18, U.S.C. Section 1030(a)(2). Because breaking into a computer begins with unauthorized access to an information system, many believe this represents the foundational computer crime offense.

Integrity of electronically stored information ensures that no one has tampered with it or modified it without authorization. Thus, any nonsanctioned corruption, impairment, or modification of computer information or equipment constitutes an attack against the integrity of that information. Many of the malicious hacking activities, such as computer viruses, worms, and Trojan horses, fall within this category. The same is true for individuals who purposefully change or manipulate data either for profit or some other motivation, such as revenge, politics, terrorism, or merely for the challenge.

" . . . computer crime has become an increasing problem."

Availability of computer data indicates the accessibility of the information and that its associated programs remain functional when needed by the intended user community. A variety of attacks, such as the often-cited denial of service incidents, constitute a set of criminal activities that interferes with the availability of computer information.

Together, computer crime incidents that attack the confidentiality, integrity, or availability of digital information or services constitute an extremely precise and easily understood foundational definition of computer crime. In effect, these offenses might represent "pure-play" computer crimes because they involve a computer system as the direct target of the attack.

These three types of crimes should form the basis for an internationally agreed-upon definition of computer crime. In reality, they already are becoming the definition of computer crime because each state has some law that prohibits these offenses. Furthermore, an analysis of penal legislation in nearly 50 nations suggests that at least one-half of those countries surveyed—including most industrialized nations—had laws in place or legislation pending that prohibited crimes affecting the confidentiality, integrity, and availability of a computer.[16] A variety of international organizations also support legislative efforts prohibiting pure-play computer crimes. Groups, such as the United Nations, the G8, the Council of Europe, the OECD, and Interpol, each have delineated confidentiality, integrity, and availability offenses as forming the minimum basis of proscribed computer criminal behavior. The Council of Europe, the 41-nation body of which the United States is an observer, has been working on a draft treaty on cybercrime for several years. If adopted as currently drafted, the treaty would ensure that confidentiality, integrity, and availability offenses were outlawed in all signatory nations to the treaty, an extremely significant step forward in policing these crimes.[17]

Computer-Mediated Offenses

Defined broadly, the term computer crime or even the more common "computer-related crime" has described a wide variety of offenses. Traditional crimes, such as fraud, counterfeiting, embezzlement, telecommunications theft, prostitution, gambling, money laundering, child pornography, fencing operations, narcotics sales, and even stalking, all could be computer related. Computer technology could facilitate or perpetrate each of these offenses.

These crimes, which represent traditional offenses perpetrated in new and, perhaps, more effective ways, differ from pure-play computer crimes, which involve a computer system as the direct target of attack. Additionally, these crimes, as a group, demonstrate that offenders can use a computer as a tool to commit the crime. The fact that a computer is not necessary to commit the crime sets these offenses apart from the pure-play computer crimes. Prostitution, counterfeiting, and frauds have taken place for hundreds of years without any computer connection. The computer-mediated forms of these crimes pose problems for law enforcement as well.

A traditional crime perpetrated with a new, high-tech twist raises the same investigative and legal challenges for police as pure-play computer offenses. The unique nature of information technology and computer networks moving at Internet speed often are highly incompatible with traditional legal models of policing. Crimes involving high technology cross multiple jurisdictions, are not covered by a single cohesive international law, become harder to track because of anonymity, result in expensive investigations, complicate efforts in obtaining forensic evidence, and require police to have specialized knowledge for a successful investigation. Because computer-related crimes pose many of the same investigative difficulties as pure-play computer crimes, documenting these criminal offenses proves useful. Once captured, these data can help police to further refine their allocation of resources and determine relevant crime trends for computer-mediated illegal activities.

Offenses where a computer is completely incidental to the crime represents the third type of criminal activity with possible computer involvement. In these cases, although a criminal might have used a computer before, during, or after the crime, it was not related directly to the offending criminal activity. For example, a man who murders his wife and confesses 3 weeks later in an electronic document has not committed a computer crime—he has committed a homicide. Leaving behind computer-related evidence that will require specialized forensic methods does not turn murder into "cyber-homicide." For this reason, police should not count offenses that generate computer-related evidence incidental to the perpetration of the offense as either a computer crime or as a computer-related crime.

Law Enforcement's Response

How can agencies capture, analyze, and report data on these offenses in an efficient manner? In 1930, the U.S. Congress required the Attorney General to produce data on the incidence of crime in America. In turn, the Attorney General designated the FBI to serve as the national clearinghouse for the statistics collected. Since that time, the FBI has administered the Uniform Crime Reporting (UCR) Program, which obtains data based on uniform classifications and procedures for reporting from the nation's law enforcement agencies and presents this information in the annual *Crime in the United States* publication.[18] While the traditional UCR Summary Reporting System[19] tracks only eight criminal offenses (murder and nonnegligent manslaughter, forcible rape, robbery, aggravated assault, burglary, larceny-theft, motor vehicle theft, and arson), the new UCR National Incident Based Reporting System[20] (NIBRS) tracks 46 criminal offenses in 22 categories, including crimes perpetrated using computers.[21] However, because the transition from the traditional system to NIBRS will take considerable time, law enforcement executives proactively should review their internal procedures to ensure that they have appropriate policies in place to track and recap pure-play computer crimes.

Agencies should consider adding the following question to crime and arrest reports: "Was a computer used in the perpetration of this offense?" Many agencies already include similar questions about the use of firearms or the occurrence of hate crimes on their internal reports. In fact, hate crimes may provide a useful lens through which to examine computer-related crime. Hate crimes often involve other crimes, such as assault, vandalism, and even murder. But, knowing what percentage hate actually motivates vandalism becomes a useful tool for police administrators attempting to understand and address community disorder problems.

Several efforts have begun to promote law enforcement's understanding of the prevalence and effects of computer crime. The FBI and the National White Collar Crime Center recently took a big step forward in counting computer-related fraud. In 2000, these organizations established the Internet Fraud Complaint Center (IFCC)[22] to create a national reporting mechanism for tracking fraud on the Internet. The center will track statistics on the number and type of complaints and forward reported incidents to the appropriate law enforcement agency. While IFCC will prove helpful in tracking Internet fraud data, it does not deal directly with pure-play computer crimes that violate the confidentiality, integrity, and availability of data. Therefore, federal, state, and local criminal justice agencies must take a more comprehensive approach.

Conclusion

To combat computer crime, law enforcement must build an internal capacity to define, track, and analyze these criminal offenses. Even if law enforcement has a highly sophisticated and well-developed system to count computer crime, agencies still must overcome the public's underreporting problem. Underreporting these crimes results from a failure on the part of the victim to realize a crime has taken place and an unwillingness to report discovered incidents to police.

To decrease the incidence of computer crime, law enforcement agencies must work with private organizations to ensure that businesses become aware of potential threats they face from computer crime. These partnerships could include working with technical experts from within and outside the government to develop solutions that improve the prevention and detection of computer crimes. Of course, even after detecting these crimes, police still must convince victims to report them.

Police agencies must work with the business community to gain trust. Many community and problem-oriented policing techniques can help law enforcement as they deal increasingly with computer crime investigations. Government and industry partnerships, and police sensitivity about businesses concerns, will help increase the number of these offenses brought to the attention of the police.

Most police agencies do not have the staff or funding to deal adequately with computer crime. Though the recent series of virus and denial of service attacks have increased public awareness of the problem, law enforcement organizations must prepare for offenses by developing a strategic and preventative approach to deal with this problem.

"Several efforts have begun to promote law enforcement's understanding of the prevalence and effects of computer crime."

Law enforcement managers must ensure that they remain capable of responding to the changing faces of criminal activity in the 21st century. When compared to murder, rape, or violent assaults, computer crime may seem trivial. But, a person who asks an executive who loses his life savings due to the theft of intellectual property from his computer hard drive will get a different answer. The teacher who receives daily calls from credit agencies because she was the victim of on-line identity theft understands the importance of policing computer related crime as well. Similarly, so does the AIDS researcher who has 5 years of work destroyed by a computer virus. The mother of the 13-year-old girl who was lured across state lines by a pedophile will certainly demand a computer-competent police force capable of helping her. Each of these computer or computer-related crimes and their victims are real. Law enforcement agencies have a responsibility to protect and serve the public, regardless of advances in technology—a role that cannot be abdicated.

Defining the problem, gathering crime data, and analyzing the nature and scope of the threat represent natural steps in any problem-oriented policing approach. New forms of criminality do not differ—a lesson law enforcement agencies must learn to make computer crime count.

Endnotes

1. Andrew Glass, "Warding Off Cyber Threat: "Electronic Pearl Harbor Feared," *The Atlanta Journal and Constitution*, June 25, 1998.
2. Anick Jesdanun, "Internet Attacks Raise Concerns About Risks of Growth," *San Francisco Examiner*, February 14, 2000.
3. Michael Zuckerman, "Love Bug Stole Computer Passwords," *USA Today*, May 10, 2000.
4. Jodi Mardesich, "Laws Across the Country Become Relevant in Connected World: Jurisdiction at Issue in Net Legal Cases," *San Jose Mercury News*, October 8, 1996, 1E.
5. Catherine H. Conly, *Organizing for Computer Crime Investigation and Prosecution*, National Institute of Justice, July 1989, 6.
6. These countries, several major industrial nations in the world, include the United States, the United Kingdom, France, Germany, Japan, Canada, Italy, and Russia.
7. "International Review of Criminal Policy: United Nations Manual on the Prevention and Control of Computer-Related Crime," United Nations Crime and Justice Information Network Vienna: United Nations, 1994.
8. Tina Kelley, "Security Fears Still Plague Cybershopping," *The New York Times*, July 30, 1998, G5; Michael Stroh, "On-line Dangers, Offspring Protection; Security: Parents Can Find Allies on the Family Computer to Protect their Children from Harm on the Internet," *The Baltimore Sun*, May 10, 1999, 1C.
9. M.E. Kabay, "ISCA White Paper on Computer Crime Statistics," International Computer Security Association (1998), *http://www.icsa.net/html/library/whitepapers/index.shtml*; accessed November 8, 2000.
10. P.A. Collier and B.J. Spaul, "Problems in Policing Computer Crime," *Policing and Society* 307, no. 2 (1992).
11. Larry Kamer, "Crisis Mode: It s About Values," *The San Francisco Examiner*, February 23, 2000, A15.
12. Carri Kirbie, "Hunting for the Hackers: Reno Opens Probe Into Attacks That Disabled Top Web Sites," *The San Francisco Chronicle*, February 10, 2000, A1.
13. "7 Days: Web Attacks Raise Security Awareness," *Computing*, February 17, 2000, 17.
14. R. Power, "2000 CSI/FBI Computer Crime and Security Survey," *Computer Security Issues and Trends* 6, No. 1, Spring 2000.
15. These three themes provide the basis for the Organization for Economic Cooperation and Development's (OECD) *Guidelines for the Security of Information Systems* and are included in most textbooks, legislative acts, and media articles on computer crime. The OECD document is available at *http://www.oecd.org/dsti/sti/it/secur/prod/reg97-2.htm*; accessed November 8, 2000.
16. Based upon research conducted by the author.
17. For further information, see *http://conventions.coe.int/treaty/EN/cadreprojets.htm*.
18. U.S. Department of Justice, Federal Bureau of Investigation, *Crime in the United States* (Washington, DC, 1999).
19. In the summary program, law enforcement agencies tally the number of occurrences of the offenses, as well as arrest data, and submit aggregate counts of the collected data in monthly summary reports either directly to the FBI or indirectly through state UCR programs.
20. In NIBRS, law enforcement agencies collect detailed data regarding individual crime incidents and arrests and submit them in separate reports using prescribed data elements and data values to describe each incident and arrest.
21. NIBRS provides the capability to indicate whether a computer was the object of the crime and to indicate whether the offenders used computer equipment to perpetrate a crime. This ensures the continuance of the traditional crime statistics and, at the same time, "flags" incidents involving computer crime. For additional information on NIBRS, contact the NIBRS Program Coordinator, Criminal Justice Information Services, 1-888-827-6427.
22. Jerry Seper, "Justice Sets Up Web Site to Combat Internet Crimes," *The Washington Times*, May 9, 2000, A6, *www.ifccfbi.gov*; November 8, 2000.

For further information regarding computer crime, contact the author at digitalpolice@yahoo.com.

ENOUGH IS ENOUGH

WHITE-COLLAR CRIMINALS: THEY LIE THEY CHEAT THEY STEAL AND THEY'VE BEEN GETTING AWAY WITH IT FOR TOO LONG

BY CLIFTON LEAF

Arthur Levitt, the tough-talking former chairman of the Securities and Exchange Commission, spoke of a "multitude of villains." Red-faced Congressmen hurled insults, going so far as to compare the figures at the center of the Enron debacle unfavorably to carnival hucksters. The Treasury Secretary presided over a high-level working group aimed at punishing negligent CEOs and directors. Legislators from all but a handful of states threatened to sue the firm that bollixed up the auditing, Arthur Andersen. There was as much handwringing, proselytizing, and bloviating in front of the witness stand as there was shredding behind it.

It took a late-night comedian, though, to zero in on the central mystery of this latest corporate shame. After a parade of executives from Enron and Arthur Andersen flashed on the television monitor, Jon Stewart, anchor of *The Daily Show*, turned to the camera and shouted, "Why aren't all of you in jail? And not like white-guy jail—*jail* jail. With people by the weight room going, 'Mmmmm.'"

It was a pitch-perfect question. And, sadly, one that was sure to get a laugh.

Not since the savings-and-loan scandal a decade ago have high crimes in the boardroom provided such rich television entertainment. But that's not for any lack of malfeasance. Before Enronitis inflamed the public, gigantic white-collar swindles were rolling through the business world and the legal system with their customary regularity. And though they displayed the full creative range of executive thievery, they had one thing in common: Hardly anyone ever went to prison.

Regulators alleged that divisional managers at investment firm Credit Suisse First Boston participated in a "pervasive" scheme to siphon tens of millions of dollars of their customers' trading profits during the Internet boom of 1999 and early 2000 by demanding excessive trading fees. (For one 1999 quarter the backdoor bonuses amounted to as much as a fifth of the firm's total commissions.) Those were the facts, as outlined by the

SEC and the National Association of Securities Dealers in a high-profile news conference earlier this year. But the January news conference wasn't to announce an indictment. It was to herald a settlement, in which CSFB neither admitted nor denied wrongdoing. Sure, the SEC concluded that the investment bank had failed to observe "high standards of commercial honor," and the company paid $100 million in fines and "disgorgement," and CSFB itself punished 19 of its employees with fines ranging from $250,000 to $500,000. But whatever may or may not have happened, no one was charged with a crime. The U.S. Attorney's office in Manhattan dropped its investigation when the case was settled. Nobody, in other words, is headed for the hoosegow.

A month earlier drugmaker ICN Pharmaceuticals actually pleaded guilty to one count of criminal fraud for intentionally misleading investors—over many years, it now seems—about the FDA approval status of its flagship drug, ribavirin. The result of a five-year grand jury investigation? A $5.6 million fine and the company's accession to a three-year "probationary" period. Prosecutors said that not only had the company deceived investors, but its chairman, Milan Panic, had also made more than a million dollars off the fraud as he hurriedly sold shares. He was never charged with insider trading or any other criminal act. The SEC is taking a firm stand, though, "seeking to bar Mr. Panic from serving as a director or officer of any publicly traded company." Tough luck.

And who can forget those other powerhouse scandals, Sunbeam and Waste Management? The notorious Al "Chainsaw" Dunlap, accused of zealously fabricating Sunbeam's financial statements when he was chief executive, is facing only civil, not criminal, charges. The SEC charged that Dunlap and his minions made use of every accounting fraud in the book, from "channel stuffing" to "cookie jar reserves." The case is now in the discovery phase of trial and likely to be settled; he has denied wrongdoing. (Earlier Chainsaw rid himself of a class-

Schemers and scams: a brief history of bad business

It takes some pretty spectacular behavior to get busted in this country for a white-collar crime. But the business world has had a lot of overachievers willing to give it a shot.

by Ellen Florian

1920:
The Ponzi scheme

Charles Ponzi planned to arbitrage postal coupons—buying them from Spain and selling them to the U.S. Postal Service at a profit. To raise capital, he outlandishly promised investors a 50% return in 90 days. They naturally swarmed in, and he paid the first with cash collected from those coming later. He was imprisoned for defrauding 40,000 people of $15 million.

1929:
Albert Wiggin

In the summer of 1929, Wiggin, head of Chase National Bank, cashed in by shorting 42,000 shares of his company's stock. His trades, though legal, were counter to the interests of his shareholders and led to passage of a law prohibiting executives from shorting their own stock.

1930:
Ivar Krueger, the Match King

Heading companies that made two-thirds of the world's matches, Krueger ruled—until the Depression. To keep going, he employed 400 off-the-books vehicles that only he understood, scammed his bankers, and forged signatures. His empire collapsed when he had a stroke.

1938:
Richard Whitney

Ex-NYSE president Whitney propped up his liquor business by tapping a fund for widows and orphans of which he was trustee and stealing from the New York Yacht Club and a relative's estate. He did three years' time.

1961:
The electrical cartel

Executives of GE, Westinghouse, and other big-name companies conspired to serially win bids on federal projects. Seven served time—among the first imprisonments in the 70-year history of the Sherman Antitrust Act.

1962:
Billie Sol Estes

A wheeler-dealer out to corner the West Texas fertilizer market, Estes built up capital by mortgaging nonexistent farm gear. Jailed in 1965 and paroled in 1971, he did the mortgage bit again, this time with nonexistent oil equipment. He was re-jailed in 1979 for tax evasion and did five years.

1970:
Cornfeld and Vesco

Bernie Cornfeld's Investors Overseas Service, a fund-of-funds outfit, tanked in 1970, and Cornfeld was jailed in Switzerland. Robert Vesco "rescued" IOS with $5 million and then absconded with an estimated $250 million, fleeing the U.S. He's said to be in Cuba serving time for unrelated crimes.

1983:
Marc Rich

Fraudulent oil trades in 1980–1981 netted Rich and his partner, Pincus Green, $105 million, which they moved to offshore subsidiaries. Expecting to be indicted by U.S. Attorney Rudy Giuliani for evading taxes, they fled to Switzerland, where tax evasion is not an extraditable crime. Clinton pardoned Rich in 2001.

1986:
Boesky and Milken and Drexel Burnham Lambert

The Feds got Wall Streeter Ivan Boesky for insider trading, and then Boesky's testimony helped them convict Drexel's Michael Milken for market manipulation. Milken did two years in prison, Boesky 22 months. Drexel died.

1989:
Charles Keating and the collapse of Lincoln S&L

Keating was convicted of fraudulently marketing junk bonds and making sham deals to manufacture profits. Sentenced to 12½ years, he served less than five. Cost to taxpayers: $3.4 billion, a sum making this the most expensive S&L failure.

(continued)

Schemers and Scams (continued)

1991: BCCI	1991: Salomon Brothers	1995: Nick Leeson and Barings Bank	1995: Bankers Trust	1997: Walter Forbes
The Bank of Credit & Commerce International got tagged the "Bank for Crooks & Criminals International" after it came crashing down in a money-laundering scandal that disgraced, among others, Clark Clifford, advisor to four Presidents.	Trader Paul Mozer violated rules barring one firm from bidding for more than 35% of the securities offered at a Treasury auction. He did four months' time. Salomon came close to bankruptcy. Chairman John Gutfreund resigned.	A 28-year-old derivatives trader based in Singapore, Leeson brought down 233-year-old Barings by betting Japanese stocks would rise. He hid his losses—$1.4 billion—for a while but eventually served more than three years in jail.	Derivatives traders misled clients Gibson Greetings and Procter & Gamble about the risks of exotic contracts they entered into. P&G sustained about $200 million in losses but got most of it back from BT. The Federal Reserve sanctioned the bank.	Only months after Cendant was formed by the merger of CUC and HFS, cooked books that created more than $500 million in phony profits showed up at CUC. Walter Forbes, head of CUC, has been indicted on fraud charges and faces trial this year.

1997: Columbia/HCA	1998: Waste Management	1998: Al Dunlap	1999: Martin Frankel	2000: Sotheby's and Al Taubman
This Nashville company became the target of the largest-ever federal investigation into healthcare scams and agreed in 2000 to an $840 million Medicare-fraud settlement. Included was a criminal fine—rare in corporate America—of $95 million.	Fighting to keep its reputation as a fast grower, the company engaged in aggressive accounting for years and then tried straight-out books cooking. In 1998 it took a massive charge, restating years of earnings.	He became famous as "Chainsaw Al" by firing people. But he was then axed at Sunbeam for illicitly manufacturing earnings. He loved overstating revenues—booking sales, for example, on grills neither paid for nor shipped.	A financier who siphoned off at least $200 million from a series of insurance companies he controlled, Frankel was arrested in Germany four months after going on the lam. Now jailed in Rhode Island—no bail for this guy—he awaits trial on charges of fraud and conspiracy.	The world's elite were ripped off by years of price-fixing on the part of those supposed bitter competitors, auction houses Sotheby's and Christie's. Sotheby's chairman, Taubman, was found guilty of conspiracy last year. He is yet to be sentenced.

action shareholder suit for $15 million, without admitting culpability.) Whatever the current trial's outcome, Dunlap will still come out well ahead. Sunbeam, now under bankruptcy protection, gave him $12.7 million in stock and salary during 1998 alone. And if worse comes to worst, he can always tap the stash he got from the sale of the disemboweled Scott Paper to Kimberly-Clark, which by Dunlap's own estimate netted him a $100 million bonanza.

Sunbeam investors, naturally, didn't fare as well. When the fraud was discovered internally, the company was forced to restate its earnings, slashing half the reported profits from fiscal 1997. After that embarrassment, Sunbeam shares fell from $52 to $7 in just six months—a loss of $3.8 billion in market cap. Sound familiar?

The auditor in that case, you'll recall, was Arthur Andersen, which paid $110 million to settle a civil action. According to an SEC release in May, an Andersen partner authorized unqualified audit opinions even though "he was aware of many of the

company's accounting improprieties and disclosure failures." The opinions were false and misleading. But nobody is going to jail.

At Waste Management, yet another Andersen client, income reported over six years was overstated by $1.4 billion. Andersen coughed up $220 million to shareholders to wipe its hands clean. The auditor, agreeing to the SEC's first antifraud injunction against a major firm in more than 20 years, also paid a $7 million fine to close the complaint. Three partners were assessed fines, ranging from $30,000 to $50,000, as well. (You guessed it. Not even home detention.) Concedes one former regulator familiar with the case: "Senior people at Andersen got off when we felt we had the goods." Andersen did not respond to a request for comment.

The list goes on—from phony bookkeeping at the former Bankers Trust (now part of Deutsche Bank) to allegations of insider trading by a former Citigroup vice president. One employee of California tech firm nVidia admitted that he cleared

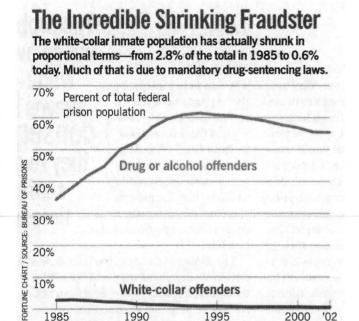

The Incredible Shrinking Fraudster

The white-collar inmate population has actually shrunk in proportional terms—from 2.8% of the total in 1985 to 0.6% today. Much of that is due to mandatory drug-sentencing laws.

FORTUNE CHART / SOURCE: BUREAU OF PRISONS

Percent of total federal prison population

Drug or alcohol offenders

White-collar offenders

nearly half a million dollars in a single day in March 2000 from an illegal insider tip. He pleaded guilty to criminal charges, paid fines, and got a 12-month grounding at home.

The problem will not go away until white-collar thieves face a consequence they're actually scared of: time in jail.

While none of those misbehaviors may rise to Enronian proportions, at least in terms of salacious detail, taken en masse they say something far more distressing. The double standard in criminal justice in this country is starker and more embedded than many realize. Bob Dylan was right: Steal a little, and they put you in jail. Steal a lot, and you're likely to walk away with a lecture and a court-ordered promise not to do it again.

Far beyond the pure social inequity—and that would be bad enough, we admit—is a very real dollar-and-cents cost, a doozy of a recurring charge that ripples through the financial markets. As the Enron case makes abundantly clear, white-collar fraud is not a victimless crime. In this age of the 401(k), when the retirement dreams of middle-class America are tied to the integrity of the stock market, crooks in the corner office are everybody's problem. And the problem will not go away until white-collar thieves face a consequence they're actually scared of: time in jail.

The U.S. regulatory and judiciary systems, however, do little if anything to deter the most damaging Wall Street crimes. Interviews with some six dozen current and former federal prosecutors, regulatory officials, defense lawyers, criminologists, and high-ranking corporate executives paint a disturbing pic-

ture. The already stretched "white-collar" task forces of the FBI focus on wide-ranging schemes like Internet, insurance, and Medicare fraud, abandoning traditional securities and accounting offenses to the SEC. Federal securities regulators, while determined and well trained, are so understaffed that they often have to let good cases slip away. Prosecutors leave scores of would-be criminal cases referred by the SEC in the dustbin, declining to prosecute more than half of what comes their way. State regulators, with a few notable exceptions, shy away from the complicated stuff. So-called self-regulatory organizations like the National Association of Securities Dealers are relatively toothless; trade groups like the American Institute of Certified Public Accountants stubbornly protect their own. And perhaps worst of all, corporate chiefs often wink at (or nod off to) overly aggressive tactics that speed along the margins of the law.

LET'S START WITH THE NUMBERS. WALL STREET, AFTER ALL, IS about numbers, about playing the percentages. And that may be the very heart of the problem. Though securities officials like to brag about their enforcement records, few in America's top-floor suites and corporate boardrooms fear the local sheriff. They know the odds of getting caught.

The U.S. Attorneys' Annual Statistical Report is the official reckoning of the Department of Justice. For the year 2000, the most recent statistics available, federal prosecutors say they charged 8,766 defendants with what they term white-collar crimes, convicting 6,876, or an impressive 78% of the cases brought. Not bad. Of that number, about 4,000 were sentenced to prison—nearly all of them for less than three years. (The average time served, experts say, is closer to 16 months.)

But that 4,000 number isn't what you probably think it is. The Justice Department uses the white-collar appellation for virtually every kind of fraud, says Henry Pontell, a leading criminologist at the University of California at Irvine, and co-author of *Big-Money Crime: Fraud and Politics in the Savings and Loan Crisis*. "I've seen welfare frauds labeled as white-collar crimes," he says. Digging deeper into the Justice Department's 2000 statistics, we find that only 226 of the cases involved securities or commodities fraud.

And guess what: Even those are rarely the highfliers, says Kip Schlegel, chairman of the department of criminal justice at Indiana University, who wrote a study on Wall Street lawbreaking for the Justice Department's research wing. Many of the government's largest sting operations come from busting up cross-state Ponzi schemes, "affinity" investment scams (which prey on the elderly or on particular ethnic or religious groups), and penny-stock boiler rooms, like the infamous Stratton Oakmont and Sterling Foster. They are bad seeds, certainly. But let's not kid ourselves: They are not corporate-officer types or high-level Wall Street traders and bankers—what we might call *starched*-collar criminals. "The criminal sanction is generally reserved for the losers," says Schlegel, "the scamsters, the low-rent crimes."

Statistics from the Federal Bureau of Prisons, up to date as of October 2001, make it even clearer how few white-collar criminals are behind bars. Of a total federal inmate population of

The SEC's Impressive Margins

Did someone say "resource problem"? The SEC is, in fact, a moneymaking machine. The U.S. Treasury keeps fees and penalties. Disgorgements go into a fund for fraud victims.

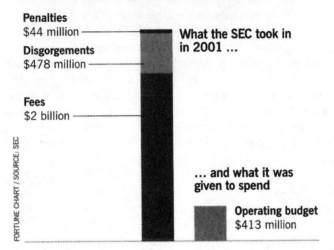

Penalties
$44 million

Disgorgements
$478 million

Fees
$2 billion

What the SEC took in in 2001 ...

... and what it was given to spend

Operating budget
$413 million

FORTUNE CHART / SOURCE: SEC

156,238, prison authorities say only 1,021 fit the description—which includes everyone from insurance schemers to bankruptcy fraudsters, counterfeiters to election-law tamperers to postal thieves. Out of those 1,000 or so, well more than half are held at minimum-security levels—often privately managed "Club Feds" that are about two steps down the comfort ladder from Motel 6.

And how many of them are the starched-collar crooks who commit securities fraud? The Bureau of Prisons can't say precisely. The Department of Justice won't say either—but the answer lies in its database.

Susan Long, a professor of quantitative methods at the school of management at Syracuse University, co-founded a Web data clearinghouse called TRAC, which has been tracking prosecutor referrals from virtually every federal agency for more than a decade. Using a barrage of Freedom of Information Act lawsuits, TRAC has been able to gather data buried in the Justice Department's own computer files (minus the individual case numbers that might be used to identify defendants). And the data, which follow each matter from referral to the prison steps, tell a story the Justice Department doesn't want you to know.

In the full ten years from 1992 to 2001, according to TRAC data, SEC enforcement attorneys referred 609 cases to the Justice Department for possible criminal charges. Of that number, U.S. Attorneys decided what to do on about 525 of the cases—declining to prosecute just over 64% of them. Of those they did press forward, the feds obtained guilty verdicts in a respectable 76%. But even then, some 40% of the convicted starched-collars didn't spend a day in jail. In case you're wondering, here's the magic number that did: 87.

FIVE-POINT TYPE IS SMALL PRINT, SO TINY THAT ALMOST everyone who remembers the Bay of Pigs or the fall of Saigon will need bifocals to read it. For those who love pulp fiction or

the crime blotters in their town weeklies, however, there is no better place to look than in the small print of the *Wall Street Journal*'s B section. Once a month, buried in the thick folds of newsprint, are bullet reports of the NASD's disciplinary actions. February's disclosures about alleged misbehavior, for example, range from the unseemly to the lurid—from an Ohio bond firm accused of systematically overcharging customers and fraudulently marking up trades to a California broker who deposited a client's $143,000 check in his own account. Two senior VPs of a Pittsburgh firm, say NASD officials, cashed out of stock, thanks to timely inside information they received about an upcoming loss; a Dallas broker reportedly converted someone's 401(k) rollover check to his personal use.

In all, the group's regulatory arm received 23,753 customer complaints against its registered reps between the years 1997 and 2000. After often extensive investigations, the NASD barred "for life" during this period 1,662 members and suspended another 1,000 or so for violations of its rules or of laws on the federal books. But despite its impressive 117-page *Sanction Guidelines*, the NASD can't do much of anything to its miscreant broker-dealers other than throw them out of the club. It has no statutory right to file civil actions against rule breakers, it has no subpoena power, and from the looks of things it can't even get the bums to return phone calls. Too often the disciplinary write-ups conclude with a boilerplate "failed to respond to NASD requests for information."

"That's a good thing when they default," says Barry Goldsmith, executive vice president for enforcement at NASD Regulation. "It gives us the ability to get the wrongdoers out quickly to prevent them from doing more harm."

Goldsmith won't say how many cases the NASD passes on to the SEC or to criminal prosecutors for further investigation. But he does acknowledge that the securities group refers a couple of hundred suspected insider-trading cases to its higher-ups in the regulatory chain.

Thus fails the first line of defense against white-collar crime: self-policing. The situation is worse, if anything, among accountants than it is among securities dealers, says John C. Coffee Jr., a Columbia Law School professor and a leading authority on securities enforcement issues. At the American Institute of Certified Public Accountants, he says, "no real effort is made to enforce the rules." Except one, apparently. "They have a rule that they do not take action against auditors until all civil litigation has been resolved," Coffee says, "because they don't want their actions to be used against their members in a civil suit." Lynn E. Turner, who until last summer was the SEC's chief accountant and is now a professor at Colorado State University, agrees. "The AICPA," he says, "often failed to discipline members in a timely fashion, if at all. And when it did, its most severe remedy was just to expel the member from the organization."

Al Anderson, senior VP of AICPA, says the criticism is unfounded. "We have been and always will be committed to enforcing the rules," he says. The next line of defense after the professional associations is the SEC. The central role of this independent regulatory agency is to protect investors in the financial markets by making sure that publicly traded companies

The Odds Against Doing Time

Regulators like to talk tough, but when it comes to actual punishment, all but a handful of Wall Street cheats get off with a slap on the wrist.

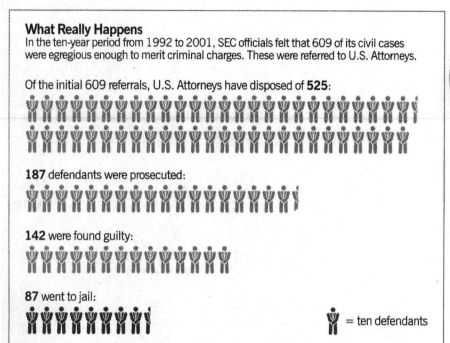

What Really Happens
In the ten-year period from 1992 to 2001, SEC officials felt that 609 of its civil cases were egregious enough to merit criminal charges. These were referred to U.S. Attorneys.

Of the initial 609 referrals, U.S. Attorneys have disposed of **525**:

187 defendants were prosecuted:

142 were found guilty:

87 went to jail:

 = ten defendants

SOURCE: TRANSACTIONAL RECORDS ACCESS CLEARINGHOUSE

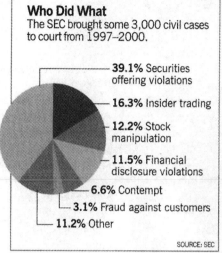

Who Did What
The SEC brought some 3,000 civil cases to court from 1997–2000.

- **39.1%** Securities offering violations
- **16.3%** Insider trading
- **12.2%** Stock manipulation
- **11.5%** Financial disclosure violations
- **6.6%** Contempt
- **3.1%** Fraud against customers
- **11.2%** Other

SOURCE: SEC

A Look at Self-Policing
Few complaints received last year by the NASD resulted in serious sanctions.

Registered reps	675,821
Customer complaints received	5,155
Individuals barred	466
Individuals suspended	346

SOURCE: NASD REGULATION

play by the rules. With jurisdiction over every constituent in the securities trade, from brokers to mutual funds to accountants to corporate filers, it would seem to be the voice of Oz. But the SEC's power, like that of the Wizard, lies more in persuasion than in punishment. The commission can force companies to comply with securities rules, it can fine them when they don't, it can even charge them in civil court with violating the law. But it can't drag anybody off to prison. To that end, the SEC's enforcement division must work with federal and state prosecutors—a game that often turns into weak cop/bad cop.

Nevertheless, the last commission chairman, Arthur Levitt, did manage to shake the ground with the power he had. For the 1997–2000 period, for instance, attorneys at the agency's enforcement division brought civil actions against 2,989 respondents. That figure includes 487 individual cases of alleged insider trading, 365 for stock manipulation, 343 for violations of laws and rules related to financial disclosure, 196 for contempt of the regulatory agency, and another 94 for fraud against customers. In other words, enough bad stuff to go around. What would make them civil crimes, vs. actual handcuff-and-fingerprint ones? Evidence, says one SEC regional director. "In a civil case you need only a preponderance of evidence that there was an intent to defraud," she says. "In a criminal case you have to prove that intent beyond a reasonable doubt."

When the SEC does find a case that smacks of criminal intent, the commission refers it to a U.S. Attorney. And that is where the second line of defense often breaks down. The SEC

has the expertise to sniff out such wrongdoing but not the big stick of prison to wave in front of its targets. The U.S. Attorney's office has the power to order in the SWAT teams but often lacks the expertise—and, quite frankly, the inclination—to deconstruct a complex financial crime. After all, it is busy pursuing drug kingpins and terrorists.

And there is also the key issue of institutional kinship, say an overwhelming number of government authorities. U.S. Attorneys, for example, have kissing-cousin relationships with the agencies they work with most, the FBI and DEA. Prosecutors and investigators often work together from the start and know the elements required on each side to make a case stick. That is hardly true with the SEC and all but a handful of U.S. Attorneys around the country. In candid conversations, current and former regulators cited the lack of warm cooperation between the law-enforcement groups, saying one had no clue about how the other worked.

THIRTEEN BLOCKS FROM WALL STREET IS A DIFFERENT KIND of ground zero. Here, in the shadow of the imposing Federalist-style courthouses of lower Manhattan, is a nine-story stone fortress of indeterminate color, somewhere in the unhappy genus of waiting-room beige. As with every federal building these days, there are reminders of the threat of terrorism, but this particular outpost has taken those reminders to the status of a four-bell alarm. To get to the U.S. Attorney's office, a visitor must wind his way through a phalanx of blue police barricades, stop by a kiosk manned by a U.S. marshal, enter a giant white tent with police and metal detectors, and proceed to a bulletproof visitors desk, replete with armed guards. Even if you make it to the third floor, home of the Securities and Commodities Fraud Task Force, Southern District of New York, you'll need an electronic passkey to get in.

This, the office which Rudy Giuliani led to national prominence with his late-1980s busts of junk-bond king Michael Milken, Ivan Boesky, and the Drexel Burnham insider-trading ring, is one of the few outfits in the country that even know how to prosecute complex securities crimes. Or at least one of the few willing to take them on. Over the years it has become the favorite (and at times lone) repository for the SEC's enforcement hit list.

And how many attorneys are in this office to fight the nation's book cookers, insider traders, and other Wall Street thieves? Twenty-five—including three on loan from the SEC. The unit has a fraction of the paralegal and administrative help of even a small private law firm. Assistant U.S. Attorneys do their own copying, and in one recent sting it was Sandy—one of the unit's two secretaries—who did the records analysis that broke the case wide open.

Even this office declines to prosecute more than half the cases referred to it by the SEC. Richard Owens, the newly minted chief of the securities task force and a six-year veteran of the unit, insists that it is not for lack of resources. There are plenty of legitimate reasons, he says, why a prosecutor would choose not to pursue a case—starting with the possibility that there may not have been true criminal intent.

But many federal regulators scoff at such bravado. "We've got too many crooks and not enough cops," says one. "We could fill Riker's Island if we had the resources."

And Owens' office is as good as it gets in this country. In other cities, federal and state prosecutors shun securities cases for all kinds of understandable reasons. They're harder to pull off than almost any other type of case—and the payoff is rarely worth it from the standpoint of local political impact. "The typical state prosecution is for a standard common-law crime," explains Philip A. Feigin, an attorney with Rothgerber Johnson & Lyons in Denver and a former commissioner of the Colorado Securities Division. "An ordinary trial will probably last for five days, it'll have 12 witnesses, involve an act that occurred in one day, and was done by one person." Now hear the pitch coming from a securities regulator thousands of miles away. "Hi. We've never met, but I've got this case I'd like you to take on. The law that was broken is just 158 pages long. It involves only three years of conduct—and the trial should last no more than three months. What do you say?" The prosecutor has eight burglaries or drug cases he could bring in the time it takes to prosecute a single white-collar crime. "It's a completely easy choice," says Feigin.

That easy choice, sadly, has left a glaring logical—and moral—fallacy in the nation's justice system: Suite thugs don't go to jail because street thugs have to. And there's one more thing on which many crime experts are adamant. The double standard makes no sense whatsoever when you consider the damage done by the offense. Sociologist Pontell and his col-

leagues Kitty Calavita, at U.C. Irvine, and Robert Tillman, at New York's St. John's University, have demonstrated this in a number of compelling academic studies. In one the researchers compared the sentences received by major players (that is, those who stole $100,000 or more) in the savings-and-loan scandal a decade ago with the sentences handed to other types of nonviolent federal offenders. The starched-collar S&L crooks got an average of 36.4 months in the slammer. Those who committed burglary—generally swiping $300 or less—got 55.6 months; car thieves, 38 months; and first-time drug offenders, 64.9 months. Now compare the costs of the two kinds of crime: The losses from all bank robberies in the U.S. in 1992 *totaled* $35 million, according to the FBI's Uniform Crime Reports. That's about 1% of the estimated cost of Charles Keating's fraud at Lincoln Savings & Loan.

"Nobody writes an e-mail that says, 'Gee, I think I'll screw the public today.' There's never been a fraud of passion."

"OF ALL THE FACTORS THAT LEAD TO CORPORATE CRIME, NONE comes close in importance to the role top management plays in tolerating, even shaping, a culture that allows for it," says William Laufer, the director of the Zicklin Center for Business Ethics Research at the Wharton School. Laufer calls it "winking." And with each wink, nod, and nudge-nudge, instructions of a sort are passed down the management chain. Accounting fraud, for example, often starts in this way. "Nobody writes an e-mail that says, 'Gee, I think I'll screw the public today,'" says former regulator Feigin. "There's never been a fraud of passion. These things take years." They breed slowly over time.

So does the impetus to fight them. Enron, of course, has stirred an embarrassed Administration and Congress to action. But it isn't merely Enron that worries legislators and the public—it's *another* Enron. Every day brings news of one more accounting gas leak that for too long lay undetected. Wariness about Lucent, Rite Aid, Raytheon, Tyco, and a host of other big names has left investors not only rattled but also questioning the very integrity of the financial reporting system.

And with good reason. Two statistics in particular suggest that no small degree of executive misconduct has been brewing in the corporate petri dish. In 1999 and 2000 the SEC demanded 96 restatements of earnings or other financial statements—a figure that was more than in the previous nine years combined. Then, in January, the Federal Deposit Insurance Corp. announced more disturbing news. The number of publicly traded companies declaring bankruptcy shot up to a record 257, a stunning 46% over the prior year's total, which itself had been a record. These companies shunted $259 billion in assets into protective custody—that is, away from shareholders. And a record 45 of these losers were biggies, companies with assets greater than $1 billion. That might all seem normal in a time of burst bubbles and economic recession. But the number of nonpublic bankruptcies has barely risen. Regulators and plaintiffs lawyers say both restatements and sudden public bankruptcies often signal the presence of fraud.

The ultimate cost could be monumental. "Integrity of the markets, and the willingness of people to invest, are critical to us," says Harvey J. Goldschmid, a professor of law at Columbia since 1970 and soon to be an SEC commissioner. "Widespread false disclosure would be incredibly dangerous. People could lose trust in corporate filings altogether."

So will all this be enough to spark meaningful changes in the system? Professor Coffee thinks the Enron matter might move Congress to take action. "I call it the phenomenon of crash-then-law," he says. "You need three things to get a wave of legislation and litigation: a recession, a stock market crash, and a true villain." For instance, Albert Wiggin, head of Chase National Bank, cleaned up during the crash of 1929 by short-selling his own company stock. "From that came a new securities law, Section 16(b), that prohibits short sales by executives," Coffee says.

But the real issue isn't more laws on the books—it's enforcing the ones that are already there. And that, says criminologist Kip Schlegel, is where the government's action falls far short of the rhetoric. In his 1994 study on securities law-breaking for the Justice Department, Schlegel found that while officials were talking tough about locking up insider traders, there was little evidence to suggest that the punishments imposed—either the incarceration rates or the sentences themselves—were more severe. "In fact," he says, "the data suggest the opposite trend. The government lacks the will to bring these people to justice."

DENNY CRAWFORD SAYS THERE'S AN ALL-TOO-SIMPLE REASON for this. The longtime commissioner of the Texas Securities Board, who has probably put away more bad guys than any other state commissioner, says most prosecutors make the crimes too complicated. "You've got to boil it down to lying, cheating, and stealing," she says, in a warbly voice that sounds like pink lemonade. "That's all it is—the best way to end securities fraud is to put every one of these crooks in jail."

Trust and Confidence in Criminal Justice

by Lawrence W. Sherman

Criminal justice in America today is a paradox of progress: While the fairness and effectiveness of criminal justice have improved, public trust and confidence apparently have not.

Criminal justice is far less corrupt, brutal, and racially unfair than it has been in the past. It is arguably more effective at preventing crime. It has far greater diversity in its staffing. Yet these objectively defined improvements seem to have had little impact on American attitudes toward criminal justice.

Understanding this paradox—better work but low marks—is central to improving public trust and confidence in the criminal justice system.

How Low Is Public Confidence?

Gallup polls over the last few years have consistently found that Americans have less confidence in the criminal justice system than in other institutions, such as banking, the medical system, public schools, television news, newspapers, big business,and organized labor.[1]

The most striking finding in the Gallup poll is the difference between the low evaluation of "criminal justice" and the high evaluation given to the police and the Supreme Court. Other sources of data show similar attitudes: Confidence in local courts and prisons is far lower than it is for the police.[2] These large differences suggest that Americans may not think of police in the same way as they do the criminal justice system.

The Racial Divide

A 1998 Gallup poll reports little overall demographic difference among the respondents saying they had confidence in the criminal justice system. But what is most clear is the difference in opinion between whites and blacks about the individual components of the criminal justice system and especially the police. Whites express considerably more confidence in the police, local court

system, and State prison system than blacks (see exhibit 1).

Race, Victimization, and Punishment. Racial differences also appear in rates of victimization and punishment: Blacks are 31 percent more likely to be victimized by personal crime than whites and twice as likely as whites to suffer a completed violent crime.[3]

The personal opinions of the survey respondents are consistent with a major theory about the declining public confidence in all government—not just criminal justice—in all modern nations, not just the United States. The concerns arise from the decline of hierarchy and the rise of equality in all walks of life. The rise in egalitarian culture increases the demand for government officials to show more respect to citizens.

Young black males are historically 10 times more likely to be murdered than white males.[4]

Arrest rates for robbery are five times higher for blacks than for whites; four times higher for murder and rape; and three times higher for drug violations and weapons possession.[5]

Blacks are eight times more likely to be in a State or Federal prison than non-Hispanic whites (and three times more likely than Hispanic whites). Almost 2 percent of the black population, or 1 of every 63 blacks, was in prison in 1996.[6]

Race and Neighborhood. What these data fail to show, however, is the extent to which the racial differences in

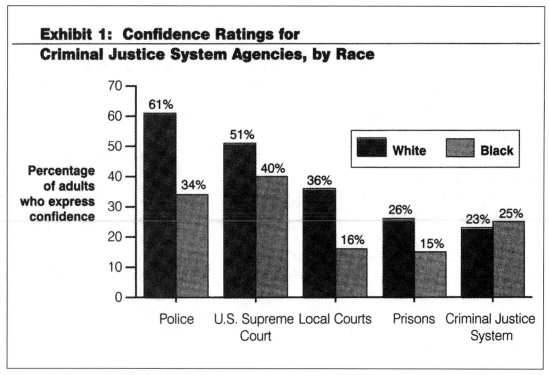

Exhibit 1: Confidence Ratings for Criminal Justice System Agencies, by Race

Source: The Gallup Organization, "Confidence In Institutions," Retrieved From The WORLD WIDE WEB SITE HTTP:// WWW.GALLUP.COM, October 10, 2000.

attitudes, victimization, and punishment may be largely related to more blacks being the residents of a small number of high-crime, high-poverty areas concentrated in a small fraction of urban neighborhoods. This is the case even though Harvard University sociologist Orlando Patterson has estimated that only 1 in every 30 black adults resides in these high-crime, high-poverty areas; the proportion is higher for children.

What we may understand as a problem of race in America may largely reflect conditions in those neighborhoods that are generalized by both blacks and whites to conditions of the larger society.

Due to limited national data, it is difficult to determine what precisely drives the lower levels of confidence in criminal justice among blacks, but insights from city-by-city analysis suggest two conclusions:

- **There is no race-based subculture of violence.** Blacks and whites who live in neighborhoods with similar conditions have similar views on the legitimacy of law. To the extent that race is associated with attitudes toward law, it may be a reflection of the greater likelihood that blacks reside in poverty areas.
- **There is no race-based hostility to police in high-crime areas.** High levels of dissatisfaction with police are endemic to high-crime areas. Whites residing in such areas express attitudes just as hostile as blacks toward police.[7] The distrust of police in high-crime areas may be related to the prevalence of crime rather than to

police practice. If negative attitudes are driven by police practice, it may be because those practices fail to prevent crime rather than because police presence or behavior is excessive. Or it may be that the practice of policing in such areas offers less recognition and dignity to citizen consumers than is found in lower crime areas.

Strong Demands for Change

The findings and responses from a random digit-dialing telephone survey of 4,000 residents of 10 northeastern States in 1998 found that more than 80 percent—four out of five respondents—preferred the idea of "totally revamping the way the [criminal justice] system works" for violent crime; 75 percent said the same for all crime.[8] The responses varied little from State to State or from one demographic group to another. The majority of respondents believed that:

- Victims are not accorded sufficient rights in the criminal justice process.
- Victims are not informed enough about the status of their cases.
- Victims are not able to talk to prosecutors enough.
- Victims should be able to tell the court what impact the crime had on them, but most victims do not get that chance.

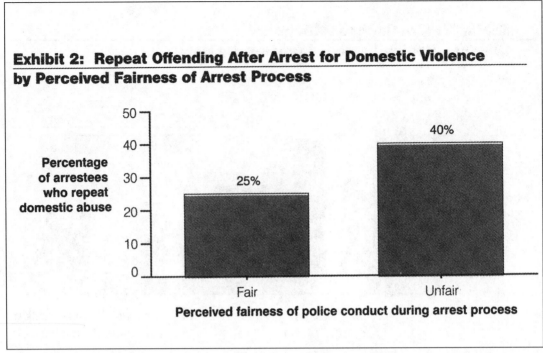

Exhibit 2: Repeat Offending After Arrest for Domestic Violence by Perceived Fairness of Arrest Process

Source: Paternoster, R., R. Brame, R. Bachman, and L. W. Sherman, "Do Fair Procedures Matter? The Effect of Procedural Justice on Spousal Assault," *Law & Society Review*, 31(1997): 185.

- Offenders, even if jailed, should reimburse victims for the cost of the crime.
- Offenders should acknowledge their responsibility for the crime.
- Victims should have the opportunity to meet with the offender to find out why the crime occurred and to learn whether the offender accepted responsibility.
- Ordinary citizens, not courts, should set penalties for non-violent crimes.
- Drug treatment should be used more widely for drug-using offenders.

The personal opinions of the survey respondents are consistent with a major theory about the declining public confidence in all government—not just criminal justice—in all modern nations, not just the United States. The concerns arise from the decline of hierarchy and the rise of equality in all walks of life. The rise in egalitarian culture increases the demand for government officials to show more respect to citizens.[9]

Egalitarianism in Modern Culture: Raised Expectations, Reduced Trust

Americans' trust in government has declined sharply in the last quarter century.[10] A similar loss of trust has been found in 18 other democracies. Citizens now expect higher levels of recognition, respect, and status from the government. Criminal justice serves as a flash point for this change in citizen attitudes because so many Americans have contact with the criminal justice system and because the hierarchical design of criminal justice institutions juxtaposes so starkly with the egalitarian demands of the public.

As the spread of equality has combined with growing freedom from want, political culture has shifted away from Puritan views of a *hierarchical* communal democracy to Quaker views of a more *egalitarian* individualistic democracy. Indeed, the consistently greater support for police than for courts may result from a perception of police as egalitarian individualists (the new cultural ideal) while judges are seen as bossy conformists (the outdated ideal).

The massive three-decade decline of public trust in liberal democratic governments suggests a deeper paradox of success: As democracies become more materially successful and better educated, the perceived need for governance declines and expectations of government for appropriate conduct increase.[11] The crisis of government legitimacy has thus been prompted less by declining quality of government conduct than by increasing public dissatisfaction with institutions in general, driven by what Ronald F. Inglehart, Professor, University of Michigan, calls "postmaterialist values."[12]

Social changes taking place around the globe appear to be resulting in challenges to the legitimacy of virtually all forms of social hierarchy of authority (although not hierarchy of wealth)—of husbands over wives, doctors over patients, schoolteachers over students and parents, parents over children, and government officials over citizens. This evolution may have led to widespread preference for the recognition of individual dignity over the recognition of communal authority.[13]

Thus, what Robert J. Sampson, Professor of Sociology, University of Chicago, and other scholars refer to as "legal cynicism"—the extent to which people feel that laws are not binding—is not the product of a criminal subculture.[14] It is a 400-year-old Christian political theology that has become globally accepted across people of all religions in a more egalitarian and individualistic modern culture.

In such a world, people are less likely to obey the law out of a sense of communal obligation, and more likely to obey laws they support through a personal sense of what is moral.

Consensus thus appears to be a much better fit to the new political culture. Standing up when judges enter a room and obeying orders barked out by police, for example, are procedural forms that may imply officials are more important than citizens. Such forms may do more to undermine legal trust than to build respect for the law.

Trust and Recognition

What changing culture may be creating is a world in which people trust *laws* but not *legal institutions*. This new world may be one in which trust in criminal justice is no longer automatic; it must be earned everyday, with each encounter between legal agents and citizens.

The research of Tom R. Tyler, Department of Psychology, New York University, shows that Americans—especially members of minority groups—are extremely sensitive to the respect they perceive and the procedures employed when they come into contact with criminal justice.[15] Tyler's evidence suggests that in building citizen trust in the legal system, it may matter less whether you receive the speeding ticket than whether the police officer addresses you politely or rudely during the traffic stop. Similarly, sentencing guidelines that punish possession of crack more harshly than possession of powdered cocaine may discriminate against blacks. But dissatisfaction may be greater with some police officers engaged in drug enforcement who treat suspects and arrestees like people who are enemies rather than like people who are equal fellow citizens.

Tyler concludes that the procedural justice perceived in treatment by legal officials affects the level of trust citizens have in government.[16] That level of trust, in turn, affects the pride we have in our government and the

degree to which we feel we are respected by other members of our democracy—including the government.

Tyler further concludes that the odds of citizens reaching the conclusion that the law is morally right are much higher when citizens feel that the law has given each of them adequate recognition and respect.

Rather than creating a willingness to *defer* to the power of the law, Tyler suggests that respectful treatment creates a stronger *consensus* about what is moral and what the law must be. The consensus model assumes more equality than the deference model on which our legal institutions were designed.[17]

Consensus thus appears to be a much better fit to the new political culture. Standing up when judges enter a room and obeying orders barked out by police, for example, are procedural forms that may imply officials are more important than citizens. Such forms may do more to undermine legal trust than to build respect for the law.

Fitting Legal Institutions to the Culture: The Canberra Experiments

For all Americans, regardless of race, the central cause of declining trust may be the misfit of hierarchical legal institutions in an egalitarian culture. In many ways, citizens may experience the conduct of judges, prosecutors, and police as being overly "bossy" and unnecessarily authoritarian.

Results of experiments in Canberra, Australia, suggest that an egalitarian, consensual procedure of stakeholder citizens deciding the sentence for a crime creates more legitimacy in the eyes of both offenders and victims than the hierarchical, deferential process of sentencing by a judge.[18]

The experiments compared traditional court sentencing of youthful violent and property offenders to an alternative community justice conference making the same decisions.

Offenders who were sent to conferences were far less likely than offenders who were sent to traditional court to say that they were pushed around; disadvantaged by their age, income, or education; treated as if they were untrustworthy; or not listened to. They also were more likely to report that their experience increased their respect for the justice system and the police, as well as their feeling that the crime they had committed was morally wrong.

Victims also were far more satisfied with community justice conferences than with court proceedings. Much of this difference may be because most victims of criminals sent to court were never informed of the offenders' court appearances, either before or after sentencing. The victims invited to community justice conferences with offenders, in sharp contrast, gained increased trust in police and justice, as well as decreased fear of and anger

Alternative Community Justice Conferences

In the Canberra experiments, the police invite victims, offenders, and their respective supporters to a meeting in which the offenders must not—for these purposes—dispute their guilt. At the meetings, everyone sits in a circle to discuss the harm the crime has caused, acknowledge the pain and emotional impact of that harm, and deliberate democratically as to how the offenders should repair that harm.

The egalitarian proceedings begin with the police officer moderating the proceedings, offering only questions, not answers. For example, what did the offender do? How did it hurt the victim? How does the victim feel about that hurt? How do the victim's friends and family feel? How do the offender's family and friends feel about what has been said? What would be the right way for the offender to repay the debt to the victim and to society? Does everyone agree? Is there anything the offender wants to say to the victim (sometimes the offender says "I'm sorry")? Is there anything the victim wants to say to the offender (possibly "I forgive you")?

One of the most important parts of the proceedings is that everyone is allowed to talk, just as in a Quaker meeting, but no one person dominates speech, as might happen in a Calvinist church or in an Anglo-American courtroom. Emotions can be intense at the conferences—unlike the restraint valued by Puritan cultures and Western courts.

No Lawyers. Lawyers are not allowed to attend the conferences as legal advocates for either an offender or the State, although they may attend as personal supporters. They are always on call, ready to act to protect anyone whose rights may seem abused. But as long as the victim-offender consensus is under discussion, everyone in the circle has equal authority, regardless of age or education.

Extra Time Required. A community justice conference takes, on average, about 70 minutes to resolve. A similar case in traditional court may take 10 minutes spread across several different appearances, which have no emotional significance for victim or offender, and thus leave citizens feeling like cogs in a wheel. A community justice conference is about the people present rather than the legal formalities. People come only once, prepared to stay until the case is resolved.

Trust in Justice. Research shows that sentences imposed in the community justice conferences and the traditional court process were fairly similar despite the major differences in the decision making procedures employed.[1] But the conferences produced far better results in terms of citizen respect for legal institutions.

[1]Sherman, L.W., H. Strang, and G.C. Barnes, "Stratification of Justice: Legitimacy of Hierarchical and Egalitarian Sentencing Procedures," unpublished manuscript, Fels Center of Government, University of Pennsylvania, 1999.

at the offender. (For more details, see "Alternative Community Justice Conferences.)

Building Trust One Case at a Time

The Canberra experiments suggest the highly personal nature of citizen trust in criminal justice. The *personal* legitimacy of legal agents may depend on a leveling of distinctions in rank between citizen and official.

As Albert J. Reiss, Jr., Professor Emeritus, Sociology Department, Yale University, observed, the legitimacy of police authority in the eyes of citizens varies widely from one situation to the next.[19] Thus, officials must earn the legitimacy of their authority one case at a time.

The most dramatic demonstration of this principle is the finding that *how* police make arrests for domestic violence affects the rate of repeat offending. Raymond Paternoster, Ph.D., University of Maryland, et al. demonstrated that offenders who were arrested for domestic violence and who perceived that the police officers' arresting procedures were fair were less likely to repeat

the offense than offenders who perceived the arresting procedures as unfair.[20] Actions that constituted "procedural justice" included the police taking the time to listen to both the offender and the victim, not handcuffing the offender in front of the victim, and not using physical force.

As exhibit 2 shows, the risk of repeat offending was 40 percent for offenders who had a low perception of police procedural fairness, but only 25 percent for those who perceived a high level of police fairness. The estimate of offending risk took prior levels of violence into account; hence the findings shown in exhibit 2 increase our confidence that *how* the police make an arrest may affect the crime rate (much of which comes from repeat offending)—through trust and confidence in the criminal justice system.

Reducing Complaints Against Police. Other tests of the hypothesis that trust in criminal justice comes from egalitarian procedures can be seen in actions that have been shown to reduce complaints against police.

In sum, a growing body of theory and evidence suggests that it is not the fairness or effectiveness of decisions criminal justice officials make that determines the public's level of trust. Changes in modern culture have made the *procedures* and manners of criminal justice officials far more important to public trust and left officials out of step with modern culture.

In the 42nd and 44th precincts in The Bronx, complaints reached a 10-year high in 1996. But after the precinct commanders instituted a program to promote respectful policing and improve police relations with community residents, complaints dropped dramatically. Among the elements of the new program was vigorous training for officers on how to treat citizens respectfully, zealous monitoring of complaints, and follow through with consequences for officers who received complaints.

In addition, the simple elimination of the precinct's high desk and bar in front of the desk in the reception area helped the precinct present a less hierarchical face to the community. Research on the effects of the strategy, conducted by the Vera Institute of Justice, found that citizens began to perceive the police as responsive to community concerns.[21]

The second test of the procedural equality theory comes from a community with a population of almost one million; 55 percent of the population is African American.

Complaints dropped in this department of 1,400 officers when a new procedure for traffic stops was initiated in 1997–99. The procedure, called "Take Away Guns" (TAG), was one part of a larger strategy to reduce gun violence. One of the first steps the department took was to increase traffic enforcement—a 400-some percent increase—so that police had an opportunity to explain the program at each traffic stop and distribute a letter from the district police captain explaining the program. The letter contained the captain's phone number and invited citizens to call the captain with complaints or questions. Officers were trained to be very polite in explaining the program to drivers and then asking permission to search the car for guns.

The program not only received a high rate of compliance with the requests, but also received praise from the drivers stopped who approved of the efforts to get guns off the street. Over the first 2 years of the program, both gun violence and citizen complaints of excessive force by police dropped substantially.

In sum, a growing body of theory and evidence suggests that it is not the fairness or effectiveness of decisions criminal justice officials make that determines the public's level of trust. Changes in modern culture have made the *procedures* and manners of criminal justice officials far more important to public trust and left officials out of step with modern culture.

This explanation gains further support from scholarship on the effect of television and other communications media on the nature of authority and trust in government. For despite Tyler's focus on personal contacts with criminal justice, most citizens have little if any personal contact with legal officials. For this majority of Americans, the level of trust in criminal justice may depend on what they hear about criminal justice encounters with other citizens, a little-studied area. But it also may depend on how legal agencies are portrayed in entertainment and news media.

Authority and Media Celebrity

The future authority of the criminal justice system may well depend on how the system appears not just to those directly involved in the system, but to all citizens. That, in turn, may depend heavily on how criminal justice manages its image in the electronic media. Legal historian Lawrence Friedman notes that modern culture has changed the very nature of authority from *vertical* (where people look up to leaders in high position) to *horizontal* (where people look in to the center of society to find leaders who are celebrities, defined by the number of people who recognize their names and faces). "Leaders are no longer distant, awesome, and unknown; they are familiar figures on TV.… The horizontal society is [one in which] the men and women who get and hold power become celebrities" and the public come to know them, or think they know them, through the media. "By contrast," Friedman writes, "traditional authority was vertical, and the higher up the authority, the more stern, distant, and remote it was."[22]

A celebrity culture creates still another paradox: Americans now feel more personal connections with celebrities living far away than they do with legal officials in their own hometown. Just as many people felt more emotional loss at the death of Princess Diana than at the death of a neighbor, the celebrity culture makes us feel personal connections to people we do not know.

Thus, for all the programs designed to foster community policing or community prosecution with legal officials in the neighborhood, Americans still are more likely to form their impressions of criminal justice from vicarious contact through friends or through television shows than from personal experience with their own legal system. The evidence is clear: On a Wednesday night when police convene a neighborhood meeting in a church basement, more local residents are home watching television than attending the meeting.

We may well ask if there are any celebrities of American criminal justice, and if so, who they are—The Chief Justice of the Supreme Court? The director of the FBI? Probably not. These positions appear to fit Friedman's characteristics of traditional authority: stern, distant, and remote. Television's Judge Judy, on the other hand, is an internationally recognized celebrity, with far greater name-face recognition than the traditional authority figures.

Unfortunately, the entertainment values of the television business conflict with the core values of legal institutions. What sells TV audiences is conflict and putdowns, tools Judge Judy uses to portray a rude, in-your-face (but perhaps egalitarian), power-control image of the bench. Audiences find this fun to watch, although Judge Judy may confirm their worst fears, leaving them reluctant to have anything to do with the legal system.

The difficulty in using celebrity power to send messages about the trustworthiness of criminal justice is the clash of cultures between law and entertainment. The reticence of the legal culture conflicts with the chattiness of celebrity culture.

One can imagine a legal official appearing weekly on a talk showwith a huge audience, saying things that could help shore up public faith in criminal justice as an egalitarian and fair system. One can equally imagine such a strategy being condemned by leaders of the American Bar Association, conservative journalists, and other defenders of traditional remoteness of authority.

The kind of public education programs that legal culture would approve of—such as tasteful PBS specials or public service announcements on radio and television—would seem unlikely to reach much of the public, let alone those citizens most distrustful of the system.

Portraying Values in the Media

The media often portray criminal justice through a morality play that explores themes of what Elijah Anderson, Charles and William L. Day Professor, Sociology Department, University of Pennsylvania, calls "street" and "decent" values. Based on years of field research in high-crime areas of Philadelphia, Anderson has observed people who exhibit "decent" values as patient, hopeful, respectful of authority, and with a belief in the predictability of punishment. Those who exhibit "street" values take on a bitter, impatient, antisystem outlook that is disrespectful of authority and demanding of deference.[23]

Television dramas that portray a hero's impatience with red tape may glorify the "street" enforcement of vengeance and personal respect. TV interviewers who ask officials provocative and insulting questions may reflect an effort to produce a "street" response.

The paradox of such media portrayals is that the more frequently legal officials are portrayed breaking the official rules out of distrust for "decent" government, the less reason the public has to believe the criminal justice system will treat citizens decently. By showing criminal justice agents pursuing street values, the media may create a self-fulfilling prophecy, defining conduct for legal officials and the public alike.

The research on respect for authority suggests that street sanctioning styles interact with different kinds of citizen personalities in ways that produce the following differences in repeat offending:

- Decent sanctioning of "decent" people produces the lowest repeat offending.
- Street sanctioning of "decent" people produces higher repeat offending.
- Decent sanctioning of "street" people may produce even higher repeat offending.
- Street sanctioning of "street" people produces the highest levels of repeat offending.[24]

The research on respect for authority consistently suggests that when people in positions of authority impose "street" attitudes or sanctions, the reaction is almost always negative. It is more productive for criminal justice officials to show more respect to, and take more time to listen to, citizens. To the extent that this message is portrayed in entertainment media and identified with celebrity authority, the criminal justice system might be able to increase its public trust and confidence. Yet to the extent that "decent" values are themselves communicated in an illegitimate way, it will be difficult to foster a more "decent" legal culture.

Half a century ago and half a world away, a French journalist observed during a 2-month tour of China in the early 1950's that police had become far more polite under Mao's early communism:

> In the olden days the Peking police were renowned for their brutality, and pedestrians frequently suffered at their hands, smacks in the face being the least form of violence offered them. Today they are formally forbidden to use any kind of force. Their instructions are to explain, to make people understand, to convince them.[25]

It may be easier to change official conduct in a dictatorship than in a democracy, but the power of electronic media may make the dynamics totally different today. Electronic communications comprise a highly democratized, free-market institution that cannot be manipulated easily for official purposes. But the media can be avenue in which celebrity power is built and put to use in fostering support for "decent" styles of criminal justice, both in the image and the reality of how criminal justice works.

The Domains of Public Trust

Three major domains appear to affect public trust and confidence in criminal justice:

- The conduct and practices of the criminal justice system.
- The changing values and expectations of the culture the system serves.
- The images of the system presented in electronic media.

Changes in each domain affect the others. Trust, as the product of all three combined, is likely to increase only when changes in all three domains can be aligned to create practices and values that are perceived to be fair, inclusive, and trustworthy.

Discovering how that can be made to happen is a daunting task. But the data suggest that fairness builds trust in criminal justice, and trust builds compliance with law. Thus what is fairer is more effective, and to be effective it is necessary to be fair.

Notes

1. Retrieved from the World Wide Web site http://www.gallup.com, October 10, 2000.

2. Maguire, K., and A. Pastore, eds., *Sourcebook of Criminal Justice Statistics, 1997*, Washington, DC: U.S. Department of Justice, Bureau of Justice Statistics, 1998 (NCJ 171147).

3. Maguire and Pastore, *Sourcebook*, 182, see note 2.

4. Reiss, A.J., Jr., and J. Roth, *Understanding and Preventing Violence*, Washington, DC: National Academy of Sciences, 1993: 64 (NCJ 140290).

5. Hacker, A., *Two Nations: Black and White, Separate, Hostile, and Unequal*, New York: Free Press, 1992: 181.

6. Maguire and Pastore, *Sourcebook*, 494, see note 2.

7. Sampson, R., and D. Bartusch, "Legal Cynicism and Subcultural Tolerance of Deviance: The Neighborhood Context of Racial Differences," *Law & Society Review*, 32 (4) (1999): 777–804.

8. Boyle, J.M.,*Crime Issues in the Northeast: Statewide Surveys of the Public and Crime Victims in Connecticut, Delaware, Maine, Massachusetts, Vermont, New Hampshire, New Jersey, New York, and Rhode Island*, Silver Spring, MD: Schulman, Ronca, and Bucuvalas, Inc., 1999.

9. Fukuyama, F., *The End of History and the Last Man*, New York: Free Press, 1992.

10. Orren, G., "Fall From Grace: The Public's Loss of Faith in the Government," in *Why People Don't Trust Government*, eds. J.S. Nye, Jr.,
P.D. Zelikow, and D.C. King, Cambridge, MA: Harvard University Press, 1997: 83.

11. Fukuyama, *The End of History*, see note 9; Heclo, H., "The Sixties' False Dawn: Awakenings, Movements, and Postmodern Policymaking," *Journal of Policy History*, 8 (1996): 50–58; Balogh, B., "Introduction," *Journal of Policy History*, 8 (1996): 25.

12. Inglehart, R., "Postmaterialist Values and the Erosion of Institutional Authority," in *Why People Don't Trust Government*, eds. J.S. Nye, Jr., P.D. Zelikow, and D.C. King, Cambridge, MA: Harvard University Press, 1997.

13. Baltzell, E.D., *Puritan Boston and Quaker Philadelphia: Two Protestant Ethics and the Spirit of Class Authority and Leadership*, New York: Free Press, 1979.

14. Sampson and Bartusch, "Legal Cynicism and Subcultural Tolerance of Deviance," see note 7.

15. Tyler, T., *Why People Obey the Law*, New Haven, CT: Yale University Press, 1990; Tyler, T., "Trust and Democratic Governance," in *Trust and Governance*, eds. V. Braithwaite and M. Levi, New York: Russell Sage Foundation, 1998.

16. Tyler, "Trust and Democratic Governance," see note 15.

17. Baltzell, *Puritan Boston*, 369, see note 13.

18. See details of the Reintegrative Shaming Experiments project at http://www.aic.gov.au/rjustice/rise.

19. Reiss and Roth, *Understanding and Preventing Violence*, 2, 3, 59–65, see note 4.

20. Paternoster, R., R. Brame, R.Bachman, and L.W. Sherman, "Do Fair Procedures Matter? The Effect of Procedural Justice on Spouse Assault," *Law & Society Review*, 31 (1997): 185.

21. A more complete description of the Vera Institute of Justice study can be found in *NIJ Journal*, July 2000, p. 24, http://www.ncjrs.org/pdffiles1/jr000244f.pdf. The authors' presentation of findings also is available on videotape from NCJRS (NCJ 181106).

22. Friedman, L., *The Horizontal Society*, New Haven, CT: Yale University Press, 1999: 14–15.

23. Anderson, E., *Crime and Justice*, Chicago: Chicago University Press, 1999.

24. Just how much harmful impact "street" conduct by agents of criminal justice can have has been revealed by experimental and quasi-experimental research on diverse situations using different levels of analysis. See, for example, Nisbett, R.E., and D. Cohen, *Culture of Honor: The Psychology of Violence in the South*, Boulder, CO: Westview Press, 1996: 46–48; Raine, A., P. Brennan, and S.A. Mednick, "Birth Complications Combined With Early Maternal Rejection at Age 1 Year Predispose to Violent Crime at Age 18 Years," *Archives of General Psychiatry*, 51 (1994): 986; Greenberg, J., "Employee Theft as a Reaction to Underpayment Inequity: The Hidden Costs of Pay Cuts," *Journal of Applied Psychology*, 75 (1990): 561–568; Makkai, T., and J. Braithwaite, "Reintegrative Shaming and Compliance With Regulatory Standards," *Criminology*, 32 (1994): 361–385.

25. de Segonzac, A., *Visa for Peking*, London: Heinemann, 1956.

about the author

Lawrence W. Sherman is the Albert M. Greenfield Professor of Human Relations and Director of the Jerry Lee Center of Criminology at the University of Pennsylvania. Contact him at 3814 Walnut Street, Philadelphia, PA 19104, 215-898-9216, lws@pobox.upenn.edu.

So You Want to Be a Serial-Murderer Profiler...

By John Randolph Fuller

As PROFESSORS, we often get caught up in the flurry of teaching and publishing and forget that we sometimes play a pivotal role in helping students decide what careers to pursue. I remember Patrick Mc-Namara of the University of New Mexico casually telling me, "John, you ought to go to graduate school."

Me? Graduate school? You mean I might actually finish college? Although no other professor, none of my friends, nobody in my family, and certainly not my girlfriend had ever suggested that I was graduate-school material, that one passing remark by a professor I respected changed the direction of my life.

I also often suggest to students that they should go to graduate school. Those suggestions come easily because the students in question demonstrate a keen intellect and a thirst for knowledge. It is the students who request practical career guidance whom I find more problematic.

Students in my criminology classes occasionally show up in my office and ask me, much like Virgil in Dante's *Divine Comedy*, to guide them through hell as they struggle with the cosmic decision of what they are going to do with their lives. I give them the best counsel I can, but I'm never comfortable doing it. They look at me as if I have all the answers. I don't. I'm not the insightful wizard that Pat Mc-Namara was.

Here is what usually happens.

I'm sitting at my desk, typing away on my computer, a Mozart CD playing on my little boombox, when I hear a knock on my door. I turn to see a young woman with an expectant look on her face.

"Dr. Fuller, are you busy?"

"Of course not. Please come in. I always have time for my students," I say. Actually I'm thinking, "Of course I'm busy. Can't you hear the rhythmic clack of the keyboard as I pound away at speeds approaching 20 words a minute? Can't you see that I'm deep in the creative process, composing a missive that could only be described as poetry?"

I motion the student to a chair.

"I want to talk about my future," she says. "I'm going to be a serial-murderer profiler. Can you help me?"

At that point, my heart sinks. I have had similar requests for help with a glamorous but unrealistic career track from at least a hundred students over the past 20 years. It is a conversation that never fails to challenge my concept of the role of adviser.

"Did you see *The Silence of the Lambs* last night?" I ask.

"That's a great movie," the young woman says. "Also, I watch the TV program *Profiler*, and I've decided that's what I want to do. I want to get inside the brains of serial murderers and help the police catch them. When I graduate next year, I plan to work with the FBI—traveling around the country to help police departments with cases."

This is where the challenge of advising comes in. Fortunately, serial murderers are rare creatures. Rare enough that there is no career track for people who want to profile them. Do I tell my student that probably only two dozen people in the country make a living out of profiling serial murderers? Do I tell her that she is not going to work for the FBI after only four years of college, with a 2.3 grade-point average and no street experience? Do I tell her that she should study accounting or go to law school if she wants to be an FBI agent? Do I attempt to convince her that her career goals are a figment of some Hollywood mogul's imagination?

Kind of. I fold my hands and smile. "Let's talk about this," I say.

What I don't tell her is that I have come to doubt myself as a source of wisdom for guiding the lives of other people. While I want my students to achieve their goals, I know that most of them will end up working in local criminal-justice agencies and not as serial-murderer profilers or even FBI agents.

Even the ones who do get the jobs they want may find themselves disappointed by the real world of criminal justice, as opposed to the made-for-television version. Recently, I spoke with a former student who was considering quitting the Secret Service. His job, of late, was guarding empty stairwells all night because the president might walk down them. My former student had realized his dream: He was protecting the president. But he found out the hard way that protecting the president involves less fighting off attackers and escorting VIP's into waiting limousines and more concentrating on blank expanses of floor and lonely flights of stairs.

So when students design glamorous careers for themselves in criminal justice, I'm often tempted to point out their unrealistic expectations. However, I always hesitate, because I have been wrong before. In fact, I missed the boat on serial murderers.

Twenty years ago, as a fresh, young assistant professor at the State University of West Georgia, I shared an office with another neophyte, Eric Hickey, who is now at California State University at Fresno. The local paper interviewed us about the murders of 29 African-American children in Atlanta, and we pontificated on the new buzzword "serial killers." While we didn't say anything profound, the interview piqued our interest. As new professors out to make our mark in the discipline, we talked about writing a book on the subject.

For several weeks, we tossed the idea back and forth. Finally, I told Eric, "This is fascinating, but we could never get this book published. By the time we're done with it, serial murderers will no longer be in vogue, and we'll be laughingstocks for jumping into pop criminology instead of concentrating on serious issues. Count me out."

Eric did. Now, two decades later, his book *Serial Murderers and Their Victims* is in its third edition. Eric is an internationally recognized expert on the subject and trots around the globe lecturing and consulting on serial murders. He has been interviewed on National Public Radio and numerous television programs. He served as a consultant in the federal search for the Unabomber and is constantly called on by law-enforcement agencies to lead workshops on profiling serial murderers. Additionally, he serves as an expert witness in both criminal and civil cases. I use his book in my graduate class on violence. It hurts.

All that could have been half mine had I had the vision. But no. I said that the book would never be published and that serial murder as a criminological topic was but a passing fad. So who am I to give career advice to my students? More than most professors I have come to appreciate the limitations of the adviser's role.

How do I tell my students that being a serial-murderer profiler isn't realistic? It turned out to be plenty realistic for Eric,

and I envy him for his wisdom in ignoring my counsel.

I do my best to help guide my students. I sketch out the various career options in criminal justice. I attempt to demystify the students' overly romantic notions. I offer them pragmatic advice on the probabilities of achieving high-profile, high-paying, and ultimately satisfying careers in the field. I try to steer them toward a realistic path, armed with some common sense as they begin their working lives. While I strive to be intellectually honest with them, I also hope, to some degree, that they will ignore me as Eric did. After all, the journey is theirs, not mine.

John Randolph Fuller is a professor of criminology at the State University of West Georgia. His latest book, written with Michael Braswell and Bo Lozoff, is Corrections, Peacemaking, and Restorative Justice: Transforming Individuals and Institutions *(Anderson Publishing, 2001).*

UNIT 2
Victimology

Unit Selections

9. **What Is a Life Worth?** Amanda Ripley
10. **Coping After Terrorism**, *OVC Handbook for Coping After Terrorism: A Guide to Healing and Recovery*
11. **Telling the Truth About Damned Lies and Statistics**, Joel Best
12. **Violence and the Remaking of a Self**, Susan J. Brison
13. **Prosecutors, Kids, and Domestic Violence Cases**, Debra Whitcomb
14. **Strengthening Antistalking Statutes**, *OVC Legal Series*

Key Points to Consider

- What is needed in order to switch from calling oneself a "victim" of crime to a "survivor" of crime?

- Why do we need good statistics to talk sensibly about social problems?

- Have the terrorist attacks of September 11, 2001, affected your sense of safety, security, and emotional well-being? If so, how? If not, why not?

 **Links: www.dushkin.com/online/**
These sites are annotated in the World Wide Web pages.

Connecticut Sexual Assault Crisis Services, Inc.
http://www.connsacs.org
National Crime Victim's Research and Treatment Center (NCVC)
http://www.musc.edu/cvc/
Office for Victims of Crime (OVC)
http://www.ojp.usdoj.gov/ovc

For many years, crime victims were not considered an important topic for criminological study. Now, however, criminologists consider that focusing on victims and victimization is essential to understanding the phenomenon of crime. The popularity of this area of study can be attributed to the early work of Hans Von Hentig and the later work of Stephen Schafer. These writers were the first to assert that crime victims play an integral role in the criminal event, that their actions may actually precipitate crime, and that unless the victim's role is considered, the study of crime is not complete.

In recent years a growing number of criminologists have devoted increasing attention to the victim's role in the criminal justice process. Generally, areas of particular interest include establishing probabilities of victimization risks, studying victim precipitation of crime and culpability, and designing services expressly for victims of crime. As more criminologists focus their attention on the victim's role in the criminal process, victimology will take on even greater importance.

This unit provides sharp focus on several key issues. The lead article, "What Is a Life Worth?" points out that the mathematics of loss was a little-known science until the terrorist attacks of September 11, 2001. Information contained in the handbook that follows, "Coping After Terrorism," is intended to help the reader to understand reactions to an act of terrorism or mass violence. The need for good statistics in order to talk sensibly about social problems is the point of the next article, "Telling the Truth About Damned Lies and Statistics." A rape victim's account of her traumatic experience follows next in "Violence and the Remaking of a Self." "Prosecutors, Kids, and Domestic Violence Cases" then outlines the special role that a prosecutor can play in helping to guarantee the safety of battered women and their children. The unit closes by focusing on a crime of intimidation known as stalking, in "Strengthening Antistalking Statutes." According to a U.S. Department of Justice report, work must be done in the future to better protect stalking victims.

WHAT IS A LIFE WORTH?

TO COMPENSATE FAMILIES OF THE VICTIMS OF SEPT. 11, THE GOVERNMENT HAS INVENTED A WAY TO MEASURE BLOOD AND LOSS IN CASH. A LOOK AT THE WRENCHING CALCULUS

By AMANDA RIPLEY

A TRAIN BARRELED OVER JOSEPH Hewins' body on a wintry evening in 1845 in the Massachusetts Berkshires. Hewins had spent the workday shoveling snow off the tracks, only to be killed on his trip back to town when a switchman got distracted. Hewins left behind a wife and three children, who were poor even before his death. His widow sued but lost at every level. Had the train merely chopped off Hewins' leg, the railroad would have paid. But in the perverse logic of that time, when a man died, he took his legal claims with him. And so the thinking went for most of the century, until something unheard of began to happen. The courts started to put a dollar value on a life—after death.

The concept of assigning a price tag to a life has always made people intensely squeamish. After all, isn't it degrading to presume that money can make a family whole again? And what of the disparities? Is a poor man's life worth less than a rich man's? Over the past 100 years, U.S. courts have crafted their answers to these questions. Forensic economists testify on the value of a life every day. They can even tell you the average valuation of an injured knee (about $200,000). But until now, the public at large has not had to reckon with the process and its imperfections. Until the terrorist attacks of Sept. 11 created a small city's worth of grieving families and the government established an unprecedented fund to compensate them, the mathematics of loss was a little-known science. Now the process is on garish display, and it is tempting to avert the eyes.

On the morning of Jan. 18, about 70 family members file into the rows of crimson seats at the Norwalk, Conn., city hall auditorium. They listen quietly to special master Kenneth Feinberg, whom the government has entrusted with dispersing its money to those most affected by the Sept. 11 tragedy. His first job is to persuade them to join the federal Victim Compensation Fund, the country's largest experiment in paying mass victims and their families without placing blame. The effort is being closely watched for the precedents it will set.

Much has been made of the enormous charity funds raised after the attacks. Donations to those groups do funnel thousands of dollars to the victims' families—in particular, the families of fire fighters and police officers. But overall, the nearly $2 billion in charity money is chump change compared with the cash that will flow out of government coffers. There is no limit to the federal fund, but the tab is likely to be triple the size of the charity pot. And while charity funds are doled out to a vast pool of people, including businesses hurt by the attacks, the government money will go exclusively to the injured and to families of the deceased.

Feinberg, in a black-and-white polka-dot tie, speaks in short, punchy sentences and a loud voice. He has already given the speech 32 times up and down the East Coast. The main thrust: The government, for the first time ever, has agreed to write large checks to victims' families without any litigation. The checks will arrive within four months after a claim is filed—no legal fees, no agonizing 10-year lawsuit. But every award will be based on a cold calculus, much the way courts handle wrongful-death claims.

That means different sums for different families. In a TIME/CNN poll taken last month, 86% said all families should receive the same amount. But that's not how it's going to work.

The calculus has several steps, Feinberg explains. First, the government will estimate how much a victim would have earned over his or her lifetime had the planes never crashed. That means a broker's family will qualify for a vastly higher award than a window washer's family. To estimate this amount, each family was handed an easy-to-read chart on the way into the meeting: Find your loved one's age and income and follow your finger to the magic number. Note that the lifetime earnings have been boosted by a flat $250,000 for "pain and suffering"—noneconomic losses, they are called. Tack on an extra $50,000 in pain and suffering for a spouse and for each child. The charts, while functional, are brutal, crystallizing how readily the legal system commodifies life.

Then—and this is crucial—don't get too excited. That first number may be quite high—in the millions for many. But you must, according to the rules of the fund, subtract all the money you are getting from other sources except charities. A court settlement would not be diminished this way, but this is not a court, Feinberg repeatedly

After Math

There are many things the new federal victims fund will not do: it will not place blame or apologize; it will not substitute for a lawsuit; and it will not dramatically affect families who will receive hefty insurance checks. It will help some families maintain a semblance of the lifestyle they had before Sept. 11. Here are the outlines:

How the Fund Works

Unlimited
Total amount of money in the fund

2
Number of years families have to file claims

$250,000
Flat payment to families for pain and suffering

246
Number of claims filed as of Jan. 31

$50,000
Additional pain-and-suffering payment for spouse and for each child

120
Number of days the special master has to decide each claim

0
Federal taxes owed on any award

0
Chances to appeal the decision

How Three Families Could Fare

To estimate these families' awards, TIME asked Gary Albrecht, head of the Society of Litigation Economists, to run some numbers based on the fund's draft rules

The Insurance Executive

Families with large insurance policies, like this one, will get much smaller awards under the rules
- **VICTIM:** James Halvorson, 56, earned $500,000 a year at Marsh & McLennan. Married with one adult son. Caretaker for mother
- **GROSS AWARD:** $1.4 million
- **DEDUCTIONS:** $2.6 million for multiple insurance policies
- **FINAL AWARD:** $0

The Currency Trader

Traditional death benefits like Social Security will shrink the award
- **VICTIM:** Thomas Sparacio, 35, earned $60,000 at Euro Brokers. Married with twins, age 2, and a baby on the way
- **GROSS AWARD:** $1.6 million
- **DEDUCTIONS:** $491,842 Social Security; $379,084 workers' compensation; $543,890 life insurance and pension
- **FINAL AWARD:** $137,842

The Security Guard

This family starts out with the smallest award, but ends up with the largest
- **VICTIM:** Samuel Fields, 36, worked for Summit Security, earning $22,000 a year. Married with four kids and one on the way
- **GROSS AWARD:** $1 million
- **DEDUCTIONS:** $215,864 Social Security; $263,757 workers' compensation; $90,236 life insurance
- **FINAL AWARD:** $444,010

points out. Deduct life insurance, pension, Social Security death benefits and workers' compensation. Now you have the total award the government is offering you for your loss.

The deductions have the effect of equalizing the differences in the awards. Critics have called this Feinberg's "Robin Hood strategy." For many people in the room, the number is now at or close to zero. Feinberg says he will make sure no one gets zero. "Leave it to me," he says. But nowhere will that be written into the rules when they are finalized in mid-February. Likewise, many fiancés and gay partners will be at the mercy of Feinberg's discretion in seeking awards. Before finding out exactly what they will get—and the rules are complex—families will have to agree never to sue anyone for the attacks. "Normally, that would be a difficult call," says Feinberg. "Not here. The right to sue in this case is simply not a reasonable alternative."

That's because Congress has capped the liability of the airlines, the airport own-ers, the aircraft manufacturers, the towers' landlord and the city of New York. In the name of the economy, the government severely restricted the victims' rights to sue—whether they join the fund or not. It is this lack of a viable option, even if they would not take it, that galls many families.

Congress created the fund as a safety net for the victims' families, to ensure that they maintain something resembling their current standard of living—whether they get assistance from private insurance or government money. The families see it as so much more. For the traumatized, the charts are like a Rorschach test. Some view the money as a halfhearted apology for the breakdown in security and intelligence that made the attacks possible. Others can't help seeing the award as a callous measure of their loved one's value. Many regard it as a substitute for the millions they think they may have got in court, had the liability not been capped. When the total comes out to be underwhelming, these families take it personally. There's a fundamental clash between the way they interpret the purpose

of the fund and the way the government sees it.

After Feinberg speaks, he stands back and braces himself for an artillery of angry rhetorical questions. Gerry Sweeney, whose brother died in Tower 2, Floor 105, points at Feinberg and explains why $250,000 is not enough for pain and suffering in the case of her now fatherless nephew. "Have you ever seen a 12-year-old have a nervous breakdown?" she asks. Another woman concocts an analogy to illustrate for Feinberg what it was like to talk to loved ones as they came to accept their imminent, violent deaths and to watch the towers collapse on live TV. "If your wife was brutally raped and murdered and you had to watch and listen to it happen, what would you think the right amount would be?" Finally, Maureen Halvorson, who lost her husband and her brother, speaks up from the front row in a quiet, bewildered voice. "I just can't accept the fact that the Federal Government is saying my husband and my brother are worth nothing." Feinberg is silent.

THE MORE THAN 3,000 VICTIMS OF THE Sept. 11 attacks are frozen in snapshots, wide-smiling men and women in crisp suits and uniforms who liked to build birdhouses on weekends and play practical jokes. In the literature of grief, they have become hardworking innocents, heroes and saints. But those they left behind are decidedly human. Some compete with others for most bereaved status; others demand an apology even when no one is listening. Some are popping pills, and others cannot leave the house. Most days, they are inconsolable. And as the rest of the country begins to ease back into normalcy, these families stand, indignant, in the way.

Already, some Americans have lost patience with them. "My tax money should not be given to someone with a $750,000 mortgage to pay who needs a set of fresh, matching towels in her bathroom every season," one person wrote anonymously to the Department of Justice's Web page on victim compensation. "I'm shocked and appalled and very disappointed," wrote a Florida resident, "that some individuals are living in such a rare and well-gilded ivory tower that they feel $250,000 is not sufficient compensation. Most of us, the working people of America, make $20,000 to $40,000 per year. Where do these wealthy, spoiled, greedy folks in New York get off, pretending that what happened to them was so uniquely horrible? I'm over it. Yeah, it was unique. Yeah, it was horrible. Yeah, I sent money to help. And after reading about them suing for more money, I begin to regret it."

It's true that some families' behavior has been less than dignified. The divorced parents of a woman killed in the Pentagon, who are eligible for money because their daughter left no dependents, have filed competing claims. Lawyers are now involved. Says her father: "I guarantee she loved her daddy as much as she loved her mom. I feel that I'm entitled to something."

And it's also a fact that these families will get more money from charities and the government combined than anyone has so far received after the Oklahoma City bombing or the 1998 bombing of the Nairobi embassy. For that matter, if these victims had been killed in a drive-by shooting, they probably would not have received more than a few thousand dollars from state victim-compensation funds.

That fact is not lost on the public, particularly people whose relatives have died in everyday tragedies. At the Wichita *Eagle* in Kansas, editorial-page director Phil

Brownlee has received calls and letters from locals disgusted by the families' complaints, and he agrees. "It's just frustrating that the goodwill demonstrated by the government seems to be deteriorating," he says. "Now you've got families who are upset with what most Americans deem to be generous contributions. It's the loss of the spirit of Sept. 11, the souring of that sense of solidarity."

But it may not be fair to compare Sept. 11 with a street crime or even Oklahoma City. After all, these recent attacks involved an orchestrated, simultaneous security breach on four airplanes, carried out by 19 men who had been living and training on our soil. A better comparison might be past international terrorist attacks and plane crashes. Those that have been resolved—and that's a major distinction— do show higher payouts than the average amount likely to come out of the Sept. 11 federal fund.

In 25 major aviation accidents between 1970 and 1984, the average compensation for victims who went to trial was $1 million in current dollars, according to a Rand Corp. analysis. Average compensation for cases settled without a lawsuit was $415,000. The biggest aviation payout in history followed the crash of Pan Am Flight 103 over Lockerbie, Scotland, in 1988. Settlements ranged all over the spectrum, with a couple dozen exceeding $10 million, according to Manhattan attorney Lee Kreindler, who acted as lead counsel. Dividing the total $500 million payout over the 270 victims yields an average award of $1.85 million. However, the families had to hand about a third of their awards to their lawyers, and they waited seven to eight years to see any money. And the families of the six people killed in the 1993 World Trade Center bombing are still waiting for their day in civil court.

IN THE END, MOST FAMILIES WILL PROBably choose the fund over litigation. The Lockerbie millions are simply not a realistic possibility. It is always extremely difficult to sue the government. And the liability for the Sept. 11 attacks was capped by Congress at about $1.5 billion per plane. So while the families of those killed in the Pennsylvania and Pentagon crashes may have enough to go around, there are far too many victims in New York. "The court model works perfectly when you don't have $50 billion in damages or 3,000 deaths," says Leo Boyle, a Boston lawyer and president of the Associ-

ation of Trial Lawyers of America, which supports the fund option and has lined up more than 2,000 attorneys to offer free help navigating its rules. Even without the caps, Boyle insists, victims could not have extracted more money by putting United and American Airlines through bankruptcy. So far, only a handful of suits have been filed.

In any event, there was no talking Congress out of the liability caps when it drafted the airline-bailout package 10 days after the attacks. The airlines could not fly without insurance, and their coverage was far short of what it would take to pay the damages. Federal Reserve Chairman Alan Greenspan privately told congressional leaders that getting the planes up again was the single biggest "multiplier" that could revive the economy on every level. So the Democrats, who usually balk at limiting the ability to sue, accepted the idea of an airline bailout—as long as it came with a mechanism to compensate victims. Oklahoma Senator Don Nickles, the No. 2 Republican in the Senate and a longtime proponent of tort reform, pushed hard to limit how much the victims' families could claim, but he did not prevail.

But once the interim rules were drawn up by Feinberg's office—in conjunction with the Department of Justice and the Office of Management and Budget—there were some surprises. In particular, the figures for pain and suffering astonished some who had backed the fund. "The numbers are low by any measure," says Boyle. Feinberg says he chose the $250,000 figure because that's how much beneficiaries receive from the Federal Government when fire fighters and police die on the job. The additional $50,000 for the spouse and each child is, he admits, "just some rough approximation of what I thought was fair." He calls the fund "rough justice."

The American Tort Reform Association, backed mostly by Republicans, has been lobbying since 1986 to limit noneconomic damages in some suits to $250,000. John Ashcroft, head of the Justice Department, pushed for such a cap on punitive damages when he was a Senator. But Feinberg, a Democrat, insists he was not pressured by the Administration to keep the numbers low.

No matter how many times tearful widows accuse him of protecting the airlines, Feinberg does not blush. A lawyer with decades of experience in the messy art of compromise (Feinberg was special master for the $180 million distributed to veterans exposed to Agent Orange), he is accustomed to rage. "On Tuesday I get whacked for this or that in New Jersey. The next day it's New York. It goes with the job." But he rejects the theory that greed is a factor. "People have had a loved one wrenched from them suddenly, without warning, and we are only five months beyond that disaster. It was nearly yesterday. And they are desperately seeking, from what I've seen, to place as much of a value on that lost loved one as they can. So here is where they seek to amplify the value of that memory. They do it by saying we want more, as a validation of the loss. That's not greed. That's human nature."

SUSAN AND HARVEY BLOMBERG OF Fairfield County, Conn., have been to three meetings on the victim-compensation fund, even though, as parents of a victim who has left a wife and kids behind, they are not in line for compensation. The rules give preference to the victim's spouse and children. But the Blombergs come to these meetings to be part of something, to be counted. And they linger after everyone else has left. "My daughter-in-law was upset when we went to the meetings," Susan says. "She said, 'It's not really about you. It's about the widows and children.' And I said, 'I want more information.' You can't compare grief, because nobody can get inside you. But I feel like an orphan. When they did this formula, why didn't they consider the parents? My daughter-in-law was married for five years. We had Jonathan for 33 years."

"It's a horrible thing that this is where our energies need to be pulled," says Cheri Sparacio, 37, the widow of Thomas Sparacio, a currency trader at Euro Brokers who died in Tower 2. In their modest house in Staten Island, littered with the toys of her twin two-year-olds, she explains why she

sees the estimated $138,000 she would get from the fund as a cheap bribe. "The government is not taking any responsibility for what it's done. This was just one screw-up after another." She is also worried about her financial stability; in less than a month, she will have their third child. Thomas was the primary wage earner, although Cheri worked as a part-time school psychologist until Sept. 11. She doesn't see how she can go back to work with an infant and two toddlers unless she hires full-time help. "Please, come step into my shoes for a minute," she says, her eyes flat and unblinking. "I am not looking to go to Tahiti."

But uptown in the apartment where Samuel Fields once lived, the fund acts like a quiet equalizer, a way for the government to guarantee that victims with less insurance emerge with basic support. Fields was a security guard for six years in Tower 1. He made $22,000 a year and lived with his family in a housing project in Harlem. On Sept. 11, he helped people evacuate the building and then went back inside to help some more. Fields never came home. Next month his widow Angela will give birth to their fifth child. Because Fields made a small salary, his family's preliminary award is less than Sparacio's. But his family's deductions are also smaller. In the end, Angela's estimated $444,010 award will probably be three times the size of Cheri's.

In valuing different lives differently—the first part of the equation—the fund follows common legal practice. Courts always grant money on the basis of a person's earning power in life. That's because the courts are not attempting to replace "souls," says Philip Bobbitt, a law professor at the University of Texas who has written about the allocation of scarce resources in times of tragedy. "We're not

trying to make you psychologically whole. Where we can calculate the loss is in economic loss." The Feinberg plan differs from legal norms in deducting the value of life insurance and pensions. Also, it allows no flexibility in determining noneconomic damages. In court, pain and suffering would be weighed individually.

Money aside, a lawsuit can be an investigative device like no other, forcing answers about what led to a death. Some Sept. 11 families say they might file suit for that reason alone, even if they never get a dime. And for other families, there is enormous value in no lawsuits at all. David Gordenstein lost his wife, Lisa Fenn Gordenstein, on American Flight 11. "Am I sad? I've had my heart torn out," he says. But he would rather devote his life to raising his two young daughters than pursuing a lawsuit. He will probably file a claim with the federal fund, which he acknowledges is not perfect. "I am proud of what my country tried to do. I think the intention is noble."

The night before Lisa died, she slipped a clipping under the door of David's home office, something she often did. It was a saying from theologian Charles Swindoll that read, "Attitude, to me, is more important than facts. It is more important than the past, than education, than money, than circumstances, than failures, than successes, than what other people think or say or do...It will make or break a company, a church, a home." David read it at her memorial. And while he jokes that it's kind of clichéd—"typical Lisa"—he says he thinks its message might help carry his family through this.

—With reporting by Nadia Mustafa and Julie Rawe/New York and Karen Tumulty/Washington

OVC Handbook for

Coping
After Terrorism

A Guide to Healing and Recovery

The information in this handbook is intended to help you understand your reactions to an act of terrorism or mass violence. It is not intended to be a substitute for the role of professionals with expertise in counseling trauma victims.

Nothing in life can prepare you for the horror of an act of terrorism that robs you of your sense of security and, in some instances, a loved one. No one expects such a thing to happen. Violent crime is an abnormal event, and terrorism is even more rare. The normal reactions to this type of traumatic disaster include a wide range of powerful feelings that may feel abnormal to the person having them or seem strange to those who have not gone through such a disaster. You may feel like something is wrong with you and that the terrible pain will never ease up.

Recovering from a traumatic event will take a long time and will not be easy. Everyone responds differently to trauma. No one reacts in a right or wrong way—just differently. It will help your recovery process if you do not expect too much of yourself and of others.

Reactions to a Traumatic Disaster

Shock and Numbness

At first you may be in a state of shock and may feel numb and confused. You also may feel detached—as if you are watching a movie or having a bad dream that will not end. This numbness protects you from feeling the full impact of what has happened all at once.

Intense Emotion

You may feel overpowered by sorrow and grief. As shock begins to wear off, it is not unusual to feel intense grief and cry uncontrollably. While some parts of our society

MESSAGE FROM THE DIRECTOR

The terrorist acts of September 11, 2001, have deeply shaken our sense of safety, security, and emotional well-being. Every one of us has been changed forever by this horrible tragedy, but we are a resilient Nation, strong in our patriotism and determined in our resolve to find ways to cope with our losses.

It is difficult to try to comprehend these heinous acts that were perpetrated against innocent people going about their daily business. It is hard to accept the profound sense of loss, and it is difficult to cope with the raw emotions felt in the wake of this devastating act of inhumanity.

We at the Office for Victims of Crime will never understand the depths of your despair, but we have relied on the experiences of other terrorism victims and the expertise of mental health, crisis counseling, and victim assistance professionals to prepare this handbook for you.

Our office grieves with all who have lost loved ones. We pledge our determination to be sensitive to your needs and to seek justice on behalf of all who were injured or killed as a result of the attacks on Americans and our country's way of life.

John W. Gillis, Director
Office for Victims of Crime

frown on emotional behavior, this emotional release is an important part of grieving for most people. It is unhealthy to hold back or "swallow" your painful feelings and can actually make the grieving process last longer. If you are uncomfortable with these feelings, you may want to seek help from a counselor or minister or other victims who understand what you are going through.

Fear

You may feel intense fear and startle easily, become extremely anxious when you leave your home or are alone, or experience waves of panic. Someone you love has been suddenly and violently killed while going about his or her daily life. You had no time to prepare psychologically for such an incident, so you may feel intense anxiety and horror. You may be afraid that the terrorist will return and harm you or your loved ones again. Crime shatters normal feelings of security and trust and the sense of being able to control events. Once you have been harmed by crime, it is natural to be afraid and suspicious of others. These feelings will go away or lessen over time.

> Ignoring feelings of anger and resentment may cause physical problems such as headaches, upset stomachs, and high blood pressure. Anger that goes on a long time may cover up other more painful feelings such as guilt, sadness, and depression.

Guilt

Victims who were injured in the traumatic disaster want to understand why the crime happened, and families wonder why they lost a loved one. Some people find it easier to accept what happened if they can blame themselves in some way. This is a normal way of trying to once again feel a sense of control over their lives. Victims often feel guilt and regret for things they did or did not say or do and that they should have protected a loved one better or have done something to prevent his or her death. Survivors spend a lot of time thinking, "If only I had.... " This guilt does not make sense because the circumstances that lead to terrorism usually cannot be controlled and are hard to predict. Get rid of imagined guilt. You did the best you could at the time. If you are convinced that you made mistakes or have real guilt, consider professional or spiritual counseling. You will need to find a way to forgive yourself. Feelings of guilt can be made worse by people who point out what they would have done differently in the same situation. People who say such things are usually trying to convince themselves that such a tragedy could never happen to them.

Anger and Resentment

It is natural for you to be angry and outraged at the tragedy, the person or persons who caused the tragedy, or someone you believe could have prevented the crime. If a suspect is arrested, you might direct your anger toward that person. You may become angry with other family members, friends, doctors, police, prosecutors, God, or even yourself and may resent well-meaning people who say hurtful things and do not understand what you—as a victim—are going through.

Feelings of anger may be very intense, and the feelings may come and go. You also may daydream about revenge, which is normal and can be helpful in releasing rage and frustration.

> Injury by terrorism carries with it a stigma for the victim that can leave him or her feeling abandoned and ashamed.

Feelings of anger are a natural part of the recovery process. These feelings are not right or wrong; they are simply feelings. It is important to recognize the anger as real but to not use it as an excuse to abuse or hurt others. There are safe and healthy ways to express anger. Many people find that writing down their feelings, exercising, doing hard physical work, beating a pillow, or crying or screaming in privacy helps them release some of the anger. Ignoring feelings of anger and resentment may cause physical problems such as headaches, upset stomachs, and high blood pressure. Anger that goes on a long time may cover up other more painful feelings such as guilt, sadness, and depression.

Depression and Loneliness

Depression and loneliness are often a large part of trauma for victims. It may seem that these feelings will last forever. Trials are sometimes delayed for months and even years in our criminal justice system. Once the trial day comes, the trial and any media coverage means having to relive the events surrounding the traumatic disaster. Feelings of depression and loneliness are even stronger when a victim feels that no one understands. This is the reason a support group for victims is so important; support group members will truly understand such feelings.

Victims of traumatic disaster may feel that it is too painful to keep living and may think of suicide. If these thoughts continue, you must find help. Danger signals to watch for include (1) thinking about suicide often, (2) being alone too much, (3) not being able to talk to other people about what you are feeling, (4) sudden changes in weight, (5) continued trouble sleeping, and (6) using too much alcohol or other drugs (including prescription drugs).

Isolation

You may feel that you are different from everyone else and that others have abandoned you. Terrorism is an abnormal and unthinkable act, and people are horrified by it. Injury by terrorism carries with it a stigma for the victim that can leave him or her feeling abandoned and ashamed. Other people may care but still find it hard or uncomfortable to be around you. You are a reminder that terrorism can happen to anyone. They also cannot understand why you feel and act the way you do because they have not gone through it.

Physical Symptoms of Distress

It is common to have headaches, fatigue, nausea, sleeplessness, loss of sexual feelings, and weight gain or loss after a traumatic event. Also, you may feel uncoordinated, experience lower backaches and chills/sweats, twitch/shake, and grind your teeth.

Panic

Feelings of panic are common and can be hard to cope with. You may feel like you are going crazy. Often, this feeling happens because traumatic disasters like terrorism seem unreal and incomprehensible. Your feelings of grief may be so strong and overwhelming that they frighten you. It can help a great deal to talk with other victims who have had similar feelings and truly understand what these feelings are all about.

Inability To Resume Normal Activity

You may find that you are unable to function the way you did before the act of terrorism and to return to even the simplest activities. It may be hard to think and plan, life may seem flat and empty, and the things that used to be enjoyable may now seem meaningless. You may not be able to laugh, and when you finally do, you may feel guilty. Tears come often and without warning. Mood swings, irritability, dreams, and flashbacks about the crime are common. These feelings may come several months after the disaster. Your friends and coworkers may not understand the grief that comes with this type of crime and the length of time you will need to recover. They may simply think it is time for you to put the disaster behind you and get on with normal life. Trust your own feelings and travel the hard road to recovery at your own pace.

Delayed Reaction

Some individuals will experience no immediate reaction. They may be energized by a stressful situation and not react until weeks or months later. This type of delayed reaction is not unusual and, if you begin to have some of the feelings previously discussed, you should consider talking with a professional counselor.

Overcoming even the greatest tragedies is possible and can help bring about change and hope for others.

Practical Coping Ideas

Other victims and survivors of traumatic disasters who have been where you are have offered some practical suggestions of things you can do to help you cope and begin to heal:

- Remember to breathe. Sometimes when people are afraid or very upset, they stop breathing. When you are scared or upset, close your eyes and take deep, slow breaths until you calm down. Taking a walk or talking to a close friend can also help.
- Whenever possible, delay making any major decisions. You may think a big change will make you feel better, but it will not necessarily ease the pain. Give yourself time to get through the most hectic times and to adjust before making decisions that will affect the rest of your life.
- Simplify your life for a while. Make a list of the things you are responsible for, such as taking care of the kids, buying groceries, teaching Sunday school, or going to work. Then, look at your list and see which things are absolutely necessary. Is there anything you can put aside for a while? Are there things you can let go of completely?
- Take care of your mind and body. Eat healthy food. Exercise regularly, even if it is only a long walk every day. Exercise will help lift depression and help you sleep better, too. Massages can also help release tension and comfort you.
- Avoid using alcohol and other drugs. These substances may temporarily block the pain, but they will keep you from healing. You have to experience your feelings and look clearly at your life to recover from tragedy.
- Keep the phone number of a good friend nearby to call when you feel overwhelmed or have a panic attack.
- Talk to a counselor, clergy member, friend, family member, or other survivors about what happened. It is common to want to share your experience over and over again—and it can be helpful for you to do so.
- Begin to restore order in your world by reestablishing old routines at work, home, or school as much as possible. Stay busy with work that occupies your mind, but do not throw yourself into frantic activity.
- Ask questions. You may have concerns about what types of assistance are available, who will pay for your travel and other expenses, and other issues

Victim Benefits and Assistance Contacts			
Organization	Contact Information	Assistance Offered	Eligible Victims
Office for Victims of Crime Victim Assistance Center	1-800-331-0075 (inside U.S.) 00-1-414-359-9751 (call collect outside U.S.) 1-800-833-6885 (TTY)	Emergency transportation, information, and referral	All victims for information and referral, transportation assistance for victims not covered by airline, military, or other sources
Bureau of Justice Assistance Public Safety Officers' Benefits Program	1-888-744-6513	Financial and emotional assistance	Families of federal, state, and local public safety officers (police, fire, EMS) killed in the line of duty

concerning compensation and insurance. Find out what will be expected of you in the days to come so you can plan ahead for any new or stressful circumstances.

- Talk to your children, who are often the invisible victims, and make sure they are part of your reactions, activities, and plans. Involve them in funerals and memorials if they want to be involved.
- Organize and plan how you will deal with the media. It may be helpful to include family, friends, or other victims or survivors in your planning process. You do NOT have to speak to the media. It is up to you to decide how much, if any, involvement you will have with the media. Any contact should be on your terms.
- Seek the help of a reputable attorney if you think you need legal advice. Take time to make decisions about insurance settlements, legal actions, and other matters that have long-term consequences.
- Rely on people you trust. Seek information, advice, and help from them. Remember that although most people are honest and trustworthy, some unscrupulous individuals will try to take advantage of victims in the aftermath of a disaster.
- Avoid doing upsetting things right before bed if you are having trouble sleeping. Designate 30 minutes sometime earlier in the day as your "worry time." Do not go to bed before you are tired. Write down your fears and nightmares. Put on quiet music or relaxation tapes. If you still cannot sleep, do not get mad at yourself and worry about not getting sleep. You can still rest by lying quietly and listening to relaxing music or by reading a good book. If your sleeping problems continue, you may want to see your doctor.
- Find small ways to help others, as it will help ease your own suffering.
- Ask for help from family, friends, or professionals when you need it. Healing grief and loss is similar to healing your body after an illness or accident. Just as there are doctors and nurses who are trained to help heal the body, there are professionals who are trained to help people recover from loss and cope with emotional pain.
- Think about the things that give you hope. Make a list of these things and turn to them on bad days.

It is important to remember that emotional pain is not endless. It does have limits. The pain will eventually ease, and the joys of life will return. There will be an ebb and flow to your grief. When it is there, let yourself feel it. When it is gone, let it go. You are not responsible or obligated to keep the pain alive. Smiles, laughter, and the ability to feel joy in the good things of life will return in time.

> Healing begins by talking about what happened with people you trust— people who support you without being judgmental or giving unwanted advice about what you should do or how you should feel.

Victims are forever changed by the experience of terrorism. They realize that although things will never be the same, they can face life with new understanding and new meaning. Many things have been lost, but many things remain. Overcoming even the greatest tragedies is possible and can help bring about change and hope for others.

Finding Help

Whatever you are facing or feeling at the moment, it is important to remember that each person copes with tragedy in his or her own way. Trust your own feelings— that what you are feeling is what you need to feel and that it is normal. Do not act like things are fine when they are not. Healing begins by talking about what happened with people you trust—people who support you without being judgmental or giving unwanted advice about what you should do or how you should feel.

Most people find it helpful to talk with a professional counselor who has worked with other crime survivors. Sometimes just a few sessions with a trained counselor will help you resolve the anger, guilt, and despair that keep you from recovering. Also, talking with other victims of violent crime may help you feel better understood and less alone.

If you feel overwhelmed by your emotions and think you may hurt yourself or others, immediately ask for support and guidance from family, friends, a minister, or a professional counselor. For crisis counseling, contact the Office for Victims of Crime (OVC) Victim Assistance Center at 1–800–331–0075. In addition, contact OVC at 1–800–627–6872 for a list of the victim assistance programs it funds in your area. The same information is available on OVC's Web site and at **www.ojp.usdoj.gov/ovc** and at **www.ojp.usdoj.gov/ovc/terrorismvictimassistance**. (The second Web address is intended for victims and family members only and will be password protected in the near future.)

For copies of this handbook and/or additional information, please contact: **Office for Victims of Crime Resource Center (OVCRC)** P.O. Box 6000 Rockville, MD 20849-6000 Telephone: 1-800-627-6872 or 301-519-5500 (TTY 1-877-712-9279)

E-mail orders for print publications to *puborder@ncjrs.org*

E-mail questions to *askovc@ncjrs.org*

Send your feedback on this service to *tellncjrs@ncjrs.org*

Refer to publication number: **NCJ 190249**

From *OVC Handbook for Coping After Terrorism: A Guide to Healing and Recovery*, September 2001, pp. 3-9. © 2001 by the U.S. Department of Justice.

Telling the Truth About Damned Lies and Statistics

By JOEL BEST

The dissertation prospectus began by quoting a statistic—a "grabber" meant to capture the reader's attention. The graduate student who wrote this prospectus undoubtedly wanted to seem scholarly to the professors who would read it; they would be supervising the proposed research. And what could be more scholarly than a nice, authoritative statistic, quoted from a professional journal in the student's field?

So the prospectus began with this (carefully footnoted) quotation: "Every year since 1950, the number of American children gunned down has doubled." I had been invited to serve on the student's dissertation committee. When I read the quotation, I assumed the student had made an error in copying it. I went to the library and looked up the article the student had cited. There, in the journal's 1995 volume, was exactly the same sentence: "Every year since 1950, the number of American children gunned down has doubled."

This quotation is my nomination for a dubious distinction: I think it may be the worst—that is, the most inaccurate—social statistic ever.

What makes this statistic so bad? Just for the sake of argument, let's assume that "the number of American children gunned down" in 1950 was one. If the number doubled each year, there must have been two children gunned down in 1951, four in 1952, eight in 1953, and so on. By 1960, the number would have been 1,024. By 1965, it would have been 32,768 (in 1965, the F.B.I. identified only 9,960 criminal homicides in the entire country, including adult as well as child victims). By 1970, the number would have passed one million; by 1980, one billion (more than four

times the total U.S. population in that year). Only three years later, in 1983, the number of American children gunned down would have been 8.6 billion (nearly twice the earth's population at the time). Another milestone would have been passed in 1987, when the number of gunned-down American children (137 billion) would have surpassed the best estimates for the total human population throughout history (110 billion). By 1995, when the article was published, the annual number of victims would have been over 35 trillion—a really big number, of a magnitude you rarely encounter outside economics or astronomy.

Thus my nomination: estimating the number of American child gunshot victims in 1995 at 35 trillion must be as far off—as hilariously, wildly wrong—as a social statistic can be. (If anyone spots a more inaccurate social statistic, I'd love to hear about it.)

Where did the article's author get this statistic? I wrote the author, who responded that the statistic came from the Children's Defense Fund, a well-known advocacy group for children. The C.D.F.'s *The State of America's Children Yearbook 1994* does state: "The number of American children killed each year by guns has doubled since 1950." Note the difference in the wording—the C.D.F. claimed there were twice as many deaths in 1994 as in 1950; the article's author reworded that claim and created a very different meaning.

It is worth examining the history of this statistic. It began with the C.D.F. noting that child gunshot deaths had doubled from 1950 to 1994. This is not quite as dramatic an increase as it might seem. Remember that the U.S. population also rose through-

out this period; in fact, it grew about 73 percent—or nearly double. Therefore, we might expect all sorts of things—including the number of child gunshot deaths—to increase, to nearly double, just because the population grew. Before we can decide whether twice as many deaths indicates that things are getting worse, we'd have to know more. The C.D.F. statistic raises other issues as well: Where did the statistic come from? Who counts child gunshot deaths, and how? What is meant by a "child" (some C.D.F. statistics about violence include everyone under age 25)? What is meant by "killed by guns" (gunshot-death statistics often include suicides and accidents, as well as homicides)? But people rarely ask questions of this sort when they encounter statistics. Most of the time, most people simply accept statistics without question.

Certainly, the article's author didn't ask many probing, critical questions about the C.D.F.'s claim. Impressed by the statistic, the author repeated it—well, meant to repeat it. Instead, by rewording the C.D.F.'s claim, the author created a mutant statistic, one garbled almost beyond recognition.

But people treat mutant statistics just as they do other statistics—that is, they usually accept even the most implausible claims without question. For example, the journal editor who accepted the author's article for publication did not bother to consider the implications of child victims doubling each year. And people repeat bad statistics: The graduate student copied the garbled statistic and inserted it into the dissertation prospectus. Who knows whether still other readers were impressed by the author's statistic and remembered it or repeated it? The article remains on the shelf in hundreds of libraries, available to anyone who needs a dramatic quote. The lesson should be clear: Bad statistics live on; they take on lives of their own.

Some statistics are born bad—they aren't much good from the start, because they are based on nothing more than guesses or dubious data. Other statistics mutate; they become bad after being mangled (as in the case of the author's creative rewording). Either way, bad statistics are potentially important: They can be used to stir up public outrage or fear; they can distort our understanding of our world; and they can lead us to make poor policy choices.

THE NOTION that we need to watch out for bad statistics isn't new. We've all heard people say, "You can prove anything with statistics." The title of my book, *Damned Lies and Statistics*, comes from a famous aphorism (usually attributed to Mark Twain or Benjamin Disraeli): "There are three kinds of lies: lies, damned lies, and statistics." There is even a useful little book, still in print after more than 40 years, called *How to Lie With Statistics*.

We shouldn't ignore all statistics, or assume that every number is false. Some statistics are bad, but others are pretty good. And we need good statistics to talk sensibly about social problems.

Statistics, then, have a bad reputation. We suspect that statistics may be wrong, that people who use statistics may be "lying"—trying to manipulate us by using numbers to somehow distort the truth. Yet, at the same time, we need statistics; we depend upon them to summarize and clarify the nature of our complex society. This is particularly true when we talk about social problems. Debates about social problems routinely raise questions that demand statistical answers: Is the problem widespread? How many people—and which people—does it affect? Is it getting worse? What does it cost society? What will it cost to deal with it? Convincing answers to

such questions demand evidence, and that usually means numbers, measurements, statistics.

But can't you prove anything with statistics? It depends on what "prove" means. If we want to know, say, how many children are "gunned down" each year, we can't simply guess—pluck a number from thin air: 100, 1,000, 10,000, 35 trillion, whatever. Obviously, there's no reason to consider an arbitrary guess "proof" of anything. However, it might be possible for someone—using records kept by police departments or hospital emergency rooms or coroners—to keep track of children who have been shot; compiling careful, complete records might give us a fairly accurate idea of the number of gunned-down children. If that number seems accurate enough, we might consider it very strong evidence—or proof.

The solution to the problem of bad statistics is not to ignore all statistics, or to assume that every number is false. Some statistics are bad, but others are pretty good, and we need statistics—good statistics—to talk sensibly about social problems. The solution, then, is not to give up on statistics, but to become better judges of the numbers we encounter. We need to think critically about statistics—at least critically enough to suspect that the number of children gunned down hasn't been doubling each year since 1950.

A few years ago, the mathematician John Allen Paulos wrote *Innumeracy*, a short, readable book about "mathematical illiteracy." Too few people, he argued, are comfortable with basic mathematical principles, and this makes them poor judges of the numbers they encounter. No doubt this is one reason we have so many bad statistics. But there are other reasons, as well.

Social statistics describe society, but they are also products of our social arrangements. The people who bring social statistics to our attention have reasons for doing so; they inevitably want something, just as reporters and the other media figures who repeat and publicize statistics have their own goals. Statistics are tools, used for particular purposes. Thinking critically about statistics requires understanding their place in society.

While we may be more suspicious of statistics presented by people with whom we disagree—people who favor different political parties or have different beliefs—bad statistics are used to promote all sorts of causes. Bad statistics come from conservatives on the political right and liberals on the left, from wealthy corporations and

powerful government agencies, and from advocates of the poor and the powerless.

In order to interpret statistics, we need more than a checklist of common errors. We need a general approach, an orientation, a mind-set that we can use to think about new statistics that we encounter. We ought to approach statistics thoughtfully. This can be hard to do, precisely because so many people in our society treat statistics as fetishes. We might call this the mind-set of the Awestruck—the people who don't think critically, who act as though statistics have magical powers. The awestruck know they don't always understand the statistics they hear, but this doesn't bother them. After all, who can expect to understand magical numbers? The reverential fatalism of the awestruck is not thoughtful—it is a way of avoiding thought. We need a different approach.

One choice is to approach statistics critically. Being critical does not mean being negative or hostile—it is not cynicism. The critical approach statistics thoughtfully; they avoid the extremes of both naive acceptance and cynical rejection of the numbers they encounter. Instead, the critical attempt to evaluate numbers, to distinguish between good statistics and bad statistics.

The critical understand that, while some social statistics may be pretty good, they are never perfect. Every statistic is a way of summarizing complex information into relatively simple numbers. Inevitably, some information, some of the complexity, is lost whenever we use statistics. The critical recognize that this is an inevitable limitation of statistics. Moreover, they realize that every statistic is the product of choices—the choice between defining a category broadly or narrowly, the choice of one measurement over another, the choice of a sample. People choose definitions, measurements, and samples for all sorts of reasons: Perhaps they want to emphasize some aspect of a problem; perhaps it is easier or cheaper to gather data in a particular way—many considerations can come into play. Every statistic is a compromise among choices. This means that every definition—and every measurement and every sample—probably has limitations and can be criticized.

Being critical means more than simply pointing to the flaws in a statistic. Again, every statistic has flaws. The issue is whether a particular statistic's flaws are severe enough to damage its usefulness. Is the definition so broad that it encompasses too many false positives (or so narrow that it excludes too many false negatives)?

How would changing the definition alter the statistic? Similarly, how do the choices of measurements and samples affect the statistic? What would happen if different measures or samples were chosen? And how is the statistic used? Is it being interpreted appropriately, or has its meaning been mangled to create a mutant statistic? Are the comparisons that are being made appropriate, or are apples being confused with oranges? How do different choices produce the conflicting numbers found in stat wars? These are the sorts of questions the critical ask.

As a practical matter, it is virtually impossible for citizens in contemporary society to avoid statistics about social problems. Statistics arise in all sorts of ways, and in almost every case the people promoting statistics want to persuade us. Activists use statistics to convince us that social problems are serious and deserve our attention and concern. Charities use statistics to encourage donations. Politicians use statistics to persuade us that they understand society's problems and that they deserve our support. The media use statistics to make their reporting more dramatic, more convincing, more compelling. Corporations use statistics to promote and improve their products. Researchers use statistics to document their findings and support their conclusions. Those with whom we agree use statistics to reassure us that we're on the right side, while our opponents use statistics to try and convince us that we are wrong. Statistics are one of the standard types of evidence used by people in our society.

It is not possible simply to ignore statistics, to pretend they don't exist. That sort of head-in-the-sand approach would be too costly. Without statistics, we limit our ability to think thoughtfully about our society; without statistics, we have no accurate ways of judging how big a problem may be, whether it is getting worse, or how well the policies designed to address that problem actually work. And awestruck or naive attitudes toward statistics are no better than ignoring statistics; statistics have no magical properties, and it is foolish to assume that all statistics are equally valid. Nor is a cynical approach the answer; statistics are too widespread and too useful to be automatically discounted.

It would be nice to have a checklist, a set of items we could consider in evaluating any statistic. The list might detail potential problems with definitions, measurements, sampling, mutation, and so on. These are, in fact, common sorts of flaws found in many statistics, but they should not be considered a formal, complete checklist. It is probably impossible to produce a complete list of statistical flaws—no matter how long the list, there will be other possible problems that could affect statistics.

The goal is not to memorize a list, but to develop a thoughtful approach. Becoming critical about statistics requires being prepared to ask questions about numbers. When encountering a new statistic in, say, a news report, the critical try to assess it. What might be the sources for this number? How could one go about producing the figure? Who produced the number, and what interests might they have? What are the different ways key terms might have been defined, and which definitions have been chosen? How might the phenomena be measured, and which measurement choices have been made? What sort of sample was gathered, and how might that sample affect the result? Is the statistic being properly interpreted? Are comparisons being made, and if so, are the comparisons appropriate? Are there competing statistics? If so, what stakes do the opponents have in the issue, and how are those stakes likely to affect their use of statistics? And is it possible to figure out why the statistics seem to disagree, what the differences are in the ways the competing sides are using figures?

At first, this list of questions may seem overwhelming. How can an ordinary person—someone who reads a statistic in a magazine article or hears it on a news broadcast—determine the answers to such questions? Certainly news reports rarely give detailed information on the processes by which statistics are created. And few of us have time to drop everything and investigate the background of some new number we encounter. Being critical, it seems, involves an impossible amount of work.

In practice, however, the critical need not investigate the origin of every statistic. Rather, being critical means appreciating the inevitable limitations that affect all statistics, rather than being awestruck in the presence of numbers. It means not being too credulous, not accepting every statistic at face value. But it also means appreciating that statistics, while always imperfect, can be useful. Instead of automatically discounting every statistic, the critical reserve judgment. When confronted with an interesting number, they may try to learn more, to evaluate, to weigh the figure's strengths and weaknesses.

Of course, this critical approach need not—and should not—be limited to statistics. It ought to apply to all the evidence we encounter when we scan a news report, or listen to a speech—whenever we learn about social problems. Claims about social problems often feature dramatic, compelling examples; the critical might ask whether an example is likely to be a typical case or an extreme, exceptional instance. Claims about social problems often include quotations from different sources, and the critical might wonder why those sources have spoken and why they have been quoted: Do they have particular expertise? Do they stand to benefit if they influence others? Claims about social problems usually involve arguments about the problem's causes and potential solutions. The critical might ask whether these arguments are convincing. Are they logical? Does the proposed solution seem feasible and appropriate? And so on. Being critical—adopting a skeptical, analytical stance when confronted with claims—is an approach that goes far beyond simply dealing with statistics.

Statistics are not magical. Nor are they always true—or always false. Nor need they be incomprehensible. Adopting a critical approach offers an effective way of responding to the numbers we are sure to encounter. Being critical requires more thought, but failing to adopt a critical mind-set makes us powerless to evaluate what others tell us. When we fail to think critically, the statistics we hear might just as well be magical.

Joel Best is a professor of sociology and criminal justice at the University of Delaware. This essay is excerpted from Damned Lies and Statistics: Untangling Numbers From the Media, Politicians, and Activists, *published by the University of California Press and reprinted by permission. Copyright © 2001 by the Regents of the University of California.*

Violence and the Remaking of a Self

BY SUSAN J. BRISON

On July 4, 1990, at 10:30 in the morning, I went for a walk along a country road in a village outside Grenoble, France. It was a gorgeous day, and I didn't envy my husband, Tom, who had to stay inside and work on a manuscript with a French colleague. I sang to myself as I set out, stopping along the way to pet a goat and pick a few wild strawberries. About an hour and a half later, I was lying face down in a muddy creek bed at the bottom of a dark ravine, struggling to stay alive.

I had been grabbed from behind, pulled into the bushes, beaten, and sexually assaulted. Helpless and entirely at my assailant's mercy, I talked to him, trying to appeal to his humanity, and, when that failed, addressing myself to his self-interest. He called me a whore and told me to shut up. Although I had said I'd do whatever he wanted, as the sexual assault began I instinctively fought back, which so enraged my attacker that he strangled me until I lost consciousness.

When I came to, I was being dragged by my feet down into the ravine. I had often thought I was awake while dreaming, but now I was awake and convinced I was having a nightmare. But it was no dream. After ordering me to get on my hands and knees, the man strangled me again. This time I was sure I was dying. But I revived, just in time to see him lunging toward me with a rock. He smashed it into my forehead, knocking me out. Eventually, after another strangulation attempt, he left me for dead.

After I was rescued and taken to the Grenoble hospital, where I spent the next 11 days, I was told repeatedly how "lucky" I was to be alive, and for a short while I even believed this myself. At the time, I did not yet know how trauma not only haunts the conscious and unconscious mind but also remains in the body, in each of the senses, in the heart that races and the

skin that crawls whenever something resurrects the buried terror. I didn't know that the worst—the unimaginably painful aftermath of violence—was yet to come.

For the first several months after my attack, I led a spectral existence, not quite sure whether I had died and the world was going on without me, or whether I was alive but in a totally alien world. The line between life and death, once so clear and sustaining, now seemed carelessly drawn and easily erased. I felt as though I'd outlived myself, as if I'd stayed on a train one stop past my destination.

After I was rescued and taken to the hospital, I was told repeatedly how 'lucky' I was to be alive. For a short while I even believed this myself.

My sense of unreality was fed by the massive denial of those around me—a reaction that is an almost universal response to rape, I learned. Where the facts would appear to be incontrovertible, denial takes the shape of attempts to explain the assault in ways that leave the observers' worldview unscathed. Even those who are able to acknowledge the existence of violence try to protect themselves from the realization that the world in which it occurs is their world. They cannot allow themselves to imagine the victim's shattered life, or else their illusions about their own safety and control over their lives might begin to crumble.

The most well-meaning individuals, caught up in the myth of their own immunity, can inadvertently add to the victim's suffering by suggesting that the attack was avoidable or somehow her fault. One victims'-assistance coordinator, whom I had phoned for legal advice, stressed that she herself had never been a victim and said I would benefit from the experience by learning not to be so trusting of people and to take basic safety precautions, like not going out alone late at night. She didn't pause long enough for me to point out that I had been attacked suddenly, from behind, in broad daylight.

I was initially reluctant to tell people (other than medical and legal personnel) that I had been raped. I still wonder why I wanted the sexual aspect of the assault—so salient to me—kept secret. I was motivated in part by shame, I suppose, and I wanted to avoid being stereotyped as a victim. I did not want the academic work I had already done on pornography and violence against women to be dismissed as the ravings of a "hysterical rape victim." And I felt that I had very little control over the meaning of the word "rape." Using the term denied the particularity of what I had experienced and invoked in other people whatever rape scenario they had already constructed. I later identified myself publicly as a rape survivor, having decided that it was ethically and politically imperative for me to do so.

But my initial wariness about the use of the term was understandable and, at times, reinforced by others' responses—especially by the dismissive characterization of the rape by some in the criminal-justice system. Before my assailant's trial, I heard my lawyer conferring with another lawyer on the question of victim's compensation from the state (to cover legal expenses and unreimbursed medical bills). He said, without irony, that a certain amount was typically awarded for "*un viol gentil*" ("a nice rape") and somewhat more (which they would request on my behalf) for "*un viol méchant*" ("a nasty rape").

Not surprisingly, I felt that I was taken more seriously as a victim of a near-fatal murder attempt. But that description of the assault provided others with no explanation of what had happened. Later, when people asked why this man had tried to kill me, I revealed that the attack had begun as a sexual assault, and most people were satisfied with that as an explanation. It made some kind of sense to them. But it made no sense to me.

A FEW MONTHS AFTER THE ASSAULT, I sat down at my computer to write about it for the first time, and all I could come up with was a list of paradoxes. Just about everything had stopped making sense. I thought it was quite possible that I was brain-damaged as a result of the head injuries I had sustained. Or perhaps the heightened lucidity I had experienced during the assault remained, giving me a clearer, though profoundly disorienting, picture of the world. I turned to philosophy for meaning and consolation and could find neither. Had my reasoning broken down? Or was it the breakdown of Reason? I couldn't explain what had happened to me. I was attacked for no reason. I had ventured outside the human community, landed beyond the moral universe, beyond the realm of predictable events and comprehensible actions, and I didn't know how to get back.

As a philosopher, I was used to taking something apparently obvious and familiar—the nature of time, say, or the relation between words and things—and making it into something quite puzzling. But now, when I was confronted with the utterly strange and paradoxical, philosophy was, at least initially, of no use in helping me to make sense of it. And it was hard for me, given my philosophical background, to accept that knowledge isn't always desirable, that the truth doesn't always set you free. Sometimes, it fills you with incapacitating terror, and then uncontrollable rage.

I was surprised, perhaps naively, to find that there was virtually nothing in the philosophical literature about sexual violence; obviously, it raised numerous philosophical issues. The disintegration of the self experienced by victims of violence challenges our notions of personal identity over time, a major preoccupation of metaphysics. A victim's seemingly justified skepticism about everyone and everything is pertinent to epistemology, especially if the goal of epistemology is, as Wilfrid Sellars put it, that of feeling at home in the world. In aesthetics, as well as in the philosophy of law, the discussion of sexual violence in—or as—art could use the illumination provided by a victim's perspective. Perhaps the most important questions that sexual violence poses are in social, political, and legal philosophy. Insight into those areas, as well, requires an understanding of what it's like to be a victim of such violence.

It occurred to me that the fact that rape has not been considered a properly philosophical subject—unlike war, for example—resulted not only from the paucity of women in the profession but also from the disciplinary biases against thinking about the "personal" or the particular, and against writing in the form of narrative. (Of course, the avowedly personal experiences of *men* have been neglected in philosophical analysis as well. The study of the ethics of war, for example, has dealt with questions of strategy and justice as viewed from the outside, not with the wartime experiences of soldiers or with the aftermath of their trauma.) But first-person narratives, especially ones written by those with perspectives previously excluded from the discipline, are essential to philosophy. They are necessary for exposing previously hidden biases in the discipline's subject matter and methodology, for facilitating understanding of (or empathy with) those different from ourselves, and for laying on the table our own biases as scholars.

WHEN I RESUMED TEACHING at Dartmouth, the first student who came to my office told me that she had been raped. Since I had spoken out publicly several months earlier about my assault, I knew that I would be in contact with other survivors. I just didn't realize that there would be so many—not only students, but also female colleagues and friends, who had never before told me that they had been raped. I continued to teach my usual philosophy courses, but, in some ways philosophy struck me as a luxury when I knew, in a more visceral way than before, that people were being brutally attacked and killed—all the time. So I integrated my work on trauma with my academic interests by teaching a course on global violence against women. I was still somewhat afraid of what would happen if I wrote about my assault, but I was much more afraid of what would continue to happen if I, and others with similar experiences, didn't make them public.

It was one thing to have decided to speak and write about my rape, but another to find the voice with which to do it. Even after my fractured trachea had healed, I frequently had trouble speaking. I lost my voice, literally, when I lost my ability to continue my life's narrative, when things stopped making sense. I was never entirely mute, but I often had bouts of what a friend labeled "fractured speech," during which I stuttered and stammered, unable to string together a simple sentence without the words scattering like a broken necklace. During the assault itself, my heightened lucidity had seemed to be accompanied by an unusual linguistic fluency—in French, no less. But being able to speak quickly and (so it seemed to me) precisely in a foreign language when I felt I had to in order to survive was followed by episodes, spread over several years, when I couldn't, for the life of me, speak intelligibly even in my mother tongue.

The fact that rape has not been considered a properly philosophical subject results in part from disciplinary biases against thinking about the 'personal.'

For about a year after the assault, I rarely, if ever, spoke in smoothly flowing sentences. I could sing, though, after about six months, and, like aphasics who cannot say a word but can sing verse after verse, I never stumbled over the lyrics. I recall spending the hour's drive home from the weekly meetings of my support group of rape survivors singing every spiritual I'd ever heard. It was a comfort and a release. Mainly, it was something I could do, loudly, openly (by myself in a closed car), and easily, accompanied by unstoppable tears.

Even after I regained my ability to speak, more or less reliably, in English, I was unable to speak, without debilitating difficulty, in French. Before my ill-fated trip in the summer of 1990, I'd never have passed for a native speaker, but I'd visited France many times and spent several summers there. I came of age there, intellectually, immersing myself in the late 1970s in research on French feminism, which had led to my interviewing Simone de Beauvoir (in Rome) one summer. Now, more than 10 years after the assault, I still almost never speak French, even in Francophone company, in which I often find myself, given my husband's interests.

After regaining my voice, I sometimes lost it again—once for an entire week after my brother committed suicide on Christmas Eve, 1995. Although I'd managed to keep my speech impairment hidden from my colleagues and students for five and a half years, I found that I had to ask a colleague to take over a class I'd been scheduled to teach the day after the funeral. I feared that I'd suffer a linguistic breakdown in front of a lecture hall full of students.

I lost my voice again, intermittently, during my tenure review, about a year after my brother's death. And, although I could still write (and type) during this time, I can see now that my writing about violence had become increasingly hesitant and guarded, as I hid behind academic jargon and excessive citations of others' work. Not only had my brother's suicide caused me to doubt whether I, who had, after all, survived, was entitled to talk about the trauma I'd endured, but now I could not silence the internalized voices of those who had warned me not to publish my work on sexual violence before getting tenure. In spite of the warm reception my writing on the subject was receiving in the larger academic community—from feminist philosophers and legal theorists, people in women's studies, and scholars from various disciplines who were interested in trauma—I stopped writing in the personal voice and slipped back into the universal mode, thinking that only writing about trauma in general was important enough to justify the academic risks I was taking. And I took fewer and fewer risks.

After getting tenure, I was given sanctuary, for nearly two years, at the Institute for Advanced Study, in Princeton. There I gradually came to feel safe enough to write, once again, in my own voice, about what I considered to be philosophically important. It helped to be surrounded by a diverse group of scholars who, to my initial amazement and eternal gratitude, simply assumed that whatever I was working on must be of sufficient intellectual interest to be worth bothering about.

My linguistic disability never resurfaced in my many conversations at the institute, although it returned later, after a particularly stressful incident at Dartmouth. That episode, more than eight and a half years after the assault, forced me to accept that I have what may well be a permanent neurological glitch resulting from my brain's having been stunned into unconsciousness four times during the attack. Although I had spoken out as a rape survivor at a Take Back the Night rally nine months after the event, it took me nearly nine years to acknowledge, even to myself, that the assault had left me neurologically disabled—very minimally, to be sure, in a way that I could easily compensate for, by avoiding extremely stressful situations, but disabled nonetheless.

PEOPLE ASK ME if I'm recovered now, and I reply that it depends on what that means. If they mean, Am I back to where I was before the attack? I have to say no, and I never will be. I am not the same person who set off, singing, on that sunny Fourth of July in the French countryside. I left her in a rocky creek bed at the bottom of a ravine. I had to in order to survive. The trauma has changed me forever, and if I insist too often that my friends and family acknowledge it, that's because I'm afraid they don't know who I am.

But if recovery means being able to incorporate this awful knowledge of trauma and its aftermath into my life and carry on, then, yes, I'm recovered. I don't wake each day with a start, thinking: "This can't have happened to me!" It happened. I have no guarantee that it won't happen again. I don't expect to be able to transcend or redeem the trauma, or to solve the dilemmas of survival. I think the goal of recovery is simply to endure. That is hard enough, especially when sometimes it seems as if the only way to regain control over one's life is to end it.

A FEW MONTHS after my assault, I drove by myself for several hours to visit my friend Margot. Though driving felt like a much safer mode of transportation than walking, I worried throughout the journey, not only about the trajectory of every oncoming vehicle but also about my car breaking down, leaving me at the mercy of potentially murderous passersby. I wished I'd had a gun so that I could shoot myself rather than be forced to live through another assault. Later in my recovery, as depression gave way to rage, such suicidal thoughts were quickly quelled by a stubborn refusal to finish my assailant's job for him. I also learned, after martial-arts training, that I was capable, morally as well as physically, of killing in self-defense—an option that made the possibility of another life-threatening attack one I could live with.

Some rape survivors have remarked on the sense of moral loss they experienced when they realized that they could kill their assailants, but I think that this thought can be seen as a salutary character change in those whom society does not encourage to value their own lives enough. And, far from jeopardizing their connections with a community, this new-found ability to defend themselves—and to consider themselves worth fighting for—enables rape survivors to move once more among others, free of debilitating fears. It gave me the courage to bring a child into the world, in spite of the realization that doing so would, far from making me immortal, make me twice as mortal, doubling my chances of having my life destroyed by a speeding truck.

But many trauma survivors who endured much worse than I did, and for much longer, found, often years later, that it was impossible to go on. It is not a moral failing to leave a world that has become morally unacceptable. I wonder how some people can ask of battered women, Why didn't they leave? while saying of those driven to suicide by the brutal and inescapable aftermath of trauma, Why didn't they stay? Jean Améry wrote,

"Whoever was tortured, stays tortured," and that may explain why he, Primo Levi, Paul Celan, and other Holocaust survivors took their own lives decades after their physical torture ended, as if such an explanation were needed.

THOSE who have survived trauma understand the pull of that solution to their daily Beckettian dilemma—"I can't go on, I must go on"—for on some days the conclusion "I'll go on" can be reached by neither faith nor reason. How does one go on with a shattered self, with no guarantee of recovery, believing that one will always stay tortured and never feel at home in the world? One hopes for a bearable future, in spite of all the inductive evidence to the contrary. After all, the loss of faith in induction following an unpredictable trauma has a reassuring side: Since inferences from the past can no longer be relied upon to predict the future, there's no more reason to think that tomorrow will bring agony than to think that it won't. So one makes a wager, in which nothing is certain and the odds change daily, and sets about willing to believe that life, for all its unfathomable horror, still holds some undiscovered pleasures. And one remakes oneself by finding meaning in a life of caring for and being sustained by others.

While I used to have to will myself out of bed each day, I now wake gladly to feed my son, whose birth gave me reason not to have died. Having him has forced me to rebuild my trust in the world, to try to believe that the world is a good enough place in which to raise him. He is so trusting that, before he learned to walk, he would stand with outstretched arms, wobbling, until he fell, stiff-limbed, forward, backward, certain the universe would catch him. So far it has, and when I tell myself it always will, the part of me that he's become believes it.

Susan J. Brison is an associate professor of philosophy at Dartmouth College and a visiting associate professor of philosophy at Princeton University. She is the author of Aftermath: Violence and the Remaking of a Self, *published by Princeton University Press.*

From *The Chronicle of Higher Education*, January 18, 2002, pp. B7-B10. © 2002 by the Chronicle of Higher Education.

Prosecutors, Kids, and Domestic Violence Cases

by Debra Whitcomb

Police and prosecutors say they sometimes feel like they are walking a tightrope when they intervene in domestic violence cases. Each step into a heated domestic situation requires careful balance. On the one hand, the justice system must hold batterers accountable for their violent behavior; on the other hand, a woman needs to control her life and find safety and security for herself and her children as best she can.

As research reveals more about the effects of domestic violence on children, prosecutors are finding that both the law and public opinion have raised expectations for what criminal justice professionals should do and actually can do.

Some States have enacted legislation to better protect children exposed to violence, but the new laws are raising concern about the impact on mothers. Critics hypothesize that battered women will be increasingly charged with criminal child abuse or failure to protect their children if they do not take action against their batterer and could eventually lose custody. Others fear that children who are exposed to domestic violence will increasingly be forced to testify and therefore to "choose sides" in the cases against their mother or father.

This article describes some of the issues prosecutors should be aware of when they handle domestic violence cases involving children, especially in light of recent legislation aimed to protect children. It is the product of an NIJ-funded exploratory study that relied on two sources of data: a national telephone survey of prosecutors and field research in five jurisdictions. (See "The Survey and Its Findings.")

The exploratory study sought answers to the following questions:

- How are new laws, now in effect in a small number of States, affecting practice?
- What challenges do prosecutors face when children are exposed to domestic violence?
- What can prosecutors do to help battered women and their children?

Why the New Laws?

Children who witness domestic violence often manifest behavioral and emotional problems, poor academic performance, and delinquency.[1] Sadly, violence against women and violence against children often coexist in families—the frequency of child abuse doubles in families experiencing intimate partner violence, compared to families with nonviolent partners, and the rate of child abuse escalates with the severity and frequency of the abuse against the mother.[2]

Domestic violence is also a known risk factor for recurring child abuse reports[3] and for child fatalities.[4] In addition, domestic violence frequently coexists with substance abuse, so that children are exposed to the effects of dangerous substances and the parental neglect that usually comes with addiction.[5] One large study involving 9,500 HMO members revealed that the 1,010 people who reported that their mothers had been treated violently also reported being exposed to other adverse childhood experiences, such as substance abuse (59 percent reported exposure), mental illness (38 percent), sexual abuse (41 percent), psychological abuse (34 percent), and physical abuse (31 percent).[6]

It is generally recognized that the well-being of children who witness domestic violence is tied closely to that of their mothers,[7] but the mother's interests and the child's may not always be identical or even compatible. A mother may face serious concerns about their financial and physical well-being if she separates from her violent partner. She may lack resources or social networks to extricate herself from dangerous relationships, and the community's support system may be inadequate. Her efforts to seek help may be thwarted by waiting lists, lack of insurance, or high fees for services. She may believe that she and her children are better off staying with the violent partner despite the consequences.[8]

Meanwhile, the children remain in perilous environments. Child protection agencies may feel compelled to intervene to forestall the escalating risk of harm to children. Unfortunately, in many jurisdictions, a referral to the child protection agency is perceived as a mixed blessing. Many child protection agencies do not have adequate resources to respond to the volume of domestic violence reports they receive when exposure to violence is defined as a form of child maltreatment by law or policy. Elsewhere, critics charge, protective services workers are too quick to remove children from violent homes, inappropriately blaming women for the actions of their abusive partners.

> Police officers are being encouraged to note the presence of children when they respond to domestic violence incidents and to collaborate with mental health professionals to address the children's trauma and anxiety.

How Are New Laws Affecting Practice?

The words of San Diego City Attorney Casey Gwinn capture the climate of growing concerns related to children and violence in the home:

> … children must be a central focus of all we do in the civil and criminal justice system… from the initial police investigation through the probationary period, we must prioritize children's issues.[9]

Police officers are being encouraged to note the presence of children when they respond to domestic violence incidents and to collaborate with mental health professionals to address the children's trauma and anxiety.[10] Battered women's shelters are hiring staff to work with children and developing policy for alerting child protection agencies when needed.[11] Juvenile and family courts are sponsoring programs to meet the needs of battered women whose children are at risk for maltreatment.[12] Child protection agencies are instituting training and protocols to better identify domestic violence; some are hiring domestic violence specialists to help develop appropriate case plans.[13] Legislators, too, are taking action by enhancing penalties when domestic violence occurs in front of children and creating new criminal child abuse offenses for cases involving children who are exposed to domestic violence.

The new laws are affecting prosecutors in different ways. For example, district attorneys in Multnomah County, Oregon, where a new law recently upgraded domestic violence offenses to felonies when children are present,[14] issued nearly 150 percent more felony domestic violence cases in the year that the new law was passed.

In both Salt Lake County, Utah, and Houston County, Georgia, where committing domestic violence in the presence of a child is a new crime of child abuse,[15] prosecutors tend to use these charges as "bargaining chips" to exert leverage toward guilty pleas on domestic violence charges.

In these jurisdictions, the new State laws remind law enforcement investigators to document children as witnesses and to take statements from them whenever possible, which may strengthen prosecutors' domestic violence cases even if the children cannot testify.

To understand how prosecutors are responding to the changing attitudes, researchers asked them to explain how they would respond to three different scenarios involving children and domestic violence:

1. An abused mother is alleged to have abused her children.
2. Both mother and children are abused by the same male perpetrator.
3. Children are exposed to domestic violence, but not abused themselves.

For each scenario, respondents answered these questions:

- Would your office *report* the mother to the child protection agency?
- Would your office *prosecute* the mother in the first scenario for the abuse of her children?
- Would your office report or prosecute the mother in scenarios 2 and 3 for failure to protect her children from abuse or exposure to domestic violence?

Many respondents noted the lack of statutory authority in their States to prosecute mothers for failure to protect their children, especially from exposure to domestic violence. Some explained that they consider mothers' experience of victimization in their decisions to report or prosecute battered mothers for their children's exposure to abuse or domestic violence.

Factors in these decisions commonly include the severity of injury to the child, chronicity of the domestic violence, the degree to which the mother actively participated in the abuse of her child, and prior history of failure to comply with services or treatment plans.

Prosecutors in States with laws either creating or enhancing penalties for domestic violence in the presence of children were significantly more likely to report battered mothers for failure to protect their children from abuse or from exposure to domestic violence, but there is no significant difference in the likelihood of prosecution. (See table 1.)

The Survey and Its Findings

The study involved a telephone survey of prosecutors and in-depth site visits to five jurisdictions to collect information about current practice and to identity "promising practices" in response to cases involving domestic violence and child victims or witnesses.

The final report, *Children and Domestic Violence: Challenges for Prosecutors,* NCJ 185355; grant 99–WT–VX–0001) is available from NCJRS for $15. To order a copy, call 1-800-851-3420.

Findings from the Telephone Survey

The 128 prosecutors who completed the telephone survey worked in 93 office in 49 States. The offices had jurisdiction over both felony and misdemeanor cases at either the county or district level. Nearly half (48 percent) of the jurisdictions had units or prosecutors responsible for all family violence cases, 38 percent had separate domestic violence and child abuse prosecutors or units. The other respondents represented the singular perspectives of domestic violence (10 percent) or child abuse (4 percent).

Specific findings include the following:

Most respondents (78 percent) agreed that the presence of children provides added incentive to prosecute domestic violence cases. A few individuals pointed to the children's capacity to testify as an important factor in their decisions.

A majority of prosecutors' offices (59 percent) are aggressively pursuing enhanced sanctions for domestic violence offenders when incidents involve children as victims or witnesses. Most commonly, prosecutors argue for harsher sentencing or file separate charges of child endangerment. Responding offices in which prosecu-

tors had received at least some training on the co-occurrence of domestic violence and child maltreatment (65 percent) were significantly more likely to report employing these avenues in applicable cases.

Most jurisdictions lack a policy for prosecutors and investigators to identify co-occurring cases of domestic violence and child maltreatment. None of the 35 responding offices with separate domestic violence and child abuse units had protocols directing prosecutors in these units to inquire about co-occurrence or to communicate with one another when relevant cases arise. About half were aware of protocols directing law enforcement officers to ask about child victims or witnesses when investigating domestic violence reports. About one-fourth knew of protocols directing investigators to inquire about domestic violence when responding to child abuse reports.

Findings From the In-Depth Site Visits

Dallas, Texas. Prosecutors in Dallas pursue a fairly strict "no-drop" policy for domestic violence cases, and the presence of children only strengthens their resolve to move cases forward. However, with reluctant women, the officials can offer the option of filing an "affidavit of nonprosecution." This document helps women who fear retribution from their abusive partners because it allows the women to demonstrate their efforts to terminate law enforcement's intervention. However, it has no effect on the prosecutor's decision making or the court's proceedings.

Where there are concurrent charges of domestic violence and child abuse, prosecutors try to coordinate the cases to optimize the sanctions against the offender and the safety of the mother and children. For example, the family violence prose-

cutor can use child abuse cases to support the domestic violence charge. Even if the child abuse is a felony and the domestic violence is a misdemeanor, prosecutors may accept a plea to jail time on the domestic violence charge and a 10-year deferred adjudication on the child abuse charge, which typically carries with it numerous conditions (e.g., no contact, participation in substance abuse treatment, and so on). This avenue ensures a domestic violence conviction while imposing strict court oversight on the child abuse charge.

Respondents observed that deferred adjudication or a probation sentence is, in some ways, more severe and more effective than jail time, precisely because of the conditions that can be imposed, the length of time that the offender can remain under the court's supervision, and the threat of revocation and incarceration.

San Diego, California. Prosecutors in San Diego are both aggressive and creative in finding ways to enhance sanctions for perpetrators of domestic violence and child abuse. For example, domestic violence offenders can be charged with child endangerment when a child:

- Calls 911 to report domestic violence.
- Appears fearful, upset, or hysterical at the scene.
- Is an eyewitness to the incident.
- Is present in a room where objects are being thrown.
- Is in a car during a domestic violence incident.
- Is in the arms of the victim or suspect during an incident.[1]

Anyone convicted of child endangerment and sentenced to probation will be required to complete a yearlong child abuser's treatment program.

(continued on next page)

Several programs support the prosecutors. For example, the Child Advocacy Project (CAP) provides services to children and families in reported incidents of abuse, neglect, exploitation, or domestic violence that are *not* investigated for criminal justice system intervention. Through a collaboration with the San Diego Police Department and Children's Hospital Center for Child Protection, the San Diego City Attorney's Office reviews these reports with an eye toward any angle that might support a misdemeanor prosecution with the goal of creating an avenue for service delivery. Most defendants plead guilty and receive informal probation with referrals to parenting and counseling programs.

Salt Lake County, Utah. In May 1997, Utah became the first State to enact legislation specifically addressing the issue of children who witness domestic violence. Notable elements of this statute include the following:

- It creates a crime of child abuse, not domestic violence.
- It does not require the child to be physically present during the incident of domestic violence. The perpetrator simply must be aware that a child may see or hear it.
- Unless the precipitating domestic violence incident is quite severe, it requires at least one previous violation or act of domestic violence in the presence of a child. A police incident report documenting an earlier act in the presence of a child will suffice for this purpose.

Although criminal justice agencies in Salt Lake County were not able to provide statistical data, anecdotal evidence suggests that:

- The law is infrequently applied to mothers. But it could be applied if the women were arrested in the underlying incident of domestic violence.

- The law is largely symbolic. It adds minimal time to the offender's sentence—perhaps 6 months if the sentences for the domestic violence and child abuse charges run consecutively.
- The crime is relatively easy to prove, requiring either (a) testimony from the responding officer, (b) testimony or excited utterances from the victim parent, or (c) a 911 tape that records children's voices.

Concurrent with the enactment of the new criminal statute, Utah's Department of Child and Family Services created a new category of child abuse and neglect: "Domestic Violence-Related Child Abuse," or DVRCA, defined as "violent physical or verbal interaction between cohabitants in a household in the presence of a child."

In adopting the new category, the department hired domestic violence advocates and developed a protocol to guide child protection workers in their determinations.

Houston County, Georgia. Prosecutors in Houston County, Georgia, actively use new provisions of Georgia's "cruelty to children" statute that pertain to domestic violence committed in the presence of children. Because cruelty to children is almost always a misdemeanor offense, it makes little difference in the penalties imposed on a batterer; indeed, the sentence typically runs by concurrently with the underlying domestic violence charge. However, the law does give prosecutors a stronger argument for no contact as a condition of bond. Violations of no-contact orders are charged as aggravated stalking, a felony offense in Georgia. Prosecutors perceive the severe consequences of violating no-contact orders as perhaps the most effective response to domestic violence among the sanctions available to them.

Also, by identifying children as victims of the family violence battery, the new law accomplishes at least three things:

- It helps to counter batterers' threats to gain custody of a child.
- It makes the children eligible for crime victims compensation.
- It enables the court to impose no-contact orders on the children's behalf.

Multnomah County, Oregon. The study team selected Multnomah County (Portland), Oregon, because Oregon enacted legislation upgrading certain assault offenses from misdemeanors to felonies when a child witnesses the crime. The felony upgrade applies only to assault in the fourth degree, a misdemeanor offense that applies to many incidents of domestic violence. Assaults in the first, second, or third degree are felonies that require more serious injuries or the use of weapons.

Even though the felony upgrade applies to defendants with prior convictions (either one against the same victim or three against any victims) regardless of the presence of children, prosecutors observe that the large majority of elevated cases are those involving child witnesses.

The felony upgrade law has had a noteworthy impact on the District Attorney's Office: The number of felonies reviewed more than tripled in 1998 (the year in which the law became effective), while the number of misdemeanors reviewed remained nearly constant. Also, the number of felonies issued exceeded the number of misdemeanors for the first time.

In that same year, the proportion of issued domestic violence cases declined. This pattern held true for misdemeanors as well as felonies. Prosecutors may have imposed higher standards as they began to interpret and apply the new law.

Note

1. Gwinn, C., "Domestic Violence and Children: Difficult Issues," Presentation for the National College of District Attorneys, 1998.

Table 1: Prosecutors' Responses to Scenarios Involving Children and Abuse

Scenario	Would *Report* At Least Sometimes	Would *Prosecute* At Least Sometimes
Mom Abuses Children	94% (n = 90)	100% (n = 82)
Mom Fails to Protect from Abuse	63% (n = 87)	77.5% (n = 80)
Mom Fails to Protect from Exposure	40% (n = 86)	25% (n = 73)

The more tangible benefits of the new laws—particularly those in Utah and Georgia—may accrue to the children. By identifying children as victims, these statutes:

- Allow children access to crime victims compensation funds to address health or mental health needs resulting from their exposure to domestic violence.
- Enable the courts to issue protective orders on the children's behalf (potentially affording prosecutors another tool for monitoring offenders' behavior).
- Signal a need to file a report with the child protection agency, even in the absence of laws naming domestic violence as a condition of mandatory reporting.

> No other institution in the community has the capacity and power to force offenders to confront and change their behavior.... Prosecutors can bring together people with disparate views and hammer out ways to overcome distrust and conflict toward a common goal: protection of battered women and their children.

What Can Prosecutors Do?

Research suggests a number of steps prosecutors can take to help children who are exposed to domestic violence:

- Employ every available avenue to enforce the terms of no-contact orders and probationary sentences. Field research suggests that these measures may offer the most powerful means of holding domestic violence offenders accountable for their behavior.
- Establish protocols within prosecutors' offices to encourage information sharing among prosecutors with responsibility for domestic violence and child abuse caseloads.
- Identify avenues for early intervention (e.g., by placing greater emphasis on misdemeanor prosecution).
- Train law enforcement investigators to note the presence of children in domestic violence incidents and to take statements from them whenever appropriate to do so.
- Encourage law enforcement agencies to adopt a model of law enforcement–mental health partnership that was pioneered in New Haven, Connecticut, as a means of ensuring that children who are exposed to violence receive timely and appropriate therapeutic intervention.[16] Be prepared, however, to develop policies or protocols to guide law enforcement officers' decisions to report these incidents to the child protection agency.
- Wherever possible, prosecute domestic violence offenders on concurrent charges of child endangerment, emotional abuse, or other available charges reflecting the danger to children who witness violence. These additional charges can be used to argue for stricter conditions of pretrial release or probation, or perhaps for upward deviation from sentencing guidelines.
- Provide training on domestic violence, child abuse, and the impact of domestic violence on children for all prosecutors, victim advocates, and other court personnel whose job responsibilities include responding to allegations of family violence.
- Promote increased attention to services for battered women. Women cannot reasonably be expected to extricate themselves from dangerous relationships if the financial and social supports are not available in their communities. Particular attention should be paid to substance abuse

treatment; one recent study suggests that substance abuse predicts noncooperation with prosecution among battered women.[17]

- Ensure that social service agencies will connect with families that have been reported for domestic violence, both to offer referrals for needed services and to monitor future incidents. Some avenues need to be available for offering needed services to children in troubled families before they suffer serious harm.

No other institution in the community has the capacity and power to force offenders to confront and change their behavior. As political leaders in their communities, prosecutors have the status and opportunity to advocate for needed change, whether legislative, fiscal, or programmatic in nature. Prosecutors can bring together people with disparate views and hammer out ways to overcome distrust and conflict toward a common goal: protection of battered women and their children.

Notes

1. For a comprehensive review, see Edleson, J., "Children's Witnessing of Adult Domestic Violence," *Journal of Interpersonal Violence,* 14 (1999): 839–870.
2. Strauss, M., R. J. Gelles, and S. Steinmetz, *Behind Closed Doors: Violence in the American Family,* New York: Doubleday/Anchor, 1980.
3. English, D. J., D. B. Marshall, S. Brummel, and M. Orme, "Characteristics of Repeated Referrals to Child Protective Services in Washington State," *Child Maltreatment,* 4 (1999): 297–307.
4. U.S. Advisory Board on Child Abuse and Neglect, *A Nation's Shame: Fatal Child Abuse and Neglect in the United States,* Washington, DC: U.S. Department of Health and Human Services, Administration for Children and Families, 1995.
5. U.S. Department of Health and Human Services, *Blending Perspectives and Building Common Ground: A Report to Congress on Substance Abuse and Child Protection,* Washington,

   DC: Administration for Children and Families, Substance Abuse and Mental Health Services Administration, Assistant Secretary for Planning and Evaluation, 1999.
6. Felitti, V. J., R. F. Anda, D. Nordenberg, et al., "Relationship of Childhood Abuse and Household Dysfunction to Many of the Leading Causes of Death in Adults," *American Journal of Preventive Medicine,* 14 (1998): 250.
7. Osofsky, J. D., "The Impact of Violence on Children," *The Future of Children: Domestic Violence and Children,* 9(1999): 33–49.
8. Hilton, N. Z., "Battered Women's Concerns About Their Children Witnessing Wife Assault," *Journal of Interpersonal Violence,* 7(1992): 77–86.
9. Personal communication, January 2000.
10. Marans, S., S. J. Berkowitz, and D. J. Cohen, "Police and Mental Health Professionals: Collaborative Responses to the Impact of Violence on Children and Families," *Child and Adolescent Psychiatric Clinics of North America,* 7(1998): 635–651.
11. Saathoff, A. J., and E. A. Stoffel, "Community-Based Domestic Violence Services," *The Future of Children: Domestic Violence and Children,* 9(1999): 97–110.
12. See, e.g., Lecklitner, G. L., N. M. Malik, S. M. Aaron, and C. S. Lederman, "Promoting Safety for Abused Children and Battered Mothers: Miami-Dade County's Model Dependency Court Intervention Program," *Child Maltreatment,* 4(1999): 175–182.
13. Whitney, P., and L. Davis, "Child Abuse and Domestic Violence in Massachusetts: Can Practice Be Integrated in a Public Child Welfare Setting?" *Child Maltreatment,* 4(1999): 158–166.
14. Oregon's legislation can be found at ORS 163.160(3)(b).
15. Utah: U.C.A. §76–5–109.1; Georgia: O.C.G.A. §16–5–70.
16. Marans, Berkowitz, and Cohen, "Police and Mental Health Professionals," see note 10.
17. Goodman, L., L. Bennett, and M. A. Bennett, "Obstacles to Victims' Cooperation with the Criminal Prosecution of Their Abusers: The Role of Social Support," *Violence and Victims,* 14(1999): 427–444.

about the author
Debra Whitcomb conducted this research while she was an NIJ Research Fellow. Whitcomb is Director, Grant Programs and Development, American Prosecutors Research Institute, 99 Canal Center Plaza, Suite 510, Alexandria, Virginia 22314, 703-519-1675, debra.whitcomb@ndaa-apri.org.

From *National Institute of Justice Journal,* Number 248, 2002. © 2002 by U.S. Department of Justice.

STRENGTHENING ANTISTALKING STATUTES

Introduction

Stalking is a crime of intimidation. Stalkers harass and even terrorize through conduct that causes fear or substantial emotional distress in their victims. A recent study sponsored by the National Institute of Justice (NIJ) (U.S. Department of Justice) and the Centers for Disease Control and Prevention estimates that 1 in 12 women and 1 in 45 men have been stalked during their lifetime.[1] Although stalking behavior has been around for many years, it has been identified as a crime only within the past decade. Most laws a the state level were passed between 1991 and 1992. As more is learned about stalking and stalkers, legislatures are attempting to improve their laws.[2]

In 1993, under a grant from NIJ, a working group of experts was assembled to develop a model state stalking law.[3] Many of its recommendations have been followed as states have amended their laws.[4]

Status of the Law

Generally, stalking is defined as the willful or intentional commission of a series of acts that would cause a reasonable person to fear death or serious bodily injury and that, in fact, does place the victim in fear of death or serious bodily injury. Stalking is a crime in every state. Every state has a stalking law, although the harassment laws of some states also encompass stalking behaviors. In most states, stalking is a Class A or first degree misdemeanor except under certain circumstances, which include stalking in violation of a protective order, stalking while armed, or repeat offenses. In addition, states typically have harassment statutes, and one state's harassment law might encompass behaviors that would be considered stalking in another state.

Significant variation exists among state stalking laws. These differences relate primarily to the type of repeated behavior that is prohibited, whether a threat is required as part of stalking, the reaction of the victim to the stalking, and the intent of the stalker.

Prohibited Behavior

Most states have broad definitions of the type of repeated behavior that is prohibited, using terms such as "harassing," "communicating," and "nonconsensual contact." In some states, specific descriptions of stalking behavior are included in the statute. For example, Michigan's stalking law provides that unconsented contact includes, but is not limited to, any of the following:

1. Following or appearing within sight of that individual.
2. Approaching or confronting that individual in a public place or on private property.
3. Appearing at that individual's workplace or residence.
4. Entering onto or remaining on property owned, leased, or occupied by that individual.
5. Contacting that individual by telephone.
6. Sending mail or electronic communications to that individual.
7. Placing an object on or delivering an object to property owned, leased, or occupied by that individual.[5]

A handful of states have narrow definitions of stalking. Illinois, for example, limits stalking to cases involving following or keeping a person under surveillance.[6]

Message From THE DIRECTOR

Over the past three decades, the criminal justice field has witnessed an astounding proliferation of statutory enhancements benefiting people who are most directly and intimately affected by crime. To date, all states have passed some form of legislation to benefit victims. In addition, 32 states have recognized the supreme importance of fundamental and express rights for crime victims by raising those protections to the constitutional level.

Of course, the nature, scope, and enforcement of victims' rights vary from state to state, and it is a complex and often frustrating matter for victims to determine what those rights mean for them. To help victims, victim advocates, and victim services providers understand the relevance of the myriad laws and constitutional guarantees, the Office for Victims of Crime awarded funding to the National Center for Victims of Crime to produce a series of bulletins addressing salient legal issues affecting crime victims.

Strengthening Antistalking Statutes, the first in the series, provides an overview of state legislation and current issues related to stalking. Although stalking is a crime in all 50 states, significant variation exists among statutes as to the type of behavior prohibited, the intent of the stalker, whether a threat is required, and the others in the Legal Series highlight various circumstances in which relevant laws are applied, emphasizing their successful implementation.

We hope that victims, victim advocates, victim service providers, criminal justice professionals, and policymakers in states across the Nation will find the bulletins in this series helpful in making sense of the criminal justice process and in identifying areas in which rights could be strengthened or more clearly defined. We encourage you to use these bulletins not simply as informational resources but as tools to support victims in their involvement with the criminal justice system.

John W. Gillis
Director

ability to carry out the threat. As understanding of stalking has grown, however, most states have modified or eliminated the credible-threat requirement. Stalkers often present an implied threat to their victims. For example, repeatedly following a person is generally perceived as threatening. The threat may not be expressed but may be implicit in the context of the case.

Only two states—Arkansas and Massachusetts—require the making of a threat to be part of stalking,[11] although a few other states require an express threat as an element of aggravated stalking. Most states currently define stalking to include implied threats or specify that threats can be, but are not required to be, part of the pattern of harassing behavior.

Reactions of the Victim

Stalking is defined in part by a victim's reaction. Typically, stalking is conduct that "would cause a reasonable person to fear bodily injury to himself or a member of his immediate family or to fear the death of himself or a member of his immediate family"[12] or "would cause a reasonable person to suffer substantial emotional distress"[13] and does cause the victim to have such a reaction. Some states refer to conduct that seriously "alarms," "annoys," "torments," or "terrorizes" the victim, although many of those states also require that the conduct result in substantial emotional distress.[14] Others refer to the victim's fear for his or her "personal safety";[15] feeling "frightened, intimidated, or threatened";[16] or fear "that the stalker intends to injure the person, another person, or property of the person."[17] In general, however, stalking statutes provide that the conduct must be of a nature that would cause a specified reaction on the part of the victim and in fact does cause the victim to have that reaction.[18]

Intentions of the Stalker

Originally, most stalking statutes were "specific intent" crimes; they required proof that the stalker intended to cause the victim to fear death or personal injury or to have some other particular reaction to the stalker's actions. The subjective intent of a person, however, can be difficult to prove. Therefore, many states have revised their statutes to make stalking a "general intent" crime; rather than requiring proof that the defendant intended to cause a reaction on the part of the victim, many states simply require that the stalker intentionally committed prohibited acts. Other states require that in committing the acts, the defendant must know, or reasonably should know, that the acts would cause the victim to be placed in fear. The latter approach was recommended in the NIJ Model Antistalking Code project. At least two courts have discussed the model's language in finding that general intent is sufficient.[19]

Maryland requires that the pattern of conduct include approaching or pursuing another person.[7] Hawaii is similar, limiting stalking to cases in which the stalker pursues the victim or conducts surveillance of the victim.[8] Connecticut limits stalking to following or lying in wait.[9] Wisconsin requires "maintaining a visual or physical proximity to a person."[10]

Threat

When stalking laws were first adopted in states across the country, many laws required the making of a "credible threat" as an element of the offense. Generally, this was defined as a threat made with the intent and apparent

Exceptions

Most states have explicit exceptions under their stalking laws for certain behaviors, commonly described simply as "constitutionally protected activity." Many also specifically exempt licensed investigators or other professionals operating within the scope of their duties;[20] however, it may not be necessary to provide such exceptions within the statute itself. The Supreme Court of Illinois interpreted that state's stalking laws to prohibit only conduct performed "without lawful authority," even though the laws do not contain that phrase. The court reasoned that "[t]his construction… accords with the legislature's intent in enacting the statutes to prevent violent attacks by allowing the police to act before the victim was actually injured and to prevent the terror produced by harassing actions."[21]

Aggravating Circumstances

Many state codes include an offense of aggravated stalking or define stalking offenses in the first and second degrees. Often, the higher level offense is defined as stalking in violation of a protective order,[22] stalking while armed with a deadly weapon,[23] a second or subsequent conviction of stalking,[24] or stalking a minor.[25] Many states without a separately defined higher offense provide for enhanced punishment for stalking under such conditions.

Challenges to Stalking Laws

Most of the cases challenging the constitutionality of stalking laws focus on one of two questions: whether the statute is overbroad or whether it is unconstitutionally vague. A statute is unconstitutionally overbroad when it inadvertently criminalizes legitimate behavior. In a Pennsylvania case, the defendant claimed the stalking statute was unconstitutional because it criminalized a substantial amount of constitutionally protected conduct. In that case, the defendant engaged in a campaign of intimidating behavior against a judge who had ruled against him in a landlord-tenant case. For nearly a year, the defendant made regular phone calls and distributed leaflets calling the judge "Judge Bimbo," "a cockroach," "a gangster," and "a mobster." During one of his many calls to the judge's chambers, her secretary asked him if his intentions were "to alarm and disturb" the judge. The defendant replied, "I would hope that my calls alarm her. I am working very hard at it. If my calls are disturbing, wait until she sees what happens next." He also called and spoke about the bodyguard hired for the judge and the judge carrying a gun "to let [her] know that he's watching and knows what is going on."

The court in that case found that the statute was not overbroad and did not criminalize constitutionally protected behavior. The court noted that "[t]he appellant cites us no cases, nor are we able to locate any,

announcing a constitutional right to 'engage in a course of conduct or repeatedly committed acts toward another person [with the] intent to cause substantial emotional distress to the person.'"[26]

Defendants have also argued that stalking laws are unconstitutionally vague. The essential test for vagueness was set out by the U.S. Supreme Court in 1926. A Government restriction is vague if it "either forbids or requires the doing of an act in terms so vague that men of common intelligence must necessarily guess at its meaning and differ as to its application."[27] Whether a given term is unconstitutionally vague is left to the interpretation of each state's courts.

In a New Jersey stalking case, the court rejected the defendant's claim that the statute was unconstitutionally vague, finding the defendant's conduct "unquestionably proscribed by the statute." In that case, the defendant had maintained physical proximity to the victim on numerous occasions, late at night, that the court found to be threatening, purposeful, and directed at the victim. He repeatedly asked for sexual contact that he knew was unwanted, and he implied that she had better agree. "To suggest, as the defendant does, that his activity could be seen as the pursuit of 'normal social interaction' is absurd. On the contrary, his conduct was a patent violation of the statute."[28]

In a Michigan case, the defendant also argued that the stalking statutes were unconstitutionally vague and violated his first amendment right to free speech. The court disagreed. "Defendant's repeated telephone calls to the victim, sometimes 50 to 60 times a day whether the victim was at home or at work, and his verbal threats to kill her and her family do not constitute protected speech or conduct serving a legitimate purpose, even if that purpose is 'to attempt to reconcile,' as defendant asserts."[29]

Claims that stalking laws were unconstitutionally vague have focused on the wide range of terms commonly used in such laws. For example, courts have ruled that the following terms were not unconstitutionally vague: "repeatedly,"[30] "pattern of conduct,"[31] "series,"[32] "closely related in time,"[33] "follows,"[34] "lingering outside,"[35] "harassing,"[36] "intimidating,"[37] "maliciously,"[38] "emotional distress"[39] "reasonable apprehension,"[40] "in connection with,"[41] and "contacting another person without the consent of the other person."[42]

Courts have also determined that terms such as "without lawful authority"[43] and "serves no legitimate purpose"[44] were not unconstitutionally vague. The Oregon Court of Appeals, however, did invalidate that state's stalking law on the grounds that the term "legitimate purpose" was unconstitutionally vague.[45] The court found that the statute did not tell a person of ordinary intelligence what was meant by the term "legitimate purpose"; therefore, the statute gave no warning as to what conduct must be avoided. The Oregon legislature later revised the statute to remove the phrase.

The Supreme Court of Kansas found that state's stalking statute unconstitutionally vague because it used the terms "alarms," "annoys," and "harasses" without defining them or using an objective standard to measure the prohibited conduct. "In the absence of an objective standard, the terms... subject the defendant to the particular sensibilities of the individual.... [C]onduct that annoys or alarms one person may not annoy or alarm another.... [A] victim may be of such a state of mind that conduct that would never annoy, alarm, or harass a reasonable person would seriously annoy, alarm, or harass this victim."[46] Kansas has since amended its statute, and the amended statute has been ruled constitutional. The court specifically found that the revised law included an objective standard, that is, the standard of a "reasonable person," and defined the key terms "course of conduct," "harassment," and "credible threat."[47]

Similarly, the Texas Court of Criminal Appeals found that state's original antistalking law unconstitutionally vague. Although there were several factors in this ruling, the expansive nature of the prohibited conduct was a key point in the decision. That conduct included actions that would "annoy" or "alarm" the victim. The court observed that "the First Amendment does not permit the outlawing of conduct merely because the speaker intends to annoy the listener and a reasonable person would in fact be annoyed."[48] The Texas Legislature subsequently revised the law to correct the problem.

Massachusetts's stalking law was also declared unconstitutionally vague because it provided that a person could be guilty of stalking if that person repeatedly harassed the victim. "Harass" was defined as a pattern of conduct or series of acts. Thus, the court found that the statutory requirement of repeated harassment meant that a person "must engage repeatedly (certainly at least twice) in a pattern of conduct or series of acts over a period of time.... One pattern or one series would not be enough." The court noted that the legislature presumably intended a single pattern of conduct or a single series of acts to constitute the crime but did not state this with sufficient clarity to meet the constitutional challenges.[49] The Commonwealth has since revised its stalking law to address the issue.

Other courts have disagreed with the reasoning of the Massachusetts decision. The Rhode Island Supreme Court declared that the Massachusetts court's "metaplasmic[†] approach... has attracted little, if any following." The court found that the statute, as drafted, met the constitutional test by giving adequate warning to potential offenders of the prohibited conduct. "It indeed defies logic to conclude that a defendant would have to commit more than one series of harassing acts in order to be found guilty of stalking."[50] The D.C. Court of Appeals reached a similar conclusion.[51]

Attempted Stalking

At least one state has grappled with the question of whether a person can be charged with attempted stalking. In Georgia, a defendant made harassing and bizarre phone calls to his ex-wife. The defendant was arrested and released under the condition that he was to have "[a]bsolutely no contact with the victim or the victim's family." A few weeks later, he called his ex-wife's office, claiming to be the district attorney, and asked personal questions about his ex-wife. He later attempted to call his ex-wife at the office, but she was out of town. He told a coworker to tell his ex-wife that "when she gets home she can't get in." The Georgia Supreme Court found that it was not absurd or impractical to criminalize attempting to stalk, which under the terms of the statute meant attempting to follow, place under surveillance, or contact another, when it was done with the requisite specific intent to cause emotional distress by inducing a reasonable fear of death or bodily injury. A concurring Justice noted that to hold otherwise would be to permit a stalker "to intimidate and harass his intended victim simply by communicating his threats to third parties who (the stalker knows and expects) will inform the victim."[52]

Current Issues

Cyberstalking

As the use of computers for communication has increased, so have cases of "cyberstalking." A 1999 report by the U.S. Attorney General called cyberstalking a growing problem. After noting the number of people with access to the Internet, the report states, "Assuming the proportion of cyberstalking victims is even a fraction of the proportion of persons who have been the victims of offline stalking within the preceding 2 months, there may be potentially tens or even hundreds of thousands of victims of recent cyberstalking incidents in the United States."[53]

Many stalking laws are broad enough to encompass stalking via e-mail or other electronic communication, defining the prohibited conduct in terms of "communication," "harassment," or "threats" without specifying the means of such behavior. Others have specifically defined stalking via e-mail within their stalking or harassment statute.

For example, California recently amended its stalking law to expressly include stalking via the Internet.[54] Under California law, a person commits stalking if he or she "willfully, maliciously, and repeatedly follows or harasses another person and... makes a credible threat with the intent to place that person in reasonable fear for his or her safety, or the safety of his or her immediate family." The term "credible threat" includes "that performed through the use of an electronic communication device, or a threat implied by a pattern of conduct or a combination of verbal, written, or electronically communicated statements." "Electronic communication device" includes "telephones, cellular phones, computers, video recorders, fax machines, or pagers."

Bail Restrictions

States are grappling with the matter of pretrial release of people charged with stalking. Because stalkers often remain dangerous after being charged with a crime, states have sought means to protect victims at the pretrial stage. Many states permit the court to enter a no-contact order as a condition of pretrial release.[55] A few give the court discretion to deny bail. For example, Illinois allows a court to deny bail when the court, after a hearing, "determines that the release of the defendant would pose a real and present threat to the physical safety of the alleged victim of the offense and denial of… bail… is necessary to prevent fulfillment of the threat upon which the charge is based.[56]

Lifetime Protection Orders

Stalkers frequently remain obsessed with their targets for years. Requiring victims to file for a new protective order every few years can be unduly burdensome. Because victims may have attempted to conceal their whereabouts from the stalkers, reapplying for a protective order may inadvertently reconnect stalkers with their victims. In New Jersey, this problem has been alleviated. A conviction for stalking in that state operates as an application for a permanent restraining order. The order may be dissolved on application of the victim.[57]

Conclusion

Stalking is a serious and pervasive criminal offense. The Nation is increasingly aware of the danger stalkers pose and of the need for effective intervention. Research into the nature and extent of stalking is ongoing. As more is learned about effective responses to stalkers, laws will continue to evolve. Victim advocates and victim service providers must work closely with law enforcement and prosecutors to identify what additional legislative changes are needed to better protect stalking victims.

---

†*Metaplasmia:* alteration of regular verbal, grammatical, or rhetorical structure usually by transposition of the letters or syllables of a word or of the words in a sentence. *Metaplasmic,* adj. (*Webster's Third New International Dictionary,* 1971).

Notes

1. Tjaden, Patricia, and Nancy Thoennes (1998). *Stalking in America: Findings From the National Violence Against Women Survey.* Washington, DC: U.S. Department of Justice, National Institute of Justice and the Centers for Disease Control and Prevention.
2. This bulletin focuses on state stalking laws. For the federal interstate stalking law, see 18 U.S.C. § 2261A (2001).
3. National Criminal Justice Association (1993). *Project To Develop a Model Anti-Stalking Code for States.* Washington, DC: National Institute of Justice. To receive a copy of the final report of this project, contact the National Criminal Justice Reference Service at 1–800–851–3420 and ask for publication NCJ 144477.
4. For more indepth information on the problem of stalking, see *Stalking and Domestic Violence: The Third Annual Report to Congress Under the Violence Against Women Act*, Washington, DC: U.S. Department of Justice, Violence Against Women Grants Office, 1998.
5. MICH. STAT. ANN. § 28.643(8) (2000).
6. 720 ILL. COMP. STAT. 5/12-7.3 (2001).
7. MD. ANN. CODE art. 27, § 124 (2001).
8. HAW. REV. STAT. §§ 711-1106.4, -1106.5 (2000).
9. CONN. GEN. STAT. §§ 53a-181d, -181e (2001).
10. WIS. STAT. ANN. § 940.32 (2000).
11. ARK. STAT. ANN. § 5-71-229 (2001); MASS. GEN. LAWS ANN. ch. 265, § 43 (2001).
12. N.J. STAT. ANN. § 2C:12-10 (2001).
13. For example, CAL. PENAL CODE § 646.9 (Deering 2001); KAN. STAT. ANN. § 21-3438 (2000).
14. KAN. STAT. ANN. § 21-3438 (2000). See also KY. REV. STAT. § 508.150 (2001); ME. REV. STAT. ANN. tit. 17-A, § 210-A (2000); MISS. CODE ANN. § 97-3-107 (2001).
15. N.H. REV. STAT. ANN. § 633:3-a (2000).
16. N.M. STAT. ANN. § 30-3A-3 (2000).
17. WASH. REV. CODE ANN. § 9A.46.110 (2001).
18. The specific terms are subject to the interpretation of each state's courts.
19. *State v. Neuzil*, 589 N.W.2d 708 (Iowa 1999); *State v. Cardell*, 318 N.J. Super. 175, 723 A.2d 111 (N.J. Super. Ct. App. Div. 1999).
20. For example, ARK. STAT. ANN. § 5-71-229 (2001).
21. *People v. Bailey*, 167 Ill. 2d 210, 657 N.E.2d 953 (1995).
22. For example, ALA. CODE § 13A-6-91 (2001); N.M. STAT. ANN. § 30-3A-3.1 (2000).
23. For example, ARK. STAT. ANN. § 5-71-229 (2001) (stalking in the first degree).
24. For example, VT. STAT. ANN. § 13-1063 (2001).
25. For example, FLA. STAT. § 784.048 (2000).
26. *Commonwealth v. Schierscher*, 447 Pa. Super. 61, 668 A.2d 164 (Pa. Super. Ct. 1995).
27. *Connally v. General Construction Co.*, 269 U.S. 385, 391, 46 S. Ct. 126, 70 L. Ed. 322 (1926).
28. *State v. Cardell*, 318 N.J. Super. 175, 723 A.2d 111 (N.J. Super. Ct. App. Div. 1999).
29. *People v. White*, 212 Mich. App. 298, 536 N.W.2d 876 (Mich. Ct. App. 1995).
30. *State v. Martel*, 273 Mont. 143, 902 P.2d 14 (1995); *State v. McGill*, 536 N.W.2d 89 (S.D. 1995).
31. *State v. Dario*, 106 Ohio App. 3d 232, 665 N.E.2d 759 (Ohio Ct. App. 1995).
32. *State v. Randall*, 669 So.2d 223 (Ala. Crim. App. 1995).
33. *State v. Dario*, 106 Ohio App. 3d 232, 665 N.E.2d 759 (Ohio Ct. App. 1995).
34. *State v. Lee*, 135 Wash. 2d 369, 957 P.2d 741 (1998); *People v. Zamudio*, 293 Ill. App. 3d 976, 689 N.E.2d 254 (Ill. App. Ct. 1997).
35. *State v. Schleirermacher*, 924 S.W.2d 269 (Mo. 1996).
36. *State v. Martel*, 273 Mont. 143, 902 P.2d 14 (1995).
37. Id.
38. *State v. McGill*, 536 N.W.2d 89 (S.D. 1995).
39. *Woolfolk v. Commonwealth*, 18 Va. App. 840, 447 S.E.2d 530 (Va. Ct. App. 1994); *Salt Lake City v. Lopez*, 313 Utah Adv. Rep. 26, 935 P.2d 1259 (Utah Ct. App. 1997).
40. *State v. Martel*, 273 Mont. 143, 902 P.2d 14 (1995).
41. *People v. Baer*, 973 P.2d 1225 (Colo. 1999).

42. *Johnson v. State*, 264 Ga. 590, 449 S.E.2d 94 (1994).

43. *State v. Lee*, 135 Wash. 2d 369, 957 P.2d 741 (1998).

44. *People v. Tran*, 47 Cal. App. 4th 253, 54 Cal. Rptr. 2d 650 (Cal. Ct. App. 1996).

45. *State v. Norris-Romine*, 134 Or. App. 204, 894 P.2d 1221 (Or. Ct. App. 1995).

46. *State v. Bryan*, 259 Kan. 143, 910 P.2d 212 (1996).

47. *State v. Rucker*, 1999 Kan. LEXIS 410 (1999).

48. *Long v. State*, 931 S.W.2d 285, 290 n. 4 (Tex. Crim. App. 1996).

49. *Commonwealth v. Kwiatkowski*, 418 Mass. 543, 637 N.E.2d 854 (1994).

50. *State v. Fonseca*, 670 A.2d 1237 (R.I. 1996).

51. *United States v. Smith*, 685 A.2d 380 (App. D.C. 1996).

52. *State v. Rooks*, 266 Ga. 528, 468 S.E.2d 354 (1996).

53. *Cyberstalking: A New Challenge for Law Enforcement and Industry*, A Report From the Attorney General to the Vice President, August 1999, p. 6.

54. CAL. PENAL CODE § 646.9 (Deering 2001).

55. For example, ALASKA STAT. § 12.30.025 (2001); MD. ANN. CODE art. 27, § 616 1/2 (2001).

56. 725 ILL. COMP. STAT. 5/110-4, -6.3 (2001).

57. N.J. STAT. § 2C:12-10.1 (2001).

From *OVC Legal Series*, January 2002. © 2002 by U.S. Department of Justice.

UNIT 3

The Police

Unit Selections

15. **The Changing Roles and Strategies of the Police in Time of Terror**, Melchor C. deGuzman
16. **Racial Profiling and Its Apologists**, Tim Wise
17. **Early Warning Systems: Responding to the Problem Police Officer**, Samuel Walker, Geoffrey P. Alpert, and Dennis J. Kenney
18. **Crime Story: The Digital Age**, John D. Cohen, Adam Gelb, and Robert Wasserman
19. **Ethics and Criminal Justice: Some Observations on Police Misconduct**, Bryan Byers
20. **Spirituality and Police Suicide: A Double-Edged Sword**, Joseph J. D'Angelo

Key Points to Consider

- Can racial profiling ever be a legitimate police tactic? Explain.

- Is police work the cause of suicides among officers, or does the availability of a gun just make it easier?

- Do local police departments have a role to play in combating international terrorism? Why or why not?

 **Links: www.dushkin.com/online/**
These sites are annotated in the World Wide Web pages.

ACLU Criminal Justice Home Page
http://www.aclu.org/CriminalJustice/CriminalJusticeMain.cfm

Introduction to American Justice
http://www.uaa.alaska.edu/just/just110/home.html

Law Enforcement Guide to the World Wide Web
http://leolinks.com/

National Institute of Justice (NIJ)
http://www.ojp.usdoj.gov/nij/lawedocs.htm

Violent Criminal Apprehension Program (VICAP)
http://www.state.ma.us/msp/unitpage/vicap.htm

Police officers are the guardians of our freedoms under the Constitution and the laws of the land, and as such they have an awesome task. They are asked to prevent crime, protect citizens, arrest wrongdoers, preserve the peace, aid the sick, control juveniles, control traffic, and provide emergency services on a moment's notice. They are also asked to be ready to lay down their lives, if necessary.

In recent years the job of the police officer has become even more complex and dangerous. Illegal drug use and trafficking are still major problems, racial tensions are explosive, and terrorism is now an alarming reality. As our population grows more numerous and diverse, the role of the police in America becomes ever more challenging, requiring skills that can only be obtained through greater training and professionalism.

The lead article in the section, "The Changing Roles and Strategies of the Police in Time of Terror," is a speech that ar-

gues that crime analysis and police strategies need to be changed in the wake of the recent terrorist attacks.

The typical offender in violent crime categories is white, as pointed out by Tim Wise in "Racial Profiling and Its Apologists." A study dealing with problem police officers is discussed in "Early Warning Systems: Responding to the Problem Police Officer" and shows that an early-warning system might have a dramatic effect on citizen complaints. A discussion of the use of new technology in community policing follows in "Crime Story: The Digital Age." The next article, "Ethics and Criminal Justice: Some Observations on Police Misconduct," discusses police misconduct in terms of ethical violations. This section concludes with a treatment of the tragedy of police suicide in "Spirituality and Police Suicide: A Double-Edged Sword."

THE CHANGING ROLES AND STRATEGIES OF THE POLICE IN TIME OF TERROR

Speech delivered at a panel discussion during the IUSB-SPEA Criminal Justice Symposium on the Changing Role of Criminal Justice Agencies in a Time of Terrorism (February 15, 2002, Northside Room 113)

by MELCHOR C. DE GUZMAN

Indiana University South Bend (IUSB)

Introduction

The disorders experienced by America in the 1960s and the 1970s pale in comparison to the *virtual* disorder that its citizens are experiencing today due to the terrorist attacks last September 11, 2001. The attacks have clearly brought to the limelight not only the false sense of security of the United States but also its vulnerability to the violence of terrorism on its domestic soil. The tragic events have undoubtedly brought to fore the need to re-examine and revise our strategic thinking and paradigms about the way domestic security is maintained.

In response, President Bush did not only embark on a military assault against terrorism but he also has called for the fortification of the United States in the domestic front. In his recent State of the Union Address, President Bush outlined four major areas where homeland security needs improvement, namely, 1) biological and chemical attacks, 2) intelligence gathering and law enforcement coordination, 3) airport and border security, and 4) emergency response.

In light of these developments and policy pronouncements, public policing has to make the necessary adjustments to contribute to the immediate security requirements of the nation. I underscore the word "immediate" to emphasize that the focus of this essay will merely involve primary steps that the police will have to undertake in response to the urgent call against domestic terrorism. In the end, when the dusts have clearly set-

tled, there should be a more elaborate change in the way the police maintain public safety in time of terror, one that is effective and least intrusive on basic individual rights.

Thus, my analyses and recommendations will revolve around current police practices and how these have to be adjusted in the fight against terror. I would argue that the police can still perform traditional strategies but must do so with a different spin. These are the spin-offs that constitute the changes for public policing to undertake.

The Traditional Strategies and Roles of the Police

For the past decade, the United States has been experiencing the evolution of the police primarily from being law enforcement-oriented agencies of the 1960s and 1970s (Goldstein, 1977; Skolnick & Bayley, 1986) to become the so-called community-oriented agencies of the 1990s. By traditional practices, however, I intend to include everything that has been employed up until the events of September 11, 2001. Therefore, even the practices introduced in the community-policing era will be referred to as traditional. The following are the enumeration and brief descriptions of how these practices are being undertaken.

Crime analysis. For a long time, crime analysis by most police departments has always concentrated on specific crimes involving specific suspects

on a specific geographical space (Bayley, 1994). This means that they have always looked at a "spot" and the "dirty" characters within that spot, analyzed the intervention strategies needed, and cleaned the spot.

Previous to the introduction of community policing, the police were primarily incident driven and they lacked the analytical framework to understand crime and its underlying conditions or causes (Goldstein, 1979). The advent of problem-oriented policing has somehow conditioned police officers to broaden their perspective in responding to crime incidents (Kelling & Moore, 1988; Trojanowitz & Bucqueroux, 1990). The most recent and elaborate application of the problem-oriented policing model is that of the CompStat experiment in New York City. However, I suspect that until now most police departments are still grappling with the concepts of problem-oriented policing and its accompanying paradigm called SARA (i.e., Scanning, Analyzing, Response and Assessment). I would say that with respect to normal crimes, the process seemed to have worked in New York City (see McDonald, 2000). As regards terrorism, I would let the events of September 11 speak for themselves. Thus, adjustments have to be undertaken by the police in the area of crime analysis. I will discuss these analytical adjustments in the next section.

Police strategies. The police have always embraced three essential roles as agents of social control. They enforce laws, maintain order, and deliver service (Bayley, 1994; Wilson, 1968). They have also consistently applied three broad strategies in the performance of their roles as law enforcers, namely, 1) patrol, 2) investigation, and 3) traffic (Moore, Trojanowitz, & Kelling, 1988). Since the inception of formal policing dating all the way from the establishment of the London Metropolitan Police, these strategic practices, except for traffic, have been primary tools used by the police in plying their trade (Langworthy & Travis, 1999). Over the years, variations of these tactics have emerged.

Let us first examine patrol. Patrol has been the primary tool of the police (Sherman, 1991). A close observer of the police will note the variety of patrol tactics that have been used by the police over the years (Langworthy & Travis, 1999). In fact, some patrol strategies come and go depending on the current advocacy and the perceived need of the time (e.g., foot patrol, horse patrol, etc.). Despite the multiplicity of patrol tactics (e.g., suspect-oriented, directed, mobilized, bike, foot, horse, random, one person, two person, etc.), the focus has always been constant for all these varieties in patrol strategies—to watch suspects and their places of trade (Bayley, 1985; Petersilia, 1987; Reiss, 1971; Sherman, 1991; Sherman & Rogan, 1995; Sherman & Weisburd, 1995).

Such orientation of patrol has to be redefined in the face of terror. Suspect-oriented or disorder-oriented patrol is probably an effective crime prevention strategy (Sherman, 1991) but may be not an effective anti-terrorist strategy. As to what alternative patrol strategy can be made and how it can be done shall be the topic for the next section.

Investigation is also being carried out in a suspect and incident-oriented fashion (Bayley, 1994; Eck, 1983; Kuykendall, 1982; Sherman, 1986). Like patrol, investigation keeps on redesigning itself from the least scientific type of investigation to the most scientific type (Greenwood & Petersilia, 1975). Similar to patrol, it has maintained one focus-specific crime solution and the apprehension of a particular suspect (Ericson, 1982). Furthermore, despite the onslaught of community policing among

many police departments, the investigation unit remains virtually untouched and unintegrated to the whole concept.

I would say that in the face of terror, investigation should redirect its functional focus and its organizational relationships with the rest of the units in the department. Investigation under the current structure remains highly individualized and disjointed from the rest of the force. Investigation units themselves are also highly fragmented. These work conditions as well as the culture in investigation hamper the effectiveness of the police in solving cases (Crank, 1999), especially cases involving terrorism.

Traffic. Traffic enforcement has also stagnated for several decades. Right now, traffic enforcement among and within police departments are highly discretionary (Bayley, 1994). Likewise, traffic enforcement appears to be completely independent and disjointed from all the other activities of police work. The latter statement means that the activities, events, and analyses involving traffic enforcement have not been smoothly interwoven with the other units of the agency. The current philosophies and practices about traffic enforcement should be redirected to respond to the demands of the war against terror.

Philosophy. The intellectual, emotional, and cultural dimensions of police work also need re-examination and redirection. The redirection of these beliefs and attitudes on how policing should be done usually translates into concrete actions (Crank, 1999). The significant influence of conviction among police officers has been shown particularly evident where sometimes police officers subvert rules and regulations (Reuss-Ianni, 1983) or set aside the education and training in favor of deeply entrenched belief on how their work should be done (Van Maanen, 1973). The current philosophy pervading in most police departments nowadays involves the community-policing model. Basic tenets of this philosophy include 1) the winning of the hearts and minds of the public, 2) strategic partnership with the community, and 3) neighborhood based policing. The incongruence of these tenets in fighting terrorism will be discussed in the next section.

Police response. The last topic that should be brought to focus is police response to emergencies, specifically terrorist emergencies. The police are trained to provide immediate responses. However, they do so in a sporadic and sometimes uncoordinated fashion (Crank, 1999). This means that almost everyone who is not tied up with another incident can rush to the incident once a call has been made. In a terrorist attack, a mad dash to the scene not only poses danger for the police officers but also to others caught in the confusing state.

In a recent survey by the National Institute of Justice (Hollis, Tillery, & Schaenman, 1999), most state and local police agencies surveyed have stated that they need to improve their means of categorizing and detecting explosives, nuclear, biological, and chemical threats. Furthermore, they also need to improve their inter-agency communications. These competencies are crucial in the proper response to terrorist incidents (McVey, 1997). Otherwise, a mad dash to the scene will have catastrophic results. The apparent deficiency of police officers involving these competencies impinges on police administrators to develop better response protocols in the event of terrorist attack. There should be a calibrated response procedure in these types of incidents and the police should be trained on this aspect.

The events of September 11, 2001, clearly demonstrated that current police philosophies, roles, and tactics are at best inadequate to prevent and respond to a terrorist attack. It is in this face of terror and in the manifest shortcoming of local law enforcement that I suggest that the police will have to redefine their tactics in using these strategies. In fact, the events of September 11 are by themselves sufficient motivation or provocation for police departments to re-examine themselves and adjust their tactics to the demands of the time.

The Roles and Strategies of the Police in Time of Terror

After discussing the traditional roles, practices, and philosophies of the police and how they need to be readjusted in the war against terrorism, let us look at the specific changes that police officers must undertake in order to square off with the current challenges.

Event analysis. I have pointed out that suspect and crime oriented crime analysis may not be enough strategic crime analysis framework for this time of terror. I believe that police should instead undertake "event analysis." By event analysis, I mean the inclusion of not only criminal incidents or even disorder incidents but also social events in analyzing the possibility of these events being connected to terrorist activities. McVey (1997) suggested that the police must be aware of gatherings in their communities as well as pay attention to the personalities, issues, and activities during those gatherings. Likewise, the police should be conscious about important celebrations, ideologies, and anniversaries of known activists, terrorists, or groups. Celebrations among terrorists are usually punctuated with a violent attack. In this time of terror, therefore, there should be a thorough analysis of the environment and events where the police operate and they should try to determine whether these incidents are connected to a possible terrorist act. Brown (1975) had earlier issued a recommendation toward changing the focus of the police. Unfortunately, the police are known to resist changes (Fogelson, 1991; Guyot, 1979).

As far as analytical requirement is concerned, the police need not reinvent the wheel in developing new approaches towards the analysis of events. The era of community policing has prepared the local police for the task. One of the central paradigms in community policing is the SARA model of problem-solving (Eck & Spelman, 1987). Through this analytical framework, police have been trained to look for the underlying causes of crime. Such analytical framework will be most appropriate and adequate for analyzing events in the community and their possible relationships to planned terrorist activities.

The police also can utilize the five-step event analysis model developed when the Integrated Criminal Apprehension Program was initiated (Bieck, 1989). This latter program is a research-oriented approach geared towards developing specific patterns of event from incidents or crime activity.

Therefore, the efforts toward event analysis should not be a daunting task for the police. For the last decade, they have been oriented about the appropriate technologies. The police must, however, sincerely apply the analytical models and they must be fully convinced of their utility in fighting terrorism. Otherwise, the police will fall back on their traditional knowledge and technologies.

Target-oriented patrolling. Several experts on terrorism have suggested that local law enforcement officers should assess likely targets in their jurisdiction (Bolz, et al., 1990; Levitt, 1988; McVey, 1997; Netanyahu, 1986). Thus, I would suggest that the police should not be only watching over obvious places of disorder and danger but be on alert where disruption of order in safe places might occur.

I believe that the focus of patrol should be redirected at this time of terror. As I said previously, our patrol tactics have been primarily focused on dangerous people and dangerous places. Instead of watching dangerous places and people, patrol should watch over safe places and significant or symbolic people.

Terrorists are bound to create disorder. Terrorists have shown patterns in their attacks where symbols of strength, stability, and peace of a nation are their favorite targets (Holmes & Burk, 2002; Levitt, 1988; McVey, 1997; Netanyahu, 1986). Cities in America abound with symbols, personalities, and artifacts that represent its sense of order. Thus, the World Trade Center and the Pentagon are rational targets for terrorists. Places like these are likely targets of terror. Police patrol then should direct their focus on these things. Instead of being suspect-oriented or disorder-oriented, they should now be "target-oriented." They should intensify their patrol efforts in guarding safe places.

In this endeavor, the police should be able to "deconstruct the obvious" (Crank, 1999; Manning, 1979) and are trained to sense danger (Skolnick, 1966; Westley, 1970). This means that they should be able to see the vulnerability of people and places and how people and places can become targets of terrorism. It is this ability to sense danger that they should employ on attacks against favorite terrorist targets. For example, we have always assumed that the airport is safe so we never took time to really evaluate the threats against the violation of its safety. The results of this failure to deconstruct the obvious were the attacks on September 11.

One would argue that this thought lacks common sense. on the contrary, this line of thinking makes a lot of sense in the war against terror. Terrorists will not target disorderly places because they will just be branded as ordinary criminals. Terrorists want drama in their actions. They get involved in shock criminality. They believe in sensationalizing their crime to dramatize their cause and attract more people to their cause (Jenkins, 1990; Sick, 1990). What then would be more dramatic than wreaking havoc in a seemingly safe and fortified place? What would be more sensational than inflicting harm on prominent personalities?

Some may argue that this patrol tactic will take away police efforts in high crime places, thereby, exposing citizens of those areas in greater danger. I will argue that if the patrol is well allocated, current services to these formerly watched places would not be severely reduced. Allow me to illustrate this point.

In a study conducted by Greene and Klockars (1991) about patrol activities in Wilmington, Delaware, they noted that about thirty-three percent of the officer's time on patrol is considered "clear time." It is this time that officers can use to conduct their own, self-directed patrol activity. It is during this time when "target-oriented" patrol may be conducted. It is clear that this extra-time of police officers can be directed to patrol or survey the potential "targets" and try to sense if there is any danger to these targets. Police will have to use their oft-quoted "sixth sense" in seeing danger and thereby note if there is anything unusual about the vicinity of the identified potential terrorist targets. Target-oriented patrol should be a strategy that the police can initiate in the ply of their trade.

Proactive investigation. Police investigation has been by nature reactive (Langworthy & Travis, 1999). This means that investigators have been trained and socialized primarily as responders to criminal events. In this age of terror, police investigation should be proactive. Proactive investigation requires the analysis of every criminal case and the conscious effort to try to create assumptions about the connections of the case to terrorist activities. In other words, evidence of a crime should not only be gathered to make a connection to a certain suspect but that there must be some effort to try to see if the evidence has some connection to a possible terrorist activity. This may be especially true if there is evidence that seems not to fit with the motive and the nature of the crime committed. Investigating officers should try to establish if there are other motives that may be attached to the offense under investigation (McVey, 1997). For example, a reported incident of someone's wife being poisoned may have occurred due to a mishandling of chemicals that the couple was preparing for a terrorist attack. The most frequent treatment of such incidents is that it is an ordinary crime against a partner. Some investigators will simply even treat this as an ordinary accident. The tendency for detectives to dismiss or close cases in a cavalier fashion should be changed. Although, the screening out of cases may be administratively efficient (Petersilia, 1987; Williams & Sumrall, 1982), the practice may not be appropriate for terrorist investigation where each event, though mundane, may be related to a terrorist plan. Again, the police will have to employ their honed talent for deconstructing the obvious. They should constantly ask the question, "Is this latter incident a random act of violence or a violence that may be related to terrorism" (McVey, 1997)?

Intensified traffic enforcement. I believe that police officers can make a big dent in the war against terror by simply intensifying their role as traffic enforcers. The police should always watch out for the abnormalities in traffic behavior and vehicles. Expired license plates, heavily tinted vehicles, odd drivers, and smoke or liquid coming out from trunks of vehicles are all flag signs for terror. Terrorists move and they move their wares with them. A no-nonsense implementation of all traffic laws will surely

make the movements of terrorists very limited. Police departments should seriously consider implementing more stringent, if not "zero-tolerance," policies regarding traffic violations.

One of the potential stumbling blocks of vigorous patrol and traffic enforcement strategy involves the sidestepping of the demands of the exclusionary rule. However, recent developments in jurisprudence seem to favor the unleashing of the police with respect to traffic stops. In several recent decisions, the "articulable suspicion" requirements were relaxed. In *Mexico State v. Cohen* (1985), characteristics such as appearing nervous, driving a rental car with a Florida license plate, driving cross-country, carrying a small amount of luggage, and driving a rental car paid with cash were considered by the court to be enough basis for conducting a search. In *New Mexico v. Mann* (1985), characteristics of driving too slow and carrying items in the backseat instead of the compartment were accepted by the court as valid reasons for police intervention and search (Crank, 1999). In *Whren v. United States* (1996), the court allowed the police to use traffic stops—whether minor or real, real or alleged—as a reason to stop and investigate a vehicle and its occupants. Furthermore, the court in its decision in *Maryland v. Wilson* (1997) gave the police the power to order passengers to get out of the car, whether or not there is any basis to suspect they are dangerous. Thus, the previously unreliable "hunch" or "sixth sense" by the police is slowly being acknowledged by the courts as legitimate grounds for police intervention. These decisions will definitely embolden the police in their traffic enforcement. However, these decisions are being assailed as violating Fourth Amendment Rights. In spite of this, given the social climate and the emerging trend in jurisprudence, I do not expect the courts to be so keen on strictly implementing the requirements of the exclusionary rule as originally outlined in *Mapp v. Ohio* (1961).

Coordinated intelligence work. Perhaps the greatest challenge for police officers is the conduct of intelligence. State and local police units identified intelligence capability as their primary defi-

ciency in the efforts to combat terrorism (Hollis, et al., 1999). Lack of coordination further contributes to the problem in intelligence gathering among local law enforcement. It has been noted that various police units are secretive of their information. Officers do not share their information with one another (Manning, 1989). There is also a culture of "territoriality" and possessiveness of officers about their cases and information (Crank, 1999). This dysfunctional behavior hampers coordination and consequently prevents effective analysis of information.

In gathering information against terrorism, every incident should be analyzed in relation with each other. Robberies, murders, accidents, and other crimes should be analyzed as a whole to see if emerging patterns of terrorist threats exist (McVey, 1997). This team effort has been done with patrol for example in New York City where they try to analyze crime in a collaborative and coordinated fashion. The New York City Police used a technology called CompStat (McDonald, 2002). The experience of New York with CompStat has been touted as a success. However, such technology or paradigm practiced under CompStat has not been fully explored in the area of investigation much less in intelligence gathering and analyses. It is not even certain whether investigation and intelligence units will appreciate the collaborative technique used in these emerging technologies. We have to realize that sometimes intelligence work is better handled by the least number of people. However, we have seen the intelligence breakdown with September 11 and we begin to question the lack of coordination along this line.

The other challenge is how to share intelligence across jurisdictions and across agencies. Many police executives who took my classes on leadership in the National Police College of the Philippines manifestly opposed the idea of intelligence sharing. Their opposition only died down when I brought out the fact that they share intelligence across the world. Although, I still believe in the maxim that intelligence should be sparingly shared and only to people who *need* to know and not generously hand it out to people who would find such information *nice* to know, I think that agencies should build a mechanism for sharing this information without necessarily compromising intelligence operations.

Philosophical readjustments. One of the significant revolutions that happened to policing is the emergence of community policing. Starting with the classical work of Herman Goldstein (1979) and supported by the empirical evaluation of community policing in six American cities by Skolnick and Bayley (1986), community policing has deeply entrenched its roots in American police psyche. Community policing became a centerpiece of President Clinton's initiative on law enforcement during his two terms where lots of resources were poured into community policing for the recruitment and training of officers, reorganization of the departments, and formation of community organizations. Numerous police departments have transformed themselves and have embraced for themselves the tenets, philosophy, and strategic paradigms of community policing.

In the context of war against terror, some tenets of community policing appear to be inconsistent with the implementation of these new police roles. The events of September 11 threaten the utility as well as the continued existence of some community policing ideals on several grounds. First, community policing involves winning the hearts and minds of the community. Such orientation and philosophical ideal will not be effective against terror. An expert in terrorisms states:

In its simplest sense, terrorism is the use of fear to force an individual or a community to act in a way contrary to reason. It is the opposite of debate, argument, or persuasion. You cannot argue with a terrorist. He is not interested in dialogue or discussion. *His mind is closed.* (Italics mine) He feels superior in every way to his victims. This feeling of superiority comes not only from feeling of an immense power to destroy or inflict great injury on others; it also springs from an imagined special

access to the truth, to God's will, or to the future (David, 2002:1).

It is, therefore, futile for the police to continue the pursuit of winning the hearts and minds as far as the terrorist is concerned. Likewise, the passage above also means that terrorists cannot be deterred. Terrorists are never deterred by anything and the only way to deal with them is incapacitation through the use of force (Holmes & Burke, 2002; Netanyahu, 1986). Thus, the police should be made aware that their patrols are being made not to deter but to detect and prevent the consummation of a violent terrorist act. Should we abandon community policing altogether? Probably not! I would, however, suggest the re-examination of the prescription that community policing should be a department-wide philosophy. Such a tenet goes against the grain of the war on terror.

Second, community-policing's main assumptions are that the community will be cooperative and that police-community relations should be founded on trust. The war and strategies against terror should negate such assumptions because any counter-terrorist measures threaten the existence of trust between the police and the public. The methods of counter-terrorism are stumbling blocks to the development of trust. Police are not supposed to trust anybody. Terrorists are constantly employing deceit and the police investing their trust on a "hidden" terrorist will have disastrous effects on their ability to detect and apprehend potential offenders.

Third, community policing is a partnership where both parties will have to reach a consensus about strategies of crime prevention and police strategies. In this partnership, the police will have to reveal their strategies to the community. If the police will decide to hold back, the community will sense this and thus trust will be breached and such partnerships will inevitably wither away.

Fourth, parochial policing is promoted in community policing but the war on terror necessitates collaborative policing. The level of collaboration should not only be within the department but includes other local departments, federal or state agencies. In the war on

terror, the planning space may be remotely located from the target phase. Thus, efforts to make communications and collaborations among and between police departments should be a constant undertaking.

Developing technical competencies and appropriate police responses. Although the repertoire of terrorism is very limited (Holmes & Burke, 2002; Jenkins, 1990), the technological turn that terrorism has taken has made our police inadequately prepared to prevent attacks as well as to effectively respond. Terrorist methods have become highly sophisticated in the technological age and its detection becomes more difficult (Holmes & Burke, 2002). Police officers must be quickly trained and educated in this new brand of terror. As long as they remain ignorant of these devices, they will be incompetent in discovering terrorist paraphernalia and employing a rational response in the event of an attack (Bolz, Dudonis, & Schulz, 1990). In a survey of local police and state agencies about their needs to combat terrorism, the respondents have listed the agenda of the Bush administration as their greatest weakness (Hollis et al., 1999). Principally, police officers severely lack competence detecting, disabling, and containing explosive devices. They are also deficient in defending against weapons of mass destruction as well as in command, control, and communications (see Hollis et al., 1999:4). These technical deficiencies were clearly visible in the events of September 11 as well as in other domestic terrorist attacks in the United States.

Unless these technical competencies are addressed, police response to terrorist attacks should be limited to crowd control and subject apprehension. They should not jump into terrorist incidents with inadequate knowledge about the situation. Terrorist attacks are not random acts of violence. They are calculated and premeditated. Police responses should also be with caution, premeditation, and calculation.

Conclusion

The war on terror has challenged not only the way of life of the American public but also the way the police carry out their business. Police will always be engaged in three fundamental strategies of patrol, investigation, and traffic. The greater challenge for the police should be on how to fine-tune these strategies. The recommendations appear to be simple. However, the reform needed requires not only a simple realignment of police strategies and resources but also a realignment of the strategic frame of mind of the police. For a start, the police should start chanting some mantras in order for them to be constantly reminded of how to handle the current problem involving terrorism.

The first mantra for the police should be *"Coordination, Coordination, Coordination."* The Bush administration has immediately realized the critical value of coordination after the attacks on September 11. In the case of local law enforcement, this coordination should be achieved not only within the police department but also with its outside environment. Several authors have described the police as being "loosely coupled" both within its units and with its environment (Hagan, 1988: Langworthy, 1986; Meyer & Brown, 1977; Murphy, 1986). It is time to re-examine what the police do and how these can be integrated with the various activities they do and ultimately to integrate them with the other agencies of law enforcement and the criminal justice system. Earlier scholars have called the attention of police administrators on this issue but they remain unheeded (Brown, 1975; Crime and Social Justice Associates, 1995).

The second mantra that the police should be chanting should be *"Focus, Focus, Focus."* The police should be able to redirect their focus on targets of terrorism and to prevent them from being targeted. They should also redirect their attention on how they analyze crime, events, people, and places. Ordinary criminals should still be watched. They still threaten the very social order. However, police resources should be realigned to focus on terrorism and their favorite targets. In this light, symbols of freedom, democracy, and American culture should be as rigorously watched as criminals and high-crime areas.

The third mantra for the police should be, *"Education, Education, Education."*

Some police officers would probably prefer the mantra, *"Training, Training, Training."* The police, however, should make a conscious effort to link their training and education with the way they perform their jobs. It has been noted that the police are known to forget their training and the formal education they receive once they are out in the streets (Van Maanen, 1973). I have illustrated that the training they receive for sensing danger and analyzing events are important technologies that they can use in the fight against terrorism. Their education and training should not be substituted by off-the-cuff policing that they will be socialized to do once they are in the field.

Finally, this article has identified and outlined the importance and utility of recent paradigms that emerged out of the community policing literature. Thus, police officers must make the conscious effort to apply their learned technologies to the job they do. Furthermore, they should continually analyze the effect of their education and training in their job performance.

The roles and strategies of the police are shaped by the need of the times (Williams & Murphy, 1990). In this time of terror, police are required to be more vigilant and perhaps more suspicious. They are required to be more proactive both in detecting and investigating acts of terrorism. The community policing roles that they have embraced for the last decade should be examined in the light of its opposing tenets to the demands of providing police service in time of terror. The police should lean toward a more legalistic (Wilson, 1968) style and begin to apply their innate talent for sensing danger (Crank, 1999). This is the philosophical shift that circumstances demand. This is probably the role that the American people demand from their law enforcement officers.

The strategies may still be the same but their strategic philosophy and thinking has to be changed. They have to execute their traditional strategies with more analysis and with a different focus. Indeed, terrorists as well as ordinary criminals have limited arsenal but law enforcement should not be as inane as they are.

References

Bayley, D. (1985). *Patterns of Policing.* New Brunswick, NJ: Rutgers University Press.
Bayley, D. (1994). *Police for the Future.* New York: Oxford University Press.
Bieck, W. (1989). Crime analysis. In *The Encyclopedia of Police Science,* W. Bayley (ed.), pp. 89–100. New York: Garland.
Bolz, Jr., F, K. J. Dudonis, and D. P. Schulz (1990). *The Counter-terrorism Handbook: Tactics, Procedures, and Techniques.* New York: Elsevier.
Brown, W. (1975). Local policing: A three-dimensional task analysis. *Journal of Criminal Justice* 3(1): 1–15.
Crank, J. P. (1999). *Understanding Police Culture.* Cincinnati: Anderson.
Crime and Social Justice Associates (1982). The iron fist and velvet glove. In *The Police and Society: Touchstone Readings,* V. Kappeler (ed.), (1995). Prospect Heights, IL: Waveland Press.
David, R. (2002, February). Terrorism and its parasites. *Philippine Daily Inquirer.*
Eck, J. (1983). *Solving Problems: The Investigation of Burglary and Robbery.* Washington, DC: The National Institute of Justice.
Eck, J. E., & W. Spelman (1987). *Problem Solving: Problem-Oriented Policing in Newport News.* Washington, DC: National Institute of Justice.
Ericson, R. (1982). *Reproducing Order.* Toronto, Canada: University of Toronto Press.
Fogelson, R. (1991). Reform at a standstill. In *Thinking about the Police: Contemporary Readings* (2nd edition), C. B. Klockars and S. Mastroski (eds.). New York: McGraw-Hill.
Goldstein, H. (1987). Toward community oriented policing: Potential, basic requirements, and threshold questions. *Crime and Delinquency* 33(1): 6–30.
Goldstein, H. (1976). Improving policing: A problem oriented approach. *Crime and Delinquency* 25: 236–258.
Greene, J. R., & C. B. Klockars (1991). What Police do. In *Thinking about Police: Contemporary Readings,* C. Klockars and S. Mastrofski (eds.), pp. 273–284. New York: McGraw-Hill.
Greenwood, P., & J. Petersilia (1975). *The Criminal Investigation Process: Volume 1: Summary and Policy Implications.* Washington, DC: U.S. Department of Justice.
Guyot, D. (1979). Bending granite: Attempts top change rank structure of American police departments. *Crime and Delinquency* 40(3): 437–368.
Hollis, S., C. Tillery, & P. Schaenman (1999). *Inventory of State and Local Law Enforcement Technology Needs to Combat Terrorism.* Washington, DC: National Institute of Justice.

Holms, P., & T. Burke (2002). *Terrorism: Today's Biggest Threat to Freedom.* New York: Pinnacle Books.

Jenkins, B. M. (1990). International terrorism: The other world war. In *International Terrorism: Characteristics, Causes, Controls,* Kegley, Jr. (ed.), pp. 27–38. New York: St. Martin's Press.

Kelling, G., & M. Moore (1988). *The Evolving Strategy of Policing.* Washington, DC: U.S. Department of Justice.

Kuykendall, J. (1982). The criminal investigative process: Toward a conceptual framework. *Journal of Criminal Justice* 10(2): 131–145.

Langworthy, R. (1986). *The Structure of Police Organizations.* New York: Praeger.

Langworthy, R., & L. Travis III (1999). *Policing in America: A Balance of Forces* (2nd edition). Columbus, OH: Prentice Hall.

Levitt, (1988). *Democracies Against Terror: The Western Response to State-Supported Terrorism.* New York: Praeger.

Mapp v. Ohio (1961). 367 U.S. 643.

Manning, P.K. (1989). The police occupational culture in Anglo-American societies. In *Encyclopedia of Police Science,* L. Hoover and J. Dowling (eds.). New York: Garland.

Manning, P. K. (1979). Metaphors of the field: Varieties of organizational discourse. *Administrative Science Quarterly* 24 (660–671).

Maryland v. Wilson (1997), 117 S. Ct.

McDonald, P. (2002). *Managing Police Operations: Implementing the New York Crime Control Model—CompStat.* Belmont, CA: Wadsworth/Thompson Learning.

McVey, P. (1997). *Terrorism and Local Law Enforcement: A Multidimensional Challenge for the Twenty-First Century.* Springfield, IL: Charles C. Thomas Publisher, Ltd.

Meyer, J., & B. Brown (1977). Institutional organizations: Formal structure as myth and ceremony. *American Journal of Sociology 83:* 340–363.

Moore, M, R. Trojanowicz, & G. Kelling (1988). *Crime and Policing.* Washington, DC: U.S. Department of Justice.

Murphy, C. (1986). *The Social and Formal Organization of Small-Town Policing: A Comparative Analysis of RCMP and Municipal Policing.* Ph.D. dissertation. University of Toronto, Toronto, Canada.

Netanyahu, B. (1986). *Terrorism: How the West Can Win.* New York: The Jonathan Institute.

Petersilia, J. (1987). *The Influence of Criminal Justice Research.* Santa Monica, CA: Rand Corporation.

Reiss, A. (1971). *The Police and the Public.* New Haven, CT: Yale University Press.

Reuss-Ianni, E. (1983). *Two Cultures of Policing: Street Cops and Management Officers.* New Brunswick, NJ: Transaction Books.

Sederberg, P. (1990). Responses to dissident terrorism: From myth to maturity. In *International Terrorism: Characteristics, Causes, Controls,* Kegley, Jr. (ed.), pp. 262–280. New York: St. Martin's Press.

Sherman, L. (1986). Policing communities: What works. In *Communities and Crime,* A. Reiss and M. Tonry (eds.), pp. 343–386. Chicago: University of Chicago Press.

Sherman, L. (1991). Police crackdowns: Initial and residual deterrence. In *Thinking*

About Police: Contemporary Readings, C. Klockars and S. Mastroski (eds.), pp. 188–211. New York: McGraw-Hill.

Sherman, L., & D. Rogan (1995). Deterrent effects on police raids on crack houses: A randomized controlled experiment. *Justice Quarterly* 12(4): 755–781.

Sherman, L., & D. Weisburd (1995). General deterrent effects of police patrol on 'hot spots': A randomized controlled trial. *Justice Quarterly* 12(4): 625–648.

Sick, G. (1990). The political underpinnings of terrorism. In *International Terrorism: Characteristics, Causes, Controls,* Kegley, Jr. (ed.), pp. 51–54. New York: St. Martin's Press.

Skolnick, J. (1966). *Justice Without Trial: Law Enforcement in Democratic Society.* New York: John Wiley and Sons.

Skolnick, J., & D. Bayley (1986). *The New Blue Line: Police Innovation in Six American Cities.* New York: Free Press.

Trojanowicz, R., & B. Bucqueroux (1990). *Community Policing: A Contemporary Perspective.* Cincinnati: Anderson.

Van Maanen, J. (1973, Winter). Observations on the making of policemen. *Human Organization 32:* 407–418.

Westley, W. (1970). *Violence and the Police.* Cambridge, MA: MIT Press.

Whren v. United States (1996). 517 U.S. 806.

Williams, H., & P. V. Murphy (1990). The evolving strategy of the police: A minority view. In *The Police and Society: Touchstone Readings,* V. Kappeler (ed.), (1995). Prospect Heights, IL: Waveland Press.

Wilson, J. (1968). *Varieties of Police Behavior: The Management of Law and Order in Eight Communities.* Cambridge, MA: Harvard University Press.

From *Academy of Criminal Justice Sciences (ACJS) Today,* Vol. XXII, Iss. 3, September/October 2002, pp. 8-13. © 2002 by the Academy of Criminal Justice Sciences.

Racial Profiling and its Apologists

Racist law enforcement is rooted in deceptive statistics, slippery logic, and telling indifference

By Tim Wise

It's just good police work." So comes the insistence by many—usually whites—that concentrating law enforcement efforts on blacks and Latinos is a perfectly legitimate idea. To listen to some folks tell it, the fact that people of color commit a disproportionate amount of crime (a claim that is true for some but not all offenses) is enough to warrant heightened suspicion of such persons. As for the humiliation experienced by those innocents unfairly singled out, stopped, and searched? Well, they should understand that such mistreatment is the price they'll have to pay, as long as others who look like them are heavily represented in various categories of criminal mischief.

Of course, the attempt to rationalize racism and discriminatory treatment has a long pedigree. Segregationists offer up many "rational" arguments for separation and even slave-owners found high-minded justifications for their control over persons of African descent. In the modern day, excuses for unequal treatment may be more nuanced and couched in calm, dispassionate, even academic jargon; but they remain fundamentally no more legitimate than the claims of racists past. From overt white supremacists to respected social scientists and political commentators, the soft-pedaling of racist law enforcement is a growing cottage industry: one rooted in deceptive statistics, slippery logic, and telling indifference to the victims of such practices.

As demonstrated convincingly in David Harris's new book *Profiles in Injustice: Why Racial Profiling Cannot Work* (New Press, 2002), racial profiling is neither ethically ac-

ceptable nor logical as a law enforcement tool. But try telling that to the practice's apologists.

According to racial separatist Jared Taylor of American Renaissance—a relatively highbrow white supremacist organization—black crime rates are so disproportionate relative to those of whites that it is perfectly acceptable for police to profile African Americans in the hopes of uncovering criminal activity. His group's report "The Color of Crime"— which has been touted by mainstream conservatives like Walter Williams—purports to demonstrate just how dangerous blacks are, what with murder, robbery, and assault rates that are considerably higher than the rates for whites. That these higher crime rates are the result of economic conditions disproportionately faced by people of color Taylor does not dispute in the report. But he insists that the reasons for the disparities hardly matter. All that need be known is that one group is statistically more dangerous than the other and avoiding those persons or stopping them for searches is not evidence of racism, but rather the result of rational calculations by citizens and police.

Although in simple numerical terms, whites commit three times more violent crimes each year than blacks, and whites are five to six times more likely to be attacked by another white person than by a black person, to Taylor, this is irrelevant. As he has explained about these white criminals: "They may be boobs, but they're our boobs."

Likewise, Heather MacDonald of the conservative Manhattan Institute has written that racial profiling is a "myth." Police, according to MacDonald—whose treatment of the subject was trumpeted in a column by George Will last year—merely play the odds, knowing "from experience" that blacks are likely to be the ones carrying drugs.

Michael Levin, a professor of philosophy at the City College of New York, argues it is rational for whites to fear young black men since one in four are either in prison, on probation, or on parole on any given day. According to Levin, the assumption that one in four black males encountered are therefore likely to be dangerous is logical and hardly indicates racism. Levin has also said that blacks should be treated as adults earlier by the justice system because they mature faster and trials should be shorter for blacks because they have a "shorter time horizon."

Conservative commentator Dinesh D'Souza says that "rational discrimination against young black men can be fully eradicated only by getting rid of destructive conduct by the group that forms the basis for statistically valid group distinctions. It is difficult to compel people to admire groups many of whose members do not act admirably."

Even when the profiling turns deadly, conservatives show little concern. Writing about Amadou Diallo, recipient of 19 bullets (out of 41 fired) from the NYPD Street Crimes Unit, columnist Mona Charen explained that he died for the sins of his black brethren, whose criminal proclivities gave the officers good reason to suspect that he was up to no good.

Putting aside the obvious racial hostility that forms the core of many if not all of these statements, racial profiling cannot be justified on the basis of general crime rate data showing that blacks commit a disproportionate amount of certain crimes, relative to their numbers in the population. Before making this point clear, it is worth clarifying what is meant by racial profiling.

Racial profiling means one of two things. First, the over-application of an incident-specific criminal description in a way that results in the stopping, searching, and harassment of people based solely or mostly on skin color alone. An example would be the decision by police in one upstate New York college town a few years ago to question every black male in the local university after an elderly white woman claimed to have been raped by a black man (turns out he was white).

So while there is nothing wrong with stopping black men who are 6'2", 200 pounds, driving Ford Escorts, if the perp in a particular local crime is known to be 6'2", 200 pounds, and driving a Ford Escort, but when that description is used to randomly stop black men, even who aren't 6'2", aren't close to 200 pounds, and who are driving totally different cars, then that becomes a problem.

The second and more common form of racial profiling is the disproportionate stopping, searching, frisking, and harassment of people of color in the hopes of uncovering a crime, even when there is no crime already in evidence for which a particular description might be available. In other words: stopping black folks or Latinos and searching for drugs.

This is why general crime rates are irrelevant to the profiling issue. Police generally don't randomly stop and search people in the hopes of turning up last night's convenience store hold-up man. They tend to have more specific information to go on in those cases. As such, the fact that blacks commit a higher share of some crimes (robbery, murder, assault) than their population numbers is of no consequence to the issue of whether profiling them is legitimate. The "crime" for which people of color are being profiled mostly is drug possession. In that case, people of color are not a disproportionate number of violators and police do not find such contraband disproportionately on people of color.

All available evidence indicates that whites are equally or more likely to use (and thus possess at any given time) illegal narcotics. This is especially true for young adults and teenagers, in which categories whites are disproportionate among users.

Although black youth and young adults are more likely than white youth to have been approached by someone offering to give them or sell them drugs during the past month, they are less likely to have actually used drugs in the last 30 days. Among adults, data from California is instructive: although whites over the age of 30 are only 36 percent of the state's population, they comprise 60 percent of all heavy drug users in the state.

Although blacks and Latinos often control large drug sale networks, roughly eight in ten drug busts are not for dealing, but for possession. Drug busts for narcotics trafficking rarely stem from random searches of persons or vehicles—the kind of practice rightly labeled profiling—but rather, tend to take place after a carefully devised sting operation and intelligence gathering, leading to focused law enforcement efforts. As such, the usage numbers are the more pertinent when discussing the kinds of police stops and searches covered by the pejorative label of "profiling."

A Department of Justice study released in 2001 notes that although blacks are twice as likely as whites to have their cars stopped and searched, police are actually twice as likely to find evidence of illegal activity in cars driven by whites.

In New Jersey, for 2000, although blacks and Latinos were 78 percent of persons stopped and searched on the southern portion of the Jersey Turnpike, police were twice as likely to discover evidence of illegal activity in cars driven by whites, relative to blacks, and whites were five times more likely to be in possession of drugs, guns, or other illegal items relative to Latinos. In North Carolina, black drivers are two-thirds more likely than whites to be stopped and searched by the State Highway Patrol, but contraband is discovered in cars driven by whites 27 percent more often.

In New York City, even after controlling for the higher crime rates by blacks and Latinos and local demographics (after all, people of color will be the ones stopped and searched most often in communities where they make up most of the residents), police are still two to three times more likely to search them than whites. Yet, police hunches about who is in possession of drugs, guns, other illegal contraband, or who is wanted for commission of a violent crime turn out to be horribly inaccurate. Despite being stopped and searched more often, blacks and Latinos are less likely to be arrested because they are less likely to be found with evidence of criminal wrongdoing.

So much for MacDonald's "rational" police officers, operating from their personal experiences. Despite police claims that they only stop and search people of color more often because such folks engage in suspicious behavior more often, if the "hit rates" for such persons are no higher than, and even lower than the rates for whites, this calls into question the validity of the suspicious action criteria. If blacks seem suspicious more often, but are actually hiding something less often, then by definition the actions deemed suspicious should be reexamined, as they are not proving to be logical at all, let alone the result of good police work. Indeed, they appear to be proxies for racial stops and searches.

Nor can the disproportionate stopping of black vehicles be justified by differential driving behavior. Every study done on the subject has been clear: there are no significant differences between people of color and whites when it comes to the commission of moving or other violations. Police acknowledge that virtually every driver violates any number of minor laws every time they take to the road. But these violations are not enforced equally and that is the problem.

In one New Jersey study, for example, despite no observed differences in driving behavior, African Americans were 73 percent of all drivers stopped on the Jersey Turnpike, despite being less than 14 percent of the drivers on the road: a rate that is 27 times greater than what would be expected by random chance. Similar results were found in a study of stops in Maryland. On a particular stretch of Interstate 95 in Florida, known for being a drug trafficking route, blacks and Latinos comprise only 5 percent of drivers, but 70 percent of those stopped by members of the Highway Patrol. These stops were hardly justified, as only nine drivers, out of 1,100 stopped during the study, were ever ticketed for any violation, let alone arrested for possession of illegal contraband.

As for Levin's claim that whites should properly consider one in four black males encountered to be a threat to their personal safety, because of their involvement with the criminal justice system, it should be remembered that most of these have been arrested for non-violent offenses like drug possession. Blacks comprise 35 percent of all possession arrests and 75 percent of those sent to prison for a drug offense, despite being only 14 percent of users.

When it comes to truly dangerous violent crime, only a miniscule share of African Americans will commit such offenses in a given year and less than half of these will choose a white victim.

With about 1.5 million violent crimes committed by blacks each year (about 90 percent of these by males) and 70 percent of the crimes committed by just 7 percent of the offenders—a commonly accepted figure by criminologists—this means that less than 2 percent of blacks over age 12 (the cutoff for collecting crime data) and less than 3.5 percent of black males over 12 could even theoretically be considered dangerous. Less than 1.5 percent of black males will attack a white person in a given year, hardly lending credence to Levin's claim about the rationality of white panic.

The fact remains that the typical offender in violent crime categories is white. So even if black rates are disproportionate to their population percentages, any "profile" that tends to involve a black or Latino face is likely to be wrong more than half the time. Whites commit roughly 60 percent of violent crimes, for example. So if 6 in 10 violent criminals are white, how logical could it be to deploy a profile—either for purposes of law enforcement or merely personal purposes of avoiding certain people—that is only going to be correct 40 percent of the time? So too with drugs, where any profile that involves a person of color will be wrong three out of four times?

Additionally, the apologists for profiling are typically selective in terms of the kinds of profiling they support. Although whites are a disproportionate percentage of all drunk drivers, for example, and although drunk driving contributes to the deaths of more than 10,000 people each year, none of the defenders of anti-black or brown profiling suggests that drunk driving roadblocks be set up in white suburbs where the "hit rates" for catching violators would be highest.

Likewise, though white college students are considerably more likely to binge drink (often underage) and use narcotics than college students of color, no one suggests that police or campus cops should regularly stage raids on white fraternity houses or dorm rooms occupied by whites, even though the raw data would suggest such actions might be statistically justified.

Whites are also nearly twice as likely to engage in child sexual molestation, relative to blacks. Yet how would the Heather MacDonalds and Dinesh D'Souzas of the world react to an announcement that adoption agencies were going to begin screening out white couples seeking to adopt, or subjecting them to extra scrutiny, as a result of such factual information?

Similarly, those seeking to now justify intensified profiling of Arabs or Muslims since September 11 were hardly clamoring for the same treatment of white males in the wake of Oklahoma City. Even now, in the wake of anthrax incidents that the FBI says have almost certainly been domestic, possibly white supremacist in origin, no one is calling for heightened suspicion of whites as a result.

The absurdity of anti-Arab profiling is particularly obvious in the case of trying to catch members of al-Qaeda. The group, after all, operates in 64 countries, many of them non-Arab, and from which group members would not look anything like the image of a terrorist currently locked in the minds of so many. Likewise, Richard Reid, the would-be shoe bomber recently captured was able to get on the plane he sought to bring down precisely because he had a "proper English name," likely spoke with a proper English accent, and thus, didn't fit the description.

The bottom line is that racial profiling doesn't happen because data justifies the practice, but rather because those with power are able to get away with it, and find it functional to do so as a mechanism of social control over those who are less powerful. By typifying certain "others" as dangerous or undesirable, those seeking to maintain divisions between people whose economic and social interests are actually quite similar can successfully maintain those cleavages.

No conspiracy here, mind you: just the system working as intended, keeping people afraid of one another and committed to the maintenance of the system, by convincing us that certain folks are a danger to our well-being, which then must be safeguarded by a growing prison-industrial complex and draconian legal sanctions; or in the case of terrorist "profiles," by the imposition of unconstitutional detentions, beefed-up military and intelligence spending, and the creation of a paranoiac wartime footing.

Until and unless the stereotypes that underlie racial profiling are attacked and exposed as a fraud, the practice will likely continue: not because it makes good sense, but because racist assumptions about danger—reinforced by media and politicians looking for votes—lead us to think that it does.

Tim Wise is a Nashville-based writer, lecturer and antiracist activist. Footnotes for this article can be obtained at tjwise@mindspring.com.

Early Warning Systems: Responding to the Problem Police Officer

by Samuel Walker, Geoffrey P. Alpert, and Dennis J. Kenney

It has become a truism among police chiefs that 10 percent of their officers cause 90 percent of the problems. Investigative journalists have documented departments in which as few as 2 percent of all officers are responsible for 50 percent of all citizen complaints.[1] The phenomenon of the "problem officer" was identified in the 1970s: Herman Goldstein noted that problem officers "are well known to their supervisors, to the top administrators, to their peers, and to the residents of the areas in which they work," but that "little is done to alter their conduct."[2] In 1981, the U.S. Commission on Civil Rights recommended that all police departments create an early warning system to identify problem officers, those "who are frequently the subject of complaints or who demonstrate identifiable patterns of inappropriate behavior."[3]

An early warning system is a data-based police management tool designed to identify officers whose behavior is problematic and provide a form of intervention to correct that performance. As an early response, a department intervenes before such an officer is in a situation that warrants formal disciplinary action. The system alerts the department to these individuals and warns the officers while providing counseling or training to help them change their problematic behavior.

By 1999, 39 percent of all municipal and county law enforcement agencies that serve populations greater than 50,000 people either had an early warning system in place or were planning to implement one. The growing popularity of these systems as a remedy for police misconduct raises questions about their effectiveness and about the various program elements that are associated with effectiveness. To date, however, little has been written on the subject.[4] This Brief reports on the first indepth investigation of early warning systems. The investigation combined the results of a national survey of law enforcement agencies with the findings of case studies of three agencies with established systems.

How prevalent are early warning systems?

As part of the national evaluation of early warning systems, the Police executive Research Forum—funded by the National Institute of Justice and the Office of Community Oriented Policing Services—surveyed 832 sheriffs' offices and municipal and county police departments serving populations of 50,000 or more.[5] Usable responses were received from 571 agencies, a response rate of 69 percent. The response rate was significantly higher for municipal agencies than for sheriffs' departments.

Approximately one-fourth (27 percent) of the surveyed agencies had an early warning system in 1999. One-half of these systems had been created since 1994, and slightly more than one-third had been created since 1996. These data, combined with the number of agencies indicating that a system was being planned (another 12 percent), suggest that such systems will spread rapidly in the next few years.

Early warning systems are more prevalent among municipal law enforcement agencies than among county sheriffs' departments.

How does an early warning system work?

Early warning systems have three basic phases: selection, intervention, and postintervention monitoring.

Selecting officers for the program. No standards have been established for identifying officers for early warning programs, but there is general agreement about the criteria that should influence their selection. Performance indicators that can help identify officers with problematic behavior include citizen complaints, firearm-discharge and use-of-force reports, civil litigation, resisting-arrest incidents, and highspeed pursuits and vehicular damage.[6]

Although a few departments rely only on citizen complaints to select officers for intervention, most use a combination of performance indicators. Among systems that factor in citizen complaints, most (67 percent) require three complaints in a given timeframe (76 percent specify a 12-month period) to identify an officer.

Intervening with the officer. The primary goal of early warning systems is to change the behavior of individual officers who have been identified as having problematic performance records. The basic intervention strategy involves a combination of deterrence and education. The theory of simple deterrence assumes that officers who are subject to intervention will change

Issues and Findings

Discussed in this Brief: A systematic study of early warning systems designed to identify officers who may be having problems on the job and to provide those officers with the appropriate counseling or training. The findings are based on a survey of 832 local law enforcement agencies and site visits to three departments with established early warning systems.

Key issues: A growing body of evidence indicates that in any police department a small percentage of officers are responsible for a disproportionate share of citizen complaints. Early warning systems help supervisors identify these officers, intervene with them, and monitor their subsequent performance.

Even though early warning systems are becoming more popular among law enforcement agencies, little research has addressed the effectiveness of such programs. This Brief reports on a study that establishes a baseline description of early warning system programs and asks some fundamental questions:

- Are early warning systems effective in reducing police officer misconduct?
- Are some types of early warning systems more effective than others?
- What impact do early warning systems have on the departments in which they operate?
- Do early warning systems have unintended and undesirable effects?

Key findings: Twenty-seven percent of local law enforcement agencies serving populations of at least 50,000 had an early warning system in 1999; another 12 percent were planning to establish such a program.

Larger agencies were more likely than smaller agencies to use an early warning system. Among agencies with 1,000 or more sworn officers, 79 percent had or planned to have an early warning system; only 56 percent of agencies with between 500 and 999 sworn officers had or planned to have such a program.

No standards have been established for identifying which officers should participate in early warning programs, but there is general agreement that a number of factors can help identify problem officers: citizen complaints, firearm-discharge reports, use-of-force reports, civil litigation, resisting-arrest incidents, and pursuits and vehicular accidents.

Data from the three case-study agencies (in Miami, Minneapolis, and New Orleans) indicate the following:

- In spite of considerable differences among the programs, each program appeared to reduce problem behaviors significantly.
- Early warning systems encourage changes in the behavior of supervisors, as well as of the identified officers.
- Early warning systems are high-maintenance programs that require ongoing administrative attention.

A caveat is in order about the findings reported here. The research design was limited in a number of ways, and each of the early warning systems studied operates in the context of a department's larger commitment to increased accountability. It is impossible to disentangle the effect of the department's culture of accountability from that of the early warning program.

Target audience: State and local law enforcement administrators, planners, and policy makers; researchers; and educators.

their behavior in response to a perceived threat of punishment.[7] General deterrence assumes that officers not subject to the system will also change their behavior to avoid potential punishment. Early warning systems also operate on the assumption that training, as part of the intervention, can help officers improve their performance.

In most systems (62 percent), the initial intervention generally consists of a review by the officer's immediate supervisor. Almost half of the responding agencies (45 percent) involve other command offcers in counseling the officer. Also, these systems frequently include a training class for groups of officers identified by the system (45 percent of survey respondents).

Monitoring the officer's subsequent performance. Nearly all (90 percent) the agencies that have an early warning system in place report that they monitor an officer's performance after the initial intervention. Such monitoring is generally informal and conducted by the officer's immediate supervisor, but some departments have developed a formal process of observation, evaluation, and reporting. Almost half of the agencies (47 percent) monitor the officer's performance for 36 months after the initial intervention. Half of the agencies indicate that the follow-up period is not specified and that officers are monitored either continuously or on a case-by-case basis.

Limitations of the survey findings

The responses from the national survey should be viewed with some caution. Some law enforcement agencies may have claimed to have an early warning system when such a system is not actually functioning. Several police departments created systems in the 1970s, but none of those appears to have survived as a permanent program.[8]

Findings from three case studies

The research strategy for the case studies was modeled after the birth cohort study of juvenile delinquency conducted by Wolfgang and colleagues.[9] They found that a small group within the entire cohort (6.3 percent of the total) were "chronic delinquents" and were responsible for half of all the serious crime committed by the entire cohort. The early warning concept rests on the assumption that within any cohort of police officers, a small percentage will have substantially worse performance records than their peers and, consequently, will merit departmental intervention. The research was designed to confirm or refute the assumption.

Three police departments were chosen for the case study investigation: Miami–Dade County, Minneapolis, and New Orleans. The three sites represent large urban areas, but the size of each police force varies considerably: At the time of the study, Miami–Dade had 2,920 sworn officers, New Orleans had 1,576 sworn officers, and Minneapolis had 890 sworn officers.

The three sites were chosen for several reasons. Each has an early warning system that had been operating for at least 4 years at the time of the study. Also, the three systems differ from one another in terms of structure and administrative history, and the three departments differ in their history of police officer use of force and accountability (see "Three cities, three stories").

One goal of the case studies was to evaluate the impact of early warning systems on the officers involved. In New Orleans, citizen complaints about officers in the early warning program were analyzed for 2-year periods before and after the initial intervention. Officers subject to early warning intervention participate in a Professional Performance Enhancement Program (PPEP) class; their critiques of the class were analyzed and a 2-day class was observed to determine both the content of the intervention and officer responses to various components.

Demographic and performance data were collected in Miami–Dade and Minneapolis on a cohort of all officers hired in certain years—whether or not they were identified by the early warning systems. The performance data included citizen complaints, use-of-force reports, reprimands, suspensions, terminations, commendations, and promotions. Other data were collected as available in each site.

These records were sorted into two groups: officers identified by the early warning system and officers not identified, with the latter serving as a control group. The performance records of the early warning group were analyzed for the 2-year periods before and after the intervention to determine the impact of the intervention on the officers' behavior. The analysis controlled for assignment to patrol duty on the assumption that citizen complaints and use-of-force incidents are infrequently generated in other assignments.

Characteristics of officers identified by early warning systems. Demographically, officers identified by the systems do not differ significantly from the control group in terms of race or ethnicity. Males are somewhat over represented and females are under represented. One disturbing finding was a slight tendency of early warning offcers to be promoted at higher rates than control officers. This issue should be the subject of future research, which should attempt to identify more precisely whether some departments tend to reward through promotion the kind of active (and possibly aggressive) behavior that is likely to cause officers to be identified by an early warning system.

The impact of early warning systems on officers' performance. Early warning systems appear to have a dramatic effect on reducing citizen complaints and other indicators of problem-

atic police performance among those officers subject to intervention. In Minneapolis, the average number of citizen complaints received by officers subject to early intervention dropped by 67 percent 1 year after the intervention. In New Orleans, that number dropped by 62 percent 1 year after intervention (exhibit 1). In Miami–Dade, only 4 percent of the early warning cohort had zero use-of-force reports prior to intervention; following intervention, 50 percent had zero use-of-force reports.

Data from New Orleans indicate that officers respond positively to early warning intervention. In anonymous evaluations of the PPEP classes, officers gave it an average rating of 7 on a scale of 1 to 10. All of the officers made at least one positive comment about the class, and some made specific comments about how it had helped them. Officers in the PPEP class that was directly observed were actively engaged in those components they perceived to be related to the practical problems of police work, particularly incidents that often generate complaints or other problems. Officers were disengaged, however, in components that they perceived to be abstract, moralistic, or otherwise unrelated to practical aspects of police work.

This study could not determine the most effective aspects of intervention (e.g., counseling regarding personal issues, training in specific law enforcement techniques, stern warning about possible discipline in the future) or whether certain aspects are more effective for certain types of officers.

The impact of early warning systems on supervisors. The original design of this study did not include evaluating the impact of these systems on supervisors. Nonetheless, the qualitative component of the research found that these systems have potentially significant effects on supervisors. The existence of an intervention system communicates to supervisors their responsibility to monitor officers who have been identified by the program. The New Orleans program requires supervisors to monitor identified officers under their command for 6 months and to complete signed evaluations of the officers' performance every 2 weeks. Officials in Miami–Dade think that their system helps ensure that supervisors will attend to potential problem officers under their command. In this respect, the systems mandate or encourage changes in supervisor behavior that could potentially affect the standards of supervision of all officers, not just those subject to early intervention. Furthermore, the system's database can give supervisors relevant information about officers newly assigned to them and about whom they know very little.

The impact of early warning systems on the rest of the department. The original design of this study did not include evaluating the impact of these systems on the departments in which they operate. Nonetheless, the qualitative component identified a number of important issues for future research. The extent to which a system changes the climate of accountability within a law enforcement agency is not known, and identifying it would require a sophisticated research design. The qualitative findings suggest that an effective early intervention program depends on a general commitment to accountability within an organization. Such a program is unlikely to create or foster a cli-

Three cities, three stories

The three early warning systems in the sites selected for the case studies have different administrative histories and program structures, and the three police departments have different histories with regard to police officer use of force and accountability.

Miami–Dade County. The Miami-Dade Police Department (MDPD) currently enjoys a reputation for high standards of professionalism and accountability to reforms instituted following controversial racial incidents in the late 1970s and early 1980s.

As a result of the real and perceived problems between police and citizens, the Dade County Commission enacted legislation that opened to the public the internal investigations conducted by MDPD. In addition, an employee profile system (EPS) was created to track all complaints, use-of-force incidents, commendations, disciplinary actions, and dispositions of all internal investigations. As an offshoot of the EPS, MDPD created the Early Identification System (EIS) under the supervision of the Internal Review Bureau.

MDPD's EIS began operating in 1981. Quarterly reports list all officers who receive two or more citizen complaints that were investigated and closed or who were involved in three or more use-of-force incidents during the previous 3 months. Annual reports list officers who were identified in two or more quarterly reports. Monthly reports list employees who received two or more complaints during the previous 60 days, regardless of disposition.

The reports are disseminated through the chain of command to the supervisors of each officer identified. As one official described the system, supervisors use the reports "as a resource to determine if job stress or performance problems exist."[1] The information is intended to help supervisors evaluate and guide an employee's job performance and conduct in conjunction with other information.

The intervention phase of EIS consists primarily of an informal counseling session between the supervisor and the officer. The supervisor is expected to discuss the report with the officer and determine whether further action is needed. Such actions may include making referrals to employee assistance programs inside or outside the department, such as psychological services, stress abatement programs, or specialized training programs.

Postintervention monitoring of officers in the early warning system is informal and conducted by supervisors. Review of officers' performance records is designed to identify officers who continue to exhibit patterns of misconduct and to make the officers aware that their performance is being closely scrutinized. Additionally, the program puts supervisors on notice that their responsibilities include the close monitoring of those whose performance is problematic.

(continued)

mate of accountability where that commitment does not already exist.

The data developed as a part of an early warning system can be used to effect changes in policies, procedures, or training. Presumably, such changes help reduce existing problems and help the department maintain and raise its standards of accountability. Thus, these systems can be an important tool for organizational development and human resource management.[10]

The nature of early warning systems. A second goal of the case studies was to describe the systems themselves. In all three sites, qualitative data gathered from official documents and interviews with key stakeholders yielded a description and assessment of the formal structure and administrative history of each program, along with an assessment of its place in the larger processes of accountability in the department.

In addition to finding that the early warning systems in the three sites vary considerably in terms of their formal program elements, the study documented that an effective system requires considerable investment of resources and administrative attention. Miami–Dade's program, for example, is part of a sophisticated data system on officers and their performance. The New Orleans program involves several staff members, including one full-time data analyst and two other full-time employees who spend part of their time entering data.

Early warning systems should not be considered alarm clocks—they are not mechanical devices that can be programmed to automatically sound an alarm. Rather, they are extremely complex, high-maintenance administrative operations that require close and ongoing human attention. Without this attention, the systems are likely to falter or fail.

Limitations of the case study findings. The findings regarding the impact of early warning intervention should be viewed with caution. As the first-ever study of such systems, this project encountered a number of unanticipated problems with the data. First, it was not possible to collect retrospectively systematic data on positive police officer performance (e.g., incidents when an officer avoided using force or citizens felt they had been treated fairly and respectfully). Thus, it is not known whether early intervention had a deterrent effect on desirable officer behavior.

Second, the early warning systems in each site studied operate in the context of a larger commitment to increased accountability on the part of the police department. Given the original research design, it is impossible to disentangle the effect of this general climate of rising standards of accountability on officer performance from the effect of the intervention program itself.

Finally, the early warning systems in two of the three sites experienced significant changes during the years for which data were collected. Thus, the intervention delivered was not consistent for the period studied. Significant changes also occurred in two sites immediately following the data collection period. In one instance, the system was substantially strengthened. In the other, it is likely that the administration of the system has deteriorated significantly; this deterioration may have begun during the study, affecting the data that were collected.

Three cities, three stories (continued)

Minneapolis. When the study began, the Minneapolis Police Department (MPD) had a mixed reputation and was in transition under the leadership of a relatively new chief. MPD has long had a national reputation as a police department receptive to research. At the same time, however, MPD had a troubled local reputation with respect to the use of force by its officers.This reputation eventually brought a number of important political and administrative changes in the 1990s. The mayor declined to reappoint the incumbent police chief, who had failed to discipline the police officers. The new police chief began raising standards of accountability; among other reforms, he instituted a version of the COMPSTAT process. These changes have had direct implications for the system of accountability within the MPD and complicate any attempt to evaluate the impact of MPD's early warning system.

The program was established in the early 1990s and has undergone a number of significant administrative changes, including a period of slightly more than 1 year in the mid-1990s when the system ceased functioning altogether. After the data collection period for this study, a new procedure was instituted that calls for reviewing all reports of potentially problematic officer performance every 2 weeks. This procedure substantially heightens the intensity of the level of supervision. Thus, the findings reported here do not reflect current practices in the department.

The only selection criterion for the system is citizen complaints. The formal selection criteria have changed over the years, however. Currently, a quarterly report lists all officers with two or more citizen complaints, whether sustained or unsustained.

The intervention phase in Minneapolis consists of only an informal counseling session between the officer and his or her immediate supervisor. In the early years, supervisors were required to document their counseling session in the form of a memorandum to the commander. There is currently no documentation requirement, and MPD's program does not include any formal postintervention monitoring. Apart from the routine supervision applied to all officers, officers who are subject to intervention are not subject to formal monitoring and no special data are collected on their performance.

New Orleans. In the mid-1990s, the New Orleans Police Department (NOPD) had a national reputation for both corruption and use of force by its officers. Between 1995 and 1998, NOPD terminated an average of slightly more than 18 officers per year and imposed an average of more than 100 suspensions per year. At the same time, 97 officers resigned or retired while under investigation by the department and 105 officers were either arrested or issued a citation for a criminal law violation. These are extremely high figures compared with police departments of similar size.[2]

The officials associated with NOPD's Professional Performance Enhancement Program (PPEP) have a strong sense of identification with the program and are committed to maintaining and improving it. The department also conducts random integrity "stings" to identify possible corrupt activities by officers. Furthermore, PPEP does not limit its focus to individual officers, but also examines training, procedures, and supervision."[3]

As in Minneapolis, changes in the program occurred after the data collection period. It is likely that the administration of the program has weakened somewhat, due largely to the retirement or departure of key individuals. Thus, the findings reported here do not reflect current practices in the department.

Officers are selected for the program on the basis of three categories of performance indicators: incidents involving conflict in arrest and nonarrest situations and referrals from supervisors. However, intervention is not automatic; commanders review performance records and exercise discretion in selecting officers.

The PPEP class consists of an overview and explanation of the program and units on human behavior, stress management, conflict management, complaint avoidance, sensitivity training, "extraneous contributors to conflict" (such as substance abuse), and techniques and assessment (which includes training related to such police activities as tactical stops, situation assessment, handcuffing, and custodial security). Each class includes a private counseling session with the instructor, during which the officer's record is reviewed and the reasons for being selected for the program are explained.

Immediate supervisors are required to monitor each officer for a period of 6 months after the intervention. During that period, the supervisor is required to observe the officer interacting with citizens while on duty and to complete a bi-weekly evaluation of the officer's performance.

1. Charette, Bernard, "Early Identification of Police Brutality and Misconduct," Miami: Metro-Dade Police Department, n.d., p. 5.
2. "Disciplinary Action Breakdown," New Orleans Police Department, February 9, 1999.
3. New Orleans Police Department, Public Integrity Division, "To Whom It May Concern," May 5, 1998.

Policing strategies and legal considerations

Early warning systems and policing strategies. These intervention strategies are compatible with both community-oriented and problem-oriented policing. Community-oriented policing seeks to establish closer relations between the police and the communities they serve. Insofar as the systems seek to reduce citizen complaints and other forms of problematic behavior, they are fully consistent with these goals.[11]

Problem-oriented policing focuses on identifying specific police problems and developing carefully tailored responses.[12] Early warning systems approach the problem officer as the concern to be addressed, and the intervention is the response tailored to change the behavior that leads to indicators of unsatisfactory performance.

Early warning systems and traffic-stop data. The issue of racial profiling by police has recently emerged as a national controversy. In response to this controversy, a number of law enforcement agencies have begun to collect data on the race and ethnicity of drivers stopped by their officers.

An officer who makes a disproportionate number of traffic stops of racial or ethnic minorities (relative to other offcers with the same assignment) may be a problem officer who warrants the attention of the department. Traffic-stop information can be readily incorporated into the database and used to identify possible racial disparities (as well as other potential problems, such as disproportionate stops of female drivers or unacceptably low levels of activity).

Legal considerations of these systems. Some law enforcement agencies may resist creating an early warning system for fear that a plaintiff's attorney may subpoena the database's information on officer misconduct and use that information against the agency in lawsuits alleging excessive use of force.[13] Several experts argue, however, that in the current legal environment, an early warning system is more likely to shield an agency against liability for deliberate indifference regarding police use of force. Such a system demonstrates that the agency has a clear policy regarding misconduct, has made a good faith effort to identify employees whose performance is unsatisfactory, and has a program in place to correct that behavior.[14]

Policy concerns and areas for further research

Each of an early warning system's three phases involves a number of complex policy issues.

Selection. Although the selection criteria for most early warning systems consider a range of performance indicators, some rely solely on citizen complaints. A number of problems related to official data on citizen complaints, including underreporting, have been documented.[15] Using a broader range of indicators is more likely to identify officers whose behavior requires departmental intervention.

Intervention. In most early warning systems, intervention consists of an informal counseling session between the officer and his or her immediate supervisor. Some systems require no documentation of the content of that session, which raises concerns about whether supervisors deliver the intended content of the intervention. It is possible that a supervisor may minimize the importance of the intervention by telling an officer "not to worry about it," thus reinforcing the officer's behavior. Involving higher ranking command officers is likely to ensure that the intervention serves the intended goals. Further research is needed on the most effective forms of intervention and whether it is possible to tailor certain forms of intervention to particular categories of officers.

Exhibit 1. *Annual average number of complaints against officers, before and after intervention*

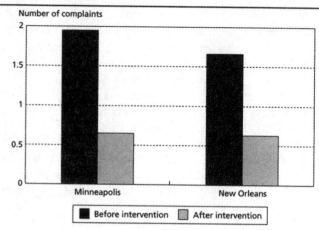

Postintervention monitoring. The nature of postintervention monitoring varies among systems. Some systems rely on informal monitoring of the subject officers; others employ a formal mechanism of observation and documentation by supervisors. The relative impact of different postintervention monitoring systems on individual officers, supervisors, and departments requires further research.

One tool among many

Early warning systems have emerged as a popular remedy for police misconduct. This study suggests that these systems can reduce citizen complaints and other problematic police behavior. Officers in the three departments investigated as case studies were involved in substantially fewer citizen complaints and use-of-force incidents after the intervention than before. In these three departments, however, the systems were part of larger efforts to raise standards of accountability. The effectiveness of such a system is reinforced by (and probably dependent on) other policies and procedures that enforce standards of discipline and create a climate of accountability.

An effective early warning system is a complex, high-maintenance operation that requires a significant investment of administrative resources. Some systems appear to be essentially symbolic gestures with little substantive content, and it is unlikely that an intervention program can be effective in a law enforcement agency that has no serious commitment to accountability. It can be an effective management tool, but it should be seen as only one of many tools needed to raise standards of performance and improve the quality of police services.

Notes

1. "Kansas City Police Go After Their 'Bad Boys,'" *New York Times*, September 10, 1991; and "Waves of Abuse Laid to a Few Officers," *Boston Globe*, October 4, 1992.

2. Goldstein, Herman, *Policing a Free Society*, Cambridge, MA: Ballinger, 1977: 171.

3. *Who is Guarding the Guardians?* Washington, DC: U.S. Commission on Civil Rights, 1981: 81.

4. Kappeler, Victor, Richard Sluder, and Geoffrey Alpert, *Forces of Deviance: Understanding the Dark Side of Policing*, Prospect Heights, IL: Waveland Press, 1998.

5. The first wave of the survey occurred in August 1998, with a second wave in October 1998 and followup in February 1999.

6. For discussions of recommended performance categories, see International Association of Chiefs of Police, *Building Integrity and Reducing Drug Corruption in Police Departments*, Washington, DC: U.S. Department of Justice, Bureau of Justice Assistance, 1989: 80; and Reiter, Lou, *Law Enforcement Administrative Investigations: A Manual Guide*, 2nd ed., Tallahassee, FL: Lou Reiter and Associates, 1998: 18.2.

7. Zimring, Franklin, and Gordon Hawkins, *Deterrence*, Chicago: University of Chicago Press, 1973.

8. Milton, Catherine H., Jeanne Wahl Halleck, James Lardner, and Gary L. Albrecht, *Police Use of Deadly Force*, Washington, DC: The Police Foundation, 1977: 94–110.

9. Wolfgang, Marvin E., Robert M. Figlio, and Thorsten Sellin, *Delinquency in a Birth Cohort*, Chicago: University of Chicago Press, 1972.

10. Mathis, Robert L., and John H. Jackson, eds., *Human Resource Management: Essential Perspectives*, Cincinnati: Southwestern College Publishing, 1999: 98–102; and Poole, Michael, and Malcolm Warner, *The IEBM Handbook of Human Resource Management*, London: International Thomson Business Press, 1998: 93.

11. Alpert, Geoffrey, and Mark H. Moore, "Measuring Performance in the New Paradigm of Policing," in *Performance Measures for the Criminal Justice System*, Washington, DC: U.S. Department of Justice, Bureau of Justice Statistics, 1993: 109–142.

12. Eck, John E., and William Spelman, *Problem-Solving: Problem-Oriented Policing in Newport News*, Washington, DC: U.S. Department of Justice, National Institute of Justice, 1987.

13. Reiter, Lou, *Law Enforcement Administrative Investigations*, chapter 18.

14. Gallagher, G. Patrick, "The Liability Shield: From Policy to Internal Affairs," in Reiter, Lou, *Law Enforcement Administrative Investigations*, chapter 20; and Beh, Hazel Glenn, "Municipal Liability for Failure To Investigate Citizen Complaints Against Police," *Fordham Urban Law Journal* XXV (2) 1998: 209–254.

15. Walker, Samuel, *Police Accountability: The Role of Citizen Oversight*, Belmont, CA: Wadsworth Thompson, 2001.

This study was conducted by Samuel Walker, Ph.D., Professor, University of Nebraska at Omaha; Geoffrey P. Alpert, Ph.D., Washington State University; and Dennis J. Kenney, Ph.D., Rutgers University. Support for the study was provided by NIJ grant number 98-IJ-CX-0002 through a transfer of funds from the Office of Community Oriented Policing Services.

Findings and conclusions of the research reported here are those of the authors and do not necessarily reflect the official position or policies of the U.S. Department of Justice.

The National Institute of Justice is a component of the Office of Justice Programs, which also includes the Bureau of Justice Assistance, the Bureau of Justice Statistics, the Office of Juvenile Justice and Delinquency Prevention, and the Office for Victims of Crime.

Crime Story:
The Digital Age

Harnessing new technologies to community policing.

by John D. Cohen, Adam Gelb, and Robert Wasserman

The crime news these days is mostly good. Over the last eight years, crime rates have plummeted to the lowest levels in decades. Sustained economic growth, reduction in the use of crack cocaine, tougher gun laws and enforcement, and more cops on the beat have combined to make America's streets safer than at any time since the first reliable statistics were collected in the 1960s. Many of these improvements can be attributed to a surge of community policing techniques around the country that have fundamentally altered the philosophy of how many police departments work and the way they interact with their communities.

Yet for all the good news there are troubling signs on the horizon. Crime numbers are not continuing to plummet everywhere (for example, in Dallas and Houston, Texas, and Tampa, Fla.). New drugs such as ecstasy may reinvigorate the narcotics trade. Racial profiling and a perception of unequal law enforcement has cast a pall over improved rela-

tions in areas where community policing was beginning to make a difference. And, perhaps most worrisome, demographers forecast by 2010 a bubble of 4.4 million more youths in the crime-prone 15-to-24-year age group.

What does this mean for the new administration in Washington? It means that an aggressive new crime-fighting strategy—and appropriate funding—must emerge from Congress to help cities and states get a handle on coming crime problems before they spin back into pre-1990s numbers. This anti-crime agenda should build on the new view of community-based crime fighting developed in the last decade and focus on three key priorities:

1. harnessing the new information and communications technologies to give law enforcement agencies new crime-fighting tools;
2. expanding community policing programs with strategies aimed at dangerous people in dangerous places;
3. replacing racial profiling with criminal targeting.

How We Got Here

To understand the choices we face today in crime fighting, it's important to understand how we got where we are. In the early 1990s the nation was mired in an ideological impasse on crime fighting, in which liberals demanded more money to attack social inequities and conservatives insisted on harsher punishment for criminals. President Clinton proposed a Third Way: a new focus on preventing crime by expanding the number of police and deploying them in more creative ways.

The cornerstone of the Clinton administration's anti-crime policy was the establishment of the Office of Community Oriented Policing Services (COPS) within the Department of Justice. COPS provided funding for 100,000 new police officers both to help undermanned police departments around the country and to encourage them to adopt the new, community-oriented policing strategies that had shown great promise in San Diego and other communities. Since its inception, the COPS office has provided more than $6 billion in grants to state and local agencies for technology and new police officers. The COPS office reports that because of its efforts, 109,139 new police officers are working with community members to make neighborhoods safer.

BEATING BAD GUYS: Digital equipment and updated software help pinpoint hot spots and repeat offenders better than old-fashioned hunches and random police cruising.

While the "100,000 cops" initiative grabbed most of the headlines, the most important accomplishment of the COPS program has been strategic: It has shifted the basic policing approach away from the old "911" model known as calls-for-service. This reactive approach is now moving toward community collaboration and preemptive problem solving. Instead of driving around randomly in cars and responding to emergency calls, police are now on foot and on bicycles so that they become visible fixtures in neighborhoods. They work with community leaders to identify conditions that breed disorder; they share information about potential problems; and they forge common strategies for preventing crime, not simply catching criminals after the fact.

In short, community-oriented policing has reconnected police with the communities they serve. It has also breached the bureaucratic barriers that prevented multi-agency responses to the quality-of-life problems that facili-

tate crime, such as broken streetlights and abandoned buildings. Effective crime prevention requires that lights be repaired so that crimes aren't cloaked in darkness and that abandoned houses be condemned and razed so that they cannot be used for prostitution and drug trafficking. Thus, "broken windows" environments are eliminated before they begin attracting or reinforcing criminal activity. Even filling potholes is good policing policy—it frees officers from directing traffic to catching criminals.

Community-oriented policing also helps break down the stovepipe mentality of public agencies. It allows government and citizens to work together to tailor solutions that fit the crime problems in individual neighborhoods. It is supported by emerging information technologies such as wireless data and the Internet to improve the delivery of government services.

Agenda for the Future

Building on these successes, the new administration should pursue a technology-driven agenda for the future that breaks into three key parts—increasing COPS funding for technology tools, targeting hot spots and repeat offenders, and replacing racial profiling with criminal targeting.

1) Boost the technology budget of the COPS program. The federal government should push crime fighting into the digital age by providing national standards that support the deployment of cutting-edge information and communication systems. Through the COPS office, it should funnel seed money to state and local governments.

> "Most police, parole officers, and courts are operating with 20-year-old information technology. Even though high-speed digital technology is already available, many cops must still wait 20 minutes for basic information about a vehicle or person they've stopped."

Rapidly collecting and disseminating good information about the people who commit crime and the places where crime occurs is the key. Yet most police, parole officers, and courts are operating with 20-year-old information technology. Even though high-speed digital technology is already available, many cops must still wait 20 minutes for basic information about a vehicle or person they've stopped (digital technology can obtain and transmit a car's record in 10 seconds). Days or weeks can pass before criminal warrants find their way into computers, leaving dangerous criminals on the street and police unaware they are wanted. Judges sentence offenders without seeing their criminal history records.

Some states, such as Pennsylvania, Maryland, and North Carolina, are working to establish statewide networks that improve information sharing and voice communication between the various components of the criminal justice community. These networks will link state and local law enforcement efforts and non-law enforcement agencies.

In addition to these initiatives, the criminal justice community must adjust to the new phenomenon of cybercrime. As criminals use communications and information technologies to commit traditional crimes in new ways (forgery, identification theft, drug trafficking, child pornography) and to devise entirely new types of crime such as cyberterrorism, law enforcement agencies need to make a techno-leap in crime fighting. This will require substantial new funds and training in areas about which police today have little knowledge.

2) Hit the bad guys where they work. Research on crime convincingly demonstrates two central facts: that crime is highly concentrated in geographic areas, with as much as 50 percent of offenses occurring at just 3 percent of locations; and that a small subset of criminals is responsible for a vastly disproportionate share of crime, with an estimated 5 percent to 7 percent of offenders committing from 50 percent to 70 percent of total offenses. To take advantage of this research, the Justice Department should establish a grant program to support local efforts to target crime hot spots and high-risk offenders.

Other research tells us that certain programs work. True community policing can shut down a drug market and keep it shut down while a traditional street-corner sweep would simply move dealers down the block. A strict regimen of drug testing and treatment, backed up by escalating penalties for violations, can dramatically cut drug use among offenders. Structured after-school activities linked to students' schoolwork can reduce juvenile crime and gangs, as well as drug use and teen pregnancy.

When well managed, each of these efforts can produce results. But used alone, no single approach can hope to turn a blighted neighborhood around, so they must be combined. Crime mapping technology can identify these crime-ridden areas and be used to track, in real time, shifting and emerging patterns so police can get a jump on new trends. Local leaders must coordinate a comprehensive effort with all government resources—policing, parole, prosecution, prevention, drug treatment, nuisance abatement, housing, and business development.

3) Eliminate racial profiling and develop criminal targeting.
Racial profiling is the single greatest threat to the progress we've made in crime reduction. To counter the practice, a number of states have passed legislation that requires police departments to track traffic stops with an eye

to patterns of profiling. Some police departments are under scrutiny by the U.S. Justice Department because of allegations of racial profiling and brutality. Yet tensions between police and minority communities continue to increase—to the point that some police chiefs fear they are just one nasty incident away from an outbreak of civil disobedience. Law enforcement action, whether stopping a motorist, prosecuting a case, or sentencing an offender, must be based on more than statistical probabilities. Police executives must support anti-profiling policies by collecting verifiable data on the contacts that their officers have with citizens and by taking appropriate action against those who exhibit prejudice.

DRIVING WHILE BLACK: Racial profiling drives a wedge between aggrieved citizens and the police. Besides being unjust, it is also poor police work. Digitally-based criminal targeting is far more effective.

Law enforcement officials must also become more much sophisticated about the nature of our cultural prejudice. They should develop a deep and meaningful appreciation of how practices based on invalid assumptions can be perceived as discriminatory by people of color. Then they can become effective and impartial enforcers of the law. They must also understand that racial profiling is ineffective as a crime prevention tool because when police devote time targeting innocent people, criminals are free to commit crimes. Finally, they must understand that racial profiling breeds distrust in the very communities that need aggressive policing, reinforcing racial stereotypes.

Among the tools necessary for color-blind law enforcement are technologies to collect data on traffic and subject stops. But data collection is not enough. The widespread belief that police routinely engage in racial profiling has more to do with outmoded reactive and random crime control techniques traditionally used by police than with overt bias. Ironically, the very Justice Department that is now at the forefront of ending racial profiling promoted the use of profiling as a tool to interdict drug shipments.

The federal government should take a leadership role in eliminating racial profiling and replacing it with criminal targeting based on faster access to good information. Washington must make it a priority to provide police officers the needed technology so that they no longer rely on hunches; then they can target the people who are actually involved in criminal activity. With real time access to information that targets people who have committed crimes as opposed to members of racial and ethnic minorities, police can do a more effective job.

Conclusion

Sixty years ago, advances in technology—the patrol car and the two-way radio—offered great promise to improve the effectiveness of law enforcement. Unwittingly, these advances separated police from the citizens they are sworn to serve.

The recent movement toward community policing has started to rebuild those bonds. Now, the technology boom must be aggressively used to exchange information and establish stronger ties between all government agencies and citizens.

Police action alone can never free neighborhoods from crime and violence. Nor by itself can it reduce fear. Only when law enforcement is viewed as an integral part of a fully accountable government structure will we be able to systematically create strong communities resistant to disorder, decline, and crime.

John D. Cohen is president and CEO of PSComm, LLC, and executive director of the Progressive Policy Institute's Community Crime Fighting Project. Adam Gelb is chief operating officer of PSComm, LLC, and a former policy adviser to Maryland Lt. Gov. Kathleen Kennedy Townsend. Robert Wasserman is chairman of PSComm, LLC, and former chief of staff of the White House Office of National Drug Control Policy.

From *Blueprint* magazine, Winter 2001, pp. 56-59. © 2001 by Blueprint. Reprinted by permission.

Ethics and Criminal Justice: Some Observations on Police Misconduct

by Bryan Byers
Ball State University

One need not look far to see evidence of the societal importance placed on ethics in criminal justice. Ethics has been a hot topic in the 1990s and promises to be equally important as we venture into the new millennium. Often, the issue of ethics in criminal justice is considered synonymous with police ethics. However, ethics touches all of the main branches of criminal justice practice as well as the academic realm. Due to the high profile nature of policing in our society, however, ethics is commonly connected with policing. Therefore, particular focus is given to this dimension in the following discussion. Within this essay the topic of ethics is addressed by first examining a general understanding of this concept. Second, a brief discussion of our societal concern over ethics and criminal justice practice is examined. Third, the discussion centers on selected scholarship in criminal justice ethics. Finally, some concluding remarks are offered.

ETHICS AND ETHICAL ISSUES: A PRIMER

According to the Merriam-Webster Dictionary, "ethics" is defined as (1) "a discipline dealing with good and evil and with moral duty" or (2) "moral principles or practice." The first definition suggests that ethics is a discipline or area of study. This certainly has been the case when we examine the academic field of Philosophy. Criminal justice is, admittedly, a hybrid discipline drawing from many academic fields—one being Philosophy. Interestingly, a good portion of the published academic scholarship in criminal justice ethics is philosophical in nature and can be found in the journal *Criminal Justice Ethics*. The other part of the definition sug-

gests that ethics is a combination of cognition ('moral principles') and behavior ('practice'). Therefore, we might conclude that ethics is the study of the principle and practice of good, evil, and moral duty.

As we consider the nature of criminal justice, and in particular policing, within contemporary society, the behavior of law enforcement officers is continually the target of ethical evaluation. The field of law enforcement has been under scrutiny during various historical epochs for behavior that has been called into question on ethical grounds. Whether it be search and seizure "fishing expeditions" prior to *Mapp v. Ohio*, the fallout from the Knapp Commission report (*à la Serpico*) or the latest instance of police misconduct to flood the media, essentially the concern is over conduct or behavior. Cognitive processes and the socialization that reinforces unprofessional and unethical conduct influence the onset and proliferation of undesirable behavior. Thus, while one must be concerned with psychological and sociological forces that help to produce police unprofessionalism and unethical behavior, we should not lose sight of the role choice has in police misconduct.

One would be hard pressed to produce credible evidence to suggest that policing has not become more professional over the past several decades. It seems equally unreasonable to suggest that the entire field of policing is corrupt and permeated with graft. However, and as most readers will know, such an explanation has been offered. The venerable "rotten barrel theory"[1] of police corruption suggests such permeation within a police department. As most readers know, the rotten barrel theory of police corruption suggests that unethical and illegal behavior not only occurs at the individual officer level but is pervasive

enough within a police department that unethical conduct may be traced to top administrative officials.

Another interpretation of police corruption is the "rotten apple theory."[2] This approach does not suggest that corruption and unethical conduct is so pervasive that it spreads to the highest ranks and throughout the organization. This approach, rather, suggests that there are a few "rotten apples" in a police department and inappropriate behavior is isolated to a few individuals. Police administrators have been keen on this explanation in the wake of police corruption because it avoids suggestion of wholesale departmental corruption, allows for a tidy response (e.g., fire the offending officer), and does not necessarily have to result in a tarnished image of an entire department.

An additional form of police misconduct has also been identified. In addition to the rotten apple and the rotten barrel, there may also be a "rotten group theory" of police corruption. According to a 1998 report by the General Accounting Office on police corruption in the United States, "The most commonly identified pattern of drug-related police corruption involved small groups of officers who protected and assisted each other in criminal activities, rather than the traditional patterns of non-drug-related police corruption that involved just a few isolated individuals or systemic corruption pervading an entire police department or precinct."[3]

Whether unethical behavior is systematic, small group, or individual, one cannot deny the importance placed on the intellectual process that allows for such conduct to take place. One might still be left wondering what it is about policing that produces opportunities to engage in unethical behavior. That is, what is it about the policing profession that affords officers the opportunity to engage in unethical conduct? The answer might be found in the concepts of "authority" and "power." Police wield a tremendous amount of power and authority within society. The powers to arrest, question and detain are entrusted with the police. The authority given to the police to protect our belongings and persons is unmatched by any other profession. Unethical or illegal behavior results when a law enforcement officer makes a conscious decision to abuse authority or wield power that is not appropriate to the situation. What is fundamental to unethical behavior by police is the conscious decision to abuse authority or power and circumstances, peer pressure, socialization, loyalty, and individual psychology are secondary in their ability to explain the behavior.

It might be best to interpret the role played by factors such as circumstances, peer pressure, socialization, loyalty, and individual psychology as a means of excusing or justifying the unethical or illegal act committed by an officer. That is, while the individual officer makes a decision to violate the public's trust and engage in unethical behavior, one might suggest that the officer's loyalty to his peers was a justification for the conduct. Let us examine this dynamic by way of an ethical dilemma. Assume that Officer X has just pulled over a drunk driver and realizes that the suspect is a fellow officer and friend. In fact, the driver has helped Officer X out of a few "tight spots" over the years. Instead of placing the colleague through a field sobriety test, Officer X helps his buddy park the car and then drives him home with the understanding from his friend that he will "sleep it off." What was the ethical dilemma? The choice between doing what was appropriate (the field sobriety test and subsequent arrest if appropriate) and being loyal to his friend. This situation, at the very least, describes a scenario ripe for abuse of discretion. Since discretion is a power that police have, it can be abused. Thus, many might examine this situation and suggest that the officer abused his discretionary authority. The officer made a decision to abuse his power but did so out of loyalty to the friend that is promoted through socialization behind the "blue curtain."

CONCERN OVER ETHICS: CAN WE CALL IT A TREND?

Media reports of police misconduct pepper us whenever there is an incident of alleged misbehavior or corruption. It might be the nightly newscaster reporting on the Rodney King incident at the start of the 1990s. It could be the recent case of the Philadelphia Police Department officers viewed on tape kicking a downed felony crime suspect at the birth of the twenty-first century. Whatever the instance, the topic of ethics and ethical behavior within the criminal justice profession grabs headlines. The media likes to report on such "ethical misadventures" because it sells. Some of the public, and powerful leaders, use such instances to legitimize their negative attitudes toward police. The police loathe the "bad press" in the wake of their self-perception of "doing good" for the community.

The media might be the only winner in the wake of police misconduct. However, the public loses and so do the fields of policing and criminal justice, in general. Even the academic field of criminal justice loses because policing is so closely linked in the public mind to it. I am reminded of this reality when recalling my flight back from the 1991 Academy of Criminal Justice Sciences meeting in Nashville. As plane passengers do, I began a conversation with the person seated next to me. We engaged in the typical small talk of "where are you from" and "where are you going." When my fellow passenger heard that I was returning from a "criminal justice" meeting, his response was immediate and unequivocal. He said, "why are cops such jerks?" The conversation occurred in the wake of the Rodney King incident and he was referring to the behavior of the L.A. police officers captured on tape. Admittedly taken aback, I was speechless. Part of the reason was personal, given my experiences in the field as a practitioner and those of close family members and friends. The other part of my speechlessness was professional and social scientific in nature, given how astounding it was to me to find a person willing to generalize so broadly from one highly celebrated incident. This seemingly innocuous exchange had an indelible impression on me. It made me think about the impact the field of criminal justice might have in the topic of ethics.

There is little doubt that real world events and their impact on the collective conscience influence the academic field. In fact, one could reasonably argue that societal events drive research agendas and define, to some degree, what is popular to investigate criminologically and what is not. Ethics may be no exception. For instance, the Rodney King incident, one might argue, had a tremendous impact not only on the practical dimensions of policing and police-community relations but also on the academic field of criminal justice. For instance, the book jacket for *Above the Law: Police and the Excessive Use of Force* by Jerome Skolnick and James Fyfe has a frame from the Rodney King video just below the title. The impact goes beyond one book, however.

Using 1991 as a pivotal year, given that the Rodney King beating occurred then, the author decided to conduct a computer search for articles on ethics in criminal justice. The findings, albeit not scientific, are interesting nonetheless. Using Periodical Abstracts, an on-line search method at my institution and offered through the university library, a search was conducted for "criminal justice" + "ethics" comparing the years 1986–1990 to 1991–1999. What I wanted to find out is this: were there more publications in criminal justice ethics prior to Rodney King or after? Since the incident occurred relatively early in 1991, that year was placed in the "post-Rodney King" group of years. From 1986 (the first year the index covers) through 1990, there were 28 "hits" or publications on criminal justice ethics. From 1991 through 1999 there were 152 publications. Admittedly, the "post" period encompassed nine years and the "pre" period only contained five years. However, it is still rather telling that such a difference exists.

Only time will tell if the aforementioned suggests a trend for the discipline. However, there is certainly every indication that criminal justice scholarship and practice will continue with an emphasis on ethics. A key reason why ethics promises to have a strong future presence has less to do with the lasting impact of Rodney King and more to do with constant reminders that ethical misadventures keep occurring. For example, during the past ten years, the cities of New Orleans, Chicago, New York, Miami, and Los Angeles, to name a few, have all reeled in the aftermath of ethical transgressions among their sworn law enforcement officers.

ETHICS AND CRIMINAL JUSTICE PRACTICE

In addition to the Rodney King case, there have been many other instances in which law enforcement officers have been found in ethically compromising or illegal positions. Every major city police force in the United States has experienced some form of unethical or illegal behavior within its ranks. Some of the situations in recent history have involved drugs and drug units. A few examples are listed below:

- A 1998 report by the General Accounting Office cites examples of publicly disclosed drug-related police corruption in the following cities: Atlanta, Chicago, Cleveland, Detroit, Los Angeles, Miami, New Orleans, New York, Philadelphia, Savannah, and Washington, DC. [4]

- On average, half of all police officers convicted as a result of FBI-led corruption cases between 1993 and 1997 were convicted for drug-related offenses.[5]

- A 1998 report by the General Accounting Office notes, "… several studies and investigations of drug-related police corruption found on-duty police officers engaged in serious criminal activities, such as (1) conducting unconstitutional searches and seizures; (2) stealing money and/or drugs from drug dealers; (3) selling stolen drugs; (4) protecting drug operations; (5) providing false testimony; and (6) submitting false crime reports."[6]

- A 1998 report by the General Accounting Office notes, "Although profit was found to be a motive common to traditional and drug-related police corruption, New York City's Mollen Commission identified power and vigilante justice as two additional motives for drug-related police corruption."[7]

- As an example of police corruption, the GAO cites Philadelphia, where "Since 1995, 10 police officers from Philadelphia's 39th District have been charged with planting drugs on suspects, shaking down drug dealers for hundreds of thousands of dollars, and breaking into homes to steal drugs and cash."[8]

- In New Orleans, 11 police officers were convicted of accepting nearly $100,000 from undercover agents to protect a cocaine supply warehouse containing 286 pounds of cocaine. The undercover portion of the investigation was terminated when a witness was killed under orders from a New Orleans police officer. [9]

Part of the fallout from a major finding of unethical or illegal behavior within a police department is a call to "clean up" the agency. As a result, departments in the aftermath of such an embarrassing situation might become more open to citizen review panels, pledge to re-examine their internal affairs division, require officers to participate in "ethics training," or reinforce the importance of "ethics codes."

The concept of citizen review panels has been in existence for several decades; the first panel may have been formed in Philadelphia around 1958. Citizen review panels, sometimes also called civilian review boards, are in place in some jurisdictions for the purpose of assisting with the investigation of citizen complaints that police officers within the jurisdiction engaged in the unfair treatment of civilians. Review panels can help to build or repair strained police-community relations. However, officers sometimes respond to such efforts with a defensive posture and resentment over "civilians trying to tell them how to do their job."

A department might also pledge to examine its own internal affairs division, the policy and procedure for investigating complaints and cases against officers, and typical responses to officers who have violated departmental policy and/or who have violated the law. It is important to note from the onset that a police department internal affairs division runs the risk of being considered "suspect" from officers and a community's citizenry alike. Officers can view internal affair or "I.A." as the "enemy" and a division that is bent on punishing officers who are risking their lives on the streets every day. From the community, there might be the perception that the police department cannot possibly take on the task of investigating itself. At the very least, this cannot be done "ethically." Thus, I.A. can find itself in a no-win situation. Whether a division in a large department or an officer charged with this responsibility in a smaller department, the I.A. role is critical. However, internal remedies are effective only if they are meted out in a fair and just fashion. I.A. recommendations that are carried out by police administration must bolster the respect of line officers. If perceptions exist that an officer has been treated unfairly, the department will lose any deterrent effect I.A. recommendations might produce.

Yet another response is the concept of "ethics training" for police officers and recruits. The notion of "ethics *training*" (with an emphasis on 'training') is an interesting one given that the concept of 'training' assumes that what a person is being "trained in" can be taught. In this case, the term

'ethics training' suggests, either correctly or incorrectly, that ethics can somehow be taught to people. I prefer the term "Ethics Awareness Training" in lieu of the aforementioned. Why? The reason is rather elementary. Is it possible to teach someone to be ethical as "ethics training" might suggest? This seems far-fetched, at best. If a department has an officer who has a propensity toward unethical behavior, and this person was not weeded out during the hiring process, the best one might hope for is a heightened awareness and sensitivity for ethical issues and dilemmas. Emphasizing codes of ethics, common today in most disciplines and professions,[10] is another avenue for police departments in the wake of ethical scandal. However, if a code of ethics[11] is printed in the departmental policy and procedure manual, never to be referred to again, it will have very little impact. A code of ethics for any department or organization must be a "living document" that is referenced often and held in high esteem. The code should be a document that officers have pride in and believe to be relevant to their lives as law enforcement officers. Otherwise, the code will have little, if any, impact on officer decision making and conduct.

THE SCHOLARS WEIGH IN

As mentioned above, a large portion of the academic scholarship in criminal justice ethics is philosophical in nature. However, a few academicians have attempted to examine ethics in criminal justice empirically and quantitatively. When discussing scholarship in criminal justice ethics, a few names immediately come to mind, including James Fyfe, Herman Goldstein, Victor Keppeler, Carl Klockars, Joycelyn Pollock, Lawrence Sherman, Jerome Skolnick and Sam Souryal. This is certainly not an exhaustive list, and we cannot possibly survey all of the literature in this field here. However, I would like to spend a few moments discussing two major studies funded by NIJ. The studies are *The Measurement of Police Integrity* by Klockars, Ivkovitch, Harver, and Haberfeld[12] and *Police Attitudes Toward Abuse of Authority: Findings from a National Study* by Weisburd and Greenspan.[13] Both studies were published in May of 2000. While the two studies do not represent the entire literature on police ethics, both studies are national in scope, recent and empirical.

The Klockars et al. study used 3,235 police officer respondents from 30 police agencies within the United States. The respondents were given 11 vignettes describing various types of possible police misconduct. In response to each vignette, officers were asked to answer six questions intended to measure "... the normative inclination of police to resist temptations to abuse the rights and privileges of their occupation." While the results indicate vast differences from agency to agency regarding the "environment of integrity," one finding is consistent with the protections afforded members of the police subculture. The survey revealed that most officers would not report a fellow officer who was engaged in "less serious" types of misconduct (e.g., running a security business on the side, receiving free meals and gifts, or even leaving a minor traffic accident while under the influence). What this suggests, even though the survey revealed little tolerance for what was defined as "serious" police misconduct, is that there is a culture of acceptance within police ranks for some forms of misconduct. While such conduct is typically referred to as "grass eating" (less serious forms of police misconduct) as opposed to "meat eating" (more serious forms of police misconduct), many members of society would find the behavior unacceptable. James W. Birch in *Reflections on Police Corruption*[14] makes an interesting observation regarding such behavior. He states that the public creates an environment for "grass eating" that makes it difficult to not accept the "discount" or the free meal. It would appear that there may be a different definition of what constitutes "misconduct" depending on whether a person is a member of the police subculture or an outsider looking in.

The second NIJ study, by Weisburd and Greenspan, entitled "*Police Attitudes Toward Abuse of Authority: Findings From a National Study*" is the result of the Police Foundation's national telephone survey of over 900 officers from various agencies across the country and addresses police attitudes concerning excessive force. The results indicate that the majority of respondents believed it was not acceptable to use more force than was legally permissible to effect control over a person who had assaulted an officer. However, respondents reported that "... it is not unusual for officers to ignore improper

conduct by their fellow officers." Other findings suggest that the majority of officers/respondents believed that serious instances of abuse were rare and that their department maintained a 'tough stand' on police abuse of citizenry. What about possible solutions to the problem of police abuse? Officers report two fruitful avenues for addressing police abuse. First, it was reported police administrators could have an impact on the occurrence of police abuse by "taking a stand" against abuse and through better supervision. Second, officers believed that training in ethics, interpersonal skills and cultural diversity would be effective in preventing abuse. What about turning fellow officers in for abuse? This was perceived as risky. While the majority of officers maintained that the "code of silence" was not essential to good policing, the majority also maintained that whistle blowing was not worth the consequences within the police subculture.

TOWARD A CONCLUSION

It is difficult to conclude this discussion because there is so much more to say about the topic of ethics in criminal justice. However, I will attempt to make a few concluding observations to make closure on this discussion. First, ethics is an important area within criminal justice practice and scholarship since criminal justice practitioners, especially the police, are continually under scrutiny. Therefore, the discipline has an obligation to remain interested in this topic and to promote the study of ethics. Second, scholars can be of assistance to practitioners by studying the sociological and psychological forces that impact ethical and unethical behavior. There is much the academy can offer criminal justice agencies in the form of research within organizations and training pertinent to ethics. Third, unethical behavior is the result of a conscious decision-making process to abuse one's authority while in a position of public trust. However, one must still take into account social forces that help to perpetuate, excuse, and justify unethical behavior. Fourth, there has been a proliferation of ethics scholarship in criminal justice since the Rodney King case but there is a need for more research of an empirical nature

much like the two studies profiled in this essay. While qualitative and philosophical literature is important to our understanding of ethics in criminal justice there is a need for additional research of a quantitative nature. With more study of ethics and ethical dilemmas faced by police, we might better understand the dynamics that propel officers into the dark side of policing and the factors that serve to justify misbehavior.

ENDNOTES

1. Police Deviance and Ethics. http://faculty.ncwc.edu/toconnor/205/205lec11.htm.

2. Knapp Commission Report. (1973). New York: George Braziller.

3. Government Accounting Office. Report to the Honorable Charles B. Rangel, House of Representatives, Law Enforcement: Information on Drug-Related Police Corruption. Washington, DC: USGPO (1998 May), p. 3.

4. Ibid. p. 36–37.

5. Ibid. p. 35.

6. Ibid. p. 8.

7. Ibid. p. 3.

8. Ibid. p. 37.

9. Ibid. p. 36.

10. The Academy of Criminal Justice Sciences (ACJS) recently adopted a code of ethics modeled after the American Sociological Association's (ASA) code.

11. The International Association of Chiefs of Police (IACP) has a model code of ethics and also publishes a training key on ethics and policing.

12. Klockars, C.B., S.K. Ivkovich, W.E. Harver, and M.R. Haberfeld. (2000, May). "The Measurement of Police Integrity." National Institute of Justice, Research in Brief. U.S. Government Printing Office: Washington, DC.

13. Weisburd, D. and R. Greenspan. (2000, May). "Police Attitudes Toward Abuse of Authority: Findings from a National Study." National Institute of Justice, Research in Brief. U.S. Government Printing Office: Washington, DC.

14. Birch, James W. (1983). "Reflections on Police Corruption." *Criminal Justice Ethics*, Volume 2.

From *Academy of Criminal Justice Sciences (ACJS) Today*, September/October 2000, pp. 1, 4-7. Reprinted with permission of the Academy of Criminal Justice Sciences.

Spirituality and Police Suicide: A Double-Edged Sword

Abstract: The stigma associated with suicide among police officers is often a reason why suicide is on the list of taboo topics for discussion. Like many other sensitive issues in law enforcement, such discussion makes us uncomfortable. Attempting to introduce the issue of spirituality into the area of suicide and law enforcement causes even more uneasiness. This article addresses the spiritual dimensions of police suicides. Spirituality is a two-edged sword; while it can be an asset in dealing with the problem, it also can be viewed as suspect. Both suicide and spirituality are emotionally charged issues, begging to be addressed in conjunction. This article explores the issues within the law enforcement profession that may have a corelationship to the prevalence of suicide among police officers. An authentic spiritual perspective on these issues may help officers who might be at risk for attempting suicide.

Key words: spirituality, police suicide, law enforcement, suicide, higher being

Joseph J. D'Angelo

INTRODUCTION

Contrary to the theme song of the long-running television series "M.A.S.H.," suicide is not painless. Every so often, daily newspapers carry a story about the suicide of a police officer. A *New York Daily News* headline recently screamed the message "His Pain Was Too Much" (August 6, 1999). According to John Marzulli, *Daily News* staff writer, police officer Salvatore Glibbery was a highly decorated officer with a bright future who took his life with a lethal overdose of pills. Subsequently, New York Police Department psychological reports disclosed that police officer Glibbery suffered from post-traumatic stress disorder (PTSD) as a result of the fatal shooting 12 years ago of an individual who was emotionally disturbed. Although he was exonerated by a grand jury, he apparently never forgave himself for his justified action. Glibbery lived with the psychological pain and its accompanying physical symptoms, insomnia, nightmares and depression, which even the prescribed Prozac could not ease. Now that he is dead, his family, friends and colleagues have inherited the pain of loss and grief.

Sadly, this is only one of all too many such stories of police officers throughout our country who commit suicide and the subsequent questions of their survivors still remain: Why did this happen? What could we have done to prevent this? Why did no one see it coming? And deeper questions exist: What do these self-destructive behaviors mean? What has happened to make this individual so incredibly hopeless that he wanted to take his own life (Turvey, 1995)?

Suicide is painful. Pain precedes it, pain is at its core and pain results for those who remain. Merely 1 week prior to this event the Surgeon General, David Satcher, declared suicide to be a serious mental health problem and the eighth leading cause of death in the United States. For the first time in our nation's history, a mental health issue has been raised as a public health concern and strategies have been called for to prevent further suffering. The article in *New York Newsday* (July 29, 1999) cited statistics indicating that 31,000 Americans committed suicide in 1966, which is about 85 people per day.

The suicide of any individual is devastating and leaves us with many painful questions, which need to be answered. For those involved in law enforcement these painful questions are compounded by the fact that these suicides have ramifications for the entire police profession. Perhaps the whole police culture needs to be examined to come to an answer to these questions as well as to find solutions to this hidden epidemic within law enforcement.

PERSPECTIVES ON THE PROBLEM

Perhaps there are elements within the police culture or the job itself that we need to ask questions about to sort out factors that seem to contribute to police suicide. One thing is certain: there is little or no formal training about suicide awareness in police academies. Like many other sensitive subjects facing the law enforcement community, the issue of suicide is often ignored by agency administrations. There is a prevailing myth that the police officer is invulnerable and indestructible. There is certainly a stigma associated with any suicide, but the suicide of a police officer is often seen as dishonor, a sign of weakness and failure and a disgrace to the profession.

Numerous studies have been conducted to attempt to determine both the extent and causes of police suicides. A study by the University of Buffalo that states that police officers are eight times as likely to die by suicide than by homicide. This happens to be the only study that compares police risk factors to other occupations. The study further indicates that police suicides often are misclassified, thus leading to an underestimation of the risks. In addition, many police suicides are reported as accidental (Baker, 1996).

What is it about the job of the police officer that might be considered a risk factor for suicide? One immediately may think of police stress. According to Hal Brown (1998), the link between police stress and police suicide has not been studied adequately; it has been misrepresented and even ignored. He further suggests that, because of possible embarrassment, life insurance considerations and potential lawsuits, police suicides often are covered up or underreported as such; thus, any possible remedial actions could not have taken place. Brown declares that there is no such thing as run-of-the-mill stress and that police officers are able to pretend that they are immune to it; what appears to be minor stress can really be the tip of the iceberg and should be taken seriously.

Stress

Even the issue of whether job stress is worse for law enforcement officers is debated by many researchers. There is both agreement and disagreement in the works of Hammett (1999), Ivanoff (1994) and Turvey (1995), which this writer has consulted for this paper. Police stress notwithstanding, research also has shown strong links between PTSD and police suicides.

If police stress is only the tip of the iceberg, then what else can be considered as possible risk factors? A review of the research and literature indicates that the following issues usually are associated with police suicide: interpersonal and relationship problems, depression and the use of alcohol and drugs (Ivanoff, 1994). Also cited are police corruption and misconduct, with its accompanying shame and humiliation, along with divorce and mental breakdown (McNamara, 1996). In addition, stress and burnout, feelings of isolation and alienation (Symonds, 1996), continuous exposure to human misery, overbearing police bureaucracy, inconsistencies in the criminal justice system, shift work, lack of control over working conditions, social strain, physical illness and impending retirement

also may play a part (Baker, 1996). According to Kirschman (1997), the loss of a relationship is perhaps the most devastating factor and often is associated with a suicide.

Some people would go so far as to suggest that a police agency that is insensitive to the needs and concerns of its officers can be considered a contributing cause of police suicide. Brown (1998) suggests that if those in command-level authority paid more attention to police morale and were more alert to signs of distress in the ranks, there would be less police officer depression. He further states that when police officers feel betrayed or abandoned by their administrators, they often feel anger, rage and resentment, which are acted upon in the form of the on-duty suicide designed to punish the administration.

According to John Violanti (1995), the greatest reason that police officers take their own lives is because they have nowhere to go for confidential help for their problems. It is no secret that police officers, due to their role and job, reluctantly seek assistance for emotional or psychological problems. They tend to be mistrustful of mental health professionals and even of the employee assistance counselors within the department (Hammett, 1999).

Turvey (1995) seems to suggest that, in addition to the aforementioned risk factors, there are two other significant issues worthy of consideration that immediately may not come to mind: control and hopelessness. These two issues seem to beat the core of police suicides and are directly related to the police culture. Police officers are taught early in their careers that they must be in control not only of the scene but also of their emotions. To be out of control threatens an officer's sense of vulnerability. Just as control is a primary element of the police culture, it is related to the issue of suicide. Because the officer's gun represents the ultimate control, as well as the officer's obligation to control the environment, the officer is trained to use it as the ultimate solution when circumstances require it. When police officers believe that they are losing control over their lives due to a personal problem, the gun provides an easy solution. Suicide may be perceived as the only means of personal control.

Hopelessness

This leads us to the issue of hopelessness. The sense that one does not have control over one's feelings, behavior, or circumstances results in a sense of self-resignation toward perceived or real elements in one's life. Hopelessness grows slowly and, left unabated, develops into an insurmountable state of mind that can be the strongest factor in suicidal ideation. As Turvey declares, when a police officer commits suicide it is most certainly an expression of hopelessness, whether perceived or real, within the perspectives defined by the police culture. It is important to note that hopelessness is indeed a factor of one's own perception and one's perception is often determined by one's cultural environment. We shall return to these concepts of control and hopelessness later.

Another possible risk factor for police officer suicide is found in the work of Blatt (1999), whose research focused on the link between perfectionism and high achievers with depression and suicide. He suggests that the very quality that drives some people toward high achievement-perfectionism—also may be the characteristic that leads them to self-destructive tendencies. This certainly would apply to the police profession, which seems to attract individuals who are either self-oriented perfectionists or become socially prescribed perfectionists due to the culture of the job. The first type of perfectionism involves setting exceedingly high and unrealistic self-imposed standards, self-scrutiny and criticism and having an inability to accept faults, flaws, or failure. The second type involves the belief that others hold exaggerated expectations that are either difficult or impossible to achieve. Some police officers seem to belong to both types at once, trying to attain both self-approval and approval from others.

THE ROLE OF SPIRITUALITY

Introducing the notion of spirituality into a discussion about suicide is fraught with many dangers. Both suicide and spirituality are extremely emotionally charged issues. Sadly, some in the field of mental health would object to such an introduction, not to mention the fact that some in law enforcement may be uncomfortable with such a discussion as well.

The subtitle of this article suggests that spirituality is a two-edged sword when applied to the topic of suicide. On the one hand, our Western cultural religious views, contained in Christianity, Judaism and Islam, categorically condemn suicide as immoral and contrary to the will and plan of God. Besides the social stigma, there is also the stigma associated with taking any human life, even if it is one's own. The consequences are seen in the prohibition against burying suicides in consecrated ground and the like. Here, for some individuals, the decision not to commit suicide may come either from guilt or from a firm belief in the dignity and value of human life. It is a curious phenomenon that some people who may be contemplating suicide might be looking for permission to do so from some religious authority. Thankfully, modern applications of religious views have taken suicide out of the realm of morality and have placed it within the realm of psychology and spiritual wellness.

Nevertheless, it is this writer's opinion that a healthy and authentic spirituality can be an asset in preventing suicide among police officers. Good spirituality is good psychology; that is to say, spirituality can aid in the psychological process of dealing with the issues related to police officer suicide. Thus, spirituality and psychology can work in concert towards spiritual and mental health. Naturally, there are also aberrations of spirituality that need to be avoided as unhealthy and detrimental to one's spiritual and mental well-being. Thus, the notion of the double-edged sword.

But, what exactly is spirituality? First, spirituality is not the same as religion. Religion is the manner in which an individual lives out his/her spirituality, usually in some type of formal structure, institution, or organization. Spirituality is, therefore, broader than religion. Spirituality can be described as one's relationship with three realities: a transcendent higher being (which some choose to call God), one's self and the universe, including other individuals. Most people would accept the no-

tion of the existence of such a transcendent higher being, even if they could not come to know such a being. This is known as agnosticism. One's relationship with one's self is usually the area associated with psychology. Nevertheless, spirituality also influences this area as well, which is the domain of the soul or spirit. Certainly, our relationship with the created universe of the world around us and its people is what living is all about; spirituality is the means whereby human beings relate to these realities and entities.

It has been said that within each human being there is a spiritual yearning for connection with these realities and that lacking these connections, human beings experience a void or emptiness within the spirit. Here is where many people get into difficulty, for when we experience such a void in any of these areas, we attempt to fill these empty spaces with something other than what is intended or healthy. Thus, things, activities and behaviors that are perceived to be fulfilling become a downfall. Drugs, alcohol, sex, money, material possessions, power, status and fame all become our gods and our universe. But alas, the void still remains and we are not fulfilled at all. Healthy spirituality can restore people to a proper and fulfilling relationship with a higher being, ourselves and the world and its people. If all is well in the spiritual realm, it stands to reason that there is a good chance that all will be well in the psychological realm as well.

Spirituality and psychology are not in conflict; in fact, they can work in harmony to alleviate the spiritual and psychic pain that people experience. Spiritual remedies can be applied to the causes or factors that result in suicide. Suicide is not about death; it is about relieving the pain and lifting the burden of suffering.

Most people would agree that the root of most of our psychological problems is found in low self-esteem. The same could be said for most spiritual problems as well, but a healthy spirituality can help raise one's self-esteem. The once-popular adage among young people, "God does not make junk," is an affirmation for building self-esteem. It implies that people are special and beloved to the Creator, that everyone is worth something and also worthy of everything life holds. If people believe that they are indeed worth something, that they are worthy of love and being loved, they will, in turn, treat themselves as having worth and deserving worth. Consequently, people also will treat others the same way and relationships will be of quality.

Many things in a police officer's life can contribute to low self-esteem: experiences deriving from childhood education and relationships with family, friends, colleagues. For many police officers, self-esteem is tied to their self-perception as a police officer. Some cops may attach more importance and worth to what they do than to who they are. The job and its stressors all play into the officer's self-esteem; it is a job in which an officer continually is being judged by colleagues, supervisors and even the public for mistakes or poor decisions. The officer can be his/her own worst critic. Feelings of self-worth are tied to judgment and the perception of judgement.

How, then, can people apply a healthy and authentic spirituality, that is, spiritual values that are life-affirming, to the contributing factors of suicide among police officers? Spirituality has something to offer toward addressing the aforementioned factors and causes. Spirituality does not attempt to offer simplistic solutions to these complex problems. Rather, it offers alternatives and choices for what seems to be a hopeless situation.

Chaplain's Role

Through pastoral counseling by a chaplain or other clergy person, healthy spirituality can be a resource for police officers in dealing with troubled interpersonal relationships and marital difficulties. The common element and major contributor to police officer suicides is the inability or refusal to seek outside assistance. In addition, the practice of spiritual love (charity), which is the expression of basic human respect for the dignity and value of each individual, can be a framework for restoring and maintaining quality interpersonal relationships. Spiritual counseling often helps people deal with issues of shame, including the shame associated with thoughts of suicide.

Feelings of isolation and alienation often are addressed in the spiritual realm. Spirituality teaches one to reach out and to rely on others for help. It attempts to engender trust in a community of believers, which can take the form of a particular church or congregational setting. The spiritual support of such a group can provide a feeling of belonging and acceptance even amidst feelings to the contrary.

Like psychological counseling, spiritual counseling plays a part in alleviating symptoms of depression and anxiety. Here is where spirituality and psychology can and should work in collaboration to address depression and its underlying symptoms of anger, fear and anxiety. The spiritual practices of prayer and mediation often are helpful to deal constructively with anger, to face one's fears with fortitude and to trust in a Higher Being.

Spirituality has much to say about control and helplessness, which are factors in police suicide. Paradoxically, spirituality suggests that to gain control, one must relinquish control. Surrender is at the heart of serenity: not surrender in the sense of hopeless resignation, which is passive, but in the sense of giving over to our higher being what we recognize as beyond their control. This is the active surrender modeled in the philosophy of Alcoholics Anonymous, where addicted individuals ask the higher power for the serenity to accept the things that cannot be changed, the courage to change what they can and the wisdom to know the difference (The Serenity Prayer).

Surrender is difficult, especially for police officers, who are taught never to surrender to anyone or anything. Active surrender is positive, not negative; it is a firm decision to face a reality that is greater than one's self and beyond one's ability to control. It is certainly a spiritual skill that needs to be taught and maintained for serenity to be attained and preserved.

Hopelessness is at the root of our self-destructive behaviors and is the enemy of our spiritual well-being. Without hope

human beings are doomed to fail in all areas of their lives and in life itself. If spirituality provides anything at all, it indeed provides hope. Instilling hope, which is so necessary as a therapeutic factor in psychological counseling, is also essential in spiritual counseling. It has been said that love is stronger than death. In this writer's opinion hope, above all else, is stronger than death. As stated before, suicide is not about death; it is about relieving pain. Hope can lift and remove the pain. Spirituality is all about hope, for it affirms that nothing in heaven or on earth can come between us and the love of God. The Jewish convert to Christianity, Paul, expresses many such affirmations in his Letter to the Romans. While this may reflect the traditional Judaeo-Christian view, most spiritual world views and religions also emphasize hope.

This writer submits that the healthy practice of the spiritual values of faith (trust), hope and charity (love) can be an invaluable foundation for alleviating the problems that can lead some people to commit suicide. Neither spirituality nor psychology can provide the so-called "magic bullet" (no pun intended) for the human spirit and psyche, but working together they can provide relief for the pain of suicide.

CONCLUSION

Spirituality does not pretend to provide simplistic solutions to life's complex problems; it is not a panacea for anxieties. Yet, denial prevents people from even admitting that there is a problem and thus from reaching any solutions. People must begin to recognize that police officer suicide is no longer a myth or a taboo topic. Police agencies must provide training and education on the early identification of potential police suicides and remove the stigma of seeking help for emotional problems. Police officers must believe that there is nothing wrong with availing themselves of confidential help from trusted peers, a chaplain, or another professional. The law enforcement community must recognize that spiritual remedies and spiritual practices can provide alternatives to traditional strategies of dealing with problems that threaten the emotional and psychological well-being of police officers. Finally, psychology and spirituality must join forces in providing sound psychological techniques and healthy spiritual practices to alleviate the pain that is at the core of police officer suicide.

Address correspondence concerning this article to Joseph J. D'Angelo, Chaplain, Nassau County Police Department, c/o *Joseph J. D'Angelo, 720 Merrick Avenue, North Merrick, NY 11566*

From *FBI Behavioral Science Unit*, 2001, pp. 503–510. Excerpted from "Suicide and Law Enforcement," by Donald C. Sheehan and Janet I. Warren, Editors. Reprinted by permission.

UNIT 4

The Judicial System

Unit Selections

21. **Jury Consulting on Trial**, D. W. Miller
22. **Opting in to Mental Health Courts**, Anne M. Hasselbrack
23. **Anatomy of a Verdict**, D. Graham Burnett
24. **Looking Askance at Eyewitness Testimony**, D. W. Miller
25. **The Creeping Expansion of DNA Data Banking**, Barry Steinhardt

Key Points to Consider

- Do you see any alternatives to "getting tough" on crime?

- Would society benefit from treating a criminal defendant's mental illness rather than just punishing the offender? Defend your answer.

- Has drug testing gotten out of hand, or is it something we should all learn to live with? Explain.

 **Links: www.dushkin.com/online/**
These sites are annotated in the World Wide Web pages.

Center for Rational Correctional Policy
http://www.correctionalpolicy.com
Justice Information Center (JIC)
http://www.ncjrs.org
National Center for Policy Analysis (NCPA)
http://www.public-policy.org/~ncpa/pd/law/index3.html
U.S. Department of Justice (DOJ)
http://www.usdoj.gov

The courts are an equal partner in the American justice system. Just as the police have the responsibility of guarding our liberties by enforcing the law, the courts play an important role in defending these liberties by applying and interpreting the law. The courts are the battlegrounds where civilized "wars" are fought without bloodshed to protect individual rights and to settle disputes.

The articles in this unit discuss several issues concerning the judicial process. Ours is an adversary system of justice and the protagonists—the state and the defendant—are usually represented by counsel.

The opening article in this section, "Jury Consulting on Trial," discusses the notion of "scientific jury selection." Following is "Opting in to Mental Health Courts," which treats the issue of alternatives to traditional courts for the mentally ill defendant. Next, D. Graham Burnett writes about his experience on a murder trial jury in Manhattan in "Anatomy of a Verdict." Then, in "Looking Askance at Eyewitness Testimony," D. W. Miller examines the problem of unreliable eyewitness evidence. Finally, Barry Steinhardt takes up the issue of DNA identification, a much more dependable method in "The Creeping Expansion of DNA Data Banking."

Jury Consulting on Trial

Scholars doubt claims that jurors' votes can be predicted

BY D.W. MILLER

"**B**eware of the Lutherans, especially the Scandinavians; they are almost always sure to convict," Clarence Darrow advised fellow defense lawyers in a 1936 *Esquire* article called "How to Pick a Jury." By contrast, the "religious emotions" of Methodists "can be transmuted into love and charity." Irishmen, he added, are "emotional, kindly, and sympathetic." But the Presbyterian juror "believes in John Calvin and eternal punishment. Get rid of him with the fewest possible words before he contaminates the others."

Judges instruct jurors to render verdicts based on evidence and law, not prejudice and sympathy. But few lawyers believe that fallible humans simply leave their backgrounds, opinions, and attitudes outside the courtroom. So they still aspire to predict how jurors' biases will affect their deliberations.

Of course, in assembling a jury or shaping an argument, lawyers no longer credit the quaint stereotypes expressed — perhaps tongue in cheek — by Darrow. Many lawyers are content to rely on experience and intuition to identify people unfriendly to their side and strike them from a jury. Those who can afford it, however, are turning to trial consultants to conduct mock trials, design community surveys, and probe the attitudes and experiences of potential jurors.

Many of the nearly 400 members of the American Society of Trial Consultants are trained social scientists. But scholars question how much trial consultants have really improved upon Darrow.

"The plausibility of being able to predict is very low," says Shari Seidman Diamond, a professor of law at Northwestern University and a leading researcher of jury behavior. "Who makes the decision is less important than how the evidence is presented," says Saul Kassin, a professor of psychology at Williams College.

"The best conclusion is that there are cases where jury-selection consultants can make a difference but that such cases are few and far between," write Neil J. Kressel and Dorit F. Kressel in *Stack and Sway: The New Science of Jury Consulting* (just out from Westview Press). "Like the fanciful stereotypes about jurors that lawyers trusted in the past, scientific jury selection can help attorneys manage their stress far more often than it helps them capture a verdict."

NO CRYSTAL BALL

The notion of "scientific jury selection" took hold in the early 1970s, when the late Jay Schulman, a sociologist at Columbia University, and a team of colleagues helped defend antiwar activists accused of plotting to kidnap Henry Kissinger. After conducting surveys and interviewing a cross section of the community, the defense used its peremptory challenges to eliminate members of the jury pool considered likely to vote for conviction. The jury ultimately hung, on a 10–2 vote for acquittal.

Since then, however, scholars have found little evidence that social science makes a big difference in jury selection. "For most cases, most of the time, people decide on the basis of evidence," says Mr. Kressel, a psychologist at William Paterson University. "We know from mock-jury research that personality variables don't matter that much."

In a study of 461 mock jurors in Ohio, Michael Saks, a professor of law and psychology at Arizona State University, measured 27 attitudes and background characteristics and then asked the jurors to render a verdict in a fictitious burglary case. The best predictor of their decisions was their answer to the question "Do you believe crime is mainly the product of 'bad people' or 'bad social conditions'?" But that explained only 9 percent of the variation among verdicts. Together, those personal attributes accounted for very little.

IT'S AN ART

Steven D. Penrod, a psychologist at the University of Nebraska at Lincoln, got similar results in a study of Massachusetts jurors. He tested the salience of 21 personal characteristics in four kinds of cases. He found that the single best predictor of an inclination to vote guilty in a rape case was whether jurors agreed that evidence of physical resistance was necessary to convict. But that predictor alone explained only 7 percent of the variation in outcomes, and the best predictors in each case were not helpful in any others.

Mr. Kressel and his wife, a lawyer, concluded that scientific jury selection matters mainly when a case is very public, the facts are inflammatory, and the evidence favors neither side.

That scholars' insight into juries is hazy should not be surprising. Courts hardly ever allow researchers to watch deliberations firsthand, so they have to rely on cruder methods to divine how personality affects jury deliberations: post-trial interviews, case studies, and mock juries among them. Furthermore, scholars have found that observations rarely apply in all situations.

"Who makes the decisions is less important than how the evidence is presented."

"It's not really a science — it's more of an art," says Neil Vidmar, a professor of psychology and law at Duke University who has himself been a consultant on pre-trial publicity. "Almost every case is unique. It's got different facts, it's got a different context." Even so, the data that the nation's trial consultants collect in hundreds of cases each year might still be valuable to scholars — except that the information is all proprietary and closely held.

In their book, the Kressels argue that the value of scientific jury selection rests on a chain of unproven assumptions: that potential jurors give honest answers to personal questions, that jurors' pretrial verdict preferences will determine their final votes, and that jurors stricken from a jury pool will be replaced by ones that lawyers find more favorable. But that hasn't deterred scholars like Linda Foley.

A trial consultant and professor of psychology at the University of North Florida, Ms. Foley also conducts academic research on decision making by jurors that may prove useful in court. She has studied, for instance, why some jurors are less sympathetic than others to rape victims who sue their assailants. She found that college-age men are much less likely to sympathize with victims the same age than with those who are older. She speculates that young men can imagine themselves being falsely accused of rape by a peer, and so defensively attribute a plaintiff's fate to her own behavior.

In theory, lawyers armed with such insights could refine their efforts to choose favorable jurors and craft effective arguments. Since the 1970s, for example, researchers have believed that people who score high on a scale of "authoritarian" attitudes seem to be more likely to convict. Even that trait, however, has counterintuitive implications. Authoritarian types, says Ms. Foley, tend to make snap judgments, but they also tend to conform to the majority. In general, researchers have failed to connect attitudes with verdicts in predictable ways.

Ms. Foley's experiments this semester exemplify both the promise and perils of efforts to put jurors' motivations under a microscope. Several times a week, she assembles a new group of North Florida students in Jacksonville to play jury in a fictitious medical-malpractice lawsuit.

On a recent Wednesday morning, seven women and three men filed into a conference room near Ms. Foley's office, in the psychology department. First they filled out a lengthy questionnaire exploring their personality traits. Then they watched a videotape of dueling experts.

"Martin Madison," a 53-year-old accountant, had died of a brain aneurysm after complaining of headaches and dizziness. Were the hospital and its emergency-room doctor negligent? In that day's version of the experiment, the expert hired by Mr. Madison's widow boasted of his years of clinical experience, while the defense expert brandished his tenured professorship at the Johns Hopkins University and a long list of publications on aneurysms.

As usual, a handful of jurors dominated the discussion that followed. The forewoman, a ponytailed student in a sweatshirt and baseball cap who said she had worked in a hospital, criticized "Dr. Hector" for failing to order timely tests once he had diagnosed the aneurysm. "People die, that's all I gotta say," said Juror 105, a young man with a brush cut, but he went along with the majority, which laid most of the blame for the patient's death on the doctor.

Courts hardly ever allow researchers to watch deliberations firsthand, so scholars have to rely on cruder methods to divine how personality affects jury deliberations.

Only Juror 98, a woman in khaki pants and a jean jacket, remained dubious. "How do we know it would have made a difference?" she said. "The aneurysm was so big, he might have died on the MRI table."

Later, Juror 98 stood alone in her reluctance to compensate the Madison family beyond lost income. Despite her misgivings, the group awarded hefty damages and apportioned fault between the doctor and the hospital in a ratio of 70:30. Before leaving, the jurors filled out another survey, to assess how influential they had found each of their peers.

After observing 32 of those mock juries, Ms. Foley will investigate whether jurors in such cases are more easily persuaded by expert witnesses with impressive credentials or by those with more clinical experience. But she

Flies on the Wall of the Jury Room

HARRY KALVEN JR. and Hans Zeisel, who pioneered academic research on juries in the 1950s, were among the first American scholars to observe real jurors deliberating. For decades, it seemed they would also be the last.

When they revealed that they had taped the deliberations of five civil juries in a federal court in Wichita, Kan., without the jurors' consent, they were unprepared for the uproar that followed. The U.S. attorney general censured the project, Congress held hearings, and dozens of jurisdictions moved to ban "jury-tapping." With few exceptions, outsiders have been unwelcome in the jury room ever since—until now.

NOT SO PASSIVE

Shari Seidman Diamond, a law professor at Northwestern University, and Neil Vidmar, a professor of law and psychology at Duke University, noticed in the mid-1990s that courts in Arizona had begun experimenting with giving jurors more latitude to participate in court, such as taking notes, asking questions of witnesses, and discussing testimony before the lawyers had rested their cases. To investigate the effects of such reforms, they won permission from courts, juries, and litigants to videotape 50 civil cases.

> In many ways, the American legal system treats jurors like empty repositories for information, holding their opinions and experiences in check.

The first findings from their Arizona Jury Project, in a paper to be published soon in the *Virginia Law Review*, seem to confirm that jurors often confound the courts' expectations of their passive role. In many ways, the American legal system treats jurors like empty repositories for information, holding their opinions and experiences in check until a judge dispatches them to the jury room. That is the premise for the legal practice of "blindfolding"—excluding certain facts, such as defendants' past criminal acts, that might unfairly influence jury verdicts.

In their paper, Ms. Diamond and Mr. Vidmar investigate two such matters thought to influence jurors'

decisions in lawsuits: whether defendants and plaintiffs are covered by insurance, and how much the parties will owe in lawyers' fees. They found some evidence that those factors might affect juries' verdicts on defendants' liability, and even more evidence that they count when juries consider damages: At that stage, the researchers found, juries frequently overlook or misunderstand judges' instructions not to speculate about those issues, and take into account testimony about insurance revealed inadvertently or through an exception to courtroom rules.

Of the 40 cases in which insurance was relevant, the scholars found that jurors raised the issue in 34. Comments like the following were typical:

"His insurance paid all his bills, so he's not really out anything."

"This is what we have insurance for…. [O]ne of the plaintiff's doctor's said she sent the claims to plaintiff's insurers so the plaintiff is probably not paying for most of this."

"Insurance usually covers chiropractic care. Why should we give her above and beyond what she is probably going to get on her insurance?"

In 16 of those cases, or 40 percent, the authors write, "the discussion was substantial enough that an effect [on the verdict] could not be ruled out." In three cases, "a juror's verdict preference can be directly linked" to the juror's expressed beliefs about a litigant's insurance coverage.

In 24 of 33 applicable cases, juries discussed lawyers' fees in their deliberations. In four cases, the fees actually affected their decisions on damages: Three juries raised their damages award to cover their estimate of the plaintiff's legal bill, and the fourth reduced its award because jurors thought the plaintiff's lawyers did not deserve the full one-third contingency that they were likely to charge.

Ms. Diamond and Mr. Vidmar believe that the problem is exacerbated by judges who respond to juries' queries about taboo subjects with terse answers. "The traditional approach of merely forbidding evidence on certain topics is of limited value when jurors draw on life experiences and peek through blindfolds," they conclude. So the authors recommend that courts confront the problem squarely. A more comprehensive instruction to juries, they write, would acknowledge their temptation to consider forbidden topics, explain why the courts have deemed them irrelevant, and remind them that any such speculation would have [to] rely on guesswork. In mock-trial studies, they say, that approach has worked.

—D.W.M.

also hopes to learn more about the effects of personality on juries' decisions: Do jurors' views of guilt and liability in particular cases correspond predictably to measurable attitudes and personality traits, such as a belief in a just world, a predilection for manipulating others, or a tendency to see issues in absolute terms? And does a juror's influence during deliberations correspond predictably to measurable leadership traits and an ease with public speaking?

MUDDY WATERS

That kind of experiment has limits. For one thing, the psychology students she relies on are hardly representative of eligible jurors in Jacksonville, much less the nation. Furthermore, with such a small pool to draw from, some of the subjects are bound to be acquainted, a fact that may muddy her analysis of how members of the group influence one another. Jurors 100 and 101 had walked in holding hands, while Jurors 103 and 104 appeared to be identical twin sisters.

As a check on those flaws, Ms. Foley is collaborating with a trial consultant in Pompano Beach who will eventually conduct similar experiments with a cross section of "real people." But that research is at least a year away.

Even if research offered lawyers a wealth of predictive information, they would often have trouble using it. For instance, they don't have utter discretion over the number and kind of questions asked during jury selection. Researchers have established, for instance, that people who support capital punishment are generally more likely to vote to convict. But lawyers aren't allowed to probe jurors' attitudes toward the death penalty unless they are trying a capital case. "Depending on the judge, the lawyers don't have a lot of leeway about what kinds of questions they can ask," says Ms. Foley. "So they try to get at the essence in one or two questions."

Those caveats hardly mean that trial consultants have no influence. Even the Kressels agree that consultants appear to be effective at post-selection tasks, such as helping lawyers hone their arguments and understand how ordinary people will see the issues. "In most instances, it's the techniques and practices of social science that are helpful, rather than any particular body of knowledge," says Duke's Mr. Vidmar.

"This is an opportunity to test the clarity and plausibility of an argument in a more systematic way," says Northwestern's Ms. Diamond. "That's a valuable thing, because there's nothing sadder than seeing an unnecessarily unintelligible presentation of evidence. That makes it harder to make a decision based on the evidence."

Opting in to Mental Health Courts

Anne M. Hasselbrack

Editor's Note: The following article does not reflect the opinions of American Correctional Association staff, leadership or members.

Diversion-oriented courts, which are alternatives to traditional courts, are equipped to offer nonpunitive options to offenders based on unique circumstances that contributed to the alleged crimes. These courts have existed since 1989, when Miami began operating the nation's first drug court. Today, there are approximately 500 drug courts in the United States and abroad. Their success has given rise to other diversion-oriented courts, such as community court to settle neighborhood disputes, and domestic violence court to assist families who would benefit from counseling rather than incarceration. Mental health courts exist for offenders whose illnesses are thought to have contributed to their alleged crimes, and who could benefit from a proactive approach involving assessment, medication, counseling, housing, training and employment, versus a strictly punitive approach with little or no access to mental health care.

Howard Finkelstein of the Broward County, Fla., Public Defender's Office recalls the landmark 1994 case that cleared the way for the nation's first mental health court, in Broward County. Aaron Wynn, a college student, was struck by a car and suffered a head injury. In the days following the accident, his behavior grew increasingly bizarre, culminating when he punched a police officer. Wynn was sentenced to a forensic hospital, in which he was held in four-point restraints for approximately two years. Upon being released, he bumped into an elderly woman, who fell and later died from her injuries. A crowd saw the woman fall and severely beat Wynn.

He spent a year in jail while the grand jury heard the case, during which time Finkelstein had to stop the facility from medicating his client. The grand jury indicted Wynn for manslaughter, but Finkelstein immediately had him declared incompetent, stating that his client was not mentally ill, as had first been thought, but had a traumatic brain injury. In a civil suit against the Department of Children and Families, Wynn's family was awarded $17 million for his terminal care in a state-of-the-art brain treatment facility.

Around the time of the Wynn case, a number of deaths occurred in the Broward County Main Jail. For example, a woman was injected with a psychotropic medication against her will and died from choking on her own vomit. As a result, a task force was convened to find ways to improve the system of justice for defendants with mental disorders. Finkelstein advocated creating a separate court, and on June 6, 1997, Broward County began operating the first mental health court in the nation.

The four original mental health courts are located in:

- Fort Lauderdale, Broward County, Fla. (June 6, 1997)
- Anchorage, Ala. (July 6, 1998)
- Seattle, King County, Wash. (Feb. 17, 1999)
- San Bernardino, Calif. (Feb. 17, 1999)

There are some similarities among the four original mental health courts, including being voluntary, allowing for prior felony convictions but carefully screening for violent offenders, and accepting offenders only if their involvement with the criminal justice system was a direct result of an illness. There are differences as well. For example, Broward County does not require a guilty plea to accept an offender into the mental health court, but the others do. San Bernardino considers low-level felons as well as misdemeanants. Among the four courts, the time between referral and the first court appearance varies from a few hours to three weeks. Further, in each of these courts, the judge makes the final decision after considering a multidisciplinary team's input — with the exception of Broward County, which requires a team consensus.

The team makeup also varies among the courts. Teams are comprised of the judge, prosecutor, public defender, court clinician or mental health court liaison, case manager and probation officer. A team approach enables members to become familiar with individual cases, and allows those with the most expertise to handle the complex legal aspects of mental illness. Also, information may be shared among members that in other circumstances, might constitute a violation of attorney-client privilege.

According to the National Alliance for the Mentally Ill, 25 percent to 40 percent of people classified as mentally ill will come into contact with the criminal justice system at some point in their lives. A Bureau of Justice Statistics survey found that in 1998, there were an estimated 238,000 mentally ill offenders in U.S. prisons and jails, most coming into contact with the criminal justice system because of drugs or "quality of life" crimes such as panhandling, sleeping on the streets and loitering.

If the first two years of King County's experience is any indication, most of those seen in mental health courts are psychotic or bipolar, 50 percent are homeless and 80 percent are substance abusers. Deinstitutionalization of the mentally ill in the 1960s and 1970s is in large part to blame. In 1970, the United States had 500,000 state psychiatric hospital beds and 300,000 prison and jail beds. By 1992, there was a stark reversal: 100,000 state psychiatric hospital beds and 1.2 million jail and prison beds (ACA, 2001).

One of the greatest challenges when dealing with the mentally ill is obtaining treatment services for those who also are substance abusers. Facilities generally are equipped to accept one or the other. This is indicative of why the mentally ill remain in jail an average of 15 months longer than the general offender population. Concern for the community leads courts to keep these offenders incarcerated rather than take the risk of releasing them without viable treatment options.

Most would agree that confinement rarely leads to adequate care, and crowded conditions cause additional stress for mentally ill offenders. Mental health courts attempt to strike a balance between an individual defendant's rights and his or her options for treatment, and the public's safety. Referred to as therapeutic jurisprudence, it is an assertion of the court's role as a "therapeutic agent in the recovery process." *Seattle Times* reporter Nancy Bartle offers a more colorful description, saying that mental health courts are "a sort of Mr. Rogers meets Sigmund Freud with a dash of Judge Judy."

A key characteristic of diversion-oriented courts, such as drug courts and mental health courts, is that offenders "opt in" to the program. Offenders are given the option of staying in a traditional court or having their trial waived and receiving a court-ordered treatment plan, which may be in conjunction with a deferred or reduced sentence. Those who choose this alternative are said to have opted in, and are then expected to follow a plan that is created to meet their individual circumstances. If it is determined that the client is not cooperating nor making an effort to follow the plan, he or she may be referred back to the traditional court.

One area of concern is the initial screening process. At that time, the decision is made, sometimes within hours of arrest, as to whether the client's mental illness contributed to the alleged crime, and if the client could benefit from court-ordered treatment. This can be a lose-lose situation, in that the person doing the screening would like to do what is best for the client, but the condition that contributed to the crime renders the client incompetent to make the decision to opt in. This especially is true when participation is contingent upon the client entering a guilty plea. Even with counsel's advice, it is sometimes impossible to determine whether a client understands the implications of his or her decision.

Another concern is that the court determines whether the client is making adequate progress, which does not necessarily translate to the treatment plan being followed to the letter. The acceptable level of effort and progress is subjective. Finally, a large contradiction exists if one considers that a mentally ill person becomes part of the criminal justice system when community resources that could have helped that person have failed to do so, and yet, the courts are using these very same resources as treatment options. Some also fear that these treatment options to which clients are being referred will, as a result, be overtaxed and rendered inefficient at their existing levels.

However, in some cases, the need for increased services has resulted in innovation, one example of which is in Broward County, where doctoral students from the Center for Psychological Studies at Nova Southeastern University perform the actual screening of offenders and determine who should be referred to a mental health court. If a person is referred, the students may subsequently perform more in-depth mental analyses, and even testify before the judge about why the defendant should be treated rather than incarcerated. The psychology students also operate an outpatient program next to the courthouse. Called OPTIONS, the program is funded by a grant from the Bureau of Justice Assis-tance and is equipped to treat up to 40 women with serious mental illnesses in conjunction with other health issues, including drug addictions, posttraumatic stress and depression. Through OPTIONS, the women are encouraged to participate in empowering activities, such as learning computer skills and practicing yoga.

Another such treatment option in Broward County is a residential facility called Cottages in the Pines. Five houses formerly occupied by doctors on the grounds of the South Florida State Hospital provide shelter and treatment to indigent, homeless and mentally ill defendants, with an average stay of five months. "We view the mental health court as a strategy to bring fairness to the administration of justice for persons being arrested on minor offenses who suffer from major mental disabilities," says Broward mental health court Judge Ginger Lerner-Wren.

The strategy of which Lerner-Wren speaks has friends in politics. In a bill introduced last summer by Sen. Mike DeWine (R-Ohio), which passed last October, $10 million in grant money will be available from the Office of Justice Programs for each of the 2001 through 2004 fiscal years. The goal is to use existing resources within the court system, such as judges and facilities, and to hire specialized case managers or other mental health professionals. With a separate docket to hear only mental health cases, and the same judges and public defenders always presiding, these courts will be better able to meet the needs of mentally ill clients. In addition, the courts may apply for grants to fund treatment programs within the community.

Ohio's first mental health court began operation in Akron on Jan. 1, 2001, and courts in both Cincinnati and Cleveland will follow. Rep. Ted Strickland (D-Ohio), an advocate for the mental health court legislation put forth by DeWine, says, "No one benefits from our current practice of incarcerating nonviolent petty offenders who are in serious need of mental health treatment."

The cases heard in mental health court may not be the high-profile felony cases reported on the nightly news, but the need for separate and well-equipped courts to address offenders with mental illnesses is serious, not only for offenders but for public safety as well. So far, it appears that offenders have not been the only ones to "opt in" to this notion.

REFERENCES

2000 Mental Health Court Report, Third Annual Mental Health Court Progress Report, July 1999-June 2000, 17th Judicial Court, Broward County, Fla. (www.broward.fl.us/ojss/ jsi00700.html.)

Bartley, Nancy. 2001. Help, not punishment, for mentally ill: King County making a difference. *The Seattle Times*. Feb. 20.

Cayce, James D. and Kari Burrell. 1999. King County's mental health court: An innovative approach for coordinating justice services. *Washington State Bar News*, June. (www.wsba. org/barnews/1999/06/mentalhealth.html.)

Lerner-Wren, Ginger. An innovative approach to the mentally disabled in the criminal justice system. Reprinted from the *Florida Defender* with permission from the Florida Association of Criminal Defense Lawyers (FACDL). (www.co. broward.fl.us/ojss/jsi01300.html.)

Rabasca, Lisa. 2000. A court that sentences psychological care rather than jail time. *Monitor on Psychology*, 31(7):July/August. (www.apa.org/monitor/julaug00/court.html.)

Robinson, Jo. 2001. Jail mental health: A joint effort. In *The state of corrections*, 51-68. Lanham, Md.: ACA Press.

U.S. Department of Justice, Office of Justice Programs, Bureau of Justice Assistance. 2000. *Emerging judicial strategies for the mentally ill in the criminal caseload: Mental health courts in Fort Lauderdale, Seattle, San Bernardino and Anchorage*. (www.ncjrs.org/pdffiles1/bja/182504.pdf.)

Anne M. Hasselbrack is editorial assistant for the American Correctional Association's Communications and Publications Department.

We, the Jury

Anatomy of a Verdict

The view from a juror's chair.

By D. Graham Burnett

Last year I served as the jury foreman in a Manhattan murder trial. The culmination of this ordeal—12 idiosyncratic individuals thrown into tight quarters for 66 hours of sequestered deliberations—pushed civics into a realm normally reserved for extreme sports. A clutch of strangers yelled, cursed, vomited, whispered, embraced, sobbed and invoked both God and necromancy. There were some moments when the scene could have passed for a graduate seminar in political theory, others that might have been a jiujitsu class.

A man's fate hung in the balance. And we, the jury—closed in our crucible; shuttled about in the dark like shades by armed officers; cut off suddenly and indefinitely from our families, friends, news, regular life—shouldered the strange double burden of jury service. We wielded fearsome power (over the young man brought before us) and yet were rendered totally powerless (before the judge, the guards and the system that had drafted us as the foot soldiers of justice). Strung between these poles, we gained perspective and understood things in new ways. Understood intimately, for instance, the great power of the state. Understood glancingly, at least, the weakness and fear of a defendant standing before it. Understood feelingly, in the end, the great, disturbing truth that lies beneath the niceties of daily life: deep down, civics *is* an extreme sport; the ultimate, primordial and extremest sport of all.

What do I mean? I mean that lives are lost and won in the courts, lost and won in the law—every day, everywhere. Most of us seldom really think about this. But in the jury room, the thought cannot be avoided, since there you learn that justice doesn't merely happen (neatly, reliably, like a crystal taking shape in a distant vacuum); justice is, rather, done, made, manufactured. Made by imperfect, wrangling, venal and virtuous human beings, using whatever means are at their disposal. In the jury room, you discover that the whole edifice of social order stands, finally, on handicraft—there is no magic, no mathematics, no science, no angelic fixer who checks our juridical homework. This is a frightening thing, not least because any one of us could be accused of a crime.

We punish one another. To live together, we must. But it is a messy business when you get up close. The jury room is as close as you can get. We expect much of this small cell, and its door seldom stands open.

August 1998

Two N.Y.P.D. patrolmen kicked in the door. (Or said they did: later evidence would show that the jamb and latch, strangely, remained intact; moreover, each officer testified that he, and not the other, had been the one to get it to give.) When the door opened—in and to the right, stopping against a low coffee table—the two men surveyed the scene: a small dark studio apartment.

Draped over the futon couch, and trailing onto the floor to the right, were two blankets, one a cream-colored knit coverlet, the other a cheap, quilted bedspread. Blood spatters stained both. The curtain of the single, street-facing, ground-level window was closed, with the exception of a small opening in the lower left corner.

Causing this aperture was the lifeless hand of an African-American male, about six feet tall and just under 200 pounds. The body lay face down, the head wedged between the arm of the couch and the radiator under the window, the legs splayed into the middle of the room. Rigor mortis had caught and preserved the victim's final gesture: his right arm reaching up to the sill—surely an effort to pull himself to the window and call for help. Under the left arm lay a wig of long, dark, kinky hair. The body was naked.

The officers did not approach the figure or check for vital signs. A multitude of stab wounds (it would turn out there were more than 20 altogether) along the right side of the victim's spine, neck and head enabled them to surmise from the doorway what the medical examiner would confirm several hours later: the man—a habitué of the West Village night life and a familiar face in the homey gay bar at the corner—was definitely dead.

Not until later, however, when crime-scene investigators rolled the body over, did anyone see the wound that actually killed him—a thin and nearly bloodless slit through his sternum, which, reaching two and a half inches into the thoracic cavity, had just nicked the upper arch of the aorta. Within minutes of his receiving the blow, blood would have filled the sac around the heart, a condition known as an "acute traumatic cardiac tamponade." It is as if the heart drowns.

Also revealed when the body was moved: two braided leather whips and two unrolled condoms, one inside the other.

January 2000

I passed through the metal detectors at 100 Centre Street. My juror card instructed me to appear at 9 a.m., but it was later than that when I finally cleared the line and the low-ceilinged lobby of the dingy court building and found my way upstairs. I caught a fragment of a conversation between two older Hispanic women in the elevator: "Just two ounces! Not some kilo or noth'n.... But he didn't care."

From the outset I had resolved to treat the unwelcome intrusion of jury duty as something like a vacation, a three-day visit to a foreign country of bureaucratic languor and vast waiting rooms, a linoleum land inhabited by a genuine demographic cross section of the Big Apple. Most of all, I was looking forward to getting some reading done.

I am a college professor, a historian of science, but that year I had been awarded a one-year fellowship in a well-appointed humanities center at the New York Public Library—books everywhere, a silent and bright office without a phone, distinguished colleagues, catered lunches. My only formal responsibilities were to read and to write. But things piled up on the desk—student evaluations, article proofs needing attention, endless e-mail—so the New York State Criminal Court began to look like an opportunity to hide in plain view.

Actually ending up on a jury never crossed my mind. The day before I reported for duty, I had a conversation with a friend, a logician, who claimed that the magic word was "philosophy": once the lawyers heard it, you were kindly asked to leave. I figured that introducing myself as an academic ought to have the same effect. With a lawyer wife who had worked for a public defender's office, I promised to give any healthy prosecutor hives.

In the twice-exhaled air of the jury waiting room, about 200 disgruntled New Yorkers had arranged themselves like a tray of magnetic monopoles: maximum space between each particle and its neighbors. Some read newspapers, others books; a few students had staked out desks in the

corner and had begun to study, wearing Walkmans. Most people simply stared into space.

This hostile levee was called to attention by the senior court clerk, who seemed a New York institution-in-the-making, to judge from the gallery of inscribed celebrity head shots on the wall outside his office. (Gwyneth Paltrow! Stephen Jay Gould?)

"Any convicted felons in the room?" he boomed happily. Snickers. "No need to jump up," he added, with the honed timing of a natural stand-up. "Just wander into the clerk's office down the hall a little later, and I'll let you go."

"Anybody not understand English?" he jawed, waving his arm over us.

He mumbled this so fast I hardly caught it. But quite a few people promptly rose and began making their way to the front to get their release cards. Out they filed.

The joke grew on everyone. Amused murmuring.

"I'll never understand it," he stage-whispered to the rest of us, over a knot of duty-dodgers bulling for the double doors.

After details (locations of restrooms, water fountains, snack machine; an exhortation not to steal the magazines), we settled in to watch the preparatory video, narrated by Ed Bradley and Diane Sawyer. In addition to offering canned testimonials to the effect that we were going to have a great time and learn a lot about our government, the program set jury duty in its historical context. This was compressed in the extreme and got under way with a memorable flash-back to the dark days of trial by ordeal: as Sawyer's wood-wind voice soothingly narrated the bleak realities of justice in a benighted age, a knot of stringy-haired plebes, smirched and scrofulous, dragged a bound man through the woods and cast him into a deep lake. A papist factotum solemnly made the sign of the cross over the disappearance of the accused, and we learned that he would be found innocent if he did not resurface. Not an outtake from Monty Python, but an educational film prepared by the state of New York, the dramatization ended with the suggestion that the accused was innocent and that his kinsmen might have succeeded in recovering him from the bottom.

The movie put everyone in a good mood and strongly suggested the possibility of human progress in matters of jurisprudence. The Centre Street court building was grim and forbidding in a Stalinist sort of way (towering, gray, squint-windowed), but it clearly beat the heck out of the Inquisition. I went back to my book.

Complacency was unwise. The next afternoon, my name came up.

The Case

How complicated was the case that absorbed my life for the weeks to come? That depends on how closely you look. For those weeks I looked very closely, so to me it seems immensely complex. And yet, the tale can be briefly told: two men are in a room; one stabs the other, first in the chest, then in the back many times; the stabber says he was acting in self-defense. There are no witnesses.

But the plot thickens. This man, the defendant, claims that when he went into the room, with that other man, the victim, he believed the victim to be an attractive woman who wanted eagerly to have sex with him. In fact, he says, it was only when they both undressed for this very purpose that he discovered something disturbing: his date's idea of sex placed the defendant on the receiving end of anal intercourse, like it or not. His date was a man.

Prevented from fleeing the room, pressed to the floor, grappling for his clothes and the exit, the defendant took a lock-blade pocket knife from the pocket of his overalls, opened it and stabbed his attacker once, in the chest. When the assault continued, so did the stabs—until, eventually, the attacker relented and the defendant gathered up his belongings and ran from the room into the street, drenched in blood, his pinkie severed from the zealous swinging of the knife.

This is what the defendant says.

But the plot thickens. The defendant didn't tell any of this to the police when they picked him up in the street and took him to the hospital to have his finger sewn back on. He told them a lie, namely that he had just been mugged by a gang of "five white males." The defendant is black.

This might have worked. Except, when the police found the victim, they did what the police do when they find a person who has been stabbed to death: they canvassed area emergency rooms for patients admitted with suspicious cuts on their arms or hands. It is hard to stab someone many times, in haste and agitation, and avoid a slip or two. The defendant slipped.

His name came up in this search, and the police paid him a visit in the hospital to ask him some pointed questions about those five white males. The detectives didn't like his answers—too vague. They asked him to come down to the station—to help jog his memory. Within a few hours he admitted to stabbing the victim (copious DNA evidence from blood at the scene would have made it hard to deny). Only now did the police hear the story of the drag seduction and the desperate fight in the small, dark room.

But the plot was thicker still by the time I and 11 other Manhattanites took up our seats in the jury box of New York State Supreme Court, Criminal Term. Because by that time the district attorney's office had sniffed around and turned up a handful of witnesses ready to testify that the victim and the defendant had long been lovers, and that they had spent the evening of the killing together in the apartment. Also, the forensics team had noticed traces of semen on the penis of the victim and the underwear of the defendant. Whose semen? They couldn't say.

Into the Open Court

We heard this evidence in the bright, high-ceilinged courtroom, under the stern eye of a sour-humored judge. Then, on a television wheeled up beside the witness stand, we were shown a grainy video of the defendant's confessional statement. After some back and forth between the judge and a court officer, the lights were dimmed; it proved impossible to lower the shades, despite several attempts. The gallery had filled in for the showing—various clerks, assistants, a visiting class from John Jay College of Criminal Justice.

A large cockroach emerged from under the prosecution's table, creating a minor disruption. It escaped the stomp of a female guard and wedged itself into an invisible crevice at the foot of the bench.

The taped statement, taken the night the police picked the defendant up from the hospital, made the evening of the killing feel immediate. In the video, the assistant district attorney—young, handsome, Asian, wearing a tie—sits across from the suspect, a narrow table between them, as in a chess tournament. As the camera frame tightens on the defendant, the A.D.A. becomes a disembodied voice, inquisitive, measured. Each question, outwardly straightforward, seems to conceal complex structures: legal implications, potential charges, due-process considerations. The A.D.A. takes his time, making it clear he has to think before he speaks. The defendant responds quickly, telling the story, his intonation rising restlessly at the end of each phrase, as if he is looking for some confirmation from his inquisitor, as if he himself is asking question after question, in an eager tumble. The difference in pace, in caution, stands out.

Asked to show how he handled the knife, the defendant obliges, raising his right arm (in a cast, from his surgery) and supporting it with his left at the elbow, through the sling. He mimes an overhand grip and makes small, apologetic pecking gestures.

He has a high voice and a Southern accent, which together give him a curiously solicitous air. He has a lisp that seems nearly a hiss; he puts his mouth around words in haste, gobbling them. "Yessir," he replies, often.

When he quotes himself as having blurted out "What the [expletive] is this?" (on spying the male sex of his erstwhile date), he excuses himself for his language, quickly, instinctively, in a whisper.

By the end of the tape, he is holding his bandaged right arm and wincing; he sucks air through his teeth in pain. Asked if he wishes to add anything to his statement, he responds, reasonably, "What's going to happen next?" And then, "Can I go home tonight?"

The A.D.A. pauses and repeats his questions: Does he wish to add anything to his statement at this time?

He declines.

The high contrast of the image erases the features of his face, making him a silhouette.

DEFENDANTS IN MURDER TRIALS SELDOM TAKE THE STAND, THEY are under no obligation to do so, and a jury is instructed to make no inferences from their choice. For one thing, testifying generally means exposing any criminal record they might have, information that is otherwise rigorously withheld from the jury.

Again and again I found myself sitting in court looking across at the defendant. Only he knew what had happened in that apartment. Day after day, I looked at the defendant, and I saw a cipher.

That changed on the last day of testimony, when, with a shrug (after requesting, unsuccessfully, more time from the judge in order to contact a no-show witness), the defense attorney called his client to the stand. As he went, long-legged, lankier than I had expected, I realized I had not yet seen him stand up. By taking the stand, he voluntarily settled the question of his criminal record. There wasn't much: some unspecified "participation" in a nonviolent robbery at the age of 13 or 14. He had graduated from high school (where he had been something of a track star) and had attended Marine Corps boot camp, from which he had been dismissed after dislocating his shoulder in a boxing competition, aggravating an older injury. After this he had apparently held several regular jobs, one at a sporting-goods store in midtown, the other doing data entry for a medical records company. He lived with his fiancé (who was pregnant at the time of his arrest, and had since borne him a child) and her mother.

In the end, the bulk of the defense case hung on these minutes of testimony. Without hesitation, even forcefully, the defendant told his story again: he insisted that he had acted in self-defense, that he had been the victim of a sexual charade. After briefly rehearsing this account under direct examination (where he seemed shy, but clear and calm, and said that he had lied in his early statements), the defense turned him over to the prosecution for the cross.

A prosecutor cannot be successful without a strong sense of how to play such a moment. This prosecutor elected to use a badgering tone and a sneeringly sarcastic mien. He dived in by accusing the defendant of being a perjurer, for having "lied on his application" to the Marines. But it appeared that this meant nothing more than that he had not alerted the Corps to his having once hurt his shoulder in high school. Since the military assesses its recruiters on the basis of how many bodies they sign up, it is easy to imagine that no one pressed him to disclose an overly detailed medical history on the forms.

Given a defendant apparently so benign—young and slight, well spoken, with a handsome, dark face and bright white in his almond eyes—the prosecutor's combative strategy ran the risk of a backfire. And that, I would say, is what happened: when the defendant maintained his composure, the prosecutor had no place to go but up, escalating his belligerence in hope of cracking this composure. By the end, the prosecutor had pulled out all the stops and found himself furiously dramatizing the state's version of the victim's final moments, as he lay helpless on his face, with the defendant poised above him, repeatedly driving the knife into his head, neck and back.

Acting all of this out a few feet from the witness stand, directly in front of the jury box, the murder weapon in his hand, the prosecutor again and again swung the open knife, rolling his head and shoulders into each exaggerated stroke as he growlingly challenged the witness to deny that this, in fact, was how the victim met his death.

"And didn't you then—like this!—stab him? And then, again! Like this? As he tried to crawl away? And—again!"

But the sensational dramatization—which the judge refused to interrupt and which sent the victim's family howling from the room as several of the jurors squirmed in disgust—built to a crashingly flat climax. To the blistering assertion that this was how it had happened, the defendant offered a simple answer.

"No."

And yet, it seemed, if anything was going to shake him, it would have been that.

So egregious did I find the whole performance that, as the defendant returned to his seat, slightly hunched, as if afraid of bumping his head on something, I felt a deep desire to see the prosecutor lose the case. How did that whisper of a thought affect what followed? It is difficult to say.

W Into a Closed Room

Walking us down the hall and into the small jury room, the short, jovial sergeant said he would take care of us: "There's water there," he nodded at a thermos, "and this is the buzzer you press if you need anything, and there's no smoking, of course, but there's windows in the bathroom.... That's all I'm saying, O.K.?"

"Oh, and, uh, you know, if you order up the knife, right? You know I bring it in, but we don't leave it with you, see?… I gotta carry it around, and you can look at it, but nobody can talk till I leave. And the knife goes with me."

He gave us a kidding smile as he prepared to close the door. "You know, we need 12 jurors for a verdict, eh?"

"Anybody want cigarettes?"

THROWING A DEFENDANT INTO A LAKE SEEMS BARBARIC TO US, or blackly funny: we are heirs of the Enlightenment, after all; we are modern, thank God. But throwing a defendant to a jury has a medieval quality all its own. Things can come out different ways; large decisions hinge on small points. People are quirky, idiosyncratic, even strange. Place a dozen individuals together in tight quarters for long enough, and nearly anything can happen.

Who were we? Four men and eight women. Perhaps as many as half of us were 30 or younger. We were white (nine), black (two) and Hispanic (one); we were, for the most part, professionals (in advertising, software development, marketing). We seemed—milling about in the hall at breaks, chatting as we took the slow elevator to the street after a long day of testimony—to get along perfectly well. Once the door to the jury room closed, I asked that we begin with a moment of silence.

How did the deliberations unfold? I am sure each of us would remember things differently; if you learn anything from a criminal trial under the adversary system, it is that sincere people can differ vehemently about events, and that there is seldom any easy way to figure out what actually went on.

This is the way I remember things: On the first day we went around the room and people said whatever they wanted about the case. That taught us two things: first, that we didn't agree; and second, that there was a great deal of confusion about the different charges we had been asked to consider (murder in the second degree under two different "theories," as well as the lesser charge of manslaughter). Did we all have to achieve unanimity on a *single* charge before we could even consider the claim of self-defense? (This made no sense to me, but it would be days before everyone was convinced that it would never work.) Could a finding of self-defense trump all of the charges? (It seemed obvious to me that it could, but we had to hash this one out too and seek clarification by means of written queries to the judge.)

By the second day a straw poll indicated we were still all over the place: a handful wanted us to find the defendant guilty of the most severe charge, and another handful voted for each of the lesser charges; but about half the room also said they had not ruled out self-defense. (Some of these people, though, had also put in a ballot for guilt, which left me scratching my head.)

We began requesting evidence we wanted to review. I had initially been reluctant to drag these items into the room (it seemed to me it would be hard enough to have a serious conversation around the table without photographs, videos and other tidbits to play with), but a pair of striking discoveries followed. One juror, looking at a video taken of the crime scene, noticed that it was impossible to see the futon couch from the hallway outside the apartment door—the angle was wrong. A small point, but one with large implications, since this meant that a key prosecution witness had lied. He had testified to seeing the defendant on the victim's couch that night. But he had also insisted he had been standing in the hall.

The other discovery turned up in one of the crime-scene photographs: a pair of what looked like panties on the corner of the couch by the body. These corroborated the defendant's story, and in doing so cast doubt on the testimony of almost all of the police and crime-scene investigators who had testified for the prosecution: they uniformly claimed that no women's clothing had been found in the searches of the apartment.

But casting niggling doubt on various witnesses was one thing. The deeper issue lay in realizing just how much the state had to prove before we could find the defendant guilty: when someone claims to have killed in self-defense, the presumption of innocence extends to this claim; in other words, the prosecution must prove, beyond a reasonable doubt, not only that the defendant killed but also that he did not do so in self-defense. When there are no witnesses, is this even possible?

It took us some time to work out just how heavy the burden of proof was. Over four days we wrestled with this problem and struggled to understand not only what happened in that cramped apartment but also what the law de-

manded of us. Three moments were decisive in this long debate, and each of them hinged on a different juror, each of whom spoke clearly at a difficult juncture and shifted the course of our deliberations.

Juror 10: Men Can Be Date-Raped, Too

Juror 10 was a raspy, dyed-blond 20-something tough girl in tight black jeans who spoke loudly and much, often well. An actress, apparently, with the hard edges of a barmaid in a Back Bay Boston Irish pub, she knew how to make herself heard and was not afraid to hold the floor. She leapt into the fray from the start, composing a long list of all the evidence that she wanted to hear again, a list that grew so long that I, as the foreman, finally felt I had to discourage her, because sending it in to the court would have obliged us to sit through nearly a week of readings from the transcript. My stalling on her requests caused trouble later: was I stringing her along? she wanted to know. She let me know that I'd better not try to jerk her around.

As the days wore on I increasingly got the sense that Juror 10's sudden, explosive interjections signaled someone quick to trigger. In addition, she was apparently taking some sort of heavily regulated prescription drug, and by the third day of deliberations she had run out. That spelled trouble.

Her moment of glory, though, came after lunch on the second day, at the end of an hour we had spent collectively trying to reconstruct the fatal fight from snippets of contradictory description given by the defendant in his videotaped statement. Replaying the tape of the defendant's account of the fight, several jurors got down on the floor and acted out the moves the defendant was describing. Juror 10 was on the floor on her back calling for someone to lie down between her legs. This and the subsequent wrangles occasioned a certain amount of joking, but our conclusion after this boisterous tangling was that the fight almost surely could not have happened in the way the defendant said. The wounds to the victim's back certainly looked as if they had been delivered from behind, when the victim was nearly motionless, lying on his face, dying, presumably, from the first blow to the chest. (The incisions in the back had the wrong penetrating angle to have been made as the defendant claimed—from underneath the victim, as the defendant claimed—from underneath the victim, as the defendant struggled in his embrace.)

We pressed the evidence. Had this been a drag seduction? Unlikely. Look at the size of that victim. Who could get within 10 feet of him and think he was a woman, wig or no?

Rape? We had lots of evidence that these men knew each other (a parade of witnesses who could have come straight out of "Paris Is Burning" swore to it), and the semen traces suggested they had just had some sort of sex before things went bad. Didn't this have all the marks of a crime of passion? Who could say why the defendant got so angry at his lover, but hadn't he clearly attacked and killed him in some sort of rage?

But not everyone agreed. Several people pointed out that even if the men had been sexually involved, that didn't prove it was murder. Juror 10 pushed this point: What difference did it make if they had just been fooling around before things got ugly? Did this make it impossible that the defendant was defending himself from rape when he swung the knife? Wasn't *that* the only question? "No means no," Juror 10 announced sharply, "even if they just had oral sex, and then his lover said he wanted more, if he said no, then it was rape."

This declaration—categorical, a little edgy, a littler holier-than-thou—visibly irritated several of the people around the table. But as the conversation continued into the afternoon, we found ourselves coming back to it. Maybe the defendant was lying about a lot of things, but if he had been cheating on his pregnant fiancée and experimenting with a homosexual relationship, his reluctance to tell the truth about much of what had happened made sense. We all agreed that a woman could be raped by a lover, could kill to protect herself in that situation; could we reject that possibility here? Place it beyond a reasonable doubt? Did we have any more reasonable account for why an apparently mild-mannered young man with no history of violent crime would have committed such a monstrous act? We did not. Then didn't self-defense remain at least a possibility? Could it be ruled "beyond a reasonable doubt"? Those were powerful words.

Juror 10's analogy to date rape cut away much of the prosecution's case and focused us on that one fatal moment—when the knife came out.

Juror 7: Law or Justice?

Juror 7 was less impressed by this argument than most of us, and because she herself was a very impressive woman, this was a problem. Juror 7 was a professor, a historian like me. From Day 1 she had been the clearest voice for the defendant's guilt, under the most severe murder charge, and she seemed a bit shocked that so many of the rest of us were hesitating. Very smart and articulate, she was evidently accustomed to holding the attention of a room. Her aspect was serious, though not at all unfriendly. Dressed comfortably—in sneakers and a shapeless sweater with loose sleeves that she pushed above her elbows—she moved with a kind of force, often lifting her short brown hair off her temples and fixing it behind her ears, rubbing her chin thoughtfully as she listened to others. Because she gave all indications of being temperamentally inclined to a pro-defendant position (urban, bookish, seemingly left-liberal), her advocacy of a guilty verdict weighed heavily.

Juror 7 simply nudged us toward a conviction with her good arguments. As a number of people were rallying round Juror 10's point, Juror 7 spoke up: "But the only evidence for that moment"—the moment the defendant said no to sex—"is this guy's word, and what's that worth?" she asked.

She proposed an exercise. "Let's make a list of everything this guy has told us, and then let's cross off everything that has turned out to be a lie. What's left on the list? Only that one moment. How can you be ready to let him walk out of here on the basis of that?" How reasonable was it to doubt that a liar was lying? And with his neck on the line?

With the room increasingly polarized, a new idea began to circulate in the wake of this strong argument for a conviction: a compromise. Since about half the jury thought the defendant should be found guilty of the most serious crime, and the other half seemed to want a total acquittal, why couldn't we agree to convict on the lesser charge of manslaughter? That way we would ensure the defendant got some punishment for all the bad things he clearly did do: abandon the scene, lie to police, etc.

"I think it would be a violation of our duty as jurors, which is to apply the law," I said. "We weren't asked to consider whether this guy is guilty of abandoning the scene. The law says we can only convict if we're persuaded, beyond a reasonable doubt, that the defendant killed this man and did not do so in self-defense. So that's the only issue. We aren't allowed to fudge the law because we'd like to see the defendant get punished."

Conversation around the idea of a compromise heated up, as we debated whether this was a legitimate way to resolve the case.

"I keep coming back to this same question," she said, "the relationship between law and justice. What I keep wanting here is for us to figure out some way to do justice, but I am starting to realize that the law itself may be a different thing. What is my real responsibility? The law? Or the just thing? I'm not sure what the answer is. We've been told that we have to 'uphold the law.' But I don't understand what allegiance I should have to the law itself. Doesn't the whole authority of the law rest on its claim to be our system of justice? So if the law isn't just, how can it have any force?"

She had gone to the heart of the matter, directly, and with great equanimity and gentleness. Gradually this new formulation—justice versus law—began to take hold. Justice: Compromise on a verdict so the defendant gets some punishment. Law: Admit that it had not been proved, beyond a reasonable doubt, that this could not have been self-defense (nearly all of us agreed that the prosecution's case had failed to meet this very heavy—absurdly heavy?—burden of proof).

Thanks to Juror 7, a new question lay before us. How could we justify applying the law if we decided that the resulting verdict was itself unjust? Were we responsible to the law? Or to our idea of justice?

It would take a born-again-formerly-crystal-meth-addicted-ex-bull-riding rodeo cowboy to answer this question for us—the improbable Juror 9.

Juror 9: Justice and God

Juror 9 was a big man: a 6-foot-3-inch God-fearing veteran of the United States Armed Forces who now repaired vacuum cleaners for a living. When I first noticed him, in the early days of jury selection, he was spitting tobacco juice behind the radiator by the elevator during a break. He had thin brown hair slicked back and a manly mustache, and wore a weathered pair of work boots. A contractor of some sort, I assumed, and I pegged him, without much thought or interest, a prime example of Susan Faludi's tragic tale of the white working-class male—big chest, big gut, big debt. I called him, irreverently, "the Faludiman" in my diary. What did I know? Before the trial ended he had blown my stereotype (indeed, any stereotype) wide open.

From the start of the trial, I thought it very likely he would take the lead in pushing for a guilty verdict, if not a hanging. I think I figured anyone wearing, apparently in earnest, a large belt buckle reading "Rodeo" had to be a law-and-order type and quite possibly a bigot too.

But at breakfast on the second day (at the hotel out by J.F.K. Airport where we had been sequestered), we got into a conversation, at first about the food, then about fasting, then about the approach of Lent and finally about the Good Lord. In addition to telling us about his victory over drugs, he began to explain that he had become a domestic missionary of his California "mother church" (of recovered addicts), part of a small cell charged to found a new community in Spanish Harlem. Almost a decade had passed since this group took up residence in the community and began pursuing its mission: wandering in and out of the heroin galleries and the crack dens of the neighborhood, handing out literature, praising the Lord, preaching the possibility of recovery and redemption. They held their first meetings in an empty storefront and circled in prayer around vomiting addicts delirious from the struggle to go cold turkey. The church now had well over 100 families, and Juror 9 had become one of its leaders, a deacon sometimes called upon to preach. He had married into the community, and he and his Guatemalan wife had two kids of their own; they were also rearing his daughter from a previous marriage.

All this helped explain his accommodating and gentle voice in our deliberations; his obvious ability to speak with authority and lead the group; his sympathy for the defendant. From the beginning, Juror 9's attitude had been that the defendant had done the wrong thing, that he had almost certainly gotten involved in something risky and stupid, but that this alone was not grounds for a conviction.

"The Lord knows," he would add, "I myself have been in the wrong place more than once."

By midafternoon on the third day, the debate over a compromise verdict of manslaughter had become testy, and several positions had hardened. We were tired, some personalities had clashed, we all felt increasingly trapped: without a verdict, would we ever be released? Could we ever agree? At least four people still pressed for a guilty verdict. About the same number seemed committed to acquit. The rest wavered. I thought we were a hung jury.

Those pushing for the compromise idea argued that the law's only purpose was justice; therefore justice had to be

the higher principle. It followed, then, that an appeal to justice must trump the mincing details of the law itself. The law might prohibit us from compromising on a manslaughter verdict unless we could all agree that the burden of proof had been met (which we could not). But we agreed that it was not just to let the defendant go unpunished for what he had done. Conclusion? The dictates of justice demanded that we circumvent the law. Q.E.D. Momentum for a guilty vote gained, even though most people in the room had by now agreed that they felt some "reasonable" doubt, however small, about the self-defense issue.

It was an odd situation. We seemed ready to ignore the law in an effort to get the verdict that so many people wanted: guilty. Or this was how I saw it.

Then Juror 9 rose to speak. "I've been listening," he began, "to these things people are saying, and I have tried to pray about all this. Now I've decided what I have to do. I believe this young man did something very, very wrong in that room. But I also believe that nobody has asked me to play God. I've been asked to apply the law. Justice belongs to God; men only have the law. Justice is perfect, but the law can only be careful."

The statement centered the room.

Here was a repudiation of sophistication that suddenly seemed overwhelmingly sage. No one spoke for several moments. He did not try to explain, or to say more. He sat down.

There was silence.

To my right I heard a whisper. Looking over, I saw brimming eyes. "He's convinced me," someone whispered. It was close to a sob. No one else spoke.

Acquit before the law; leave justice to God—could we do this?

Was this like throwing the defendant in a lake? A lake in the sky?

A Setback

We knew we were close. We took a poll, and the numbers hovered at the brink of an acquittal: 10 to 2. Juror 9's powerful declaration had played a role in killing the drive for a compromise conviction and had won converts. But the day did not end there.

Juror 10, missing her medication and exhausted by the stresses of the past three days, had been looking worse and worse. The pharmacy she had asked the court to contact claimed her prescription could not be refilled. She had been struggling with a bad cold sore for several days, and a number of ulcers could be seen on her face. Though she had applied heavy daubs of makeup to conceal them, several had opened, and she had been forced to stanch them with tissue. Her makeup bottle lay open on the table, and she had slumped into morose silence after complaining of a coming migraine.

Now from the men's bathroom came the strangled sound of gags. She was throwing up.

At that, one juror stood up and said that he wanted to leave, and that he would vote for anything that would get us out of the room—he didn't care.

When the judge was informed of Juror 10's illness, he called us into the courtroom. He had decided to have Juror 10 taken to the hospital; we would suspend deliberations until further notice and were strictly prohibited from discussing the case until the full jury could reassemble.

It was shortly before 5 p.m. on Friday evening.

The hours that followed were the most painful of the whole trial. A new complement of court officers took charge, paunchy weekend cops who had oversize highway patrol sunglasses and gonzo equipment belts. They exuded a palpable sense of armed delight. On the judge's orders they herded us into a cavernous empty courtroom down the hall, where, for almost three hours, we waited without any sense of what to expect. Could the deliberations be suspended indefinitely? Could we be kept in custody all weekend? What if Juror 10 got worse? Would the judge ever let us go?

Several jurors began to lose their composure. One, increasingly desperate, wanted to contact her own lawyer, in the hope of winning release. No chance. The judge later apparently threatened the same juror with contempt. The powerlessness of her situation—indeed, the powerlessness of our shared situation—had been made painfully clear. We, it seemed, had become the prisoners.

So this was what incarceration felt like. No wonder the burden of proof set the bar so high. When Juror 10 rejoined us later that evening, there was a feeling that the ordeal had to end, and soon.

The Last Day

It was Saturday, the fourth day of our deliberations. I took 12 index cards out of my pocket and passed them around. There was silence as they started to come back, each folded in half.

I counted the cards. Nine. We waited, and two more came in. Eleven. We waited. Still 11.

At this point there was no confusion about who still held a card. Juror 7, my fellow historian, the eloquent voice for justice, sat at the corner of the table to my left, where she had sat for four days. She had a pencil in her hand, and the card on the table in front of her. She was looking fixedly away, up, behind her, out the window.

No one spoke. One juror adopted a contemplative posture, her fingers prayerfully arranged at her brow. Several others closed their eyes and clasped their hands to wait. One man put his head down on his folded arms. There was the sense that everyone in the room was concentrating on the blank card in rapt meditation. Juror 7 breathed audibly, wrote something rapidly on the card, closed it on itself and pushed it into the middle of the table.

I placed it, consciously, and more or less conspicuously, at the bottom of the pile. I wanted the full dismay of the room to land on her if she had voted for a conviction in this, the first poll of the fourth day. We knew we were close on the previous evening, but Juror 10's trip to the hospital had forced us to suspend deliberations right at that critical moment.

I began to open the cards and read them: not guilty, not guilty, not guilty, not guilty, not guilty, not guilty, not guilty, not guilty, not guilty, not guilty, not guilty. And the last one: not guilty.

The taut silence of the room broke in a gust of relief. There was absolutely no joy, no celebration, no delight. There was only an imprecise emotional surfeit. People were overwhelmed. I think there were only a few who were not crying, though I cannot remember everyone's face, because I was choked up myself.

Rapidly, I went to the wall next to the door and buzzed for the bailiff. I returned to my seat only for a moment, to take out a sheet of the paper we used for corresponding with the court and to write on it the message I had been told to give when our deliberations had ended: "The jury has reached a verdict."

I looked around the room. Several people were embracing, and two of the young women were gathered around Juror 7, saying encouraging things to her. She looked around over the shoulder of someone giving her a supportive hug, and she said suddenly, tearfully, "If we are doing the right thing, why are we all crying?"

At that instant, the knock came solidly at the door, followed by the requisite bark, "Cease deliberations!" The officer swung the door open, and I stood there with the sheet in my hand.

But as I reached to hand it to him, Juror 7 cried out: "No! Wait, we're not ready! Not yet."

I stood there dumbly, with my arm out-stretched. I hesitated and then turned to him, apologized and asked him to leave.

With this back step, the room teetered on the brink of an unrecoverable collapse. At the prospect of snatching defeat from the jaws of victory like this, several jurors looked ready to go wild. I returned to my place and remained standing, asking for people to stay calm, if they could, and to hear a proposal.

"What we might do," I said, "is write a message to the court that makes explicit that we are unhappy, in a way, with our own verdict, that we feel we are doing the right thing before the law, but something that is not, in the end, really *just*."

I proposed a message, a sort of disavowal of our own verdict: "What if we wrote something like, 'We the jury wish it to be known to the open court that we feel most strongly that the strict application of the law to the facts established by the evidence in this case does not lead to a truly just verdict.'" I had scribbled this statement in my diary, early that morning, as an expression of despair.

I looked up. A nod here and there. Yes. Several others. Yes. No one said no, not even Juror 7.

So that was what we did. I wrote out that statement, concluding by saying that we had, nevertheless, reached a verdict. People consoled one another, and conversation turned to how this, at least, would be a way we could communicate our struggle to the family of the victim (who had sat mournfully through every day of the trial) and let them know that we had not accepted the demonized portrait the defense painted of him, but rather that we found ourselves bound by the strictures of the law. We could tell them that we were not unsympathetic toward their plea for justice.

In the half-hour it took for the court to assemble, our gray solemnity gradually brightened into the camaraderie of a parting of the ways. Laughter broke here and there, as the idea that it was over began to sink in. People started exchanging business cards, and someone had the idea that we ought to circulate an address sheet, so that we would all be able to stay in touch.

After we had taken our seats in the courtroom, the judge read my note aloud, without the least trace of inflection, slowly, mechanically, pausing momentarily after each word as if to strip the sentences of meaning.

"Have I read that correctly, Mr. Burnett?"

I said he had.

"Has the jury reached a verdict?"

I said yes.

The judge turned to the clerk and asked him to begin.

"On the charge of murder in the second degree with intent," the clerk began, "how finds the jury?"

"Not guilty."

I looked at the defendant, whose head was resting against his hands, clasped in front of him, his elbows on the table. His head dropped when the answer came.

"On the charge of murder in the second degree under the theory of depraved indifference, how finds the jury?"

"Not guilty."

His head dropped farther, and a distinct wailing went up from the back of the room.

"On the charge of manslaughter, how finds the jury?"

"Not guilty."

And the young man looked straight up, with tears streaming down his face, and his fists clenched at his throat.

The wailing from the back of the room grew louder.

The defense attorney showed no emotion; the prosecutors sat impassive.

I could hear sobbing in the jury box behind me and to my left. The judge spoke more words, the clerk spoke more words. I was asked a question. Was this the verdict of the jury? I said it was, aware that the moment was collapsing for me, that I was not able to maintain any distance from what was happening, that I was no longer seeing what was going on.

The attorneys approached the bench for a conference, and we were told that the jury would be polled. Each of us would be asked to affirm the verdict individually. Did I

speak? I do not remember. I heard the voices around me. Yes. Yes….

And so it went. I watched the defendant, who had again frozen in a posture of silent expectation, his hands clasped in front of him. Tears were visible, dripping down his nose, onto the table. His head again dropped, slightly, each time an answer came: Yes. Yes.

Once Juror 7, behind me, had spoken, the thing felt done. But five answers remained. Yes. Yes. Yes. Yes. Yes.

And it was over. We had let him go.

Epilogue

We let the defendant go.

Several weeks later, at a party on the Lower East Side, I fell into conversation with someone who turned out to be a cop. He pumped me for the story, and then, in a good-natured way, expressed his dismay that we had voted for acquittal. How had we decided to do that, when it sounded to him as if we all basically thought it had probably been a murder?

I thought about trying to explain. Trying to explain what it means to say you are convinced beyond a reasonable doubt. Trying to explain that not guilty doesn't mean innocent. Trying to explain that after four days of sequestration, you have a new understanding of the power of the state, and of the reason that the people's burden of proof is so heavy—to protect citizens from this thing, this leviathan. Trying to explain how you might think you were probably looking at a murderer but decide the law would not permit you to convict him. Trying to explain what it felt like to go home in tears, to sit in the dark, wondering if you had done the right thing.

I thought about trying to explain. Because if I explained all that, I could tell him the remarkable thing that happened next, that first night at home, in the dark. The phone rang, and I answered it, and heard the voice of a fellow juror, a young woman who had stayed around the court to talk to the lawyers after it had all ended. She told me, her voice trembling, that she had learned of additional information we had not been allowed to hear because it had been ruled inadmissible by the judge. Evidence that the victim had been in trouble with the police before—for a sexual-misconduct charge. Once upon a time, he was accused of dressing like a woman, luring a young man to his apartment and pressing sex on him.

It was a great deal to explain. The party was loud. I nodded again. "Do you want to hear the whole story?" I shouted.

D. Graham Burnett is a historian of science currently at Princeton University. This article is adapted from "A Trial by Jury," published in September 2001 by Alfred A. Knopf.

Looking Askance at Eyewitness Testimony

Psychologists, showing how errors reach the courts, offer advice on handling such evidence

BY D. W. MILLER

RONNIE BULLOCK was sentenced to 60 years in jail for kidnapping and raping a young Illinois girl. Edward Honaker spent a decade in a Virginia prison for sexually assaulting a woman at gunpoint. Kirk Bloodsworth was shipped off to Maryland's death row for raping and strangling a 9-year-old girl.

All three of those men were convicted in part because eyewitnesses or victims firmly placed them at the scene of the crime. But not one of them was guilty. They were among the first convicts to be exonerated by DNA tests proving that someone else was responsible.

Some psychologists believe that such mistakes happen in thousands of courtrooms every year. But most crimes leave no DNA traces to rule out the innocent. For more than two decades, psychological researchers have asked, How could so many witnesses be wrong, and what can be done about it? Only recently have they seen their findings influence the way the criminal-justice system handles eyewitness testimony.

Psychologists have conducted hundreds of studies on errors in eyewitness identification. In some cases, of course, witnesses simply lie. But research has shown that flawed police procedures and the vagaries of memory often lead witnesses to identify the wrong person, and that credulous jurors too easily credit their testimony.

To those familiar with the mountain of evidence about the way the human mind works, that comes as no surprise. "Why should people make good eyewitnesses?" asks Gary L. Wells, a psychologist at Iowa State University who is widely considered the dean of eyewitness research. In the presence of danger, he says, "we're wired for fight or flight. What helped for survival was not a quick recall of details."

The findings of Mr. Wells and his colleagues are finally gaining currency in the halls of criminal justice. In part

that is due to the gradual acceptance of expert testimony on eyewitness identification.

Far more crucial, however, is the growing roster of convicts cleared by DNA evidence. In 1996, the U.S. Department of Justice released a report on the first 28 known cases of DNA exoneration. After studying those and 12 subsequent cases, Mr. Wells discovered that mistaken eyewitness testimony had played a part in about 90 percent of the convictions.

MISSING THE KEY DETAILS

Concerned about the high rate of eyewitness error in the DNA cases, U.S. Attorney General Janet Reno invited him to a meeting in early 1997. As a result of their conversation, the department's National Institute of Justice asked Mr. Wells and five fellow scholars to join a panel of law-enforcement officials, criminal-defense lawyers, and prosecutors created to write guidelines for handling eyewitness testimony.

The guide, published in October, gave scholars the opportunity to show that human memory is not a highly reliable tool for determining guilt in the courtroom. For example, contrary to popular belief, people under stress remember events no better than, and often less well than, they do under ordinary circumstances. Witnesses also perceive time as moving more slowly during traumatic events. That, in turn, leads them to overestimate how much time they had to notice details, a key factor of their credibility in court. And studies have found that witnesses to a crime are so distracted by the presence of a weapon—a phenomenon called "weapon focus"—that they remember little else with accuracy.

Researchers cannot ethically recreate the trauma of real crimes. But plenty of field research suggests that witnesses are apt to misidentify people.

Gary L. Wells: "Why should people make good eyewitnesses?" In times of danger, "we're wired for fight or flight. What helped for survival was not a quick recall of details."

For example, many studies have tested the ability of convenience-store clerks and bank tellers to recall customers they encountered in non-stressful situations. Around a third of the time, the employees wrongly identified faces from "lineups" that did not include the person they had actually met.

THE DETERIORATION OF MEMORY

In addition, all sorts of factors inhibit our ability to recognize and recall facial detail. For instance, psychologists have established that most of us have more difficulty recognizing people of a different race. And memory deteriorates very quickly over time.

Elizabeth F. Loftus, a psychologist at the University of Washington and a pioneer in research on false memory, has discovered that it's remarkably easy to alter one's recollection without realizing it. Human beings are highly susceptible to incorporating "post-event information"—newspaper articles, comments by police, conversations with other witnesses—into their recollections.

Witnesses also have been known to identify as criminals people they recognized from some other encounter, a process called "transference." In one bizarre example, an Australian psychologist and memory researcher named Donald Thomson was himself once identified by a rape victim as her attacker. Not only was his alibi airtight—he was being interviewed on live television at the time—but she had mistaken him for the rapist because she had seen his face on her television screen during the assault.

IMPROVING POLICE PROCEDURES

Of course, policymakers can't do much to improve the flaws in our memories. So scholars like Mr. Wells, who wanted to reduce eyewitness mistakes, began to focus on things that the justice system can control—particularly police procedures.

One of the biggest problems with eyewitness identification, researchers have found, is that uncertain wit-

nesses are often prompted to finger the person whom police have detained, even when the suspect is not the same person they spotted at the scene. Witnesses viewing a lineup tend to assume that police have caught the person they saw. So they think their job is to find the face that most resembles the description they gave to police.

The police sometimes exacerbate that tendency by designing lineups poorly. Imagine a witness to a liquor-store robbery who says the robber was white, stocky, and bearded. Based on that description, the police identify a suspect and ask the witness to look at a lineup of live individuals or at a spread of photos (known as a "six-pack").

Too often, say researchers, the "distractor" faces used by police do not closely match the witness's description, or the suspect's photo looks different from the others. If the suspect stands out in any way—if his is the only color photo in the six-pack, for instance—the witness is far more likely to say, "That's the guy."

Lineups are also fraught with the possibility of mistaken identity, researchers report, because of our tendency to overlook differences in facial appearance among people not of our race. Not only are white witnesses, say, more likely to mistake one black suspect for another (and vice versa), but police officers may overestimate the degree to which the distractors they choose match the suspect's description.

Recently, Mr. Wells has raised the alarm about the way a witness's confidence can be manipulated. Witnesses are easily influenced during and after the lineup—by talking with other witnesses or police interviewers—to be more certain of their choice than their recall warrants. Police investigators, for example, may praise a witness for "picking the right guy" out of the lineup.

That taint frequently makes its way to the jury box. Understandably, jurors put a lot of stock in a witness who can point to the defendant and say, "He's the one. I'll never forget his face." But scholars have learned that the degree of confidence during trial is a poor predictor of a witness's accuracy. And, they warn, jurors ought to be particularly skeptical if they learn that a witness professed more confidence on the witness stand than in the squad room. Recall, they say, doesn't improve over time.

ASKING THE RIGHT QUESTIONS

Until recently, the criminal-justice system made little use of those findings. Defense lawyers, of course, have embraced and exploited them at least since the 1980's. But according to Brian L. Cutler, a psychologist at Florida International University, they have rarely been able to use the research to cross-examine eyewitnesses or police.

"Defense lawyers have no special training—they don't know what questions to ask," says Mr. Cutler. "If they do ask the right questions, how well-equipped are jurors to

As Expert Witnesses, Psychologists Have an Impact —but Only a Case at a Time

UNTIL a few years ago, when the U.S. Department of Justice invited six psychologists to help reshape police procedures for eyewitness identification, scholars had only one way to influence criminal justice: one defendant at a time. Many have themselves testified to educate juries about the pitfalls of witness memory.

Like a lot of his colleagues, Gary L. Wells, a psychologist at Iowa State University who testifies four or five times a year, got into that line of research in part to save innocent defendants from false imprisonment, and to force police to improve methods for interviewing witnesses and identifying suspects. "There was a time 20 years ago when I was so naive as to think that all I had to do was document the problem and the police would change their procedures," he says. But eventually he decided that "the courtroom was never the place to have that kind of impact."

"Judges are reluctant to tell police how to do their jobs," he says. And judges tend to hew to the established view that juries are the arbiters of witness credibility.

That has been changing slowly. In 1993, the U.S. Supreme court ruled in *Daubert* v. *Merrell Dow Pharmaceuticals, Inc.* that new federal rules of evidence permitted a broader standard for allowing expert psychological testimony. Since then, says Solomon Fulero, a psychologist at Sinclair Community College, in Dayton, Ohio, several convictions have been overturned because the trial judge had not allowed such experts to testify.

Still, there's a limit to the broad change that scholars can effect by testifying. According to Mr. Wells, there just aren't that many experts: About 50 to 75 psychologists testify in court regularly, and only about 25 of them actually do original research in the field.

Furthermore, their services can be pricey. While rates vary widely, the psychologists themselves report fees of up to $3,500 a case, although most will take some clients *pro bono*.

WITNESS CREDIBILITY

In general, the experts try to avoid challenging the credibility of individual witnesses or the conduct of the police officers who worked with them. "The goal of the defense is to cast doubt on the credibility of a particular witness. But that's not my job," says Mr. Fulero, who was invited to join the Justice Department's eyewitness-testimony panel because of his courtroom experience, not his scholarly *vitae*. What he can testify to, he explains, is that "eyewitnesses are not as accurate, over all, as the jurors believe them to be."

Unfortunately for defendants, that means the research doesn't always help their cause.

"The deep problem," says James M. Doyle, a Boston defense lawyer who served on the panel, "is that the research is all statistical and probabilistic, but the trial process is clinical and diagnostic." In other words, a jury expects the experts to say whether a witness is right or wrong, when all an expert can really do is explain how to assess the odds.

Mr. Wells echoes many of his colleagues when he says that he's not really in it for the money. He was among the half-dozen scholars who helped to fashion the new Justice Department guidelines for handling eyewitness testimony. If they are widely adopted, he says, "we have no business in the courtroom on this issue. My purpose is to make expert testimony unnecessary."

He may get his wish. According to participants, prosecutors on the Justice Department panel were concerned that quick-witted defense lawyers would use the new guidelines to impeach eyewitness testimony.

Mr. Doyle, who has co-written a lawyer's guide to the research, *Eyewitness Testimony*, calls that a reasonable fear. In the past, his colleagues have had difficulty incorporating the science into their cross-examination techniques, because they haven't taken the trouble to understand the research methods, he says. Now they won't have to.

On the other hand, he doubts that's a bad thing. "One thing police and defense lawyers share is that we don't really want to deal with innocent people. It's not necessarily easier or better for me to represent innocent people. I would just as soon the police did their jobs."

—D. W. MILLER

evaluate the questions?" Unfortunately, jurors cling to a belief that "the way memory works is a matter of common sense," he says. "It just isn't so."

"People expect it's like videotape, that we attend equally well to everything out there," says Roy S. Mal-

pass, a psychologist at the University of Texas at El Paso who served on the Justice Department panel. In fact, he says, "we're highly selective."

No one knows how often eyewitness error leads to false convictions, but some scholars have taken a stab at the question. In their book *Mistaken Identification: The Eyewitness, Psychology, and the Law* (Cambridge University Press, 1995), Mr. Cutler and Steven D. Penrod, of the University of Nebraska at Lincoln, do some courtroom calculations: If just 0.5 percent of America's yearly 1.5 million convictions for serious crimes are erroneous—a rate suggested by some studies—then other research allows the authors to infer that well over half of those defendants, or around 4,500 innocent people, are convicted on false eyewitness testimony.

All that may change now that the nation's top law-enforcement officials have created new guidelines for police conduct. The Justice Department report, "Eyewitness Evidence: A Guide for Law Enforcement," reads like a primer on eyewitness research. Among other things, it instructs investigators who assemble a lineup to:

- Select "distractors" that match the witness's description, even simulating tattoos or other unusual features if necessary.
- Remind the witness that the suspect they saw may not even be in the lineup, and that the lineup is intended to clear the innocent as much as it is to identify the guilty.
- Avoid any comments that might influence the witness's selection.
- Ask for and record the witness's degree of certainty immediately.
- Photograph or film lineups to make the police more accountable to the defense.

Before they can take their new influence for granted, psychologists say, there is more to be done. For one thing, police officers and prosecutors need to be educated about the guidelines, which do not have the force of law. But Mr. Wells and others believe that both groups will embrace them once defense lawyers in the courtroom begin to hold the guidelines up as the gold standard of diligent police work.

NO DOUBLE-BLIND LINEUPS

The social scientists didn't win every battle. Despite their urgings, law-enforcement officials on the Justice De-partment panel batted down two key suggestions for improving police lineups. Research suggests that lineups are more accurate when they are double-blind—in other words, when the investigator in charge doesn't know which person is the suspect—and sequential—when the witness sees faces one at a time.

According to participants, police representatives nixed the former idea, because logistically it would be difficult to round up investigators who didn't know who the suspect was. More important, they said, it would be a tough sell to their fellow cops, because it smacks of mistrust and requires them to cede control of an investigation to someone else.

After scholars lost the battle to include double-blind procedures, participants say, they gave up on demanding sequential lineups. Without the first precaution, they explained, sequential lineups might be even more vulnerable to manipulation than simultaneous lineups are.

John Turtle, a panel member and a psychologist at the Ryerson Polytechnic Institute, in Toronto, believes that he has a high-tech solution to all those concerns. He has developed computer software that purports to take the bias out of the photo-spread lineups, which constitute about 80 percent of those in the United States and virtually all of those in Canada.

All a police investigator would need to do is scan a photo of the suspect into a computer and sit the witness down in front of the screen. The machine would then automatically choose photos of others who match the witness's description from a large database, and offer standardized, neutral instructions that wouldn't nudge the witness toward a particular response.

Psychologists deny they are imputing bad faith to police investigators. It's human nature, they say, to want your results to match your expectations. The scholars are simply urging police officers to treat their procedures for handling witnesses with all the care of scientific experiments. "Human memory is a form of trace evidence, like blood or semen or hair, except the trace exists inside the witness's head," says Mr. Wells. "How you go about collecting that evidence and preserving it and analyzing it is absolutely vital."

From *The Chronicle of Higher Education*, February 25, 2000, pp. 19-20. © 2000 by *The Chronicle of Higher Education*. Reprinted with permission. This article may not be posted, published, or distributed without permission from *The Chronicle*.

The Creeping Expansion of DNA Data Banking

By Barry Steinhardt

I want to explain my fears about the creeping expansion of DNA data banking and the uses that this information will be put to. I want to explain what those fears are based on and to challenge those who advocate the use of DNA evidence in the criminal justice system to prove me wrong—to demonstrate that the lid can be firmly kept on Pandora's box.

Let me start with a point that I hope we can all agree on. Drawing a DNA sample is not the same as taking a fingerprint. Fingerprints are two-dimensional representations of the physical attributes of our fingertips. They are useful only as a form of identification. DNA profiling may be used for identification purposes, but the DNA itself represents far more than a fingerprint. Indeed, it trivializes DNA data banking to call it a genetic fingerprint; in Massachusetts, lawmakers have specifically rejected that term.[1]

I understand that the CODIS system[2] contains only a limited amount of genetic information compiled for identification purposes. But the amount of personal and private data contained in a DNA specimen makes its seizure extraordinary in both its nature and scope. The DNA samples that are being held by state and local governments can provide insights into the most personal family relationships and the most intimate workings of the human body, including the likelihood of the occurrence of over 4,000 types of genetic conditions and diseases. DNA may reveal private information such as legitimacy at birth and there are many who will claim that there are genetic markers for aggression, substance addiction, criminal tendencies and sexual orientation.

And because genetic information pertains not only to the individual whose DNA is sampled, but to everyone who shares in that person's blood line, potential threats to genetic privacy posed by their collection extend well beyond the millions of people whose samples are currently on file.

It is worth bearing in mind, too, that there is a long, unfortunate history of despicable behavior by governments toward people whose genetic composition has been considered "abnormal" under the prevailing societal standards of the day.

Genetic discrimination by the government is not merely an artifact of the distant past. During the 1970s, the Air Force refused to allow healthy individuals who carried one copy of the sickle-cell gene to engage in flight training, even though two copies of the gene are needed for symptoms of sickle-cell disease to develop. This restriction was based upon the then untested (and now known to be incorrect) belief that people with a single such gene could display symptoms of sickle-cell disease under low oxygen conditions, even though they would not actually have sickle-cell disease.[3]

Genetic discrimination by private industry is becoming increasingly commonplace as well. A 1997 survey conducted by the American Management Association found that six to ten percent of responding employers (well over 6,000 companies) used genetic testing for employment purposes.[4] The Council for Responsible Genetics, a nonprofit advocacy group based in Cambridge, Mass., has documented hundreds of cases in which healthy people have been denied insurance or a job based on genetic "predictions."

In short, there is a frightening potential for a brave new world where genetic information is routinely collected and its use results in abuse and discrimination.

Now, I am certainly aware that the primary purpose of forensic DNA databases like CODIS is identification and that the profiles are of 13 loci that currently provide no other information. However, I reject the term "junk DNA" because as the Human Genome Project and other studies continue those loci may well turn out to contain other useful genetic information.

The question then is why I am skeptical that we can hold the line and ward off the brave new world of genetic determinism?

In general, I am skeptical because of the long history of function creep. Of databases, which are created for one discrete purpose and, which despite the initial promises of the their creators, eventually take on new functions and purposes. In the 1930s promises were made that the Social Security numbers would only be used as an aid for the new retirement program, but over the past 60 years they have gradually become the universal identifier which their creators claimed they would not be.

Similarly, census records created for general statistical purposes were used during World War II to round up innocent Japanese Americans and to place them in internment camps.

We are already beginning to see that function creep in DNA databases. In a very short time, we have witnessed the ever-widening scope of the target groups from whom law enforcement collects DNA and rapid fire proposals to expand the target populations to new and ever greater numbers of persons.

In a less than a decade, we have gone from collecting DNA from convicted sex offenders—on the theory that they are likely to be recidivists and that they frequently leave biological evidence—to data banks of all violent offenders; to all persons convicted of a crime; to juvenile offenders in 29 states and now to proposals to DNA test all arrestees.

I am skeptical because too many state statutes allow evidence which has been purportedly collected only for identification purposes, to be used for a variety of other purposes. The Massachusetts law that the ACLU is challenging, for example, contains an open-ended authorization for any disclosure that is or may be required as a condition of federal funding and allows for the disclosure of information, including personally identifiable information for "advancing other humanitarian purposes."[5]

I am skeptical because there are proponents of these DNA database laws who continue to cling to notions of a genetic cause of crime. In 1996, the year before the Legislature's enactment of the law authorizing the Massachusetts DNA database, the Legislature commissioned a study to research the biological origins of crime that focused on the genetic causes.

That report specifically focused on genes as the basis for criminal behavior, stating: The report foresaw a future where "genetics begin… to play a role in the effort to evaluate the causes of crime," and even cited two articles regarding the debunked "XYY syndrome."[6]

I am skeptical too because too many holders of DNA data refuse to destroy or return that data even after the purported purpose has been satisfied.

The Department of Defense, for example, has three million biological samples it has collected from service personnel for the stated purpose of identifying remains or body parts of a soldier killed on duty. But it keeps those samples for information for *50 years*—long after the subjects have left the military. And the DOD refuses to promulgate regulations which assure that no third parties will have access to the records. Isn't it likely that once the genetic information is collected and banked, pressures will mount to use it for other purposes than the ones for which it was gathered, such as the identification of criminal suspects or medical research? In fact, on several occasions, the FBI has already requested access to this data for purposes of criminal investigations near military bases.

Similarly, many state laws do not require the destruction of a DNA record and/or sample after a conviction has been overturned or—in the case of Louisiana's incipient law—do not require that a person arrested for a crime of which he is not convicted automatically has his DNA records expunged.

The existence of private DNA databases in testing laboratories and government offices, that operate outside the relatively strict CODIS framework, also gives me reason for concern and skepticism.

I am also skeptical, when I hear from Professor Barry Scheck of discussions he has had with law enforcement officials who are considering DNA "dragnets" of neighborhoods or classes of people without informed consent. And I am particularly distressed by the trumpeting of the British model, with its expansive testing and where in one case all the young male inhabitants of a whole village were required to submit to blood or saliva tests.

And I am made more skeptical by sloppy practices that indicate that too few jurisdictions take seriously their obligations under the data bank regime to carefully preserve and test the samples that they do have. Only two state statutes, for example, mandate outside proficiency testing of DNA labs.

In short, the trend is away from limited-purpose forensic data banks. The purposes and target populations are growing and the trend is ominous.

Compounding this problem is that there are few laws, and certainly none at the federal level, which prohibit genetic discrimination by employers, insurers or medical care providers. More and more DNA is being collected, and with the advances in genetic research that make that DNA more and more valuable, instances of discrimination and misuse will grow as well.

Now let me turn to the specific question of DNA data collection from arrestees. Aside from supporting my suspicions that we will see an ever-widening circle of DNA surveillance, these proposals are fundamentally unfair, they violate the Constitution and even from a law enforcement perspective they are not practical—at least not at the moment.

Let's start with what I thought would be the obvious. Arrest does not equal guilt and you shouldn't suffer the consequences of guilt until after you have been convicted. The fact is that many arrests do not result in a conviction.

For example, a national survey of the adjudication outcomes for felony defendants in the 75 largest counties in the country revealed that in felony assault cases, half the charges were dismissed outright, and in 14 percent of cases, the charges were reduced to a misdemeanor.

A study released by the California State Assembly's Commission on the Status of African American Males in the early 1990s revealed that 64 percent of the drug arrests of whites and 81 percent of Latinos were not sustainable, and that an astonishing 92 percent of the black men arrested by police on drug charges were subsequently released for lack of evidence or inadmissible evidence.

Indeed, there is a disturbing element of racial disparity that runs throughout our criminal justice system that can only be compounded by the creation of databases of persons arrested but not convicted of crimes.

Racial profiling and stereotyping is a reality of our criminal justice system. One study of police stops on a strip of interstate in Maryland gives some insight into the nature of the problem. Over several months in 1995, a survey found that 73 percent of the cars stopped and searched were driven by African-Americans, while they made up only 14 percent of the people driving along the interstate. While the arrests rates were about the same for whites and persons of color (approximately 28 percent), the disproportionate number of stops of minorities resulted in a disproportionate number of persons of color being arrested.

Now I make no secret of the ACLU's opposition to DNA data banking, even for convicted felons. We have argued and will continue to argue in cases like *Landry*[7] in Massachusetts that these are intrusive, unreasonable searches made without the individualized suspicion required by the Fourth Amendment and analogous provisions of state constitutions. But even if you accept the rulings that DNA data banking for convicted felons is permissible, either because a special need is present where persons have been convicted of crimes with high recidivism rates and the presence of biological evidence like sexual assaults, or that convicted felons have a diminished expectation of privacy, neither of those circumstances apply to persons who have simply been arrested.

To find otherwise is to equate arrest with guilt and to empower police officers, rather than judges and juries, with the power to force persons to provide the state with evidence that harbors many of their most intimate secrets and those of their blood relatives. Under the current circumstances of mistrust, that is an especially chilling notion for a New Yorker.

Take, for example, the "diminished expectations" argument on which most of the post-conviction DNA testing cases rest. Under this doctrine, the rights of persons who have been convicted of crimes become "diminished," only to the extent that those rights are "fundamentally inconsistent"[8] with the "needs and exigencies" of "the regime to which they have been lawfully committed."[9]

It cannot be argued that forcing arrestees to provide blood samples serves any legitimate security concern, even if they are in pre-trial detention. There are ample other means of confirming their identity. Nor by definition can DNA samples be used to insure compliance with any specified term of post-conviction supervised release. Put simply, these persons have not been convicted of any crime and may never be.

The only possible justification is investigatory and if law enforcement has reason to suspect an individual arrestee then it can and should seek a warrant.

If the special-exception doctrine makes any sense in the context of the post-convicted, it is based on the assumption that they have been found to have committed a crime where the recidivist rate is high and the presence of biological evidence is likely. How can you justify forced testing of a person arrested for jaywalking, or taking part in a political demonstration under that doctrine?

Now let me turn to the most practical of considerations—indeed the only consideration that gives me reason to hope that we will not move further down the path of DNA surveillance. As I read the literature, the single greatest obstacle to implementation of existing DNA data bank regimes is the large backlog of unprocessed samples. If I read the literature correctly, there is a backlog of 450,000 unprocessed samples and only 38,000 have been processed.[10]

There were 15 million arrests last year. From the law enforcement perspective does it really make sense to put the next dollars into collecting and processing samples for persons who have never been convicted of a crime; let alone a crime of the sort where DNA evidence is most likely to be probative. Wouldn't it make more sense to put scarce resources into processing the samples you already have and will generate in the future under the existing programs.

Let me say that I would love to be proved wrong. I would be more than happy to find that my fears are misplaced and that the civil liberties community is wrong about the likely future. If the advocates of DNA data banking can, in fact, restrict the uses of the data to forensic identification, if the data banks only cover persons convicted of a small number of crimes like sexual assault, if testing practices and data security are improved, all to the better. I won't mind being wrong. Pandora's box can be closed.

But the stakes are high and the risks are great. Every expansion of the data banks and every new use for the data increases those risks. The Commission has an obligation not just to assist law enforcement, but to protect the privacy interests of all Americans.

We may not agree on what has come before, but I hope you will agree that if the line is not held here, it may never be held at all.

Notes

1. *Commonwealth v. Curnin*, 409 Mass. 218, 219 n. 2 (1991) (rejecting the use of the phrase "'DNA fingerprinting' because (1) it tends to trivialize the intricacies of the processes by which information for DNA comparisons is obtained (when compared to the process of fingerprinting) and (2) the word fingerprinting tends to suggest erroneously that DNA testing of the type involved in this case will identify conclusively, like real fingerprinting, the one person in the world who could have left the identifying evidence at the crime scene.").

2. Combined DNA Index System, "[a] collection of databases of DNA profiles obtained from evidence samples from unsolved crimes and from known individuals convicted of particular crimes. Contributions to this database are made through State crime laboratories and the data are maintained by the FBI." Jeremy Travis & Christopher Asplen, National Commission on the Future of DNA Evidence, NCJ Pub. No. 177626, Postconviction DNA Testing: Recommendations for Handling Requests 67 (1999).

3. F. Donald Shapiro & Michelle L. Weinberg, *DNA Data Banking: The Dangerous Erosion of Privacy*, 38 Clev. St. L. Rev. 455, 480 n. 132 (1990).

4. American Management Association, Workplace Testing & Monitoring (1997), *quoted in* Rosemary Orthmann, *Three-Fourths of Major Employers Conduct Medical and Drug Tests*, Employment Testing—Law & Policy Reporter (Jul. 1997).

5. Mass. Gen. Laws Ann. ch. 22E, 10 (West 1999).

6. "Questions Concerning Biological Risk Factors for Criminal Behavior" (1996), *cited in* Brief of Amicus Curiae, Council for Responsible Genetics, *Landry v. Harshbarger* (No. SJC-07899), http://www.aclu.org/court/landry/harshbarger_crg.html.

7. *Landry v. Attorney General*, 429 Mass. 336 (1999) *cert. denied*, 68 U.S.L.W. 3153 (U.S.Mass. Jan 10, 2000) (No. 99–359) (holding that involuntary collection of DNA samples from persons subject to Massachusetts' DNA statute did not result in unreasonable search and seizure under the 4th Amendment and the State Constitution).

8. *Hudson v. Palmer*, 468 U.S. 517, 523 (1984).

9. *Wolff v. McDonnell*, 418 U.S. at 555–556 (1974).

10. National Commission on the Future of DNA Evidence, *CODIS Offender Database Backlog Reduction Discussion* (last modified Jan. 17, 2000) http://www.ojp.usdoj.gov/nij/dnamtgtrans3/ trans-k.html.

Barry Steinhardt, Esq., is the Associate Director, American Civil Liberties Union.

This article is based on the author's testimony before the National Commission on the Future of DNA Evidence on Monday, March 1, 1999. Transcripts of his and other testimony before the Commission are available on line at http://www.ojp.usdoj.gov/nij/dna.

UNIT 5
Juvenile Justice

Unit Selections

26. **Sentencing Guidelines and the Transformation of Juvenile Justice in the 21st Century**, Daniel P. Mears
27. **Hard-Time Kids**, Sasha Abramsky
28. **Gangs in Middle America: Are They a Threat?** David M. Allender
29. **Trouble With the Law**, Tina Susman
30. **Doubting the System**, Tina Susman

Key Points to Consider

- What reform efforts are currently under way in the juvenile justice system?

- What are some recent trends in juvenile delinquency? In what ways will the juvenile justice system be affected by these trends?

- Is the departure of the juvenile justice system from its original purpose warranted? Why or why not?

 **Links: www.dushkin.com/online/**
These sites are annotated in the World Wide Web pages.

Gang Land: The Jerry Capeci Page
http://www.ganglandnews.com

Institute for Intergovernmental Research (IIR)
http://www.iir.com

National Criminal Justice Reference Service (NCJRS)
http://virlib.ncjrs.org/JuvenileJustice.asp

National Network for Family Resiliency
http://www.nnfr.org

Partnership Against Violence Network
http://www.pavnet.org

Although there were variations within specific offense categories, the overall arrest rate for juvenile violent crime had remained relatively constant for several decades. Then, in the late 1980s, something changed, which brought more and more juveniles charged with violent offenses into the justice system. The juvenile justice system is a twentieth-century response to the problems of dealing with children who are in trouble with the law or who need society's protection.

Juvenile court procedure differs from the procedure in adult courts because juvenile courts are based on the philosophy that their function is to treat and to help, rather than to punish and abandon, the offender. Recently, operations of the juvenile court have received criticism, and a number of significant Supreme Court decisions have changed the way that the courts must approach the rights of children. Despite these changes, however, the major thrust of the juvenile justice system remains one of diversion and treatment, rather than adjudication and incarceration, although there is a trend toward dealing more punitively with serious juvenile offenders.

This unit's opening essay, "Sentencing Guidelines and the Transformation of Juvenile Justice in the 21st Century," makes the argument that the past decade witnessed dramatic changes to juvenile justice in America, and that these changes are altering the focus and administration of juvenile justice as it enters the twenty-first century.

The article that follows, "Hard-Time Kids," asserts that handing down adult prison sentences to juvenile criminals is not solving their problems—or ours. Next, David Allender asks whether any community is totally immune from the threat of gangs. The answer is "no," according to "Gangs in Middle America: Are They a Threat?" Then, in "Trouble With the Law," parents and various groups decry a justice system that treats juveniles as adults. Finally, in a companion essay, "Doubting the System," which closes this unit, Tina Susman describes how laws about juveniles stir a debate over punishment and racism.

Sentencing Guidelines and the Transformation of Juvenile Justice in the 21st Century

As we enter the 21st century, many states have introduced fundamental changes to their juvenile justice systems. The changes focus on jurisdictional authority, especially transfer to adult court; sentencing guidelines and options; correctional programming; interagency information sharing; offender confidentiality; and victim involvement. At the same time, attention has turned increasingly to prevention, early intervention, rehabilitation, and the use of specialized courts. Because of their special significance in the historical context of the juvenile court, this article focuses on the emergence of sentencing guidelines to identify underlying trends and issues in the transformation of juvenile justice. In so doing, the article argues that the considerable attention given by policy makers and researchers to transfer rather than other changes provides a distorted picture of current juvenile justice practice.

DANIEL P. MEARS
The Urban Institute

The past decade witnessed dramatic changes to juvenile justice in America, changes that have altered the focus and administration of juvenile justice as it enters the 21st century (Butts & Mitchell, 2000; Feld, 1991; Harris, Welsh, & Butler, 2000). In contrast to the philosophical foundation and practice of the first juvenile courts, punishment and due process today constitute central features of processing. These emphases, which run counter to the rehabilitative *parens patriae* ("state as parent") foundation of the first juvenile courts, emerged in the 1960s with a series of U.S. Supreme Court decisions. In cases such as *In re Gault*, the Supreme Court recognized that juvenile courts served not only a rehabilitative function but also a punishment function, and that consequently due process rights and procedures should figure more prominently in juvenile proceedings (Feld, 1999). In recent years, the transition has become more pronounced, with states enacting sweeping legislative changes affecting all aspects of the juvenile justice system (National Criminal Justice Association, 1997; Torbet et al., 1996; Torbet & Szymanski, 1998).

It is important to recognize, however, that the changes have not been entirely or even primarily focused on punishment. One would not know this from a review of research, the bulk of which has examined patterns, correlates, and effects of transfer (for a review, see Butts & Mitchell, 2000). The focus is understandable—transfer provides an easily identifiable symbol for debates about the merits of maintaining two separate juvenile and adult systems (Feld, 1999; Hirschi & Gottfredson, 1993). Indeed, why have a juvenile justice system if youth are being sent into adult courts? But the fact is that only about 1% of all formally processed delinquency cases ultimately are transferred (Snyder & Sickmund, 1999, p. 171).

Focusing solely on transfer ignores the fact that other equally, if not more significant, transformations have occurred in juvenile justice. These include enactment of sentencing guidelines; creation of blended sentencing options for linking the juvenile and criminal justice systems; enhanced correctional programming, with an increasing emphasis on treatment; greater interagency and cross-jurisdiction cooperation and information sharing; reduced confidentiality of court records and proceedings; and increased participation of victims in juvenile justice processing (Fagan & Zimring, 2000; Guarino-Ghezzi & Loughran, 1996; National Criminal Justice Association, 1997; Torbet et al., 1996). In addition, states increasingly are turning their attention to prevention, early intervention, rehabilitation, and the use of specialized courts to address juvenile crime (Butts & Harrell, 1998; Butts & Mears, 2001; Cocozza & Skowyra, 2000; Coordinating Council on Juvenile Justice and Delinquency Prevention, 1996; Cullen & Gendreau, 2000; Howell, 1995; Lipsey, Wilson, & Cothern, 2000; Rivers & Anwyl, 2000).

It is apparent that juvenile justice has been evolving along many dimensions. With all of these changes, the question arises: What, if any, are the common trends and issues underlying these different changes? To answer this question, I examine sentencing guidelines, showing that they reflect many of the major trends and issues in juvenile justice. I focus on guidelines because typically they apply to all juvenile offenders and embody a range of goals, thus reflecting many of the conflicts and tensions inherent in attempts to modify the focus and administration of juvenile justice. By contrast, transfer laws, which have received much more attention in the research literature, focus only on select age groups and offenders and have the delimited purpose of punishing and deterring offenders.

The primary goal of this article, in short, is to use an analysis of sentencing guidelines to highlight a range of critical underlying trends and issues in juvenile justice. A secondary goal is to show that research on transfer laws provides little insight into juvenile justice as it is practiced today and, in the absence of research on or attention to other reforms, can provide a distorted picture of current practice. To achieve these goals, I begin by briefly describing the history of the juvenile court and the emergence of juvenile sentencing guidelines. I then use this discussion to identify key trends and issues in juvenile justice.

FOUNDATION OF THE JUVENILE JUSTICE SYSTEM

Juveniles have not always been viewed the same way throughout U.S. history. For example, in the 18th century, juvenile offenders were treated as adults and received the same types of punishments. During the 19th century, a movement began that focused on the unique, less-than-adult capacities and needs of youth. This movement highlighted the need for a specialized sanctioning process, one that emphasized rehabilitation and deemphasized punishment.

The result of this movement was the development of the first U.S. juvenile court in Cook County, Illinois, in 1899. By 1925, juvenile courts were established in all but two states, with most courts defining juveniles as individuals who were aged 17 years or younger. (For histories of the juvenile court, see Platt [1977], Bernard [1992], Feld [1999], and Butts and Mitchell [2000].)

These new youth-centered courts were grounded in the doctrine of parens patriae. The guiding rationale was that states had an obligation to intervene in the lives of children whose parents provided inadequate care or supervision. Juvenile court interventions were to be benevolent and in the "best interests" of the child.

For this reason, court processing entailed fundamentally different notions of procedural and substantive justice. Unlike adult court proceedings, juvenile court proceedings were to be informal and conducted on a case-by-case basis, with the aim of improving the lives of children through individualized treatment and varying dispositional options, ranging from warnings to probation to confinement.

The basis for intervening in the lives of juvenile offenders derived not from criminal law but civil law, further highlighting the focus on helping youth rather than sanctioning them for their crimes. Similarly, the philosophy of parens patriae clearly suggested that the courts had an obligation to help youth who committed crimes or who clearly needed help. As a result, juvenile courts could use coercive means to help youth, even when relatively minor crimes had been committed or when there was insufficient basis for determining that a crime in fact was committed.

The potential for abuse of this discretionary authority is evident in critiques of the juvenile court (see Feld, 1999). Indeed, as many scholars have shown, the transition to establishing a juvenile justice system was not motivated entirely by benevolent concerns. Under the guise of providing social services and crime control, juvenile courts could, for example, be used instead to provide a form of social control over "undesirable classes," including minorities, immigrants, and indigents (Butts & Mitchell, 2000).

By the 1960s, deep-rooted concerns arose about the procedural and substantive unfairness of juvenile court proceedings, leading the U.S. Supreme Court, through a series of decisions, to emphasize greater procedural parity with criminal court proceedings. The result was an increasingly criminal-like juvenile court. This trend, coupled with tougher transfer provisions in the 1990s, led to considerable debate about the merits of having two separate court systems, one for juveniles and one for adults (Feld, 1999).

JUVENILE SENTENCING GUIDELINES: AN OVERVIEW

The early juvenile court emphasized individualized, offender-based treatment and sanctioning. Indeed, almost every justification of the juvenile court rests on the notion that the most appropriate and effective intervention for youth is one that takes into account their particular needs and resources. Ironically, despite the establishment of this view more than 100 years ago, recent research provides considerable empirical support for it—the most effective interventions are those premised on addressing the specific risk, needs, and capacities of youth (Cullen & Gendreau, 2000; Lipsey, 1999).

Under the Office of Juvenile Justice and Delinquency Prevention's (OJJDP's) Comprehensive Strategy for Serious, Violent, and Chronic Juvenile Offenders (Howell, 1995; Wilson & Howell, 1993), states have been encouraged to adopt individualized sanctioning and to emphasize risk and needs assessment. Many have responded by enacting guideline systems that are modeled to a considerable extent on the Comprehensive Strategy.

In some states, these guideline systems are voluntary, in others there are incentives to use them, and in still others they are required. In each instance, the guidelines typically are offense-based and outline a sequence of increasingly tougher sanctions, while at the same time emphasizing rehabilitative interventions when appropriate.

In 1995, for example, Texas enacted what it termed the Progressive Sanctions Guidelines. The Guidelines outline seven tiers of sanctioning, with each linked to the instant offense and the offender's prior record. Once the appropriate level of sanctioning is established, courts are encouraged to include additional, nonpunitive interventions. Although the Guidelines are voluntary, Texas documents the extent to which county-level sanctioning deviates from the recommendations of the Guidelines (Texas Criminal Justice Policy Council, 2001). Similar approaches have been implemented in other states, including Illinois, Kansas, Nebraska, New York, Utah, Virginia, and Washington (Corriero, 1999; Demleitner, 1999; Fagan & Zimring, 2000; Lieb & Brown, 1999; National Criminal Justice Association, 1997; Torbet et al., 1996).

State guideline systems often identify their goals explicitly. In Texas, for example, the Progressive Sanction Guidelines are used to "guide" dispositional decision making in providing "appropriate" sanctions and to promote "uniformity" and "consistency" in sentencing (Dawson, 1996). At the same time, the Guidelines are seen as furthering the newly established and explicitly stated goal of the Texas Juvenile Justice Code—namely, punishment of juveniles. But they also promote rehabilitative sanctioning by encouraging appropriate treatment and interventions for each recommended sanction level. In addition, the Guidelines implicitly promote certain goals, including public safety through incapacitation of the most serious or chronic offenders and reduced crime through get-tough, deterrence-oriented sanctioning.

Other states have followed similar paths. For example, Washington established sentencing guidelines aimed directly at reducing the perceived failings of a system founded on practitioner discretion (Lieb & Brown, 1999). The guidelines focus not only on offense-based consider-

ations but also on the juvenile's age, with younger offenders receiving fewer "points" and thus more lenient sanctions. Similarly, Utah has enacted sentencing guidelines focusing on proportionate sentencing, early intervention, and progressively intensive supervision and sanctioning for more serious and chronic offenders (Utah Sentencing Commission, 1997).

Because many states increasingly are adopting sentencing guidelines and because the guidelines focus on all youth rather than simply those who may be transferred, an examination of them can help to identify underlying trends and issues emergent in juvenile justice. By contrast, a focus on transfer, typical of most research on recent reforms, provides relatively little leverage to do so. Transfer laws typically focus on "easy cases," those in which the seriousness of the offense largely vitiates, rightly or wrongly, concerns many would have about individualized or rehabilitative sanctioning. Any resulting debate therefore centers on extremes: Should we retain or eliminate the juvenile court?

But a broader issue in juvenile justice is how to balance individualized, offender-based sanctioning with proportional and consistent punishment. These issues, among several others, are a consideration in almost every case coming before the juvenile court. It is appropriate, therefore, to focus on a recent reform, such as sentencing guidelines, that typically target, in one manner or another, all youth and that reflects attempts to shape the entire juvenile justice system. For this reason, the remainder of this article uses a focus on sentencing guidelines to identify key trends and issues in the transformation of juvenile justice.

JUVENILE SENTENCING GUIDELINES: TRENDS AND ISSUES IN THE TRANSFORMATION OF JUVENILE JUSTICE IN THE NEW MILLENNIUM

Balancing Multiple and Conflicting Goals

The motivation for transforming juvenile justice has come from many sources. Scholars cite a range of factors, including the desire to address violent crime, inconsistency and racial/ethnic disproportionality in sentencing, financial burdens faced by counties versus states, and public support for get-tough and rehabilitative measures (Bazemore & Umbreit, 1995; Bishop, Lanza-Kaduce, & Frazier, 1998; Butts & Mitchell, 2000).

As suggested by the different motivations for reform, a key trend in juvenile justice is the move toward balancing multiple and frequently competing goals, only one of which includes the punitive focus associated with transfer (Bazemore & Umbreit, 1995; Guarino-Ghezzi & Loughran, 1996; Mears, 2000). Today, many juvenile justice codes and policies focus on retributive/punitive sanctioning (through get-tough sanctions generally), incapacitation, deterrence, rehabilitation, individualized as well as consistent and proportional sentencing, and restorative sanctioning.

Reduced crime is a broad goal underlying many but not all of these more specific goals. For example, get-tough sanctions are viewed as a primary mechanism to instill fear and achieve specific or general deterrence (i.e., reduced offending among sanctioned or would-be offenders) or to reduce crime through temporary incapacitation of offenders. In many instances, retribution serves as the primary focus of sanctioning, irrespective of any potential crime control impact.

Some goals, like rehabilitation, serve as steps toward enhancing the lives of juveniles, not simply reducing their offending. Others, such as restorative sanctioning, focus on reintegrating offenders into their communities while at the same time providing victims with a voice in the sanctioning and justice process. Still others, including proportional and consistent sentencing, focus primarily on fairness rather than crime control. That is, the motivation is to provide sanctions that are proportional to the crime and that are consistent within and across jurisdictions so that juveniles sanctioned by Judge X or in County X receive sanctions similar to those administered by Judge Y or in County Y.

Historically these different goals, including what might be termed intermediate goals leading to reduced crime, have overlapped considerably with those of the criminal justice system (Snyder & Sickmund, 1999, pp. 94–96). In general, though, criminal justice systems have given greater weight to punishment than rehabilitation, whereas juvenile justice systems generally have favored rehabilitation more than punishment.

In reality, the goals in each system are diverse, as are the weightings given to each goal. Indeed, the diversity of goals and their weighting can make it difficult to determine how exactly the two systems differ, especially if we focus only on new transfer laws (see, however, Bishop & Frazier, 2000). But one major difference between the two is that juvenile justice systems—as is evident in their sentencing guideline systems—are actively struggling to balance as wide a range of goals as possible. By contrast, most criminal justice systems have veered strongly toward retribution and incapacitation (Clark, Austin, & Henry, 1997).

Giving Priority to Punishment Through Offense-Based Guidelines and Changes in Discretion

Most state guideline systems use offense-based criteria for determining which types of sanctions to apply (Coolbaugh & Hansel, 2000). Once the punishment level has been established, the court is supposed to consider the needs of the offender and how these may best be addressed. However, these needs frequently are only vaguely specified and rarely assessed. One result is that priority implicitly and in practice may be given to punishment.

This priority can be reinforced through various mechanisms that place greater discretion in the hands of prosecutors rather than judges. For example, laws that stipulate automatic sanctions for certain offenses do not eliminate discretion; instead, they shift it to prosecutors, who can determine whether and how to charge an offense (Feld, 1999; Mears, 2000; Sanborn, 1994; Singer, 1996). Consequently, in practice, many guideline systems make punishment a priority not just for youth who may be transferred but for all youth referred to juvenile court.

Sentencing guidelines have not gone unopposed. For example, research on the Texas Progressive Sanction Guidelines indicates that many judges resisted enactment of the Guidelines and then, once they became law, resisted using them (Mears, 2000). One reason is their belief that offense-based criteria provide too limited a basis for structuring decision making. Thus, even though compliance with the Guidelines is voluntary, some judges feel that the Guidelines symbolize too narrow a focus, one that draws attention from factors they believe are more important, such as the age and maturity of the youth and their family and community contexts. Such concerns have been expressed about adult sentencing guidelines (e.g., see Forer, 1994). One difference with juvenile sentencing guidelines is that, despite the views of opponents, they generally state explicitly that there are multiple goals associated with sanctioning and that practitioners should consider a range of mitigating factors (Howell, 1995).

Balancing Discretion Versus Disparity and Consistency, and Procedural Versus Substantive Justice

In stark contrast to the early foundation of the juvenile court, many states today are intent on eliminating disparity and inconsistency in sentencing (Feld, 1999; Torbet et al., 1996). The widespread belief, evident in many sentencing guidelines, is that (a) judicial discretion causes disparity and inconsistency and (b) that offense-based systems can eliminate or reduce these problems. Both beliefs prevail despite the fact that little empirical evidence exists to support them (Mears & Field, 2000; Sanborn, 1994; Yellen, 1999).

But the fact that such strategies may not work does not belie that underlying trend toward discovering ways to promote fairness and consistency in sentencing. Nor does it belie the fact that, as with adult sanctioning, there likely will continue to be an ongoing tension between the use of discretion and the need to have sanctions that are relatively similar for different populations and within and across jurisdictions.

This tension is captured in part by the distinction in the sociology of law between procedural and substantive justice. From the perspective of procedural justice, fairness emerges from decisions that are guided by established rules and procedures for sanctioning cases that exhibit specific characteristics. By contrast, from the perspective of substantive justice, fairness emerges from decisions that are guided by consideration of the unique situational context and characteristics of the defendant (Gould, 1993; Ulmer & Kramer, 1996).

In recent years, and as exemplified by the creation of offense-based sentencing guidelines, juvenile justice systems increasingly are focusing on procedural justice. In the case of transfer particularly, the Supreme Court and state legislatures have attempted to ensure that there is procedural parity with adult proceedings. Yet despite the increased proceduralization, for most cases facing the juvenile courts, substantive justice also remains a priority, especially when sanctioning first-time and less serious offenders. In these instances, states have devised strategies, outlined in their guidelines, that promote diversion, rehabilitation, and treatment.

Maintaining the View That Most Youth Are "Youth," Not Adults

Public opinion polls show that whereas most people consistently support rehabilitative sanctioning of youth, they also support punitive, get-tough measures for serious and violent offenders (Roberts & Stalans, 1998). Moreover, even when the public supports transferring youth to the adult system, they generally prefer youth to be housed in separate facilities and to receive individualized, rehabilitative treatment (Schwartz, Guo, & Kerbs, 1993).

The apparent contradiction likely constitutes the primary reason that wholesale elimination of the juvenile justice system has not prevailed. In the debate about abolishing the juvenile court, this fact frequently is omitted, perhaps because so much attention has centered on changes in transfer laws. Indeed, were one to focus solely on recent trends in transfer, one might conclude that an eventual merging of juvenile and adult systems is inevitable (Feld, 1999).

Yet the focus and structure of juvenile sentencing guidelines, which explicitly call for rehabilitation and early intervention, suggest otherwise. In contrast to get-tough developments in the criminal justice system (Clark et al., 1997), most states—even those without guideline systems—have struggled to maintain a focus not only on the most violent offenders but also on efficient and effective intervention with less serious offenders.

This trend is reflected in the proliferation of alternative, or specialized, courts, including community, teen, drug, and mental health courts (Butts & Harrell, 1998; Office of Justice Programs, 1998; Santa Clara County Superior Court, 2001). These courts focus on timely and rehabilitative sanctioning that draws on the strengths of families and communities and the cooperation and assistance of local and state agencies.

Some authors suggest that these courts threaten the foundation of the juvenile court (Butts & Harrell, 1998). But specialized courts can be viewed as symbolic of the reemergence of the juvenile justice system as historically

conceived—namely, as a system designed to intervene on an individualized, case-by-case basis, addressing the particular risks and needs of offenders (Butts & Mears, 2001). Indeed, to this end, many guidelines promote diversion of first- and second-time, less serious offenders from formal processing to informal alternatives available through specialized courts.

Limited Conceptualization and Assessment of the Implementation and Effects of Changes in the Juvenile Justice System

One last and prominent trend in juvenile justice bears emphasizing—the lack of systematic attention to conceptualizing and assessing the implementation and effects of recently enacted laws. A focus on sentencing guidelines illustrates the point: Few states have systematically articulated precisely what the goals of the guidelines are, how specifically the guidelines are expected to achieve these goals, or what in fact the effects of the guidelines have been (Coolbaugh & Hansel, 2000; Fagan & Zimring, 2000; Mears, 2000).

One example common to many guidelines is the focus on consistency. Several questions illustrate the point. What exactly does *consistency* mean? Is it identical sentencing of like offenders within jurisdictions? Across jurisdictions? Does it involve similar weighting of the same factors by all judges or judges within each jurisdiction in a state? Across states? Apart from definitional issues, does consistency lead to reduced crime or increased perceptions of fairness? If so, how? What precisely are the mechanisms by which increased consistency would lead to changes in crime or perceptions of fairness? The failure to address these questions means that it is impossible to assess whether there has been more or less consistency resulting from guideline systems.

Similar questions about many other aspects of recent juvenile justice reforms remain largely unaddressed, with two unfortunate consequences. First, as noted above, it is impossible to assess the effects of the reforms without greater clarity concerning their goals and the means by which these goals are to be reached. As a result, it is difficult if not impossible to make informed policy decisions, including those focusing on maintaining or eliminating the juvenile justice system (Schneider, 1984; Singer, 1996). Second, without conceptualization and assessment of the effects of recent reforms, there is an increased likelihood that research on delimited aspects of juvenile justice systems will be generalized into statements about entire systems, even though there may be little to no correspondence between the two.

CONCLUSION

Recent changes to juvenile justice systems throughout the United States indicate a trend toward developing more efficient and effective strategies for balancing different and frequently competing goals. This trend is evident in recent juvenile sentencing guidelines. As the above discussion demonstrates, guidelines focus on more than transferring the most serious offenders to the criminal justice system. They also focus on balancing competing goals, reducing discretion and promoting fair and consistent sanctioning, and tempering procedural with substantive justice. More generally, guidelines aim to preserve the notion that youth are not adults.

One result of such trends is increasing interest in alternative administrative mechanisms for processing youthful offenders. Specialized "community," "teen," "drug," "mental health," and other such courts have been developed to do what the original juvenile court was supposed to do—provide individualized and rehabilitative sanctioning. But the "modern" approach involves doing so in a more timely and sophisticated fashion, and in a way that draws on the cooperation and assistance of local and state agencies as well as families and communities.

In the new millennium, juvenile justice thus involves more than an emphasis on due process and punishment. It also involves substantive concerns, including a range of competing goals, a belief in the special status of childhood, and the desire to develop more effective strategies for preventing and reducing juvenile crime.

By focusing on sentencing guidelines, these types of issues become more apparent, highlighting the need for researchers to look beyond transfer laws in assessing recent juvenile justice reforms. Indeed, there is a need for research on many new and different laws, polices, and programs in juvenile justice, most of which remain unassessed. As we enter the new millennium, it will be critical to redress this situation, especially if we are to move juvenile justice beyond "juvenile" versus "adult" debates and to develop more efficient and effective interventions.

REFERENCES

Bazemore, G., & Umbreit, M. (1995). Rethinking the sanctioning function in juvenile court: Retributive or restorative responses to youth crime. *Crime & Delinquency, 41,* 296–316.

Bernard, T. J. (1992). *The cycle of juvenile justice.* New York: Oxford University Press.

Bishop, D. M., & Frazier, C. E. (2000). Consequences of transfer. In J. Fagan & F. E. Zimring (Eds.), *The changing boundaries of juvenile justice: Transfer of adolescents to the criminal court* (pp. 227–276). Chicago: University of Chicago Press.

Bishop, D. M., Lanza-Kaduce, L., & Frazier, C. E. (1998). Juvenile justice under attack: An analysis of the causes and impact of recent reforms. *Journal of Law and Public Policy, 10,* 129–155.

Butts, J. A., & Harrell, A. V. (1998). *Delinquents or criminals? Policy options for juvenile offenders.* Washington, DC: The Urban Institute.

Butts, J. A., & Mears, D. P. (2001). Reviving juvenile justice in a get-tough era. *Youth & Society, 33,* 169–198.

Butts, J. A., & Mitchell, O. (2000). Brick by brick: Dismantling the border between juvenile and adult justice. In C. M. Friel (Ed.), *Criminal justice 2000: Boundary changes in criminal justice organizations* (Vol. 2, pp. 167–213). Washington, DC: National Institute of Justice.

Clark, J., Austin, J., & Henry, D. A. (1997). *"Three strikes and you're out": A review of state legislation.* Washington: DC: National Institute of Justice.

Cocozza, J. J., & Skowyra, K. (2000). Youth with mental health disorders: Issues and emerging responses. *Juvenile Justice, 7,* 3–13.

Coolbaugh, K., & Hansel, C. J. (2000). *The comprehensive strategy: Lessons learned from the pilot sites.* Washington, DC: Office of Juvenile Justice and Delinquency Prevention.

Coordinating Council on Juvenile Justice and Delinquency Prevention. (1996). *Combating violence and delinquency: The national juvenile justice action plan.* Washington, DC: Office of Juvenile Justice and Delinquency Prevention.

Corriero, M. A. (1999). Juvenile sentencing: The New York youth part as a model. *Federal Sentencing Reporter, 11,* 278–281.

Cullen, F. T., & Gendreau, P. (2000). Assessing correctional rehabilitation: Policy, practice, and prospects. In J. Horney (Ed.), *Criminal justice 2000: Policies, processes, and decisions of the criminal justice system* (Vol. 3, pp. 109–175). Washington, DC: National Institute of Justice.

Dawson, R. O. (1996). *Texas juvenile law* (4th ed.). Austin: Texas Juvenile Probation Commission.

Demleitner, N. V. (1999). Reforming juvenile sentencing. *Federal Sentencing Reporter, 11,* 243–247.

Fagan, J., & Zimring, F. E. (Eds.). (2000). *The changing borders of juvenile justice.* Chicago: University of Chicago Press.

Feld, B. C. (1991). The transformation of the juvenile court. *Minnesota Law Review, 75,* 691–725.

Feld, B. C. (1999). *Bad kids: Race and the transformation of the juvenile court.* New York: Oxford University Press.

Forer, L. (1994). *A rage to punish: The unintended consequences of mandatory sentencing.* New York: Norton.

Gould, M. (1993). Legitimation and justification: The logic or moral and contractual solidarity in Weber and Durkheim. *Social Theory, 13,* 205–225.

Guarino-Ghezzi, S., & Loughran, E. J. (1996). *Balancing juvenile justice.* New Brunswick, NJ: Transaction.

Harris, P. W., Welsh, W. N., & Butler, F. (2000). A century of juvenile justice. In G. LaFree (Ed.), *Criminal justice 2000: The nature of crime: Continuity and change* (Vol. 1, pp. 359–425). Washington, DC: National Institute of Justice.

Hirschi, T., & Gottfredson, M. R. (1993). Rethinking the juvenile justice system. *Crime & Delinquency, 39,* 262–271.

Howell, J. C. (1995). *Guide for implementing the comprehensive strategy for serious, violent, and chronic juvenile offenders.* Washington, DC: Office of Juvenile Justice and Delinquency Prevention.

Lieb, R., & Brown, M. E. (1990). Washington state's solo path: Juvenile sentencing guidelines. *Federal Sentencing Reporter, 11,* 273–277.

Lipsey, M. W. (1999). Can rehabilitative programs reduce the recidivism of juvenile offenders? An inquiry into the effectiveness of practical programs. *Virginia Journal of Social Policy and Law, 6,* 611–641.

Lipsey, M. W., Wilson, D. B., & Cothern, L. (2000). *Effective intervention for serious juvenile offenders.* Washington, DC: Office of Juvenile Justice and Delinquency Prevention.

Mears, D. P. (2000). Assessing the effectiveness of juvenile justice reforms: A closer look at the criteria and impacts on diverse stakeholders. *Law and Policy, 22,* 175–202.

Mears, D. P., & Field, S. H. (2000). Theorizing sanctioning in a criminalized juvenile court. *Criminology, 38,* 101–137.

National Criminal Justice Association. (1997). *Juvenile justice reform initiatives in the states: 1994–1996.* Washington, DC: Office of Juvenile Justice and Delinquency Prevention.

Office of Justice Programs. (1998). *Juvenile and family drug courts: An overview.* Washington, DC: Author.

Platt, A. M. (1977). *The child savers: The invention of delinquency.* Chicago: University of Chicago Press.

Rivers, J. E., & Anwyl, R. S. (2000). Juvenile assessment centers: Strengths, weaknesses, and potential. *The Prison Journal, 80,* 96–113.

Roberts, J. V., & Stalans, L. J. (1998). Crime, criminal justice, and public opinion. In M. Tonry (Ed.), *The handbook of crime and punishment* (pp. 31–57). New York: Oxford University Press.

Sanborn, J. A. (1994). Certification to criminal court: The important policy questions of how, when, and why. *Crime & Delinquency, 40,* 262–281.

Santa Clara County Superior Court. (2001). *Santa Clara County Superior Court commences juvenile mental health court.* San Jose, CA: Author.

Schneider, A. L. (1984). Sentencing guidelines and recidivism rates of juvenile offenders. *Justice Quarterly, 1,* 107–124.

Schwartz, I. M., Guo, S., & Kerbs, J. J. (1993). The impact of demographic variables on public opinion regarding juvenile justice: Implications for public policy. *Crime & Delinquency, 39,* 5–28.

Singer, S. I. (1996). Merging and emerging systems of juvenile and criminal justice. *Law and Policy, 18,* 1–15.

Snyder, H. N., & Sickmund, M. (1999). *Juvenile offenders and victims: 1999 national report.* Washington, DC: Office of Juvenile Justice and Delinquency Prevention.

Texas Criminal Justice Policy Council. (2001). *The impact of progressive sanction guidelines: Trends since 1995.* Austin, TX: Author.

Torbet, P., Gable, R., Hurst, H. IV, Montgomery, I., Szymanski, L., & Thomas, D. (1996). *State responses to serious and violent juvenile crime.* Washington, DC: Office of Juvenile Justice and Delinquency Prevention.

Torbet, P., & Szymanski, L. (1998). *State legislative responses to violent juvenile crime: 1996–97 update.* Washington, DC: Office of Juvenile Justice and Delinquency Prevention.

Ulmer, J. T., & Kramer, J. H. (1996). Court communities under sentencing guidelines: Dilemmas of formal rationality and sentencing disparity. *Criminology, 34,* 383–407.

Utah Sentencing Commission. (1997). *Juvenile sentencing guidelines manual.* Salt Lake City, UT: Author.

Wilson, J. J., & Howell, J. C. (1993). *Comprehensive strategy for serious, violent, and chronic juvenile offenders: Program summary.* Washington, DC: Office of Juvenile Justice and Delinquency Prevention.

Yellen, D. (199). Sentence discounts and sentencing guidelines. *Federal Sentencing Reporter, 11,* 285–288.

Correspondence concerning this article should be addressed to Daniel P. Mears, The Urban Institute, 2100 M Street, Washington, D.C. 20037; phone: (202) 261-5592; fax: (202) 659-8985; e-mail: dmears@urban.org. The views in this article were those of the author and do not necessarily reflect those of The Urban Institute, its board or trustees, or its sponsors. The author gratefully acknowledges the constructive comments of the anonymous reviewers.

Daniel P. Mears, Ph.D., is a research associate in The Urban Institute's Justice Policy Center. His research focuses on the causes of crime and effective ways to prevent and intervene with crime and justice problems. He has conducted research on delinquency, juvenile and criminal justice programs and policies, domestic violence, immigration and crime, correctional forecasting, and drug treatment in prisons. Recent publications include articles in Criminal Justice and Behavior, Criminology, Journal of Research in Crime and Delinquency, Law and Society Review, *and* Sociological Perspectives.

From *Journal of Contemporary Criminal Justice*, February 2002, pp. 6-12. © 2002 by Sage Publications, Inc. Reprinted by permission.

Hard-Time Kids

Handing down adult prison sentences to juvenile criminals isn't solving their problems—or ours.

SASHA ABRAMSKY

An INTERNATIONAL OUTCRY AROSE LAST WINTER when the state of Florida tried 14-year-old Lionel Tate as an adult and sentenced the boy to life in prison for killing a playmate two years earlier during what Lionel said was a mock wrestling game. Within days of his sentencing—with the photograph of his chubby, tear-stained face etched into the national consciousness—Lionel was moved from an adult prison to a juvenile facility. A clutch of high-powered appellate attorneys, led by the inimitable Johnnie Cochran and Barry Scheck, had taken up the case. And Florida Governor Jeb Bush was letting it be known that he might be amenable to eventually signing some sort of clemency deal in this unusual situation.

But in fact, Lionel Tate's case was not so exceptional. In recent years, 47 states and the District of Columbia have revamped their juvenile justice systems either to require that certain crimes be tried in adult court or to give prosecutors (instead of juvenile court judges) the discretion to try minors as adults. Such changes mean that juveniles are increasingly being tried in adult courts and given adult sentences—often to be served, as Lionel Tate's was supposed to be, in adult prisons.

Legislators and prosecutors are presumably aware that brutality is common in these prisons and that they have no specialized rehabilitative programs like those that juvenile facilities are supposed to provide. Nonetheless, according to the federal Bureau of Justice Statistics (BJS), there are only two states—California and North Dakota—that still prohibit the incarceration of children under the age of 16 in adult facilities. Only six states require that inmates under 18 be housed in separate units from the adult prison population.

THE SUPERPREDATOR MYTH

The get-tough movement supposedly was driven by the terrifying surge of juvenile violence that spiked toward the end of the crack epidemic between 1991 and 1993. Politicians claimed that a hard-time approach was the only way to deal with the specter of unredeemable juvenile "superpredators," as they were called by sociologist John DiIulio (who is now in charge of President George W. Bush's faith-based charity initiative). But in fact, the rash of new legislation came largely after crack and after violent-crime rates among teenagers began plummeting. As a result, the last decade has seen *less and less* teenage violence but *more and more* teens sent to adult jails and prisons across the country.

Nationally, the BJS estimates, some 7,400 teens under the age of 18 were admitted to state prisons in 1997, the last year for which such statistics have been compiled. This was up from 3,400 admissions in 1985. In 1997, the agency reports, 33 adolescents were sentenced to adult prison for every thousand arrested for violent crimes, up from 18 per thousand arrested in 1985. And these sentences were not to be quick, scare-'em-straight experiences. On average, minors convicted of violent crimes were expected to serve a minimum of five years in adult prison. In addition, nearly 10,000 minors were held in adult jails for some period in 1997.

Atiba FARQUHARSON, A 17-YEAR-OLD FROM A POOR black neighborhood in Miami, was sentenced as an adult three years ago for robbing a gas station with a friend and shooting the attendant in the arm. Clearly Atiba, who had been sticking up local dope dealers and businesses for several years by then, needed to be removed from society. But if he was ever going to change, the disturbed, hyperactive teenager, who had been on Prozac for years, also needed intensive counseling, a structured education, and a sense of hope. In adult prison, he's gotten none of that.

At the Zephyr Hills Correctional Institution, 20 miles north of Tampa, prison authorities send Atiba to work raking leaves and mowing grass on the compound. He is not required to enroll in school, as is standard practice in juvenile facilities. He's been in and out of prison psychiatric wards over these three years, but there he's been medicated, not counseled. Oftentimes, when his temper gets the better of him, he fights or cusses out the guards and as a punishment then spends weeks in isolation in the wing of the prison that inmates call "the box." Unlike juvenile facilities, at Zephyr Hills there are no legal limits on the amount of time a kid can be confined in these physically and psychologically destructive isolation cells.

To be sure, the country's overburdened and often malfunctioning juvenile justice systems can fall well short of their goals. But the point is, the new, hard-time approach to juvenile crime does not even attempt to achieve these goals.

"In prison," Atiba says, "I ain't really get no education. I get my learning from inmates. When I was on the street, I couldn't read well or write; only thing I was good at was math. In prison, I learned to read and write. I learned from different inmates."

The problem is that in addition to the three Rs, Atiba—whose parents were drug addicts and who learned to rob and steal before he was 10 years old while living in a two-bedroom house with his grandmother, his aunt and her several children, his uncle's family, and his own brothers and sisters—is also being taught the ethos of the street. "Prison's like a school and a gladiator prison," he explains, sitting in his blue uniform in an interview room at Zephyr Hills. "It's bad, because you've got to watch your back or you'll be killed in here. I've got beaten lots of times." One time, when he was 16, he says, an officer slammed his head against a Plexiglas window. Another time, at a different institution, a rival stabbed him in the chest with a shank. Inmates wielding socks filled with metal padlocks have hit friends of his over the head. "You're surrounded by different types of criminals," the teenager says. "People who know how to burgle houses, rob banks. You've got rapists here. Murderers. Young people, some don't have the mind I do. They'll listen to the older inmate: 'This is how you do a robbery.' He might go out there and try it again. He might get away, or he might end up dead or back in here."

Atiba is scheduled to be released sometime next year. He will be barely 19 years old; he will lack a high school education; and he will have an inexpungible adult felony record and only the most dysfunctional of families to turn to for support. His father, the one relative who has kept in regular contact with him, is terminally ill with brain cancer. Atiba talks of wanting to study medicine or psychiatry if he can ever get his high-school-equivalency diploma. But according to the grim statistics for teenagers who have spent time in adult prison, it's far more likely that he will return to the Florida penal system not long after he is released.

LUNCH-MONEY FELON

So far Florida has taken "adult time for adult crime" further than any other state. Following a rash of high-profile teen crimes in 1992, Janet Reno, then serving as the state attorney for Miami-Dade County, began pushing for more adult-court filings against violent juveniles. And in 1994, after gun-toting teenagers murdered several tourists, the state legislature gave prosecutors (rather than juvenile judges) the deciding hand as to whether to charge kids 14 and older as adults. By the late 1990s, Palm Beach County prosecutor Barry E. Krischer was trying 15-year-old Anthony Laster in adult court for allegedly stealing lunch money from a schoolmate. "Depicting and treating this forcible felony, this strong-arm robbery, in terms as though it were no more than a $2 shoplifting fosters and promotes violence in our schools," Krischer wrote in a February 1999 op-ed. "There should be 'zero tolerance' for such acts. I believe that prosecuting this robbery in juvenile court would have diminished the seriousness of the crime."

Professor Paolo G. Annino of the Children's Advocacy Center at Florida State University College of Law estimates that on any given day nearly 500 minors are now incarcerated in Florida's prisons. There are, he says, more than 1,000 Florida inmates presently serving time in prison for crimes committed when they were 15 or younger.

All told, according to University of Minnesota law professor Barry Feld (a former prosecutor and the author of *Bad Kids: Race and the Transformation of the Juvenile Court*), some 70,000 teens have gone through Florida's adult courts in the last decade. Thousands of these juveniles have ended up in adult prison. Thousands more have been sent to adult probation programs, where they are provided with far less supervision than they would have been under the state's juvenile probation system. The Florida Department of Juvenile Justice reports that between 1998 and 1999 the average caseload of juvenile probation officers was 45; in the adult system it was 78. For high-risk offenders, average caseloads were 15 to 1 in the juvenile system and 25 to 1 in the adult system. Not surprisingly, youths in the adult system fail probation more often. And for violating adult probation, they are sent to adult prison.

In addition to those serving time in the general prison population, thousands of juveniles tried as adults in Florida over the last decade have been sentenced to serve time in age-segregated prisons known as "youthful offender" institutions, or YOs. These are adult maximum-security facilities in which all inmates are under the age of 26. Apart from that, however—down to the razor-wire fencing, the uniformed guards, and the stunningly casual violence—the YOs are indistinguishable from adult prisons. And there—so much for age segregation—15-year-old muggers can be made to share a cell with killers in their twenties.

BREVARD CORRECTIONAL INSTITUTION AND WORK CAMP, 20 minutes from the Kennedy Space Center at Cape Canaveral, is one of these youthful-offender institutions. It houses more than a thousand youths, the majority of them blacks or Latinos from poor parts of Miami and other large Florida cities. Their crimes range from drug violations to murder.

"I robbed," says 17-year-old Ernest Causey, who has been in YOs since he was convicted of armed robbery at the age of 14, "because I ain't seen no other alternative. I went out there and did what I hadda do." Mostly, Ernest says, the profits from the robberies he carried out when he was 12 and 13 went to buy clothes. But sometimes, he says, he gave his mother money so she could pay the rent. It seemed normal. Most of his friends, he recalls, were in and out of juvenile facilities, jail, and prison.

Now he thinks that his years running with the tough crowd were good preparation for his life behind bars. Brevard, says Ernest, "is really no different from the street. Just no guns. You've still got knives. You've still got drugs. When you go to sleep, you've got to keep one eye open, be prepared. You don't know who's gonna take you to the bathroom and rape you. It's real dangerous."

Inmates at Brevard walk around the yard in blue uniforms with youthful versions of the blank "prison stare." They have the option to enroll in high-school-equivalency programs, but there is no mandatory school regimen. Mainly they spend their time in prison jobs or playing games with their friends. At night they sleep in dormitories divided into double rooms and are prey to violent attack. Often teenage prisoners are confined with a cellmate all day for days at a time.

"Every roommate I got, I beat him up," says 16-year-old Enrique Esquerre, whose family moved to Florida from Peru nine years ago. He was imprisoned at 14 after using what he says was an unloaded .357 Magnum to rob a liquor store. "I did 59 days in confinement one time because I got an assault charge after hitting my roommate lots of times. Bruised him up."

Brevard provides little counseling, and the inmates' relationship to prison staff is extremely antagonistic. "Gunning" at female officers—an obscene prison sport in which inmates masturbate at passing guards—simply earns the offender 30 days in isolation. Inmates report that guards routinely resort to physical force and gas to subdue them. "When they gas you," says Enrique, "you can't breathe. It goes in your pores. You can't see. I got used to it after the third time. I just got sprayed every day."

Ernest Causey remembers one guard slamming his right hand in a heavy door during a dispute. His palm still bears a jagged scar where 12 stitches closed the wound. "It makes you feel like shit," he says. "Like the lowest of the low. If the officer don't like you, he spit in your food. Yeah, it make you angry!"

Ernest hopes he won't have to resort to crime when he is released. But "if I do have to go back to what I was doing and the police come," he explains slowly, deliberately—a lanky kid talking with an adolescent combination of awkwardness and bravado—"it'll be me or them. I'll kill them. I won't come back here. If I do have to, they're going to have to kill me."

YOUNGSTERS IN PRISON FACE DAUNTING ODDS. ALTHOUGH they generally do not spend longer inside than kids convicted of similar crimes who are sent to juvenile facilities, government statistics show that those sent to adult prisons are more likely to be raped or beaten (in Florida a 17-year-old was strangled to death by an adult prisoner in 1997); they are more likely to attempt suicide; they are less likely to receive education or skills training. And according to recent research, they are more likely to return to crime upon their release.

In 1996 a research team led by Donna M. Bishop, then a professor in the Department of Criminal Justice and Legal Studies at the University of Central Florida, compared two groups of Florida teenagers matched for similar backgrounds and similar crimes. The study found that the teens who were processed through the adult courts returned to crime sooner, committed more crimes, committed more serious crimes, and ended up back behind bars sooner than did their peers who went through the juvenile system. In a four-year follow-up study, the team found that minors tried as adults for one specific category of property crimes reoffended less often than their counterparts who had been sent to juvenile court, but in every other instance and by every other measure, the researchers' early results were confirmed over the longer term. "On the face of it," says Bishop, now at Northeastern University in Boston, "these are kids who look very similar. And yet the transferred youth [those sent through the adult system] reoffended at a higher incidence."

Possibly all this shows is that the prosecutors were making good judgment calls in picking out the worst of the bad apples to prosecute as adults in the first place. But Bishop says her team found no evidence of this. Instead, they identified a pattern of prison living conditions—and of relationships with prison guards—that helped to cement a teenager's criminal identity.

A 1995 study by Jeffrey Fagan, who directs the Center for Violence Research and Prevention at Columbia University's School of Public Health, compared a matched sample of New Jersey teenagers handled in the juvenile courts with New York teenagers tried as adults. It similarly found that the kids dealt with in adult court reoffended as often or more often than those sent through the juvenile courts.

Indeed, as far back as the early 1980s experts were decrying New York's 1978 law, which defined 16-years-olds as adults for criminal justice purposes. The research then, as now, suggested that the new law would be counterproductive. Adult prison seems to be a criminogenic toxin to adolescents—one that leads in the long run not to less crime but to more.

"These kids come from backgrounds of family dysfunction, mental illness, a whole host of things. They need appropriate intervention," says Steve Harper, a Miami public defender. "Most of the teenagers are going to get out [of prison]. They went in damaged. The damage isn't addressed. It's worsened because they're in a tough place." Harper remembers a mentally ill teenager he represented a decade ago who was sent to prison rather than to a secure mental institution. Following his release, he killed someone.

Says James Milliken, the chief judge in the San Diego juvenile court system: "I can't help but think [that those sent to prison as minors] will be far more of a risk when they're released than the population of ex-cons who went to prison as adults."

REFORMING REFORM

Last year voters in California continued the get-tough onslaught by passing Proposition 21. The measure allows prosecutors to bring adult charges against teenagers arrested for relatively minor property and drug crimes. It also lowers the age at which teenagers can begin accumulating the "strikes" that could ultimately result in a life sentence under the state's "three strikes and you're out" law. And Prop 21 drastically increases the sanctions for crimes carried out by gang members. Because local police departments have spent years building secret computer databases containing the names of tens of thousands of alleged gang members—"identified" by signs as trivial as wearing certain clothing, hanging out with known gang members, using gang hand signs, or gathering with three or more friends in a public space—this provision alone poses important civil-liberty problems.

But Proposition 21 may, paradoxically, prove to be the turning point in juvenile justice policy. It has already aroused organized political opposition—including among inner-city youths like 17-year-old Maria Perez of South Central Los Angeles's Youth United for Community Action. "Here," she says, "you're guilty until proven innocent. I'm walking down the street and they can stop me because of the way I'm dressed. Me, a straight-A student. Because of my pants, my makeup. Let's say I'm 15 or 17 and commit a crime. That record's going to stay. Let's say I'm 19 or 21 and want to improve myself; that record's going to stay. They check your record even when you apply for a job at McDonald's. I'm going to just keep going back to jail."

Even many big-city prosecutors find Prop 21 excessive. "It wasn't reform," says Steve Cooley, Los Angeles's newly elected district attorney. "It was a power grab by police and prosecutors. It's a reaction to violent juvenile crime. People take that fear and try and capitalize on it and end up with things like Prop 21. Bad lawmaking. An exploitation of people's legitimate fears."

A recent court ruling, in response to a lawsuit filed by the parents of several white San Diego teenagers charged as adults for beating elderly Mexican migrant laborers, has blocked the discretionary aspects of Proposition 21. And that, combined with the hostility of prosecutors such as Cooley and public attention to the Lionel Tate case in Florida, just may provide a chance to open a debate over the use of adult courts and prisons to punish and control difficult, sometimes dangerous teenagers.

For two crucial reasons, the country must take advantage of this opportunity. The first is sheer self-interest. Current policies risk creating thousands of extremely maladjusted, crime-prone adults. The second reason has more to do with our sense of justice as a nation—for current policies are prematurely condemning as unredeemable enormous and disproportionate numbers of inner-city black and Latino youngsters.

A recent report by the Justice Policy Institute (JPI), a progressive watchdog organization, found that in Chicago's Cook County 99 percent of juveniles tried in adult court for drug crimes in 1999 and 2000 were black or Latino, although 15 percent of juveniles arrested for drug crimes in Cook County were white. In Los Angeles County, JPI found, Hispanic and black youths were transferred to adult court at six times the rate of whites and, once there, were far more likely to be sentenced to adult prison than their white peers. In Florida three-quarters of the teens in adult prison (both general-population facilities and YOs) are nonwhite.

"The harsh attitudes toward kids right now in the United States," argues JPI researcher Dan Macallair, "is a harsh attitude to black and Latino kids. Those *other* kids." Kids like Taylor Maxie, Jr., in Los Angeles, who was given a second chance under the old juvenile-justice system that he wouldn't have had in the adult system. And just when he might have looked most unredeemable, he took that chance.

Maxie was 18 when a rival gang member shot him five times while he was out walking. Viewing his survival as practically a miracle, he figured it was a message that he should start afresh. He took on a new name, Johnny Tremain, and contacted a young artist named Chris Henrickson, who runs an intervention program for juvenile delinquents called DreamYard. Maxie and Henrickson had met a couple of years before, when the gang-banger was serving time in a juvenile facility where Henrickson was running a poetry workshop. Under Henrickson's guidance, Maxie had begun writing prose and discovering the intellectual side of his personality; and while he hadn't initially heeded Henrickson's advice to stay away from the gang life, he had those resources to fall back on when he was ready to try.

"It's a very hard thing to make that transition," Tremain recalls, sitting in an office at the film company in downtown Los Angeles where he now works. "I had to change everything, down to the way I talked to people. A lot of shit. I moved, stopped coming in contact with the police, cut off communication with a lot of my friends."

Henrickson helped. He got Tremain a job as an outreach associate at DreamYard and made himself available for a talk whenever Tremain felt that he was slipping back. Now, four years later, the 22-year-old former gang member has a girlfriend, a young daughter, and a stable job. If he hadn't met someone like Henrickson, "I'd probably still be out there with a ski mask on, trying to rob somebody," he says matter-of-factly.

But "second chance" is no longer popular rhetoric. We are a country reeling under a changing definition of childhood, shifting views about redemption and rehabilitative potential, and an increasingly pre-Enlightenment notion of punishment as an emotional catharsis for victims and an automatic response to violations of the moral code. The public perception that crazed, Uzi-toting teens are roaming the countryside seems to remain in place despite the facts. And because adolescent murderers are relatively uncommon, whereas adolescent robbers, burglars, car thieves, and vandals are far more prevalent, it is these less serious offenders who have ended up bearing the brutal brunt of the laws we've changed. They are the ones treated as hopeless under the new hard-time model. For reasons of justice, that's a criminal mistake.

SASHA ABRAMSKY's *book on the American prison system was published in January 2002 by St. Martin's Press. Research for this article was supported by a grant from the Center on Crime, Communities, and Culture at the Open Society Institute.*

Gangs in Middle America
Are they a threat?

By DAVID M. ALLENDER

In the past 30 years, changes have occurred in how the police and the public view, define, and discuss gangs.[1] In the late 1960s and early 1970s, police in large cities generally acknowledged the existence of gang activity within their jurisdictions. During the 1970s, the public was recovering from the Vietnam War and dealing with a wide variety of important social issues and changes. Gangs and crime did not demand the same attention as these other matters.

By the middle of the 1980s, however, the public became increasingly concerned with safety issues. The interest continued into the 1990s, partially due to an aging population. In response to the electorates' concern, federal grant programs and monies proliferated. Several of these projects, such as Operation Weed and Seed and the Office of Community-Oriented Policing Services (COPS) antigang initiative,[2] had as a core ingredient the need to control or dismantle criminal street gangs. Increased attention and discussion also brought new legislation to deal with the gangs. Many states enacted statutes to assist police and prosecutors and mandated that new police officers attending basic police academies receive at least a minimal amount of training in gang topics. Media interest mirrored audience appetite and boosted coverage of gang-related subject matter. Increased reporting of such incidents had the effect of making it appear that gang activity was on the rise. But, is this truly the case, especially in middle America? Are states, such as Indiana, "the crossroads of America,"[3] at risk of becoming infected with the gang menace or has it occurred already? An examination of gang history, gang migration, and gang structure, along with the efforts of law enforcement to combat and prevent gangs may provide some answers. In addition, a review of Indianapolis, Indiana's experience with gangs illustrates how a "big small town" in the heart of the United States can become a new target for gangs from other areas of the country.[4]

GANG HISTORY

Historical literature makes frequent reference to groups that engaged in criminal activity. Ancient Egyptians talked about bands of robbers who preyed upon those transporting goods along the caravan routes. China had gangs who committed robberies and kidnappings for profit. Folklore romanticizes pirates on the high seas that made their living by murder, robbery, and kidnapping. According to Hollywood and some authors, large numbers of outlaw gangs populated the American West. As with the pirates, many of these outlaws became folk heroes. Endless examples exist of gangs, bound together through the commission of criminal acts.

A well-documented gang case comes from the British who, from 1834 to 1848, were dealing with what they identified as a gang of robbers and murderers in Budhuk, India.[5] Unable to deal with the gang because of its size and complexity, local authorities turned to the army for help. To gain control of the situation, the government passed legislation prohibiting gang membership, associating with known gang members, and deriving profit from a gang's criminal activity. The military convinced the government to pass additional laws allowing a federalist approach, including permission to house prisoners in jails far from the gang's home territory. Extensive use of informants, working for both pay and sentencing considerations, comprised a main component of the successful effort. Interestingly, police investigating gangs today deal with some of the problems troops encountered during this operation.

America's first identified gang, however, was formed in 1820 in the Five Points District of New York City. Named the Forty Thieves, the gang operated along the waterfront, engaging in acts of murder, robbery, assault, and other violent acts. Composed of recently arrived Irish immigrants, the Forty Thieves recruited a group of young imitators, who called themselves the Forty Little Thieves. To complete the equation, a rival gang, the Kerryonians, organized to ensure that they got their share of the ill-gotten gains. This pattern repeated itself many times over the years.

> ## "Without a standardized reporting system, it proves impossible to accurately determine the level of gang activity."

Lieutenant Allender serves with the Indianapolis, Indiana, Police Department.

The end of the Civil War saw large-scale criminal activity on the part of a few veterans who had trouble returning to a peaceful society. Some of these men formed gangs to increase the profits from their illegal actions, such as the infamous brothers Jessie and Frank James who recruited men, often boyhood friends or relatives, to assist them as they traveled to commit robberies. Media reports often attributed crimes to the James Gang that they could not possibly have committed due to the acts occurring great distances apart and on the same day. Although authorities knew where the James family lived, they were unsuccessful in apprehending the brothers. The gang finally met its ruin through a couple of events. The members ventured far from their familiar territory in Missouri to commit a robbery in Northfield, Minnesota. The robbery went awry and degenerated into a running gun battle leaving several residents and holdup men dead or wounded. Captured gang members received long prison sentences. Unrelated to the robbery, but not long after, an associate murdered Jessie. Faced with the loss of so many of the gang's members, Frank surrendered to authorities. The governor of Missouri later pardoned Frank James, and he escaped punishment for his criminal acts.

Moving from the notorious and infamous to those with more in common with gangs today, a 1927 study of street gangs in Chicago[6] identified 1,313 active gangs in the city at that time. The findings have a common thread that links these historical groups to present-day gang members. For example, many of those who formed or joined gangs felt disenfranchised by society. Many members of Forty Thieves, comprised of recently arrived immigrants, had problems adjusting to a new culture and experienced prejudice due to their immigrant status and ethnicity. In India, the gang's members had to live closely together to avoid arrest. In time, the rest of society would not accept anyone tied to the gang. Thus, they had to remain within the group to support themselves. Pirates often were seamen who had been shanghaied, escaped from authorities, or were estranged in some manner from a normal lifestyle. The James' brothers and their support system of friends and relatives felt strong resentment toward established authority because of their wartime experiences. More examples exist, but the feeling of estrangement exhibited by these groups represents an important theme. These same feelings often occur in modern gangs. The gang often exists prior to entering into any type of profit-making criminal activity. The opportunity to make money from crime comes about *because* the gang exists. The gang, with the exception of some drug gangs, does not normally form to make money.

The world of outlaw motorcycle gangs illustrates how the gang came first and then the criminal actions. Veterans returning from World War II formed motorcycle clubs. While most were social groups, a few, such as the Hell's Angels, began to engage in criminal activities. As the Angels grew in power and influence, rival gangs, such as the Pagans, Banditos, and the Outlaws, formed in other parts of the nation. Because of their organization, the motorcycle gangs controlled certain types of criminal activity within their areas of dominance. Bikers, by their bylaws, actions, and appearance, seek to force their members to remain outside the mainstream of society. In doing so, the leadership bonds the membership closer together as the group mentality becomes one of "us versus them."

> ## "Not all street gangs exist to sell drugs or commit criminal acts."

Ethnic gangs represent another illustration of gangs forming before any criminal activity takes place. Hispanic gangs grew in strength and influence following the Zoot Suit Riots of 1943. In California, white, off-duty military personnel attacked Hispanic males who they felt were benefitting from the war while evading the dangers of combat. The physical danger from the rioters, coupled with other acts of prejudice and discrimination, caused the Latino community to band together more tightly. The criminal element, usually present in every group of people, then took over some of the gangs to further unlawful enterprises.

Other ethnic groups, including Asians, Italians, Jews, Jamaicans, and many others, formed gangs because they too had to deal with prejudice and discrimination which alienated them from mainstream society. The organizations they formed had varying degrees of sophistication. Many of the groups faded away as the ethnic groups assimilated into mainstream culture. A lawful alternative for those that continued to exist was the transition into social or fraternal organizations, promoting cultural identify and positive civic actions. A small percentage mutated into criminal enterprises, which the media and entertainment industry often have romanticized.

The extreme example of this genre being the Italian Mafia, portrayed in a positive or humorous fashion in numerous movies, television programs, advertising commercials, and even news reports. The trend continues with the influx of Russian immigrants into the United States. A small percentage of these new arrivals are criminals and gang members, dubbed the "Russian Mafia" by the popular media. In short, the formula for creating and maintaining gangs is not a new concept and is ongoing. The real problem facing law enforcement is identifying the amount of criminal gang activity present and limiting the damage these groups can do to society.

GANG MIGRATION

How does the idea of establishing a gang spread? Where do aspiring members get information on how to form and structure the gang? Must gang members follow certain rules? How does a potential leader pick and recruit followers? Are there role models in this subculture? To understand the gang subculture, law enforcement officers, school administrators, social workers, and parents must become familiar with the basic concepts that these questions address.

Who Joins a Gang?

Not all street gangs exist to sell drugs or commit criminal acts. Instead, young people normally seek gang involvement for some combination of the following five reasons:

1. Structure: Youths want to organize their lives but lack the maturity to do so on their own. The gang provides rules to live by and a code of conduct.

2. Nurturing: Gang members frequently talk of how they love one another. This remains true even among the most hardened street gangs. These young people are trying to fill a void in their lives by substituting the gang for the traditional family.

3. Sense of belonging: Because humans require social interaction, some young people find that the gang fulfills the need to be accepted as an important part of a group.

4. Economic opportunity: Gang members motivated by this consideration alone probably would become involved in criminal activity anyway. Finding it hard to draw away from the lifestyle, but due to a lack of loyalty for the group, they often will provide authorities with information in exchange for some personal benefit.

5. Excitement: This often represents a motivation for suburban and affluent youths. Gangs composed of these types of individuals usually have very fluid membership, with associates joining and leaving to be replaced by others with a passing interest.

> ## "A new street gang often will form because young people have an interest in the gang lifestyle and will look for sources of information."

Few young people that enter into the gang subculture do so for evil or criminal reasons. They are looking for something that they feel is lacking in their lives. For this reason, gangs can form in any city, town, neighborhood, or region. No hard-and-fast rule says that all gang members do one thing or another. To understand the gang operating in any given area, law enforcement agencies must determine what motivates the gang's members and how the gang leadership maintains authority over, and loyalty from, its members.

At present, the most visible criminal street gangs operate in the nation's inner cities. When depicted by either the news media or the entertainment industry, these groups have almost exclusively young black or Hispanic males as members, often portrayed as violent and prosperous because of their involvement in the drug trade. In reality, not all street gangs are involved heavily in drug trafficking; very few street gang members are prosperous; and no shortage of white male gang members exists in inner-city, suburban, or rural areas. Moreover, females often join the gang subculture for the same reasons males do. They may link themselves to a male-dominated gang, or, in some cases, form their own associations. The urban legend about prosperity has grown, however, and many young people see the street gang as a method of achieving both financial and social success. Unfortunately, a few gangsters involved with street gangs are successful, both financially and socially. They become role models to less fortunate young people who are shortsighted and fail to realize the danger and the damage criminal gang activity can do to them, their families, and their neighborhoods.

How Do Gangs Spread?

Criminal street gangs can spread by what some have labeled the "imperialist method." A large street gang will dispatch members to start a chapter in a new city or neighborhood to further some form of criminal activity. For example, in 1999, the Indianapolis Safe Streets Task Force concluded a multiyear investigation of a drug-dealing gang called the New Breed. This gang arrived as an established enterprise from Chicago and only allowed local residents to fill lower levels of the organization. Members would rotate between Chicago, Indianapolis, and at least six other cities. The group had a set of rules and a belief system, which they brought with them. At the conclusion of the investigation, 15 gang members were charged with federal drug trafficking offenses, based on crimes committed in Indianapolis. Numerous New Breed members operating in other cities were unaffected by this case.[7] Two problems arise from this type of gang movement. First, surviving gang members in other locations will, after modifying their methods, move to fill the void left by those arrested. Second, local residents who were either gang members or associates will recreate the operation to take advantage of the available profits. Presently, both of these situations may be occurring in Indianapolis.

Some Gang Web Sites

Gangs and Security Threat Group Awareness: *http://www.dc.state.fl.us/pub/gangs/index.html*

Created and maintained by the Florida Department of Corrections, this Web site contains information, photographs, and descriptions on a wide variety of gang types, including Chicago- and Los Angeles-based gangs, prison gangs, nation sets, and supremacy groups from many parts of the United States.

Gangs or Us: *http://www.gangsorus.com*

A comprehensive Web site that offers a broad range of information, including a state-by-state listing of all available gang laws, gang identities and behaviors applicable to all areas of the United States, and links to other sites that provide information to law enforcement, parents, and teachers.

Southeastern Connecticut Gang Activities Group (SEGAG): *http://www.segag.org*

A coalition of law enforcement and criminal justice agencies from southeastern Connecticut and New England, this group provides information on warning signs that parents and teachers often observe first, along with a large number of resources and other working groups that are part of nationwide efforts to contain gang violence.

Another way an established street gang can spread its influence can be referred to as "franchising." Often done to realize a profit from criminal activity, this method calls for an existing gang to contact local residents and recruit them into the enterprise. If, for example, a Chicago-based gang, such as the Four Corner Hustlers, develops contacts that they trust in Indianapolis, they may work an arrangement to supply drugs in exchange for a substantial share of the profits. Both groups benefit—the locals get a dependable supply of product, and, in this example, the Four Corner Hustlers realize a profit with minimal risk. Most prevalent in drug-dealing enterprises, franchising also can involve such crimes as theft, forgery, or fencing stolen goods.

A new street gang often will form because young people have an interest in the gang lifestyle and will look for sources of information. If possible, the curious will find someone who was, or claims to have been, a gang member in another location (e.g., a young person who recently moved into the area from a city, such as Chicago or Los Angeles). This person now becomes the resident "gang expert," and the gang will shape its structure and rules by this person's information. In addition, gang members and

their associates watch movies and television programs depicting gang life from which they convert information for their purposes. Conversations with former gang members revealed that they also viewed television news reports, read news stories, and watched reality-based television programs to see how gangs in other places operated. Finally, the Internet represents an important source for emerging gangs. Simply by searching the word *gang*, the inquirer can receive a wealth of Web sites, as well as several chat rooms for gang members. Such numerous and varied sources, many of which give conflicting information, account for the wide diversity in street gang structure and methods of operation.

GANG STRUCTURE

Just as there are numerous gangs for aspiring gangsters to imitate, uncounted sources of information exist on how to establish, structure, and rule a street gang. East Coast and Hispanic gangs generate some interest, but the dominant influences in the Midwest are from the West Coast, especially Los Angeles, and from the Chicago area. Observers also will encounter other types of criminal gangs throughout the area, including

prison groups, outlaw motorcycle clubs, as well as Asian criminal enterprises and ethnic street gangs. Perhaps, the most recognizable of these latter sets are the outlaw bikers because of their attire, community activities, and Web sites. However, their sophistication and secretive nature concerning their operations and structure prevent the average street gang member from obtaining enough information to imitate them.

The Four Nations

In the 1980s, West Coast black gangs formed two loose confederations—the largest, the Crips, and their rivals, the Bloods. Contrary to what many believe, there is neither one Crip nor one Blood gang. Rather, numerous sets of each have joined together to either protect themselves or facilitate their criminal activities. These represent two of the Four Nations. The other two originate from Chicago. In the late 1970s, a very large criminal street gang, known as the Gangster Disciples, formed a coalition with several other street gangs to maximize drug profits and protect their members from violence perpetrated by rivals. The consolidation called itself the Folk Nation. Other gang sets in Chicago felt the need to form an alliance to ensure their share of the drug market. Led by the Vice Lords and the El Rukins, this band dubbed themselves the People Nation, thus creating the big four street gang nations, in no particular order of influence, the Crips, Bloods, Folks, and People.

The Indianapolis Connection

In Indianapolis, the West Coast message from the Crip and Blood Nations arrives through a variety of mediums. Evidence shows that a few California area gang members have migrated to Indianapolis. Authorities speculate that these gangsters came to the city to spread their illegal enterprises. However, officials have not documented this nor have they determined if the gangs sent these people to the Midwest or if the gangsters are acting from personal interests. The more common means of transmission for West Coast ideas and models come from the entertainment industry, including music artists who encourage violence and gang values; movies glorifying gangs and their lifestyle; and books, television programs, the Internet, and the news media all publicizing the gang subculture.

> *"The gang problem is not an exclusive law enforcement problem nor can police deal with it in a vacuum."*

Many Indianapolis residents look to Chicago for important legitimate influences, such as business, cultural pursuits, and sports teams. Many people have friends and relatives living in the Chicago area and frequently travel between the cities. With these active methods of communication present, information concerning the gang subculture often occurs by word of mouth. The closeness enables Chicago gangs to exert a measure of control over some of those operating in Indianapolis. For these reasons,

the Folk and People Nations dominate the Indianapolis gang landscape, confirmed by area street gang graffiti almost exclusively composed of Chicago-area gang names and symbols.

GANG PREVENTION AND INTERVENTION

Before addressing ways of handling the gang problem or preventing the formation of such groups, authorities need to determine the prevalence of gangs in America and whether their number is on the rise. However, for a variety of reasons, it is difficult, if not impossible, to prove that criminal street gang activity is on the increase in the United States. Confusion results from the lack of a clear definition of what constitutes a gang, past and present denial by both law enforcement and other officials about gang activity, no baseline data to determine what gangs did in the past, and a myriad of reporting problems. Several sources suggest that gang activity declined in the 1970s. The basis for this claim appears to rest with the lack of information published on gangs during that decade. Without a standardized reporting system, it proves impossible to accurately determine the level of gang activity. What is observable, however, is the growing public appetite for information on crime, in general, and gangs, in particular. For example, a 5-year study (1990 through 1994) conducted in Rochester, New York, attributed 86 percent of youth violence in that city to individuals involved with the gang subculture. The same study contended that gangs controlled the majority of drug trafficking within Rochester. Gary and other Indiana cities advance the same theory.[8] Upon considering these responses, it becomes clear that gangs are a real problem, even though the actual extent remains unknown. The question then becomes how can a gang be effectively dismantled or controlled? More important, parents, teachers, law enforcement officials, and social workers want to know how to discourage young people from joining a gang and how to disengage them from the gang subculture once they become involved.

Prevention Methods

An educated group, with diverse talents and responsibilities, working together constitutes the first ingredient to an effective gang prevention program. The gang problem is not an exclusive law enforcement problem nor can police deal with it in a vacuum. Important factors that influence people to enter the gang subculture are not enforcement issues. Boredom, a need for attention, a desire for structure, and the yearning to feel important are not areas that police have the tools to deal with effectively. Society must provide young people with meaningful alternatives that will draw them away from the gang lifestyle. These alternatives should vary and include educational programs, social interaction, recreational activities, and employment opportunities. Obviously, the provision of these services will take co-operation among families, local schools, government-funded social services, area businesses, religious organizations, and other neighborhood resources.

Unfortunately, most communities do not become interested in gang prevention until one or more gangs appear in the area. Because parents and teachers usually have the first interaction with new gang members and their sets, they need to educate themselves on what signs and behavior changes indicate gang membership. Police need to be aware of the indicators and the types of criminal activity of local gang sets. They must scrutinize incidents involving gangsters to see if arrests or enhanced charges based on criminal gang activity are appropriate. Officers need to alert prosecutors when a gang member is arrested or if a crime is gang related. Prosecutors then have the necessary tools that will enable them to effectively present the case to the court. Sentencing for those gangsters convicted of crimes can include orders forbidding association with other gang members, counseling designed to discourage gang participation, anger control classes, and, when appropriate, drug counseling.[9]

Intervention Strategies

Law enforcement agencies must structure their efforts to combat active criminal street gangs based on the targeted gang set. No program imported from another agency will prove effective without modification. Each gang set has a different level of member dedication based on how strongly members have bought into the belief system that provides the basis for the gang. No two criminal street gangs commit exactly the same crimes. Police need to make cases based on the offenses in their jurisdiction and not try to follow another agency's success story too closely. Police administrators must keep in mind that the experts on area gangs are the uniform officers and detectives who deal with them on a day-to-day basis. To develop an effective plan, the intelligence possessed by departmental personnel represents a vital component. To learn how to apply the information already in their possession, managers need to study the psychology behind gang membership. Officers then should review a number of different successful programs to gain ideas on what might work for them.

The first step in planning a response is to determine if there is a problem. A group of young people who decide to call themselves a gang and then engage in disruptive behavior in the classroom, but stop short of criminal activity, are not yet a police problem. Due to recent events around the country, however, some school officials may panic and request police intervention. The law enforcement agency must identify what they are dealing with.

One popular method employed by many agencies is the SARA technique: scanning, analysis, response, and assessment. After identifying the problem (scanning), the planners must decide what combination of ideas will be most effective (analysis). Implementation of the plan follows (response). The last step (assessment) is not designed to be the final ingredient in the plan. The planners must review what approaches were used, what worked, what did not work, and then decide if the problem was resolved. If the problem was not resolved, the planners go back to the original step and start over. Agencies can complete this process as many times as necessary until the gang ceases to be a problem.

> **"Society must provide young people with meaningful alternatives that will lead them away from the gang lifestyle."**

In addition to law enforcement intervention, the entire social structure must deal with the underlying issues. A working partnership must form to handle the problems faced by the youthful offenders who make up the gang. Many informational sources exist that can provide guidance on where and how to deal with the criminal street gang member. The working group would do well to investigate as many sources as possible, including the Internet, government reports, news stories, and other publications. A number of training programs geared to meet the needs of different audiences are available. Funding sources can sometimes be found to provide training for educators and officers. For example, Indiana schools have a small amount budgeted for training to help stop school violence, and some law enforcement grants provide training for officers involved with gang investigations.

CONCLUSION

No city, town, or neighborhood is totally immune from the threat of gangs. The first step in prevention is for those in authority to study the underlying reasons for gang formation—structure, nurturing, need to belong, economic opportunity, and excitement. If communities meet these needs, gangs will have a hard time establishing a foothold. However, once gang involvement is suspected, authorities must take time to study the situation to determine the extent and type of problem they need to deal with. A variety of social and law enforcement agencies need to become involved in the discussion process from the beginning. Police and community members need to arrive at a consensus of how serious the gang problem is and then work together to combat any criminal activity.

The police must act as the point group to bring an operating criminal street gang under control. Officers must target the gang in a variety of ways, including the criminal activities normally associated with the gang. Less apparent, but just as important, is the need to deal with other criminal and antisocial actions on the part of gang members. Officers also should develop strong working relationships with prosecutors and probation officers so that, when arrested, gang members receive special attention and appropriate sentences. Finally, a standardized reporting system to capture the true extent of gang activity in America remains a goal that all concerned citizens should work toward. Protecting this nation's youth from the dangers of gang involvement requires the effort of all facets of the society. If America's heartland is facing the threat of gangs, the entire country is at risk.

Endnotes

1. The author based this article on his experience investigating gang-related cases and on information he and his fellow officers have gathered for presentations to the law enforcement community and the general public, contained in a department training guide.
2. Weed and Seed has existed since 1991 as a comprehensive effort between law enforcement and health and human services to prevent and deter crime in high-risk areas. COPS began as a 6-year, $9 billion federal initiative designed to spur the hiring of more police and promote community policing.
3. The state motto of Indiana.

4. Indianapolis, the capital of Indiana, has a population of approximately 750,000 and hosts the annual Indianapolis 500 auto race, considered the largest 1-day event in the world.

5. Lieutenant Colonel W.H. Sleeman, *Report on Budhuk Alia Bagree Decoits an Other Gang Robbers by Hereditary Profession and on the Measures Adopted by the Government of India for Their Suppression* (Calcutta, India: J.C. Sherriff, Bengal Military Orphan Press, 1849).

6. Frederic M. Thrasher, *The Gang: The Full Original Edition* (Peotone, IL: New Chicago School Press, 2000).

7. David M. Allender, "Safe Streets Task Force: Cooperation Gets Results," *FBI Law Enforcement Bulletin*, March 2000, 1–6.

8. U.S. Department of Justice, National Drug Intelligence Center, *National Street Gang Survey Report* (Johnstown, PA, 1998).

9. Lisa A. Regini, "Combating Gangs: The Need for Innovation," *FBI Law Enforcement Bulletin*, February 1998, 25–31.

Trouble With the Law

Parents, groups, decry system treating juveniles as adults

By Tina Susman
STAFF CORRESPONDENT

Atlanta—The phone shrilled through the two-story, suburban house at about 2 a.m., waking up parents who knew that when the phone rang at that hour, it was either a wrong number or bad news.

This wasn't a wrong number.

As Glenwood Ross, an economist and college professor, groggily held the receiver to his ear, a detective announced down the line that his 15-year-old son was under arrest for an armed robbery committed earlier that night.

"They said, 'We've got your boy here.' I said, 'No you don't, he's in bed!' I even went to the bedroom to check," said Ross, who recites the details as if they happened yesterday, not six years ago. But Ross' son, Glenwood Ross III, known to family and friends as Trey, wasn't in bed. As his parents would learn while the dark yielded to dawn, Trey had finished a baby-sitting job at a nearby house, come home and then sneaked out after midnight to go riding in a car with two 19-year-old friends. Somewhere outside the tranquility of the comfortable, tree-lined neighborhood where Trey lived with his parents and younger sister, one of the three hatched the idea of robbing someone, changing the family's lives forever.

According to Trey, it was his older companions' idea, a way to get money so they could rent an apartment together. Cruising the dimly lit streets, they spotted a lone woman in a motel parking lot and steered the car in. Trey says he remained in the back seat while the two men, one holding a gun, forced the woman to give up her purse.

By the time the case had gone to court, the men had both blamed their 15-year-old passenger for the holdup, saying that, even though he didn't have a driver's license, he had developed the robbery plan and had prodded them to carry it out. All they wanted to do was look for girls, one of the older defendants said when he testified against Trey in exchange for lenience.

As a juvenile charged with armed robbery, Trey was automatically treated as an adult under Georgia law, and he faced a mandatory 10-year prison term, with no chance of parole. But the case against Trey was shaky, Ross said. The victim couldn't identify him, he had no prior record and the prosecution's key witnesses were the two others accused. Both testified against Trey and received less jail time than he did.

"We wanted to go through with the trial process because we believed him. There was no evidence that said he did it," said Trey's mother, Billie Ross, the president of Mothers Advocating Juvenile Justice, which is lobbying to overturn laws requiring juveniles to be tried as adults. "There was nothing that made us think if we went to trial they'd be able to prove he did anything. He felt the same way."

They were wrong. After a four-day trial, Trey was convicted. Now 21, he is six years into his 10-year prison term, a situation his parents believe could have been averted if they were white. "I hesitate to say it, but a part of me says yes, that is the case," Billie Ross said. "If he had been white, I think they would not have automatically taken the word of those older boys. They'd have looked at his life, his family, looked at us, seen that he came from a stable home life with two parents in a decent neighborhood."

They also might have considered Trey's health problems: He had spent much of the previous school year at home with Crohn's disease, a serious intestinal ailment that ultimately required surgery. "If we'd have come from a prominent white family, they might have done that," Billie Ross said. "But I think part of it is there seems to be this conspiracy against young black males. People are afraid of them because so many of them have committed crimes. There's this assumption that, because he's black, he must have done it."

As studies show that more than 75 percent of the youths charged with felonies in Georgia are black, parents and human rights advocates are placing much of the blame on a legal system that they say views black teenage boys as throwaway kids without considering their backgrounds. Since the Georgia legislature passed Senate Bill 440 in May 1994, requiring that 13- to 16-year-olds be treated as adults for certain crimes, 76 percent of the more than 3,800 juveniles arrested for SB440 offenses have been black. Cases involving white teenagers were twice as likely to be transferred out of the adult system back into juvenile court, according to a random sample of cases studied by the Georgia Indigent Defense Council.

"I think the numbers indicate race is a factor," Trey's father said. "Who's the district attorney? Who are the judges? They're white men. They're not going to identify with some black kid."

Supporters of harsher treatment for juveniles, and some researchers who have studied the racial disparities, warn against attributing the numbers to racism. In deciding whether to try a case in juvenile or adult court, factors such as a juvenile's history of trouble with the law may come into play. In such instances, black juveniles living in crime-ridden neighborhoods with more police patrols than white suburbs are more likely to have rap sheets, said Howard Snyder of the National Center for Juvenile Justice, who has directed several studies looking at racial disparities in the treatment of teenage offenders. Even if those rap sheets are for minor or nonviolent crimes, they can affect the decision on how to handle a more serious case.

"If a kid has been to juvenile court 15 times before, it's easier to argue he's not going to be amenable to treatment," said Snyder, who acknowledges that the heavier policing of mainly black urban areas starts the bias ball rolling against black children even before they reach court.

In New York State last year, for example, 654 black juveniles were arrested for felonies compared with 87 whites, a disparity critics attribute to differences in police patrols from neighborhood to neighborhood. "And if there is a bias, even with minor crimes, that's a way of developing a longer record and having your case transferred to adult court," Snyder said.

Wording of laws also can have an unintended racial bias. An Illinois state law mandates adult treatment for juveniles charged with weapon or drug offenses within 1,000 feet of public housing projects, resulting in some counties with 99 percent black conviction rates under the law. The law is guaranteed to nail blacks, say critics, because few whites are found around public housing projects.

After arrest, the bias continues into the courtroom. When faced with white and black teenagers accused of the same offenses, judges are more likely to show lenience toward those whose home lives are considered stable, said Melissa Sickmund of the National Center for Juvenile Justice. Again, she said, bias that does not necessarily constitute blatant racism comes into play. "You might have a kid standing in front of the judge and he's black and he's got a single mom who's raising him and she works three jobs and is hardly able to supervise that kid at home, and he lives in a terrible neighborhood," Sickmund said. "And then you have a kid who's white, and his family is standing behind him in court and the father has a good job and the mother promises she can be home for him in the afternoon and he's just been accepted to college. Which kid are you going to take a chance on? It may not be a race decision, but it is one compounded by race. It's not fair, but the juvenile justice system can't change that."

But parents such as the Rosses say that it all adds up to racism and that thousands of young, black men are paying outlandish prices for teenage misbehavior that might have been handled far differently were they white. "At first I was angry he'd sneaked off," Glenwood Ross said. "He had violated our rules. Then I said, 'Wait a minute! He's a kid, and kids do dumb stuff.' Then I got angry at the harshness of the system. It just doesn't seem fair to me."

Since Trey went to prison, his sister has turned 16. His mother has earned her master's degree in social work. His father has earned his doctorate in economics. He has missed family vacations, including a Christmas cruise to the Cayman Islands. He didn't graduate high school with his classmates, get a driver's license or attend his prom, and he marked his 21st birthday behind bars. For the rest of the family, living in a quiet neighborhood of winding, tree-lined roads and spacious homes with long driveways, it's as if a vital link of the chain binding them together has been broken. "There's just this opening, this gap, that he's not able to fill," says his mother, struggling to explain the ache that comes with each family milestone Trey misses. "Sometimes I look at it as, OK, maybe he needs this, maybe something needed to happen so he'll grow up and be successful. But then I get really, really angry and sad about the things he's missing out on."

If the system works against professional, relatively moneyed black families such as Trey's, it's far worse for those without such advantages.

From the moment of arrest to the sentencing, parents and researchers say, black minors are at a disadvantage. For some, the problem is in the defense. More black teens than whites come from families that cannot afford top-rate attorneys, leaving them to rely upon overworked public defenders or cut-rate private lawyers. Building Blocks for Youth, a Washington organization, studied 1998 arrest records of juveniles in 18 counties and found that whites were twice as likely as blacks to have private lawyers. The same study indicated that youths represented by private lawyers were less likely to be convicted and more likely to have their cases sent back to juvenile court.

A sample of SB440 cases surveyed by Georgia's Indigent Defense Council showed that about 40 percent of black minors pleaded guilty, compared with 29 percent of whites. That could be a result of more black juveniles having long rap sheets that prompted a plea deal to avoid a longer sentence, or it could be that more black teens have less-aggressive defenses than whites.

"When you don't have any experience in the justice system, you're clueless. I didn't know what we were dealing with until we were in court," said the mother of one 17-year-old prisoner, who was 14 when he was pulled out of his ninth-grade class and arrested for rape. The Department of Correction's mug shot shows a serious but baby-faced teenager carefully holding a card in front of his chest that reads in large, black letters: JUVENILE.

His mother, who requested anonymity to protect her son, remembers trying to navigate her way through a confusing legal system and trying to find a private investigator to help defend her son. "It was like playing eenie, meenie, mynie moe," she said. "You don't know who to ask. You don't know who's good and who's not. I went through the whole yellow pages looking for someone who specialized in juvenile crime. There wasn't anyone."

'I'm angry. I wanted to see my children go to college. I missed their graduation. I missed their prom. I missed their birthdays. I missed having something to brag about. I even miss them messing with their little brothers.'

—Janice McDaniel

Janice McDaniel hired a private attorney for her son, Jonathan David Barnett, 16, who was arrested in 1998 and accused of helping rob a man delivering Chinese food to a friend's house. Also arrested was McDaniel's older son, Christopher. At 17, he was already an adult under Georgia's penal code, but Jonathan's age made him an SB440 case.

The lawyer she hired tried to persuade Jonathan to plead guilty to armed robbery. The alternative was a probable life sentence, because the charges included kidnapping and aggravated assault, the lawyer warned McDaniel. But Jonathan and Christopher insisted on a trial. Christopher was convicted of armed robbery and given 15 years. Jonathan was found guilty of armed robbery, criminal trespass and false imprisonment and is serving 20 years.

McDaniel believes that her being a black, single mother put her and her sons at a disadvantage from the start, leading everyone from police to prosecutors and the judge to railroad them through the system. She charges that a team of detectives burst into her house late one night after pounding on the door, ransacked the home and never read her sons their rights before handcuffing them and taking them away.

"From Day One I've been saying this. We were not treated right," McDaniel said. Nearly three years after the arrests, she is still confused about the laws that sent her sons to prison for so long. Neither of them wielded the gun used in the robbery, nor the frying pan used to hit the deliveryman. Court testimony shows that Jonathan was outside the house when the robbery took place and that Christopher suggested calling the whole thing off when the group of teenagers began getting cold feet.

Still, Jonathan got twice as many years as the friend who slammed the victim in the head with the pan, and Jonathan and Christopher both got more time than the co-defendant with the gun.

"We don't understand what happened. Why us?" McDaniel asked, shaking her head back and forth. "We don't understand what happened." What's worse, she said, is that her sons are jailed 100 miles apart from each other, and each prison is about a two-hour drive from Atlanta. Without a car, she's able to visit Jonathan only by catching a ride with another woman who visits the prison regularly. She hasn't seen Christopher in several months, McDaniel admits, breaking down in sobs that subside when bitterness takes hold. "I'm angry. I wanted to see my children go to college. I missed their graduation. I missed their prom. I missed their birthdays. I missed having something to brag about. I even miss them messing with their little brothers."

It's not just her sons who have been sentenced, she said. "It's like when they're sentencing the children, they're sentencing the whole family."

Robert Keller, the district attorney in Clayton County, where the crime occurred, rejects McDaniel's argument that her sons should have been either acquitted or convicted of lesser crimes.

Their participation on the fringes of the crime—by helping plan it and by sharing in the proceeds—makes them as culpable as the rest, Keller said. "The activity of one is the activity of all," he said, explaining the law that critics say leads to a disproportionate number of black arrests. That's because far more black children than white fall into gangs and under the spell of gang leaders—often older companions who lure them into crime.

"Is it fair for the kid who's riding with someone who commits an armed robbery to serve the same amount of time as the kid who pointed the gun?" asked Billie Ross, who watched Trey's adult co-defendants lay the blame on him and then walk away with lighter sentences. One of them pleaded guilty to robbery, got 7 years, and was paroled in February. The other served less time. Trey's earliest possible release date is January 2007.

The Rosses remember one juror coming to them in tears after the trial, saying she didn't know that the law required Trey to spend at least 10 years in prison if found guilty.

Now, as leaders in the struggle to repeal SB440, the Rosses live with the frustration of trying to convince other families who don't have children in prison that SB440 is a law that should be changed before it hits them, too. Even among blacks, whose children are most at risk of arrest, it's a battle. Glenwood Ross remembers trying to get a meeting of black clergymen to see SB440 from his point of view. "One guy stood up and said, 'You spare the rod, you spoil the child,'" Ross said, adding that he might have thought the same thing before Trey's problems began.

McDaniel acknowledges her sons did wrong and deserved punishment. So do the Rosses, and so does Kim Williams, whose son is serving 10 years for armed robbery. But they say they were cut down by laws and by people who assumed the worst of their sons because of skin color and didn't give them the same benefits white teens accused of the same things might have enjoyed.

"A lot of children get caught up in the system, but they don't take time to find out anything about what's going on in the child's home. There could be something in their school or home. He might be in depression. And one thing you're not going to do is tell me I didn't raise my kids the right way," McDaniel said, her voice rising in anger and her eyes filling with tears. "I know I did it right. You can't tell me that because I'm a single parent, my kids were automatically bad."

Paying a High Price for the Crimes of Youth

By Tina Susman
STAFF CORRESPONDENT

Savannah, Ga.—Most mothers convinced of a son's innocence would rejoice if 20 years were sliced off his prison sentence. Not Ilona Griffin. There's not much to celebrate when life plus 65 years becomes life plus 45 years.

"The only luck I've had so far is that he's kept his sanity," she says of her son, Melvin, now 26, who was a 16-year-old high school student when he was arrested in July 1992. Melvin was accused of taking part in the robbery and shooting death of a man on a Savannah street. This was two years before passage of Senate Bill 440, which requires 13- to 16-year-olds charged with such crimes to be charged as adults, so Melvin might have been expected to be treated as a juvenile and spared an adult prison sentence.

But the events that led to his case ending up in adult court are, critics say, evidence that even before SB440, black minors were far more likely than whites to have their cases treated as felonies.

Though Melvin was a juvenile at the time of the crime, he wasn't charged with the murder for several months, until he had turned 17 and become an adult in the eyes of the Georgia penal code. He was convicted in a jury trial.

Ilona Griffin, who met Melvin's American father when he was serving in the Army in her native Germany, still doesn't understand fully what happened. "They put him in juvenile for being in possession of a gun. When he turned 17, he was moved to county jail. Then he was tried as an adult. That's the part I can't comprehend," says Griffin, who estimates she has spent about $40,000 on attorneys and private investigators in her attempts to appeal the case's outcome. Not being familiar with the ways of the court system has led to missteps.

The first attorney was recommended by a colleague, but Griffin didn't realize he had no experience in criminal cases. She could afford him, though, so she hired him, only to learn he wanted Melvin to work out a plea bargain. He did not fight vigorously enough to have the case waived back to juvenile court, Griffin says, or explain to her why prosecutors waited until Melvin had reached adulthood before filing charges.

Martina Correia of Amnesty International in Georgia says a better attorney would have fought to have Melvin charged as a juvenile, before prosecutors had the time to build a bigger case against him. By the time he went to trial,

Melvin faced at least four charges—murder, aggravated assault, armed robbery and possession of a firearm—virtually guaranteeing a stiff sentence even if he made a plea bargain. The best offer prosecutors had in exchange for a guilty plea was life in prison. "In this case, Melvin just got the short end of the stick," Correia says.

> **'You can't just take all the kids and put them in a prison and throw the key away. In the long run it's not going to work out. You're going to have too many of them in there.'**
>
> *—Ilona Griffin*

The Griffins hired a new attorney to handle an appeal, which was based, in part, on the recanting of the key prosecution witness' testimony. The witness, Melvin's co-defendant, wrote a statement in 1997 saying he had accused Melvin of being the gunman to avoid a harsh sentence for himself. But the new attorney ended up in jail himself, sentenced to 10 years in 1998 after admitting he stole hundreds of thousands of dollars of clients' fees.

"I retained an attorney. I paid the attorney. I paid the private detective. I even paid for my transcripts," says Griffin, whose files on the case are as thick as two large phone directories. "I've been paying and paying ever since I can remember. I really don't understand why this is going on, and there never, ever seems to be an end to it."

Melvin is scheduled to go before the parole board in 2007. In the meantime, Griffin says he has obtained a high school diploma, but spends most of his time cutting grass and making license plates. The most she has to show for her persistence has been the 20-year sentence reduction.

"Putting him in prison—I thought that was like telling me to just throw him out in the garbage," Griffin says, shaking her head in disgust. "You can't just take all the kids and put them in a prison and throw the key away. In the long run it's not going to work out. You're going to have too many of them in there."

But that is often what happens to people such as McDaniel's son when they come before judges, the overwhelming majority of whom are white and have preconceived notions of what constitutes a solid family life, said Kim Taylor-Thompson, a former public defender and now a law professor at New York University's law school. Taylor-Thompson is also the academic director of the criminal justice program at NYU's Brennan Center for Justice and has done research on racial differences in the handling of juvenile offenders in New York State. New York's laws regarding juveniles are considered among the toughest in the nation, with all teenagers considered adults once they reach 16 and those 14 to 16 automatically charged as adults for selected crimes that range from arson to murder.

Sometimes, even if a teenager has a working mother and no father at home, there might be other authority figures that could warrant a teenager being treated as a juvenile rather than sent into adult court, Taylor-Thompson said, but this is rarely considered by those making such decisions.

"I think we make presumptions based on what we think is… a safe choice, and that is often based on our own cultural biases and experiences," she said. "The fact that a mother is present and may be available at home in the afternoon gives you some sense there's a structure in place. But if you took a kid of color, even if a mother is working a number of jobs, it doesn't mean there aren't other structures in place for that kid. It may not be the conventional structure—it may be there is an uncle, or grandparents, or other extended family members. But because it's not our idea of the conventional norm, it's not considered, and that's racism."

'We're not saying they shouldn't pay some price, but there's the question of equality in terms of race, and there's the question of humanity. How are we going to resolve street crime—by arresting a bunch of kids?'

—Elaine Brown

Keller, the Clayton County district attorney, bristles when he hears accusations of racial bias in the handling of Georgia's youngest offenders. If anything, Keller said, prosecutors try to find mitigating circumstances to warrant sending cases back into the juvenile system, something they are permitted to do with SB440 cases. He acknowledges that the cases most likely to be waived back to juvenile court—aggravated sodomy and aggravated child molestation offenses—are also the most likely to involve white defendants. That's because of the defendants' backgrounds, not their skin color, he said.

"In child molestation cases, we've found that a lot of the time the defendants have been victimized in the past, so what we end up doing is looking at the circumstances and trying to see if there is any way we can keep this in juvenile court," Keller said. "But quite candidly, when it is an armed robbery, we can't make the guns disappear. We don't care if you're black or white or whatever."

The cases least likely to be waived to juvenile court are those involving mainly black defendants, such as armed robbery.

Parents and opponents of SB440 say that the consideration given to alleged child molesters should be granted to all juvenile defendants and that not giving them all equal consideration is unfair. If anything, they say, children accused of violent crimes such as assault and armed robbery are the most in need of counseling and special consideration, rather than incarceration with hardened criminals.

"I was just a kid," said Glenn Sims, now 20 and serving 10 years for an armed robbery committed at age 16. In the years leading up to the crime, he lived with an abusive uncle, saw his father fall victim to drug addiction and witnessed his mother being beaten repeatedly by a stepfather.

It's the sort of background that opponents of SB440 say prosecutors should take into consideration. "You just don't have a child do something like this and not look at that child's environment. Something very messed up is going on in their lives," said Elaine Brown, a one-time leader of the Black Panther Party and a writer who helped found Mothers Advocating Juvenile Justice. Her book, "The Condemnation of Little B," examines the case of Michael Lewis, who was charged with murder in Atlanta in 1997 when he was 13 and sentenced to life in prison. "We're not saying they shouldn't pay some price, but there's the question of equality in terms of race, and there's the question of humanity. How are we going to resolve street crime—by arresting a bunch of kids?"

From *Newsday*, Vol. 62, No. 353, August 22, 2002. pp. A1, A26. © 2002 by Newsday Inc.

Doubting the System

Laws on juveniles stir debate over punishment and racism

By Tina Susman
STAFF CORRESPONDENT

Morrow, Ga.—Maybe if she had been stricter with him. Maybe if she hadn't married an abusive man. Or maybe if she hadn't let him live with a dad who was a drug addict and an uncle who she says beat him up. Maybe if, as a 16-year-old girl growing up in Roosevelt, Long Island, she had stayed in school and not dropped out to have a baby.

Kim Williams recites the "maybes" of her life like a wistful mantra as she discusses her son, Glenn Sims, who was 16 in November 1998 when he was arrested in an Atlanta suburb and charged with holding up a convenience store. Williams was stunned. Sims was no angel, but Williams said she'd never expected him to be accused of such a thing.

'He was scared, and I'll tell you, when the judge said 10 years, the tears fell out of his eyes. I cried, I guess, for about two years.'

—Kim Williams, of the day her son Glenn Sims… was sentenced.

"He knew better, because we never raised him that way," said Williams, sitting in the small, one-bedroom apartment she was sharing with her 13-year-old daughter until money worries led them to move in with her parents in May. Williams assumed that Sims' young age would bring time in a juvenile facility, or perhaps house arrest and probation. She urged him to confess, thinking honesty would be rewarded with lighter treatment. "I thought there was some kind of a law for first-time offenders," she said.

What Williams didn't know, and what she and thousands of other parents have come to find out, is that under a law passed with little fanfare in 1994 under the benign name of the "School Safety and Juvenile Justice Reform Act" Sims was an adult in

the eyes of Georgia's penal code. His guilty plea brought a mandatory 10-year prison term with no chance of parole.

"He was scared, and I'll tell you, when the judge said 10 years, the tears fell out of his eyes," Williams said. "I cried, I guess, for about two years," she added, only half-jokingly.

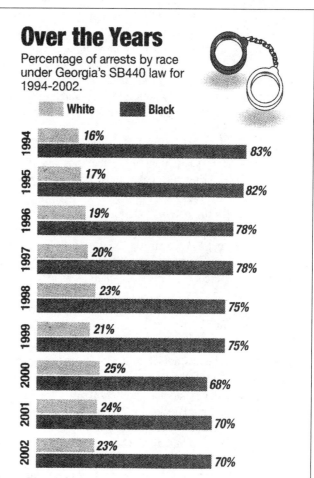

Over the Years

Percentage of arrests by race under Georgia's SB440 law for 1994-2002.

☐ White   ■ Black

Year	White	Black
1994	16%	83%
1995	17%	82%
1996	19%	78%
1997	20%	78%
1998	23%	75%
1999	21%	75%
2000	25%	68%
2001	24%	70%
2002	23%	70%

NOTE: Some juveniles may be arrested with more than one offense so the percentages may exceed 100%

SOURCE: Georgia Indigent Defense Council

And like most youths caught up in the law, charged and convicted of one of the "seven deadly sins"—murder, voluntary manslaughter, rape, armed robbery, aggravated sodomy, aggravated child molestation and aggravated sexual battery— that automatically turn 13- to 16-year-olds into adults in Georgia's courts, Sims is black. Since Senate Bill 440 was passed in May 1994, 76 percent of the more than 3,800 teenagers arrested for SB440 offenses have been black, although they comprise 34 percent of the state's teenage population, according to the Georgia Indigent Defense Council, a state agency that tracks SB440 cases.

Proponents of keeping juveniles in juvenile courts say the nationwide trend toward pushing them into the adult system is tainted by racism—sometimes blatant, sometimes unintentional—because the laws are passed by mainly white legislatures and enforced by judges and prosecutors, the overwhelming majority of whom are white.

"There really is in operation an unspoken sense that these are throwaway kids. If they didn't think they were throwaway kids, they wouldn't treat them that way," said Malcolm Young, executive director of the Sentencing Project, a Washington, D.C., think tank that studies criminal justice issues.

Proponents of tougher treatment for juveniles deny institutional racism and say black teens simply commit more, and more serious, crimes. "If you took all the black males between the ages of 16 and 25 and put them on an island in the Pacific, crime would drop 80 percent overnight," said Brian Silverman, the former chief of the juvenile division at the Cook County, Ill., Public Defender's office, who acknowledges the racial disparities in prisons. "I'm not convinced it's caused by racism. If it is, that's bad and we should do something to change it. But if the cause is something other than racism, then it's a problem maybe society can't handle."

Researchers say that both sides are looking at it too simplistically, that factors such as policing methods and the prior records juveniles bring into court must be considered when weighing the level of racial bias.

Nobody denies the numbers, though, and even if blacks do account for a higher number of teens arrested for violent crime, figures from the nation's 75 largest counties in 1998 indicated a difference in the treatment of them. In the counties surveyed, whites were 48 percent of the youths charged as juveniles with violent crimes—exactly the same as the figure for blacks. They exceeded blacks charged with murder in juvenile court, 59 percent to 36 percent.

But in those same counties, whites accounted for 25 percent of juveniles charged as adults with violent crimes, compared with 73 percent for blacks.

For nonviolent drug and public order offenses, the disparities were greater. Building Blocks for Youth, a Washington, D.C.-based organization that studies juvenile justice issues, surveyed 18 counties in 1998, including Queens, Bronx, Kings and New York in New York State and found that while blacks were 64 percent of youths arrested for felony drug offenses, they represented 76 percent of the drug offenses handled in adult courts. They were 68 percent of those arrested for public order crimes

such as gun possession and rioting, but accounted for 76 percent of youths charged as adults with such offenses.

In many states, the population of black youths in adult prisons is several times that of white youths. In Georgia, blacks account for 83 percent of the minors in adult prisons, and whites 17 percent. In Alabama, Mississippi, South Carolina and Virginia, blacks account for about 75 percent of the minors in adult prisons, while whites are about 20 percent. Studies show that minors housed in adult prisons are several times more likely to be physically assaulted and to attempt suicide, and are more inclined to commit crimes again once they have been released.

Yet throughout the 1990s, state after state passed laws making it easier to try young offenders as adults, spurred in part by criminologists' thunderous warnings that social and demographic changes had combined to create a new breed of child and teenage "superpredator."

In fact, juvenile crime has dropped since the theory swept the country, following an increase in the 1980s and early 1990s that was blamed on factors ranging from the crack cocaine epidemic to the economy. According to the FBI, violent crime arrest rates for youths ages 15 to 17 declined 44 percent from 1994 to 2000. Criminologists' ominous words, however, had struck a chord with legislators who had witnessed rising juvenile crime rates, including Georgia's then-Gov. Zell Miller. His state saw juvenile arrests for violent crime jump from about 1,900 in 1990 to 3,000 in 1993.

"Kids who commit adult crimes ought to be tried and sentenced as adults," Miller, now a U.S. senator, said after the bill passed in 1994. Among other things, he said the law would let teachers focus on teaching, rather than "worrying about whether little Johnny is packing a gun."

Critics of such laws say that they were thrown together haphazardly by politicians more concerned about public support than public safety, and that there was no thought of what sort of people the jails would turn loose on society once the young prisoners' sentences were fulfilled. But for legislators pressured by public fears of crime, repealing such laws, even those that have proved to be the most racially skewed, is out of the question, leaving thousands of young black men such as Sims to spend their developmental years behind bars.

"The unfortunate thing is that it's across-the-board mandatory. Some child who might benefit from counseling or treatment won't get it. Juvenile facilities offer schools, mental help, counseling, to a much greater degree than an adult would get," said Susan Teaster of the Georgia Indigent Defense Council, who was a public defender when SB440 passed. "They weren't thinking about the consequences 10 years down the road when they passed this law. You tell a 13- or 14-year-old he's getting 10 or 12 years in jail, and you're taking all hope away from him. We'll be looking at people who've been incarcerated all the years when they're supposed to learn to be productive members of society. They'll have been surrounded by other people convicted of crimes. They'll have no probation, no parole, and they'll have no idea how to function in society."

The Office of Juvenile Justice and Delinquency Prevention, part of the Department of Justice, said a host of unforeseen problems had arisen as more states treated juvenile offenders as

Two Mothers' Stories

KAMEELAH SHABAZZ-DIAAB

When most boys his age were idolizing rap stars, sports stars and action-movie stars, Kameelah Shabazz-Diaab's son, Joshua, was idolizing Ben Carson, a black brain surgeon.

It re-enforced Shabazz-Diaab's belief that she had done the right thing in moving the family in the early 1990s from Philadelphia to the southern suburbia of Decatur, Ga., in a middle-class neighborhood of nice houses with backyards. She liked that there were other black families in the neighborhood and she hoped this would show Joshua that life for a young, black man could stretch beyond the cacophonous, concrete jungle he had known.

"I came to Georgia so I could get my son away from the urban, city life, to give him an opportunity to be in a good environment, to let him have some better opportunities," said Shabazz-Diaab, a devout Muslim who raised Joshua the same way. When she takes time out for her daily prayers these days, Shabazz-Diaab appeals for something far more basic for her son: simply that he'll make it home before Feb. 8, 2012, the date he's scheduled to be freed from prison.

To hear Shabazz-Diaab tell it, Joshua was an ideal 15-year-old, an honor student at a private Islamic high school whose strict upbringing had served him well. She never let him play with guns. She says he disdained the often lewd, violent and obscenity-laced lyrics of the rap music that appealed to other boys his age. He liked being with his family.

In 1997, as Shabazz-Diaab was preparing a feast for Ramadan, the police called and told her that Joshua and another 15-year-old had been arrested and accused of robbing a couple at gunpoint.

"I was devastated. I couldn't believe it, because this was the day before a big celebration," said Shabazz-Diaab, a soft-spoken customer service representative at a large company. "Usually that's a day when you're happy and jovial. I was just numb."

The feeling lasted as Joshua's case slowly wound it's way through the courts. Shabazz-Diaab closed herself off from other families with children, because they were too painful a reminder of Joshua's absence. "There was just always that void that he wasn't there, " she said. "It took me a couple of years to shake myself out of it."

She hired a private attorney in hopes of getting the best defense for Joshua but admits that if she'd been able to pay more than $5,000, she might have found a better one. In the end, Joshua was convicted and sentenced to 15 years in prison. Shabazz-Diaab, who has two other children, both in college, tries to visit him each week at Hancock State Prison in Sparta, Ga., which is about a two-hour drive, and she tries to keep her spirits up. She doesn't always succeed. As she addressed a birthday card to Joshua to mark his 21st on July 24, she began to scrawl "happy birthday" on it. Then she stopped herself. "It wasn't really a happy event," she explained.

A'SHEERAH WALKER

There are just a few days left before her son's 17th birthday, and A'Sheerah Walker is watching the calendar with a growing sense of anxiety. For more than two years, since he was charged and convicted of manslaughter in the shooting of a man called Psycho, her son, Immanuell Williams, has been housed at a youth detention facility. On Aug. 24, though, when he becomes old enough to enter an adult prison, he could be moved to a state penitentiary unless Walker can prevent it.

She's trying her best, collecting hundreds of signatures on a petition urging that Immanuell be held in a youth detention center until he is 21 and then released. A judge is scheduled to make a decision Friday. If she succeeds, Walker hopes to help not only her son but hundreds of other minors convicted of crimes under Senate Bill 440, which automatically treats 13- to 16-year-olds as adults and puts them in adult prisons.

She had never heard of the bill until her son was caught by it. That was on Jan. 15, 2001, Martin Luther King Day. Immanuell was playing video games at a friend's house in southwest Atlanta.

From what Walker and Immanuell say, he was attacked by a 39-year-old street tough who allegedly tried to steal the gold medallion Immanuell wore around his neck. Immanuell, who had argued with the man's girlfriend earlier that day, says he was trying to defend himself. He was sentenced to 15 years in prison. Like other SB440 convicts, he has no chance for parole.

Many parents of young inmates prefer to keep low profiles, fearing for their jobs, their privacy or for their son's safety in prison if they complain too loudly about the law. Walker has taken the opposite approach. "I'm not afraid," said Walker, who has nine children—six adopted and three biological, including Immanuell. Two are in college. "They can't do anything more to Immanuell than they've already done to him. The only thing they can do to him now is put a bullet through his heart, and he would probably be better off with a bullet in his heart than in prison."

So far, her willingness to go out on a limb appears to have saved Immanuell from being sent directly to prison, as are most SB440 kids after conviction. Instead, the judge allowed him to remain in the youth facility at least until he's 17.

Walker says she has spent $20,000 on lawyers and investigators, not to mention the phone bills from Immanuell's collect calls home. Last month, the bill was about $600. She also has filed a motion for a new trial, arguing that the jury that convicted her son was coerced into doing so by a judge who didn't want to accept that it was hung.

So determined is Walker that she has enlisted her sister in Flushing to collect signatures on the petition asking that Immanuell be spared prison time.

adults. These included the issue of how to obtain quick medical treatment in prison for minors needing parental consent for surgery or medication; the added workload on criminal courts forced to handle formerly "juvenile" offenders; and the addition of thousands of new and immature inmates to already crowded prison systems. It also noted the overrepresentation of minori-

ties among juveniles charged as adults, and it questioned the deterrent effect of the laws, saying few states had taken steps to educate juveniles of the sanctions they might face from breaking the law.

Even get-tough advocates who favor trying some juveniles as adults, such as Silverman and Peter Reinharz, a former prosecutor in Manhattan who was chief of the city's Family Court, say that laws that treat all juveniles the same without considering an individual's circumstances and that impose minimum sentences without allowing judges to consider alternative punishments, are misguided.

"Automatically treating them as adults in every situation is ludicrous," said Reinharz, now the managing attorney for Nassau County. "If someone is 14 and doing an armed robbery, I certainly don't want to be in the community with him. Something has to be done. On the other hand, the idea of saddling this guy with a felony conviction for the rest of his life is really stupid. He's going to wind up not being able to get a job and having no other choices down the road than a life of crime. There has to be some common sense kind of plan, and unfortunately there isn't a lot of common sense type of planning with these laws."

Such arguments haven't convinced Miller, who said Georgia's drop in juvenile arrests since 1994 proves the law is deterring young offenders. "The juvenile justice system we had was not adequate to handle the violence of today's young criminals," Miller said in a written reply to questions. "These are not the Cleaver kids soaping up some windows. These are middle school kids conspiring to hurt their teachers, teenagers shooting people and committing rapes, young thugs running drug gangs and terrorizing neighborhoods."

As for the racial disparity in SB440 offenses, Miller said there will always be critics who oppose all punishment for young offenders, black or white. "I trust the prosecutors and judges in my state and believe they have exercised the proper discretion in enforcing this law."

Not everyone believes this, least of all parents of black teenagers jailed in Georgia. They share the belief that because of race, their sons were caught in a system that equates young black men with thuggery and assumes black teens arrested for serious crimes ended up in jail because they came from ghetto neighborhoods without adult supervision. And while they all acknowledge that their sons are not blameless, they agree with the experts who say putting them in prison for at least 10 years for a crime committed as a teenager will do more harm than good.

"When you're dealing with children, it's just so idiotic," said Billie Ross, the president of Mothers Advocating Juvenile Justice, a group of parents with children convicted under SB440. Ross is convinced that if her son were white, police and prosecutors would have considered his parents' professional backgrounds and their stable lifestyle when they arrested him in 1996 for armed robbery. Glenwood Ross III, better known as Trey, was a slightly built 15-year-old then. He was convicted and sentenced to the mandatory 10 years. His mother was spurred to get her master's degree in social work, in part, by Trey's arrest. His father, Glenwood Ross, is a professor of economics at Morehouse College in Atlanta.

"I think they just have this box that they put a lot of these black kids into, and he fell into it," Billie Ross said of Trey. "Let's face it, if you're a black person in America, particularly a young black man, you have to worry about this."

Few did, however, until they collided with laws such as SB440.

Williams never imagined she'd spend a decade of weekends and holidays crisscrossing Georgia's rolling, monotonous countryside to visit Sims in prison for a crime committed when he was 16. She never imagined he would be forced to fight off rapists in the first prison where he was held, the maximum-security Arrendale State Prison in Alto, Ga., where all boys convicted as adults are housed.

"He got cheated because I was young when I had him," said Williams, who was 16 when Sims was born. "All I knew was partying and running in the streets. I wasn't the best parent. I was too young to know what a parent was."

That's not to say Sims was trouble free or that Williams considers him without fault. The move from Long Island to Georgia when Sims was 10 didn't go well for the boy who preferred hanging out with his cousins and friends back in New York. He missed going out for Chinese food, ice skating, playing sports on his old school teams and the snowy winters. He also missed his father, who never married his mother but who lived around the corner from them in Roosevelt. Life in Atlanta seemed dull by comparison.

"He came down here with that New York mentality, that no one could tell him what to do. And he found out that Georgia doesn't play that way," said Williams, whose cheerful nature belies the difficulties of her life. Now 36, she works as a secretary by day and a security guard on weekend nights to support herself and her daughter, and to set aside money for both kids' futures. At least twice a month and on holidays, she makes the two-hour drive to Hancock State Prison in Sparta to spend a few hours with Sims, who was transferred there in October 2000 after nearly two years at Arrendale.

The visits aren't easy. "My mom works too hard to be coming up here every two weeks," said Sims, a tall, gregarious young man who wears the outfit issued to all inmates: white pants with a black stripe down the side and a short-sleeved white shirt with a stripe up the front. "She cries a lot. I tell her, look, I did what I did, and I'm gonna do my time for it.' "

For Williams, Sims' arrest was a crushing blow in a yearslong battle to establish a stable life. Her first husband, to whom she was married for seven years, beat her so badly, she said, that she fled with the children to a shelter. Sims said he remembers his first stepfather pummeling his mother until she was bruised and bleeding, even going to her workplace to drag her out and hit her.

Thus began a series of moves, which ended in 1990 when Williams decided to follow other family members who had gone to Georgia. As Sims struggled with the upheaval, she granted his wish to return to Long Island to live with his biological father for a while. When his father was jailed for drugs, Sims' uncle was in charge. His answer to Sims' behavior problems was violence.

"His uncle wasn't into let's whip you with a belt.' His uncle was into let's beat you up with the fists,'" Williams said.

By the time Williams brought Sims back to Georgia, his path to disaster was set. "I kept hate in my heart. Hatred, hatred, hatred," he says now. "I don't know if it just came out in my teens or what." He returned to Atlanta more troubled than when he had left.

"He [Sims] wanted to stay out all night. I'd go check on him and find a bunch of clothes under the sheets to make it look like someone was in bed," Williams said, laughing at the things that angered her then but that now bring back memories of a time when Sims was home, not sleeping on a prison cot.

When the police arrived at Williams' home that night in November 1998 to question her son, Sims admitted his involvement in the robbery. Williams and her husband thought it best to come clean. They hoped a judge would take Sims' youth, turbulent past and family ties into consideration. They didn't know about SB440.

"We really, really did not put up a fight," Williams said. "I don't know what I was thinking when I had him confess. Something in my mind told me they were not going to take that boy away. I knew he'd get time, but I didn't think it would be 10 years. Maybe five years tops."

Sims is scheduled for release in December 2008. He will be 26 years old. His grandmother has a room set aside for him in her house. His mother has been trying to gently nudge him to think about going to college when he gets out. "We're hoping to just shelter him with love," she said.

If studies of offenders are anything to go by, Sims will have a hard time avoiding trouble again. Research in New York, New Jersey and Florida comparing re-offense rates among juveniles treated in adult versus juvenile courts shows that those sent to criminal court are more likely than others to become repeat offenders. "It's scandalous. We're sowing the seeds of having these kids grow up to be violent criminals," said Herschella Conyers, a public defender in Cook County, Ill., where a law mandating adult trials for youths accused of certain drug and weapons offenses has been criticized for producing racially skewed results. One portion of the law requires adult court for juveniles charged with drug and weapon offenses within 1,000 feet of public housing projects, areas that are predominantly black. More than 90 percent of the teenagers convicted as adults under the law are black.

"It's really incredible," Conyers said. "We CAN do better things than that with kids, even if they're guilty. It's just crazy. The consequences are both inhumane and disastrous."

Even the Georgia Department of Corrections, whose prison system has absorbed at least 574 minor inmates since SB440 took effect, acknowledges it was passed without much consideration for the pasts and futures of the youngsters caught up by it. Whereas lawmakers saw 13-, 14- and 15-year-olds as street-smart and mean as adults, they didn't take into consideration other factors, said department spokesman Mike Light. "What we see is kids who've led very hard lives for the most part, and who've made bad decisions. What drives these individuals to commit crimes so early? What are we going to do with these kids?" asked Light, who worries that unless such issues are addressed, prison could become the "grad school" for the next level of crime.

With a growing inmate population and limited staffing and resources, the special needs of children behind bars, such as mentoring, counseling and education, simply cannot be adequately met, he said.

"I'm surprised he can read at all," Williams said of Sims shortly before his last birthday. "He's going to be 20 years old on Aug. 9, without an education and that really hurts me."

"I wouldn't feel so bad if they prepared the kids for when they get out," Glenwood Ross, Trey's father, said bitterly. "But these kids are just sitting around doing nothing, so what's society going to get when they come out? A bunch of dummies who've been sitting around doing nothing."

Still, there appears to be little chance laws such as SB440 will be overturned. Child advocates concede that they are fighting an uphill battle. Families of children in prison represent a tiny constituency, and they are trying to persuade people who have no interest in juvenile justice issues to rally on behalf of juveniles accused of serious crimes.

"We're not saying don't punish the kids. We're saying use discretion, use judgment. But people don't want to hear that," said Billie Ross, who admits that until Trey was arrested, she had no interest in juvenile justice issues. "It wasn't anything I felt like I needed to be concerned with. Then all of a sudden this hit me. I guess I'm like a lot of other people—dumb and blind to a lot of what's going on until it strikes you directly."

Mothers Advocating Juvenile Justice is lobbying to introduce a parole possibility for juveniles convicted under SB440 but hasn't gotten far. The proposed amendment, House Bill 269, never made it out of the legislature's Judiciary Committee last year.

From *Newsday*, Vol. 62, No. 353, August 21, 2002. pp. A6, A34, A36. © 2002 by Newsday Inc.

UNIT 6
Punishment and Corrections

Unit Selections

31. **Kicking Out the Demons by Humanizing the Experience—An Interview With Anthony Papa**, Drugwar.com
32. **Trends in State Parole**, Timothy A. Hughes, Doris James Wilson, and Alan J. Beck
33. **Inmate Reentry and Post-Release Supervision: The Case of Massachusetts**, Anne Morrison Piehl
34. **Rethinking the Death Penalty**, Kenneth Jost

Key Points to Consider

- What issues and trends are most likely to be faced by corrections administrators at the beginning of this new century?

- How does probation differ from parole? Describe any similarities.

- Discuss reasons for favoring and for opposing the death penalty.

 **Links: www.dushkin.com/online/**
These sites are annotated in the World Wide Web pages.

American Probation and Parole Association (APPA)
http://www.appa-net.org
The Corrections Connection
http://www.corrections.com
Critical Criminology Division of the ASC
http://www.critcrim.org/
David Willshire's Forensic Psychology & Psychiatry Links
http://members.optushome.com.au/dwillsh/index.html
Oregon Department of Corrections
http://www.doc.state.or.us/links/welcome.htm

In the American system of criminal justice, the term "corrections" has a special meaning. It designates programs and agencies that have legal authority over the custody or supervision of people who have been convicted of a criminal act by the courts. The correctional process begins with the sentencing of the convicted offender. The predominant sentencing pattern in the United States encourages maximum judicial discretion and offers a range of alternatives, from probation (supervised, conditional freedom within the community) through imprisonment, to the death penalty.

Selections in this unit focus on the current condition of the U.S. penal system and the effects that sentencing, probation, imprisonment, and parole have on the rehabilitation of criminals.

The lead article, "Kicking Out the Demons by Humanizing the Experience," is an interview with Anthony Papa, an artist and activist who uses his art to promote prison and drug-war reform. Convicted under the Rockefeller drug laws, Papa spent 12 years in Sing Sing prison. The essay that follows, "Trends in State Parole" asserts that the more things change in the parole system, the more they stay the same. Next, Anne Morrison Piehl, in "Inmate Reentry and Post-Release Supervision: The Case of Massachusetts," points out that mandatory sentencing laws and restrictions on community placement keep those most in need of parole supervision from receiving it. The concluding article in this unit and the book, "Rethinking the Death Penalty," raises serious questions about the fairness and reliability of the system for meting out death sentences.

Kicking Out the Demons by Humanizing the Experience— An Interview With Anthony Papa

"I want to write directions, 'How to be an agent of change and transformation.' Take posters and place them all over in public places. You know, educate."
Anthony Papa, April 30, 2002

by Preston Peet

May 1, 2002

Anthony Papa is an accomplished artist and ardent activist living and working in NYC, using his art to promote prison and Drug War reform. After being set up, then arrested in a drug sting operation in 1985, he received two concurrent sentences of 15 years to life in New York State's Sing Sing prison for his first offense under the Rockefeller Drug Laws' mandatory minimum sentencing guidelines. After gaining widespread attention through the harrowing and beautiful paintings he was creating from inside his prison cell, he received clemency after serving 12 years from NY Governor George Pataki in 1997. Papa, a friendly, intelligent, and very articulate man, graciously took time to sit down for a long and illuminating discussion with Drugwar.com, covering such topics as his art, the benefits of art for rehabilitation of prisoners, who the real targets of the War on Drugs really are and why the War continues, and some of the efforts he and friends are making to instigate positive changes in the system.

P- Have you seen the NORML ads out on the streets yet? What do you think of that idea?

AP- I think it's a great idea, putting the Mayor on the spot, but I don't think it's going to change anything.

P- You don't think it's going to change much, but you're not opposed to the idea of putting the Mayor's face out there?

AP- They should, he smoked pot. See, the whole problem with the War on Drugs is they demonize drugs, and they target specific populations and individuals, disenfranchise and marginalize blacks and Latinos, who always get pinned for these drug crimes, yet the majority of users are white individuals. That's the whole beef man. I think it's positive to use the media in a creative way, to use the arts, to enlighten people as to what the real issues are. Like with this installation we did at the Drug War Race and Party on 4-20, 'Faces of the Drug War— American Dreams, American Tragedy,' what I try to do is humanize the experience through the creative arts. This is what I do with my art. I have two websites, www.15yearstolife.com, and www.prisonzone.com, where you can take a tour in prison through the web with my friend Chris Cozzone's photography and my art. My own website, 15yearstolife.com, is basically a site that people from around the world come into. They come not necessarily because they want to know about it, they come by chance because of the art. The art drew them in, and that's what I do with the art. The whole thing with my art now, I'm not into the scene of showing my art in galleries because I'm not with those politics man. At first it's a big deal, you get a show, you sell some work, you know, every artist's dream. I've been through that, I did it, it's gone. I just don't like the politics involved. I like to freewheel, do what I like to do with no limitations. That's the greatest thing for me.

P- You were arrested in 1985 for passing an envelope of cocaine. Was it a setup, or were you just unlucky?

AP- It was a sting operation. What had happened in 1984 was I was married, had a child, was self-employed with a radio business in the South Tremont section of the Bronx. I belonged to a bowling team in Westchester County. Business was slow, my car kept breaking down,

so I kept showing up late to the leagues. So one of my teammates asked me what was going on. I told him about my car, he asked why didn't I fix it, and I told him I couldn't, things were slow. He said, "Do you want to make some money? I know somebody." He introduced me to this guy who was a drug dealer, dealing in the bowling alleys in Westchester. So to make a long story short, the guy asked me if I wanted to deliver an envelope, to Mt. Vernon from NYC. He'd give me $500, and said it might become a steady thing. At first I said no, I'm not into that.

P- You pretty much knew it was drugs then?

AP- Yeah, I knew what it was about. A couple months went by, he came back around Christmas time and asked me again. Now things were really bad financially, so I asked him what I had to do. He said I just had to deliver this package to Mt. Vernon. I did, brought it to Mt. Vernon NY and walked into a sting operation. Twenty narcotics officers came out from everywhere. The individual who actually set me up was working for the police. He had three sealed indictments against him, so what his thing was, the more people he got involved, the less time he was supposed to get. So he reached out for everybody he knew. For me it was a bad mistake and afterwards I did everything wrong. I got this shyster lawyer. They offered me a cop-out to three to life because they knew I wasn't dealing the drugs, that I was just the courier, a mule. I didn't take it because I was desperate, didn't want to leave my wife and kid and wound up listening to this attorney, going to trial, and ended up with two 15 year to life sentences.

P- You get a worse sentence if you fight it , right?

AP- Yeah, in NY State. The Rockefeller Drug Laws were enacted in 1973. The legislative intent was to catch the drug kingpins and curb the drug epidemic. They're a dismal failure. We're going to the 30 year anniversary on May 8th of this year. The kingpin is still out there, the prisons are bursting at the seams. Of 72,000 in prison, 24,000 are incarcerated under the Rockefeller Drug laws. The prison population in 1973 was 12,500, now it's 72,000. 94 percent of those incarcerated under these Rockefeller Drug Laws are black and Latino. Marginalized, disenfranchised individuals, they come from 7 inner city neighborhoods in NYC, 75 percent of those individuals are non-violent offenders.

P- Wait a minute. How many come from those 7 inner city neighborhoods?

AP- Seventy Five percent come from 7 communities in NYC, and 94 percent of them are black and Latino. So there's definitely racism involved in these issues. From my perspective, I was in prison for 12 years under the Rockefeller Drug Laws, sentenced 15 years to life. The only way I survived it was my discovery of my art. From there I transcended the negativity of the imprisonment

through the art. It became for me meaning, gave me purpose in life and helped me maintain my humanity, my self-esteem, which is very essential in order to positively interact with society upon release. I met an individual who turned me onto painting, and it created this positive but crazy energy, but a crazy energy in a socially acceptable way.

P- Ok, let me come back to that. Did you use drugs personally at the time of your arrest?

AP- I did. I was a casual user, I never really used cocaine, I smoked pot and drank. Couldn't afford hard drugs, coke, stuff like that, but yeah, I was a drug user at the time.

P- In your case, prison turned you onto creating art, which is obviously a positive result of your imprisonment. Are you the exception, or the rule?

AP- I say there's plenty of individuals in prison who experience what I experienced because of the existential nature of imprisonment. What I mean by that is there's something mystical about spending a lot of time in a 6 by 9 cell. You get to discover who you are. So for me, I pull this artist that lay dormant inside. There's plenty of individuals who do that. That's why in prison, I believe in a restorative approach of justice as opposed to a punitive approach. Where punitive approach is strictly a terrible approach because it sleeps in the shadows of life itself. To lock them up type of mentality that doesn't think of the future of the incarcerated individual as opposed to restorative justice which maintains an individual yet allows him or her to hold onto their self-esteem which is very important.

P- That could lead to rehabilitation.

AP- Right. Rehabilitation exists only if you have the programs available to someone to take advantage of, to turn their lives around.

P- You earned two degrees, one in paralegal studies, and another Behavioral Sciences, as well as earning a graduate degree in ministry from the NY Theological Seminary while in prison. How does that education help you now in spreading your message?

AP- Oh, tremendously, because it gives me credibility when I speak. In reference to say, my job. I'm a legal assistant for a patent trade firm, Fish and Neave. I've been here 5 years. The reason I got the job was because I was prepared. I had a college education and a graduate degree so it made things easier for me to be released and to interact with society. I think also that my education, especially in my theological background, well, I studied liberation theology.

P- Which is?

AP- Which is a theology which is sort of created in third world countries as opposed to white man theology. It's a main belief of my liberation theology that you can talk about the bible, you can talk about tradition all you want, if there's no tangible change or challenge to the principalities, to the powers that be, nothing is going to happen, no change is going to occur. We believe in the hands on, the hermeneutical approach, the study of the nucleus of liberation theology. What it talks about is practical change practical use of problems and challenge in a way that's tangible, not just talking about the issues, but reacting and taking care of business in a positive and tangible way. This has helped me with my art. What really turned me onto art is when I studied art at first, I got into the French impressionists, and then somebody told me art is nice, but there's more to art than pretty beach scenes and frilly white dresses. I said, what do you mean? I was into Manet, Monet, all these French impressionist artists, and he says art can be used for political purposes. He sent me a book about the Mexican muralist, Diego Rivera, who used art showing the oppressors against the oppressed, basically challenging the powers that be. So I took that and used my art. In prison I became a political artist. I saw the artist in his role as a social commentator.

P- *What do think of current art, and in that I include music, film, literature, as well as fine arts. Do you find that those artists using their art to promote a message, such as yourself, are not given as much attention, nor funding, as those artists who create the emptiest of art, art without any message whatsoever?*

AP- You're exactly right. There's a body of art out there, a collection of artists who are political artists, who use art as a vehicle for social commentary, which is what I think art is for, yet because of the politics involved, they are not getting the grants, from foundations, they're just considered part of the elite as the handful of artists are who paint diabetic art. By that I mean sugar and spice, sweet stuff kind of art. I just went to the Whitney Biennial, and I was amazed at the crap they showed there. I didn't see one political piece in the whole show. There is a problem of breaking out with your art and getting discovered if you are going to use your art in a political context. In society today, mainstream artists really don't do that way.

P- *Yeah, my girlfriend overheard a conversation between two guys on the bus the other day, where one was telling the other how he hates it when a musician tries to "get all political, it's just a song." She was struggling not to light into this guy.*

AP- That's what art is for, to use it as a vehicle to get that social message out. I think it is very important. You really interact with society that way. I think it's positive. Film makers, musicians, visual artists, performance artists, all can be positive in using their art to promote social change.

P- *So what's the deal with the new anti-art policies in the NY State prison system? Why do you think they were initiated, and do you think it a smart move to stifle positive creativity in people locked in cages?*

AP- On March 29, 2002, Glen Goord, the Commissioner of Corrections for NY State made a declaration where he prohibited the sale of art by prisoners, doing away with a yearly art show, the Correction On Canvas exhibit that was in existence for 35 years in the NY State prison system. Every year prisoners had the opportunity to show and sell their work at this exhibit that was run by the State Senate and the Department of Corrections in the legislative office building in Albany. Fifty percent of the proceeds went to crime victims.

P- *To a crime victims' fund, or to those specific individuals hurt by the artist/criminals?*

AP- A crime victims' fund. What happened was that Goord made a statement that it wasn't worth the anguish that crime victims would feel for the little money that they raised through the show, allowing prisoners to profit from their art. Behind the scenes it was a political issue that started when Pataki took office in 1995. At that time 100 percent of the profits went to the prisoners, so an agreement was worked out where 50 percent of the money raised would go to a crime victims. It worked for almost 7 years, but last year, a mass murderer who killed something like 11 prostitutes and chopped up their bodies was allowed to show his work in the annual show that is run by the State Senate and the Corrections Dept. The Daily News got a hold of it and blew it up into a big story. An assembly man from Schenectady took hold of the issue and from there the politics went into overdrive. A year later, because of 1 individual, 72,000 individuals were punished. When I heard about it, from my point of view I was really angry because I was in that show for 12 years. I know how important art is for prisoners. I actually have a ribbon on my wall that I got in 1997 for best donated work.

When I got clemency from the Governor, I donated 15 pieces of art, and won this ribbon. I took it very personally, and started this campaign to challenge the Commissioner's decision. I got the NYCLU involved. They've taken the case, which is in the early stages of litigation. The NY Times came out with a beautiful editorial, Newsday is supposed to come out with one, as well as the Christian Science Monitor. We have a major rally planned May 8, also challenging the Governor on both the Rockefeller Drug Laws, and have a petition going around demanding that the show be reinstated and the ability of prisoners be allowed to sell their art be reinstated. The petition is up on my website. I actually got a call from this woman who was so angry that Goord used crime victims as the reason for his decision, a woman whose son and daughter were both murdered and was appalled that Goord was using someone like her for the excuse to take away the art show. I actually hooked her up with a Christian Science Monitor. This is what we've been doing with this issue, and a lot of people are angry. We're challenging the Governor and not the Commissioner, since that's an appointed position, we're challenging the Governor as voters, saying we the voters of NY demand you reinstate it, because it is a political year, he's up for reelection. Hopefully something will happen in a positive way. But artist prisoners are the lowest of the low. No one cares about prisoners. So what if you take away art and music programs? They're in prison, it's there for punishment, but these same people don't realize that these are the same individuals that you have to return to society.

P- You touched on this a little earlier. Do you feel that prisons are at all concerned with rehabilitation?

AP- Not at this point. It used to be a concern, but all it is now is warehousing individuals because I was there, I know personally, and I speak from that viewpoint. If prisons were meant to rehabilitate, every step of the way would be rehabilitative in value and therapeutic.

P- You took your own initiative?

AP- Yeah, I took it upon myself to take advantage of what was available. In 1995 they cut out college education, they did away with Pell and Tap, because again, politicians used crime as a political issue, where first federal money was taken away, then state followed.

P- So prisoners in prison now are not getting an education?

AP- There's a small movement in NY State where there's volunteers, colleges working at Bedford Hills for woman, and at Sing Sing for men, instructors work on a volunteer basis and it is run strictly on private donations.

P- Which would you say is more damaging to individuals and society as a whole—drug use, or the War on Drugs?

AP- I would say the War on Drugs. We've been involved with drug use for thousands of years. It's nothing new, we've dealt with it, there's always going to be an inkling for an individual to escape reality. so we can't control it in that capacity. But I think by creating the War on Drugs, which is a War on People not on Drugs, it's a bigger problem, because the black market exists. What it has become now is a vehicle to fuel the prison-industrial complex. Money raised from State, local and federal level through people's misery. By creating this fictitious war it's caused all sorts of problems. Now we've become comfortable with locking up non-violent offenders. NY State for example, 90 percent of the prisons upstate are in Republican territory where they fight each other to build the next prison. They have become a commodity, prisons. What happens is they keep them filled with non-violent offenders. In 1995, when Clinton's Crime Bill was passed it was a big mistake, because it gave millions of dollars to states to build

prisons. Advocates spoke out against this, because when these prisons are built you're going to have to keep them filled. And what do you fill them with? Drug users. Drug users today are like communists in the McCarthy era. It's a stigma, they demonize drug use.

P- Do you have a position on decriminalization or legalization?

AP- At this point if we tried legalization right now, we wouldn't do it, it wouldn't work. I think we should try out decriminalization first, as a society, see how that works, especially with marijuana. Hard drugs are always going to be a problem. Personally I think we have the right to self-medication. I believe in harm reduction, that theory. Some people will always be addicted to drugs, but let's make it easy for them, let's give them treatment. Let's do it the right way.

P- You're talking about the option for treatment, not mandated treatment.

AP- Right. I don't believe in mandated treatment at all. But again, when you put it all together in the big picture, it becomes part of the War on Drugs, which fuels the prison-industrial complex, because there's more money involved when you mandate. That's the whole story on that.

P- And they keep people in the system.

AP- It's a constant, vicious cycle that continues because of the monetary gain made into the whole issue.

P- Do you see any shift among police and politicians in how them themselves are perceiving the way?

AP- My personal point of view, 5 years ago, when I first got out of prison there wasn't a lot going on in the form of politicians taking stances, because it was a sure fire way to look soft on crime, which is advocating for say, reduced sentencing, or against the Rockefeller Drug Laws. But in the 5 years we've been out here, me working with my organization, the William Kunstler Fund for Racial Justice, and other groups, like the Drug Policy Awareness Project, which teaches people about the war through art and education. Through the efforts of groups like these, people are beginning to understand there's a significant problem. But they look at it in a different way. Why? Because these groups and what we do, we humanize the experience, we don't demonize the experience. We tell people that these are human beings that deserve second chances. Then we have the issue of mandatory minimum sentencing, which was really enacted with the Rockefeller Drug Laws in 1973, and they in turn became the catalyst for the federal government to make the mandatory minimum sentencing the laws in the federal government, and went to all 50 states where there's some form of mandatory minimum sentencing. It really got out of hand. It took the judges ability to look at totality of the facts of each case, where everybody is just pigeonholed by the weight itself. My case for instance, the judge didn't want to sentence me to 15 years to life, but he had no choice because I went to trial and lost. Under mandatory sentencing he could give me in my case 15 years to life, and could of sentenced me to 25 years to life, but he sentenced me to two 15 years to life sentences because it was my first offense.

P- 15 years to life? For your first offence?

AP- Right, first offence, non-violent, no criminal record at all.

P- Not even a smudge on your record?

AP- I have a violation, but that's not a criminal record. I had a stolen license plate on my car I'd borrowed from my boss. 5 years earlier he's forgotten he put it in his trunk and called the police to report it stolen. 5 years later he found it and gave it to me. I got a $25 fine for that. I'd also actually gotten another violation for a joint back in 1973, again not a criminal offense, but a violation.

P- You were arrested in 1985?

AP- I was arrested in 1985.

P- You did 12 years? Then Gov. Pataki gave you clemency in 1997?

AP- Yeah. I painted my way out of prison I like to say, when in 1995, my self portrait that I did in 1988 while sitting in my cell one night. First I looked in the mirror and saw this individual who was going to be spending the most productive years of his life in a cage.

P- How old were you?

AP- I was 30 years old when I went into prison. I picked up this canvas and painted this self portrait titled 15 years to life, where 7 years later it wound up in a show at the Whitney Museum of American Art as part of a retrospective of Mike Kelly's work.

P- Where did you keep your art?

AP- I kept it in my cell. At a certain point where they made it a rule where they said we couldn't keep too much art in our cells. They were constantly making rules. It was a platonic view of the artist, they didn't like artists in prison because they were too individual, they weren't part of the collective. Which was against that whole rap about behavior modification, where the individual goes out you become part of the collective, they train you the way they want, but I wasn't about that. My art helped me transcend that. They had these rule where we couldn't keep finished pieces of art in our cells. I met this girl through an art show that every year I went into at this church. She became the keeper of my art. Every time I finished a piece I would send it out to her and she would keep it for me. A lot of work I have I wasn't able to finish because they forced me to send it

out, like one piece called metamorphosis, with barbwire and hands reaching out that turn into butterflies. I wasn't able to finish that one, because one day this lieutenant by my cell. I used to paint with a nail, hanging the painting on the nail. This piece was a huge, 40 by 50 piece, the biggest I ever did. He told me I had to get rid of it because it was a risk that I could use it to escape. I asked what he meant, and he said I could easily put a hole through the wall. I said, "but lieutenant, if I wanted to go to the other side of the wall, all I had to do was open my cells door, and open the guy's cell door and go in his cell. He said, "no, no, I don't care it's got to go."

P- What, you were going to escape from one cell to the next?

AP- That was the mentality. As a matter of fact, the first ribbon I ever won, in 1986, the first year I went into the Corrections on Canvas exhibit, I won a blue ribbon, my first time trying and I won it. I worked hard. I was a watercolorist, and I won for this piece called, "Pink Bathroom Sink." When I got the ribbon, well, when I got the package at the package room, I got a catalogue, and a letter from a Senator congratulating me on winning first prize, over 5,000 people viewed your piece, congratulations, blah, blah, blah, but when I looked in the package the ribbon wasn't there. I called the guard, and asked him where my ribbon was. He said, "you can't have it." I asked "what do you mean I can't have it?" He said you can't have it because it's blue, and blue isn't allowed. Now, blue is a color considered contraband, blue orange gray, these were colors that police uniforms were made of.

P- They must have had a lot of faith in your artistic abilities to think you'd be able to create a police uniform and make your escape using a 2 inch blue ribbon.

AP- Yeah, with a two inch ribbon I was going to try to weave this uniform. So I tried to explain to the guard but he didn't want to hear it. He called the sergeant, who said he'd go check on it with his superiors, and I figured cool, I'll get the ribbon no problem. But he came back and said, "look, you can't have it because it's blue." What eventually happened was I wrote the Senator who sent me the ribbon, who wrote me back. I'd told him I'd grieved it. There's a process where a prisoner can write a grievance, sort of like a process where you let some steam off. Prisoners rarely win, but in this case I figured I had to win. The Senator wrote back and asked me to let him know what happened with my grievance because they might have to change the color of the ribbon.

P- And did they?

AP- No, eventually someone came to their senses. The grievance hearing didn't happen, it didn't get to that point. I got the ribbon after a while. The ribbon was given by a guard to the hobby shop teacher to give to me because I was too low on the ladder for him to personally give me my ribbon. That's the kind of mentality you deal with in prisons.

P- So, do you see any shift in how politicians and police perceive and/or wage the War on Drugs?

AP- I do see a shift especially among the black and Latino caucus in the NY State Assembly, not in the Senate, not among the Republicans. Maybe some, but not a lot, of moderate Republicans. I lobby a lot in Albany, and there's a different opinion behind closed doors as to these drug laws. "Yeah, these are terrible laws, I don't support them," but they can't go out and support changes because they'd loose their constituency but behind the doors they all know it doesn't work right. But now there's a lot of black and Latino caucuses especially that support a change in the Rockefeller Drug Laws. For the first time in 30 years, we have the Governor, the Senate, and the Assembly that all want change, but at the end of the last session that couldn't come to an agreement, at this point there's a stalemate on it, which is why it is so important for us activists and advocates to go out and protest, to raise out voices and make a lot of noise to let them know we're still involved in this issue.

P- Now aren't they on the one hand moving towards small reforms and on the other trying to increase penalties for things like marijuana?

AP- It's always about that. The Governor wants to change the Rockefeller Drug Laws, in some ways, really watered down. I'd rather have no changes at all. They want to do away with parole, they want to increase penalties for marijuana. Politicians never want to give up anything for free. They always something for something.

P- Do you really think that it would be political suicide even today if a politician stood up and said flat out, "these laws are fucked up, let make some changes"? I mean among their voters. Their financial backers are probably going to be upset at this kind of stance, but there does seem to be a lot of groundswell among the common people that the War is wrong.

AP- It depends on their constituency and where you live. If you live in redneck Republican territory where everybody is conservative, if a politician came out suddenly, like say Dale Volker, a staunch Republican who is all for the Rockefeller Drug Laws, who has 9 prisons in his district, the 59th NY Senate District. This is why he supports the Rockefeller Drug Laws. Let's say he came out and was opposed to the Rockefeller Drug Laws, his constituency wouldn't be too happy.

P- Because he's got all those prisons.

AP- Right, He would probably loose his office. But let's say someone from like the South Bronx, from an area like that, where drugs are prevalent so people know about the issue, it's not going to hurt the politician that much to advocate for changing the drug laws.

P- Plus people in those areas see a lot of families broken apart.

AP- Exactly. So I think there's a difference now. I think that since the Senate, the Assembly, and the Governor all want change, I think it's different than it was 5 years ago when no one wanted change. I think then it would have been total political death. Right now I think it's really not, it's a smart issue to get involved with, but politics are politics. Some people are just not going to do it because of their politics.

P- Do you yourself hold any political affiliation?

AP- I'm a registered Democrat. I was actually registered for 5 years but couldn't vote because I was on parole. I just got off parole in February, so now is the first time I'm going to be able to vote coming up so I'm definitely going to exercise that right.

P- Now, I know that Bush and his ilk are talking about ratcheting up the War on Drugs, and already have in many ways. But under Clinton we also had this huge explosion in the prison population and in the Drug Laws. He himself might not have admitted inhaling, but he at least held the marijuana in his hand and put it to his lips. Do you see much of a difference between the Democrats and the Republicans on this issue?

AP- On the federal level? I think basically there's not too much difference, because we're talking about politics across the board, so politicians are afraid of supporting change at that level. There's some, like Democrats who support some change in mandatory minimum sentencing laws, but at the federal level I don't think there's much difference.

P- Do you have any ideas on how to build more and stronger ties between the different ethnic communities on this issue? I know that in NY, well actually, most all of the conferences and events on the Drug War, with the notable exception of Drug War Awareness Project's recent party on 4-20, that there are almost all white faces in the audience, and almost all white faces up on stage speaking and presenting. Very rarely do I see blacks and Latinos at these events. Do you have any ideas on how to bridge the cultural divides, or whatever it is that's keeping the communities apart?

AP- Well, in my experience, in the places that I've gone to in reference to conferences, I've seen a majority of black and Latinos, with whites, so I don't know the audiences you're talking about.

P- That's precisely what I'm talking about. The places I'm going to, as a white guy, I see mainly white folk, but you, a Latino, see mainly blacks and Latinos. How do we get these groups together, to work together?

AP- I really can't answer that.

P- No ideas?

AP- I think it's a universal issue that everyone should be involved with because the War on Drugs, although clearly racist in many ways, has no class barriers, no color barriers. It affects everybody. The prosecutorial tools that were created to curb the drug epidemic then in turn those laws are used against the average citizens who doesn't even use drugs, like exclusionary rules, the 4th Amendment, search and seizure…

P- Asset Forfeiture.

AP- Yeah, forfeiture laws, these are all tools that prosecutors use. They use them beyond their intended purposes. They go to the average citizen, where you can even lose your home for something like a marijuana cigarette.

P- Do you focus your efforts mainly in NY State, or do you also work on national efforts for reform?

AP- I work with the Kunstler Fund for Racial Justice mainly on the Rockefeller Drug Laws, and at the federal level I work with groups like FAMM, (Families Against Mandatory Minimum Sentencing), I've been to Washington DC and lobbied on Capitol Hill. Because the Rockefeller Drug Laws really touched me on a personal level, that's my main area of concentration. Plus, I live in NY. I've been involved with different groups, November Coalition, FAMM, groups that do work more on a national level.

P- Ok. Does being an ex-con hinder you in any way, say in your work as a legal assistant?

AP- Oh, a lot. For instance, let's say in this community here, this job. There's a lot of people here with PhD's, attorneys, people from sort of the higher echelons of society, went to the best schools. What I've calmed down is promoting what I'm about here at the firm. At first people used to hear about me and knew I was an artist. But they really didn't know what kind of artist, so when I exposed myself and they saw the art and heard the story that I was in prison, it created a stigma.

P- Just like that?

AP- Just like that. It's a stigma I'll live with all my life. They look at me different, maybe they won't even say hi to me. That's some people. Not all people, but a majority of people in this firm. I think it's a stigma. My next door neighbor doesn't know I'm an ex-prisoner. I'm always paranoid. I've been living there in this private house, with a little Italian couple who love me, yet they don't know my past. I remember when people would be coming over to do interviews, with all their production equipment, and I used to freak out because I have a small apartment and all this stuff would be out in the hall, and there's a knock on the door. Who is it but my landlord. She asked what was going on and I told her they were making a film about my art. She said, "ooh, can I see it when it's done?" I said sure, but I never showed it to her. Things like that. I always live with this stigma, carrying a Scarlet Letter as I call it. It's universal the stigma I carry, it tainted me, but it also gave me courage and strength to go on in a positive way. I use it as a tool now. Because what happens when you do an extraordinary amount of time, many people want to put it aside and go on with their life. But with me, I use it as a vehicle to become who I am, this activist involved in change, positive change and transformation to make things better for people still inside and people outside, yet still wear this Scarlet Letter, that label as a convicted felon.

P- One last question. Do you find it a bit ironic that you served 12 years in prison under the Rockefeller Drug laws, and now you work in the Rockefeller Center?

AP- I work at Rockefeller Center. I think it's very appropriate that I help stage rallies at 50th and 5th at the Rockefeller Center. Everything has evolved around the Rockefeller Center, so this is the place for me to be.

From *Drugwar.com* May 1, 2002. © 2002 by Kalyx.com.

Trends in State Parole

The More Things Change, the More They Stay the Same

BY TIMOTHY A. HUGHES, DORIS JAMES WILSON AND ALAN J. BECK, PH.D.

AT YEAR-END 2000 more than 652,000 adults were under state parole supervision, up from 509,700 ten years earlier. During the year 441,600 adults entered parole supervision and 432,200 exited. Although prison release rates dropped sharply early in the decade, the number under parole supervision grew exponentially (averaging ten percent per year) before peaking in 1992. At the same time, despite a decade of reform and change, including enhancements in sentencing, added restrictions on prison releases and experimentation with community supervision and monitoring, parolee success rates remained unchanged. Among state parole discharges, 42 percent successfully completed their term of supervision in 2000, 45 percent successfully completed their term in 1990.

These findings and others appeared in *Trends in State Parole, 1990–2000*, a special report issued by the Bureau of Justice Statistics in October 2001. The report not only documents the nature and extent of growth of state parole populations but presents statistics on parole success and failure. The report, updated specially for *Perspectives*, underscores the complex interaction between incarceration and post-release supervision policies.

Growth in parole linked to incarceration trends

Changes in sentencing laws and prison release policies, as well as the increased likelihood of a conviction and incarceration if arrested, spurred the growth of the prison population in the 1980s and early 1990s. Since 1980 incarceration rates have soared but are now beginning to stabilize. At mid-year 2001, the rate of incarceration in federal or state prisons and local jails was 690 inmates per 100,000 adult U.S. residents up from 458 in 1990. However, the 1.1 percent growth in the number of prison inmates for the 12 months ending June 30, 2001 was significantly lower than the 5.8 percent average annual increase since 1990. It was also the lowest annual rate recorded since 1972.

A consequence of the growth in imprisonment is a corresponding change over time in the number of people under community supervision. Of the people who are admitted to prison, most return to the community at some point—either released from prison by completing their sentence, by discretionary parole or by mandatory parole. In general, parole is a period of conditional supervision after serving time in prison. Discretionary parole exists when a parole board has authority to conditionally release prisoners based on a statutory or administrative determination of eligibility. Mandatory parole generally occurs in jurisdictions using determinate sentencing statutes in which inmates are conditionally released from prison after serving a specified portion of their original sentence minus any good time earned. About 95 percent of all inmates currently in state prison will be released, and 80 percent will have a period of parole or post-custody supervision.

The number of adults under state parole supervision more than tripled between 1980 and 2000 (from 196,786 to 652,199). While growth in the state parole population had nearly stabilized by yearend 2000, the largest increase occurred between 1980 and 1992. During this period, the number of adults on parole grew ten percent annually. After 1992, following more than a decade of rapid growth, annual increases in the number of adults on state parole slowed dramatically, increasing at an average annual rate of 0.7 percent **(Figure 1)**.

From 1990 to 2000, the state parole population grew at a slower rate than the state prison population. During this period, parolees increased 30 percent, compared to a 75 percent increase in state prisoners. On average, the parole population increased 2.6 percent per year, while the prison population rose 5.7 percent per year. The lower rate of growth in parole supervision reflects changes in sentencing and parole release policies that have resulted in increasing lengths of stay in prison and declining prison release rates. However, growth in the prison population has slowed since 1995 and recent data suggest

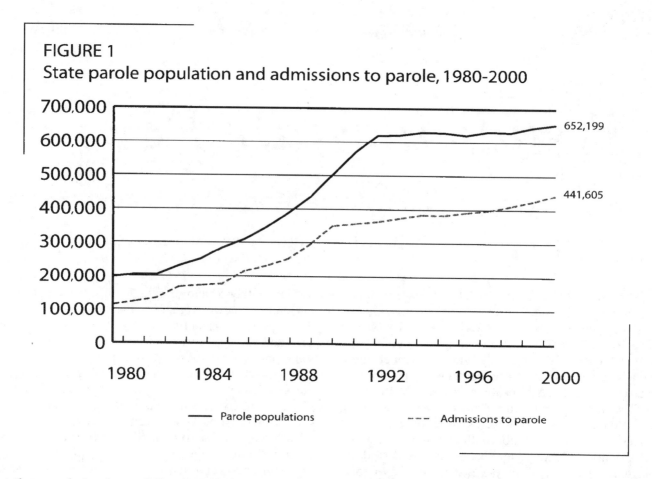

FIGURE 1

State parole population and admissions to parole, 1980-2000

— Parole populations   - - - Admissions to parole

that the population has stabilized. Underlying the dramatic slow down in the rate of growth in state prison populations has been a rise in the number of prison releases. In the last six months of 2000, the state prison population actually dropped by 0.1 percent, the first measured decline since 1972. In the last 12 months ending June 30, 2001, the number under state jurisdiction increased 0.4 percent. (Figure 2).

States reduced the discretion of parole boards

Trends in state parole populations have been affected by a movement from discretionary release toward mandatory parole release and by the enactment of truth-in-sentencing legislation. Historically, most state inmates were released to parole supervision after serving a portion of an indeterminate sentence based on a parole board decision. In 1977, 69 percent of offenders released from state prison were released by a parole board. Good time reduction and other earned time incentives permitted officials to individualize the amount of punishment or leniency an offender received and provided a means to manage the prison population.

This discretion led to criticism that some offenders were punished more harshly than others for similar offenses and to complaints that overall sentencing and release laws were lenient on crime. By 1989, eight states

(California, Florida, Illinois, Indiana, Maine, Minnesota, Oregon and Washington) had abolished discretionary parole and in 20 others, the majority of prison releases were through expiration of sentence or mandatory parole release.

Continuing the shift away from release by a parole board, an additional eight states (Arizona, Delaware, Kansas, Mississippi, North Carolina, Ohio, Virginia and Wisconsin) abolished discretionary parole in the 1990s. Most of the remaining states further restricted parole by setting specific standards offenders must meet to be eligible for release. As a result, parole boards are no longer the dominant mechanism by which inmates are released from state prison. More inmates are now released by state statutes that mandate release after inmates serve a specified portion of their sentence. After 1980, mandatory parole increased from 19 percent of releases from prison to 39 percent in 2000, while discretionary parole decreased from 55 percent to 24 percent.

In absolute numbers, releases by state parole boards peaked in 1992 (at 170,095), dropping to 136,130 in 2000 (Table 1). Mandatory parole releases steadily increased, from 26,735 in 1980 to 116,857 in 1990. By 1995 the number of mandatory releases exceeded the number of discretionary releases. In 2000, 221,414 state prisoners were released by mandatory parole, an 89 percent increase from 1990. The number of annual releases via mandatory parole is

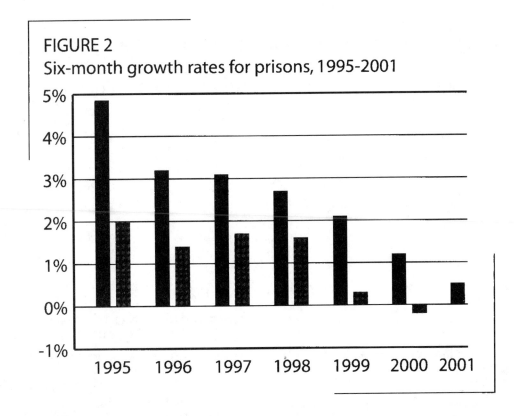

FIGURE 2
Six-month growth rates for prisons, 1995-2001

expected to continue to grow over the next several years. Instead of entering prison faced with an uncertain sentence suggestive of a rehabilitative model of criminal justice, more and more inmates are virtually guaranteed a release date upon admission to prison.

Growth in releases expected as inmates complete enhanced sentences

Several factors influenced the flow of offenders from prison to parole supervision, such as fluctuations in prison release rates, an increase in elapsed time served by offenders, and changes in release policies. Prison release rates declined from 37 percent in 1990 to 32 percent in 2000. Though this is a modest percentage difference, when applied to the growing number of inmates in prison at some time during the year, the drop implies at least 90,000 fewer releases in 2000 as a result of the five percent drop in the annual release rate since 1990. Nevertheless, the number of prisoners released from state prison has grown from 405,400 in 1990 to an expected 595,000 in 2001. (See box, State Prison.)

While violent offenders accounted for most of the growth among those in prison, drug offenders comprised an increasing percentage of prison releases as well as entries to parole. Nearly 33 percent of state prison releases in 1999 were drug offenders (up from 26 percent in 1990 and 11 percent in 1985) **(Figure 3)**. In contrast to drug offenders, the release of violent offenders has remained stable, while property offenders have dropped sharply.

Approximately 24 percent of releases were violent offenders in 1999 (compared to 26 percent in 1990), and 31 percent were property offenders (down from 39 percent).

State Prison	
Year	**Releases***
1990	**405,400**
1995	**455,100**
1999	**543,000**
2000	**571,000**
2001 (projected)	**595,000**

Excluding escapees, AWOL's and transfers.

Drug law violators increasing among parole entries

Between 1990 and 1999, annual releases from state prison to parole supervision grew by an estimated 78,900 inmates. Drug offenders accounted for 61 percent of that increase, followed by violent offenders (23 percent), and public-order offenders (15 percent). The number of property offenders released to parole declined from 1990 to 1999. Among the nearly 424,000 entries to parole in 1999,

TABLE 1

Method of release from state prison, for selected years, 1980–2000

YEAR	All Releases	Discretionary Parole	Mandatory Parole Parole	Other conditional	Expiration of sentence
1980	143,543	78,602	26,735	9,363	20,460
1985	206,988	88,069	62,851	15,371	34,489
1990	405,374	159,731	116,857	62,851	51,288
1992	430,198	170,095	126,836	60,800	48,971
1995	455,140	147,139	177,402	46,195	66,017
2000	570,966	136,130	221,414	66,958	110,441

Note: Based on prisoners with a sentence of more than one year who were released from state prison. Counts are for December 31 of each year.

drug offenders accounted for 35 percent, followed by property offenders (31 percent), violent offenders (24 percent) and public-order offenders (9 percent).

Offenders serve more time and a greater portion of their sentence before release

Reflecting statutory and policy changes that required offenders to serve a larger portion of their sentence before release, all offenders released for the first time in 1999 served on average 49 percent of their sentence, up from 38 percent in 1990. Among all state inmates released from prison for their first time on their current offense (first releases), the average time served in prison increased from 22 months in 1990 to 29 months in 1999. Released inmates had also served an average of five months in local jails prior to their admission to prison. Overall, released inmates had served a total of 34 months in 1999, compared to 28 months in 1990. Of the four major offense categories, violent offenders served the highest percentage of their sentence (55 percent) in 1999, followed by public-order (51 percent), property (46 percent) and drug offenders (43 percent).

Much of the increase in time served is likely due to the enactment of the truth-in-sentencing standards that in general specify a portion of the sentence an offender must serve in prison. By the end of 2000, the federal truth-in-sentencing standard that requires that Part 1 violent offenders serve not less than 85 percent of their sentence in prison before becoming eligible for release had been adopted by 29 states and the District of Columbia. Part 1 violent offenses, as defined by the Federal Bureau of Investigation's Uniform Crime Reports, include murder, non-negligent manslaughter, rape, robbery and aggravated assault.

By adopting this standard, states could receive truth-in-sentencing funds under the Violent Offender Incarceration and Truth-in-Sentencing (VOITIS) incentive grant program as established by the 1994 Crime Act. VOITIS

TABLE 2

Time served in prison and jail for first releases from State prison, by method of release, 1990 and 1999

Type of release and offense	Mean time served	
	1990	1999
Discretionary release	29 months	35 months
Violent	49 months	59 months
Property	25 months	31 months
Drug	20 months	28 months
Public-order	18 months	21 months
Mandatory release	27 months	33 months
Violent	41 months	47 months
Property	23 months	30 months
Drug	20 months	27 months
Public-order	19 months	25 months
Expiration of sentence	31 months	36 months
Violent	44 months	52 months
Property	27 months	30 months
Drug	21 months	29 months
Public-order	28 months	25 months

Note: Based on prisoners with a sentence of more than one year. Excludes persons released from prison by escape, death, transfer, appeal or detainer.

grants can be used by states to build or expand prison capacity. States not adopting the federal standard may have other truth-in-sentencing policies that specify a certain percentage of the sentence to be served prior to release.

At year-end 2000, nearly three-quarters of the parole population was in states that met the federal 85 percent standard. Nine of the ten states with the largest parole

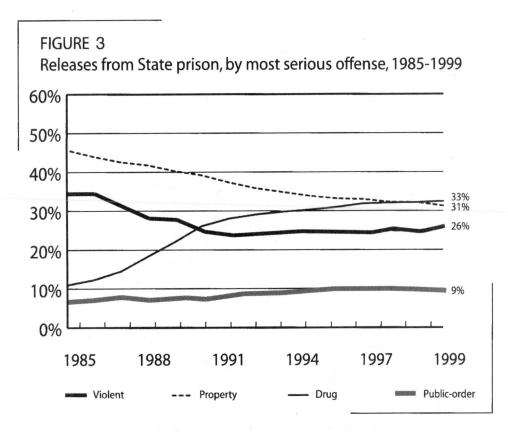

FIGURE 3

Releases from State prison, by most serious offense, 1985-1999

populations in 2000 met the federal truth-in-sentencing standard for violent offenders. Texas, with the second largest parole population, required violent offenders to serve 50 percent of their sentence before becoming eligible for release.

The result of longer lengths of stay due to truth-in-sentencing (in combination with the increased average age of prison admissions) has been an aging of the parole population. The average age of prisoners released to parole increased from 31 years in 1990 to 34 years in 1999. An estimated 109,300 state prisoners paroled in 1999 (26 percent of all entries to parole) were age 40 or older. This was more than double the number of prisoners age 40 or older who entered parole in 1990.

Inmates released by a parole board serve longer than mandatory parolees

Contrary to the widespread perception that reliance on parole board discretion implies early release, data from 30 states participating in BJS's National Corrections Reporting Program reveal that offenders released by parole boards actually serve more time in prison than other parolees. Overall, prisoners released in 1999 by discretionary parole for the first time on the current sentence had served an average of 35 months in prison and jail, while those released through mandatory parole had served 33 months **(Table 2)**. In 1990, and in every other year during the 1990s, the average time served by discretionary re-

leases exceeded the time served by mandatory parole releases. The largest disparities appear among violent prisoners released in 1999—those released through discretionary parole served an average 59 months, those released through mandatory parole served 47 months.

Though time served by discretionary releases exceeded the time served by mandatory releases, discretionary releases served a smaller percentage of their prison sentences before release. In 1999 discretionary releases served 37 percent of their total prison sentence (up from 34 percent in 1990); mandatory releases served 61 percent of their sentence (up from 55 percent).

Re-releases an increasing portion of parole entries

Among all parole entries, the percentage that had been re-released rose between 1990 and 1999. Re-releases are persons leaving prison after having served time either for a violation of parole or other conditional release or for a new offense committed while under parole supervision. In 1990, 27 percent of entries to parole were re-releases; in 1999, 45 percent were re-releases. During 1999 an estimated 192,400 re-releases entered parole, more than double the 94,900 re-releases in 1990.

These data highlight the significant number of individuals cycling through our nation's prisons. Underlying the dramatic growth in state prison populations has been a rise in parole violators returned to prison. Between 1990

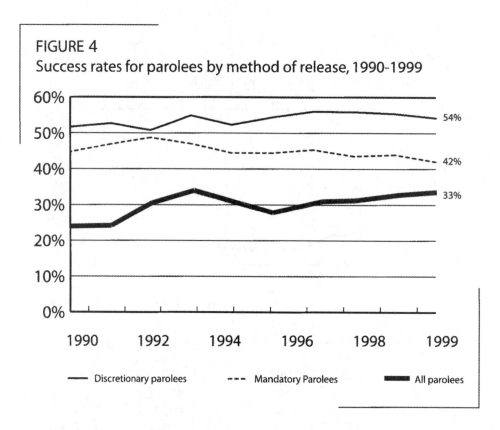

FIGURE 4
Success rates for parolees by method of release, 1990-1999

Discretionary parolees — — — Mandatory Parolees ▬▬ All parolees

and 2000, the number of returned parole violators increased 52 percent (from 133,900 to 203,600), while the number of new court commitments increased 8 percent (from 323,100 to 350,400). As percent of all admissions to prison, parole violators totaled 35 percent in 2000. As a consequence, these previously released offenders, who have failed under parole supervision in the past, represent a growing portion of subsequent parole entries.

After having been returned to prison for a parole or conditional release violation, re-releases served on average 13 months in prison in 1999. From 1990 to 1999 their average time served in prison following re-admission increased by two months.

Success rates stable despite changes in release policies

A comparison of the rates of success on parole reveals a complex relationship between the methods of parole (discretionary or mandatory), the type of offender (first release or re-release) and the length of time served. Success rates also vary by other risk factors, including age, gender and type of offense.

Despite dramatic changes in the criminal justice system over the last decade, the outcomes of parole supervision remained relatively consistent with the levels observed in 1990. Of the 410,613 discharges from State parole in 1999, 42 percent successfully completed their term of supervision, 43 percent were returned to prison or jail, and ten percent absconded (**Figure 4**). In 1990, 45 percent

of state parole discharges were successful. Between 1990 and 1999 the percent successful among state parole discharges has ranged from 42 percent to 49 percent, without any distinct trend.

A successful discharge occurs when the offender is released by the parole authority after completing the term of conditional supervision. Unsuccessful discharges include revocations of parole, returns to prison or jail and absconders. Parolees who are transferred to other jurisdictions and those who die while under supervision are not included in the calculation of success/failure rates.

Success rates highest among parole board releases and first releases

In every year between 1990 and 1999, state prisoners released by a parole board had higher success rates than those released through mandatory parole. Among parole discharges in 1999, 54 percent of discretionary parolees were successful compared to 33 percent of those who had received mandatory parole. Between 1990 and 1999 the percent successful among discretionary parolees varied between 50 and 56 percent, while the percent successful among mandatory parolees ranged between 24 and 33 percent.

Success rates also varied by type of release. In every year during the 1990s, first releases to state parole were much more likely to have been successful than re-releases. Among state parole discharges in 1990, 56 percent of first releases successfully completed their supervi-

TABLE 3

Percent successful among parole discharges in California and all other states, 1995–1999

YEAR	California	Parole in all other States		
	All Parole	All	Mandatory	Discretionary
1995	22.7%	52.8%	64.0%	54.2%
1996	23.8%	56.6%	71.6%	55.8%
1997	22.8%	55.9%	67.2%	55.8%
1998	24.3%	54.5%	65.7%	55.2%
1999	25.2%	53.3%	63.9%	53.9%

Note: Based on prisoners with a sentence of more than one year who were released from State prison.

sion, compared to 15 percent of re-releases. Of offenders exiting parole in 1999, 63 percent of first releases were successful, compared to 21 percent of re-releases.

Among parole discharges in 1999 that had been released from prison for the first time on their current offense, mandatory parolees had a higher success rate (79 percent) than discretionary parolees (61 percent). Discretionary parolees in 1999 who had been re-released from prison were more likely to be successful (37 percent) than mandatory parolees (17 percent).

Success rates higher if California is excluded

The size and make-up of California's parole population, combined with the low percent of successful terminations (25 percent in 1999), affect the national rate of success for parole discharges **(Table 3)**. When data from California are removed from the analysis, the comparative rates of success for discretionary and mandatory parole change dramatically.

Overall, California accounted for nearly 30 percent of all state parole discharges during 1999. Discretionary parole, though available as a method of release, is rarely used in California. In 1999 more than 99 percent of California's parole discharges had received mandatory parole. When California data are excluded, the success rate for all parole discharges rises to 53 percent (from 42 percent), and the rate for mandatory parolees increases to 64 percent (from 33 percent) in 1999. In states other than California, success rates are found to be higher among prisoners released through mandatory parole than by a parole board.

Nevertheless, the differences in outcomes vary by type of release. Parole boards achieve significantly higher suc-

cess rates when releasing offenders who have previously violated parole. In 1999 37 percent of discretionary parolees who had been re-released were successful, compared to 17 percent of mandatory releases. Throughout the decade, success rates among discretionary re-releases were at least twice those of mandatory re-releases.

Half of all revoked parolees returned for technical violations

During 2000 more than 203,000 offenders were returned to prison for parole violations.

Based on interviews of inmates in state prison in 1997, approximately half of those returned annually are technical violators without a new sentence. Among technical violators, seven percent had an arrest for a new offense, 36 percent had a drug violation (including a positive test, possession, or failure to participate in treatment), 50 percent had absconded or failed to report to a parole office, and 40 percent had some other violation of parole (including failure to maintain employment, to pay fines, fees or restitution, having contact with known felons, or possessing a gun). Since violators often have more than one reason for revocation, the total of all reasons exceeded 100 percent.

As a consequence of the growing number of admissions for parole violations and the longer length of stay for the most serious of these violators, nearly a quarter of all state inmates in 1997 reported having been on parole at the time of the offense for which they were serving time. Nearly 70 percent of these violators reported having been arrested or convicted of a new offense. The percent with new offenses was higher among inmates in prison than among those returned each year, due to the longer time served by violators with new offenses.

Findings have implications for prison and paroling authorities

The changing characteristics of offenders entering parole may have important implications for developing policies and programs to adequately assist offenders when they return to the community. Such changes underscore the need to have pre-release treatment programs and adequate follow-up for drug offenders who represent the largest portion of the growth in parole entries. Though the largest source of growth in state prison populations has been the increased numbers of violent offenders entering prison and staying longer once incarcerated, drug offenders represent a major portion of those inmates cycling through prisons annually.

Other changes, including the aging of parole entries, increased length of time in prison, and statutorily-mandated release, have implications for strategies to transition offenders from prison to community supervision. A growing proportion of offenders both in prison and on parole are middle aged. In part, the aging of the prison and parole populations is due to longer lengths of stay in prison combined with higher numbers of returns to prison.

The expected reductions in recidivism due to age are offset by the growing percent of older inmates who previously violated parole. Since mandatory release policies may not permit an assessment of risk when inmates who previously failed are re-released, the risk of failure would be significantly higher for this new group of older inmates. The opportunity to conduct adequate risk assessments is undercut by statutory release requirements that replace the judgments of parole boards.

Regardless of the amount of discretion to determine who gets released and when, parole failure rates remain high and unchanged for nearly a decade. Correctional authorities have relatively little time to address the often complex array of problems inmates bring with them to prison and on to parole. A third of all released prisoners serve 12 months or less. On average, inmates released from prison spend nearly three years incarcerated and about two years on parole. Along with their criminal records, many have extensive histories of drug and alcohol abuse, mental illness, homelessness, illiteracy, joblessness and domestic violence. These factors are strongly related to success or failure following prison release and must be addressed if parole success rates are to be improved.

Despite efforts to improve public safety through incapacitation and enhanced punishment, the vast majority (95 percent) of today's inmates will be released. While a sudden wave of prison releases is not expected the number of inmates released annually will continue to grow. Without new efforts and added resources directed to community supervision, the flow back to prison will likely remain steady and troubling.

The report from which this article was derived, *Trends in State Parole, 1990–2000* (October 2001, NCJ 184735), can be viewed online at: http://www.ojp.usdoj.gov/bjs/.

Timothy A. Hughes and *Doris James Wilson* are statisticians at the Bureau of Justice Statistics and work in the Corrections Statistics Program Unit.

Allen J. Beck, Ph. D. is the chief of the unit, which is responsible for the collection and analysis of all national-level data on incarcerated and community-based populations.

INMATE REENTRY

and Post-Release Supervision:
The Case of Massachusetts

BY ANNE MORRISON PIEHL, PH.D.

Two stylized facts nominate prisoner reentry as essential to public safety: the large numbers of inmates released from correctional institutions and their high rates of recidivism. The tremendous expansion in the use of incarceration at the end of the last century has resulted in large numbers of inmates being released from prisons and jails. Of all those incarcerated in the nation's state prisons, 40 percent are expected to be released within 12 months and 73 percent in five years or less. Few inmates have life sentences, and few others die in prison, suggesting that over 95 percent of inmates expect to be released at some point in the future (Beck 2000). Nationwide, some 600,000 inmates are released from state and federal prisons each year. That means that approximately one out of every 300 adult Americans will be released from prison this year.[1]

Recently released inmates are likely to continue to be involved in crime and with the criminal justice system. A new report from the Bureau of Justice Statistics reveals that recidivism rates are high, regardless of how they are measured. Within three years of release, 67 percent of former inmates were rearrested for a serious offense, 47 percent were convicted of a new crime, 25 percent were

sentenced to a prison term for a new crime, and 52 percent were returned to prison for a new sentence or a violation of the terms of release (Beck and Levin 2002). The data in Table 1 show that much of the recidivism happens quite quickly. Nearly 30 percent of releases were rearrested within six months, and an additional 14 percent were arrested in the subsequent six months. Even for the recidivism measures reconviction and new sentence to prison, which one would expect to take longer to occur, rates of recidivism are higher in the first year than in later years. The period just following release appears to be particularly important in preventing recidivism. An earlier BJS study, of those released in 1983, showed arrest rates in three month intervals, finding the highest levels in the period just following release (Beck and Shipley 1989, Table 12).

Other research provides descriptions of the time following prison release, emphasizing the importance of the period immediately following release, including the first day out (Nelson, Deess and Allen 1999). It appears that the time from release through the first year is a pivotal time for ex-offenders, determining whether they resort to old habits or make a fresh start.

Table 1

Recidivism rates of prisoners released in 1994, BJS data from 15 states

(In each category, the cell indicates the percent recidivating for the first time during that period.)

Time after release	Rearrested	Reconvicted	New sentence to prison
6 months	29.9%	10.6%	5.0%
6 mo.–1 year	14.2%	10.9%	5.4%
1 year–2 years	15.1%	14.9%	8.4%
2 years–3 years	8.3%	10.5%	6.6%

Source: Langan and Levin (2002), Table 2.

Table 2
Terms of Release from the Massachusetts Department of Correction, 1999

Type of Release	Proportion of Releases
None/Release to Street	56%
Parole	29%
Release to Other Authority	15%

Source: Author's calculations from Table 21 of Massachusetts Department of Correction, A Statistical Description of Releases from Institutions in the Jurisdiction of the Massachusetts Department of Correction During 1999, September 2000.

Note: N = 3548.

The high recidivism numbers may not be surprising given that those behind bars tend to be poorly positioned to succeed in conventional society (Travis 2000. Travis, Solomon, and Waul 2001. LoBuglio 2001). Inmates generally have low levels of educational attainment, are quite likely to have substance abuse or mental health problems, generally do not have access to permanent housing, and may or may not have family support to assist them in the transition from life behind bars to civilian life. Their term of confinement may make locating employment and housing more difficult, as some employers and landlords are excluded from hiring or renting to ex-offenders and many others prefer not to interact with this population. Given past criminal behavior and these barriers, it is no surprise that many of those released from prison and jail end up returning, some of them quite soon after release.

These recidivism statistics indicate that those newly released from confinement are committing a substantial number of crimes, representing a substantial threat to public safety. The BJS study found that the fewer than 300,000 offenders they studied had accumulated nearly five million arrest charges within three years of release. It seems reasonable to extrapolate that number (double it) to correspond to the current nationwide figure of 600,000 newly released inmates. To give some context, the total is in the same ballpark as the number of index crimes reported annually by the FBI. At the same time, reincarcerating those who do re-offend brings with it substantial costs to the taxpayer, on the order of $30,000–$50,000 per year. Anything that we can do to improve the rate of successful reintegration of newly released prisoners is likely to pay substantial social dividends in safer streets, healthier families, more productive citizens, higher tax receipts and lower governmental expenditures. Yet, with the policy and political emphasis in past decades on fighting crime and implementing tougher sentencing laws, the topic of prison release has often been overlooked. In fact, as will be discussed later, some of the very actions taken to toughen the treatment of convicted offenders have actually made it harder to manage their eventual release.

Inmate Release

A combination of sentencing law and correctional practice determines the timing and conditions under which inmates are released, and these vary substantially from state to state. Through most of the century in most states, the management of the release of inmates fell to a parole board. Traditional parole served two distinct functions: discretionary release and post-release supervision. Discretionary release occurs when a parole board determines that an inmate should be released from confinement to serve the remainder of his or her sentence in the community. The second function concerns the supervision of ex-inmates who have been released by the parole board.

A variety of legislative and bureaucratic decisions over the past 25 years have changed this picture dramatically (Ditton and Wilson 1999 and Burke 1995). A move to greater predictability in sentencing substantially reduced the discretion of parole boards to grant release to inmates. Mandatory sentencing and truth in sentencing laws eliminated discretionary release for large numbers of inmates, as these laws specify mandatory release dates. Whatever their purpose, these changes weakened parole and, as a result, reduced the opportunity for post-incarceration supervision. Even in states that did not eliminate discretionary release, parole boards became more hesitant to grant it (Petersilia 1999). In sum, these reforms effectively eliminated discretionary release in many states. At the same time, some states have introduced programs of mandatory post-incarceration supervision. By 2000, the most common method of release from state prison was mandatory parole (Hughes, Wilson and Beck 2001). Under mandatory parole (or mandatory post-release supervision), the date of release is determined by statute and supervision is provided by the parole agency after release.

The introduction of mandatory post-incarceration supervision notwithstanding, the proportion of inmates released with no further supervision has increased. If a prisoner is released under the authority of a parole board, the conditions placed can include curfews, drug testing, mandatory programs to manage anger or improve other deficits, requirements of employment, and payment of restitution to victims. These conditions are intended to help former inmates "practice" civilian life, improve their chances of success in civilian life, and reduce their chances of further criminal activity.

Parole boards have to balance several, sometimes competing, goals. Decisions to grant discretionary release impact the individual inmate, of course, but also the community into which they are released. If the inmate released to the street unconditionally at the expiration of his term, the opportunity to craft an individualized program is lost and only usual policing activities will provide a restraint on subsequent criminal activity. The extent to which parole boards grant discretionary release provides incentives to current and future inmates to take full advantage of their time incarcerated to improve their chances of pa-

Table 3
Terms of Release by Security Level of the Correctional Institution

Type of Release	Maximum Security	Medium Security	Minimum Security	County/Out of State	Total
None/Release to Street	162 (68%)	1161 (56%)	608 (55%)	64 (50%)	1,995
Parole	19 (8%)	469 (23%)	500 (45%)	33 (26%)	1,021
Release to Other Authority	56 (24%)	441 (21%)	3 (<1%)	32 (25%)	532
Total	237	2071	1111	129	3,548

Source: Tabulations performed by the Research Department of the Massachusetts Department of Corrections.

role release. Thus, the existence and use of paroling authority can have an important impact on the success of rehabilitative programming within correctional facilities, and therefore on the rate of successful inmate reintegration. States generally release some portion of their inmates with conditions and some without, depending upon state sentencing law, the actions of the parole board, and the behavior of the inmate.[2] Nationally, of those released from state prison in 1999, 18 percent were released at the expiration of their sentence with no conditions placed on the former inmate (Hughes et al. 2001, Table 3).

Inmate Release in Massachusetts

Although national trends are instructive, variation across jurisdictions means that, necessarily, the general picture does not accurately represent any given locality. In this section, the state of Massachusetts is used as a case study to illustrate in somewhat more detail the policy questions around inmate release. It is somewhat difficult to compare Massachusetts to other states due to the particularly prominent role counties play in the housing of sentenced criminal offenders. In most states, counties hold only those convicted of misdemeanor (less serious) offenses, generally with sentences of one year or less. But in Massachusetts, criminal sentences requiring terms in secure facilities are often served both in state prisons run by the Department of Correction and in Houses of Correction run by the county sheriffs. While it is true that, as in other states, those with longer sentences are sent to the state prisons and those with shorter sentences tend to go to county facilities, the split is different. (For more detail on prisons and jails in Massachusetts, see Keough 1999 and Piehl 2002.) The current rule is that convicted offenders sent to county Houses of Correction will have sentences no longer than 2 1/2 years for any single count, which means that county facilities in Massachusetts hold many inmates who would be sent to state prisons if they had committed the crime in any other state.[3] When both the county and state systems in Massachusetts are considered together, changes in incarceration over time generally mimic the national trends.

In the commonwealth of Massachusetts, approximately 20,000 inmates are released from state and county facilities per year, a number which has increased nearly 25 percent since 1990.[4] Due to the shorter sentences in the counties, the majority of those released come from the various county facilities. (In 1998, 87 percent of those released were released from county facilities and 13 percent came from state prisons.) The number of releases per year is greater than the year-end number of inmates in the counties, while among state inmates, approximately 25 percent are released each year. Rates of recidivism appear to be somewhat lower in Massachusetts, but again, in the same ballpark (Massachusetts Department of Correction 2000).

Truth in Sentencing

Truth in sentencing reform in 1993,[5] among other things, greatly reduced the scope for supervision of former inmates. The law eliminated the "Concord" sentence, in which offenders were sentenced to terms at a state reformatory with wide latitude for the parole board to determine actual time served. The law also eliminated the split sentence to state prison, in which inmates were given a term to be served in prison as well as a term of probation to be served following release. The split sentence had been a common avenue through which the probation department supervised inmates following release. The probation department is part of the court system, and offenders with split sentences were supervised by probation officers upon their release from confinement. Because the probation department also establishes conditions of satisfactory behavior and provides surveillance, it functions somewhat like parole supervision. Although truth in sentencing removed this sentencing option of a split sentence (prison and probation) for state sentences, we will see below that judges have adapted to this provision, so that probation remains an important avenue under which ex-inmates are supervised. Truth in Sentencing also eliminated parole eligibility at one-third or two-thirds of the minimum sentence for state prison sentences and it eliminated statutory good time, in which inmates were granted a certain amount of time off their stated sentence.

These changes drastically reduced the scope for parole release, with the result that more prisoners were released without supervision. Another consequence of this legislation was a reduction in the incentive for inmates to conform to expectations of non-disruptive behavior and rehabilitative efforts while in prison. Although good time continues to be granted for program participation, inmates now have less reason to adapt their behavior to the desires of the parole board in anticipation of review of their case for discretionary release.[6]

Mandatory minimum sentencing laws for various crimes further reduced the scope of a variety of mechanisms to aid prisoner reentry. The legislature passed a number of laws in the 1980s and 1990s covering particular offenses that prohibited (for a specified time period) probation, parole, furlough, work release and earned good time. When these mandatory minimum sentences are long, judges are reluctant to give terms that are longer than the minimum. As a result, there is no scope for discretionary release and thus no post-incarceration supervision for those inmates convicted of these offenses, the very ones that were determined to require more stringent punishment. One way to look at this phenomenon is to compare the minimum sentence to the maximum sentence. If there is a large gap between the two, the parole board uses its discretion to determine the actual release date. Among those sentenced to state prison for offenses other than mandatory drug offenses in fiscal year 1999, 31 percent had minimum and maximum release dates that were less than one month apart. There has been a dramatic increase in this statistic over time—in fiscal year 1994, only 2 percent of such offenders had such little scope for discretionary release. For those sentenced for drug offenses under mandatory minimum sentencing laws, 57 percent had less than one month between the minimum and maximum. This proportion had doubled since 1994 (Massachusetts Sentencing Commission 2000b, Table 23). For these offenders, Massachusetts has effectively joined those states that have legislatively eliminated or gutted post-release supervision.

The Practice of Parole

The most important element of the charge of the Massachusetts Parole Board governing discretionary release is the criterion to be used. In order to grant conditional release, the parole board must judge that "there is a reasonable probability that, if such prisoner is released, he will live and remain at liberty without violating the law, and that his release is not incompatible with the welfare of society" (Massachusetts General Law chapter 127, section 130). Given the myriad responsibilities of the parole board, it is not surprising that actual practice changes somewhat over time.

During the same period when the number of inmates eligible for parole consideration declined, the parole board in Massachusetts, as in other parts of the country, reduced the rate at which it granted discretionary release. This change may reflect a change in public sentiment, a new view of the role of discretionary release within crim-

Table 4
Type of Release from Suffolk County House of Correction, January 2001

Type of Release	Proportion of Releases
None/Release to Street	49%
Parole	8%
Release to Other Authority	19%
Probation	23%

Source: Author's communication with Suffolk County House of Correction, October 2001.

Notes: N = 212. Those released to street include two people whose sentences were revoked.

inal justice, and/or a new fear among public officials of being seen as responsible for the release of criminal offenders. From 1990 to 1999, the likelihood of a state inmate receiving parole at a given hearing dropped by nearly a half (from 70 percent to 38 percent). During the same period, the likelihood of receiving parole for county inmates fell much more modestly (Massachusetts Parole Board 1999).

Perhaps an even more telling statistic about the operation of the parole board, however, is the impact on the behavior of inmates. Over this same period, an increasing number of inmates declined to have a parole hearing. Of those eligible for a parole hearing, 15 percent waived their right to a hearing in 1990 and 32 percent waived their right in 1999 (Massachusetts Parole Board 1999). In effect, waiving the right to a hearing eliminates the possibility of being granted discretionary release and, thus, being supervised after release. It is likely that at least some inmates were discouraged by the low rates of parole and decided not to bother seeking a hearing. It is also possible that some inmates decided it was better to finish their sentences in confinement, since the total amount of time available for parole release was not very substantial. It is also possible that some inmates find community supervision sufficiently unpleasant that they prefer institutional confinement (Petersilia and Deschenes, 1994). Whatever their reasons, in 1999, 4,744 inmates chose to be released with no supervision. It is an unusual law enforcement policy to allow inmates the responsibility for making the determination of how to serve their sentences.[7]

Pre-Release Practice of Correctional Institutions

Before release from the jurisdiction of the state department of correction or a county House of Correction, inmates often receive some preparation for that release. Some inmates spend a period of time in a halfway house, working during the day, spending evenings in substance abuse recovery meetings, and nights in the halfway house. Some inmates make plans for the release, perhaps initiating relationships in the community to ease their transition.

Some inmates have used their time behind bars to develop educational or vocational skills that will improve their employment prospects upon release. Existing evidence suggests that these programs are effective at reducing recidivism (LoBuglio 2001). Efforts to prepare inmates for release and supervision of those in halfway houses or other lower-security pre-release settings gives correctional institutions much in common with the parole board.

If these kinds of initiatives are universal, the transition from a correctional sentence to the community will not be abrupt. Rather, the transition will largely have occurred prior to release. One way to view the abruptness of the transition is to look at the security level from which a prisoner is released. In 1999, 13 percent of those released from the Massachusetts Department of Correction came from maximum security institutions, 43 percent from medium security and 44 percent from lower security. Over the decade of the 1990s, there has been a substantial decline in the proportion being released from the lowest levels of security. It is only in the lower-security prisons where there is some chance that inmates have the opportunity to begin to make the transition to living in the community. The high and growing proportion of releases coming from medium and maximum security indicates that there is more work to be done to help inmates successfully reenter civil society.

Conditions of Release

An inmate released from custody may or may not have conditions placed on their behavior, depending on the sentencing regime and the actions of the parole board. In addition, there are other ways in which inmates are released from prison under the authority of some law enforcement entity. One important reason for this is that inmates have complicated legal histories, some of which require further law enforcement action after the expiration of a given sentence. For example, the Immigration and Naturalization Service (INS) has been actively seeking to deport criminal aliens, particularly following the passage of several laws in the early 1990s that expanded its authority, responsibility and funding. Another example is that judges have developed sentencing practices that provide for post-incarceration supervision. They have done this primarily by structuring sentences that include terms of probation in addition to the terms of confinement. Therefore, while it is important to consider parole when studying what happens to inmates upon release from state and county correctional facilities, it is insufficient to stop at parole. One must consider other avenues of release.

Table 2 describes categories of release from the Massachusetts Department of Correction (DOC) in 1999. Given the length of terms served, this release cohort reflects sentencing law and practice from the early to mid-1990s. While only 29 percent of releases were paroled, 15 percent were released to other legal authorities: 6 percent to the INS, 7 percent to jurisdictions in which there were outstanding warrants for their arrest, and the remaining 2 percent to another federal or state authority. Of the 56 percent that were released to the street, some were supervised by the probation department. Despite diligent efforts, the author was unable to find any agency with knowledge of the number of inmates released from the DOC who were under probation supervision.[8] Note that for those who were not paroled, the timing of their release was determined by the original sentence (and the earning of good time for participation in productive activities while incarcerated), rather than by a discretionary decision.

More detail about those released from the DOC is reported in Table 3, in which the term of release is broken out by the security level of the prison that the inmate was held in at the time of release. The first cell of the table shows that 162 people were released directly to the street from maximum-security prisons in 1999. The majority of people paroled came from medium- and minimum-security prisons. It makes sense from the perspective of the parole board that the paroling rate from maximum-security prisons would be low. Nonetheless, from a larger policy perspective, all inmates are released from confinement at the expiration of their sentences and, from these numbers, we see that many are coming from higher levels of security (2308 of the 3548 released from DOC jurisdiction came from medium or maximum security). Table 3 indicates that more than half of the prisoners released from maximum- and medium-security prisons were released directly to the street. Among those released directly to the street, 8 percent came from maximum security while among those paroled (which implies post-incarceration supervision) fewer than 2 percent were from maximum security. (Recall that it is possible that some of the people released directly to the street are under probation supervision as well, but there is no information about the extent of this phenomenon.)

Comparable data are not collected from the various counties. Therefore, to get a sense of the forms of release from county Houses of Correction (HOC), information was collected about those released from the custody of the Suffolk County HOC in January 2001. Suffolk County has historically been the county housing the greatest number of inmates in the commonwealth and is the jurisdiction covering Boston. Table 4 reports the release types for those leaving the Suffolk County HOC in January. Of this group, only 8 percent were paroled. However, only 49 percent were released with no further law enforcement involvement. Twenty-three percent of releases were on probation following release and the remaining 19 percent went to other authorities (due to outstanding warrants or immigration problems). While it is important to bear in mind that other counties (or other times of year) may yield somewhat different proportions, these numbers clearly suggest that inmates leave correctional facilities under a variety of forms of supervision. Thus, an analysis of post-incarceration supervision must consider more than simply parole.

191

The importance of probation supervision following incarceration, particularly in recent years, can also be seen in sentencing data. Among those sentenced in 1999, approximately 40 percent of those sentenced to counties and about 40 percent of those sentenced to state prison have terms of probation to serve following release (Piehl 2002). In some situations, judges sentencing an inmate to state prison can require a term of probation following release by issuing a "from & after" (also known as "on & after") sentence. In these sentences, a judge can impose a sentence of incarceration for one criminal charge and a sentence of probation (to be served after the term of incarceration) for another criminal charge. Thus, while the split sentence to state prison was eliminated, offenders convicted of multiple charges may be sentenced to prison and probation. As current inmates come to the end of their prison terms, this use of post-incarceration probation will affect an increasing percentage of the releasee population, particularly for state prisoners.

It is worth noting that the individuals on probation following a term of incarceration constitute a small part of the probation department's workload. Among all probation sentences imposed, 16 percent are for post-release probation while the remainder is for community supervision and, perhaps, fines for less serious offenders (Massachusetts Sentencing Commission 2000b, Table 27). Those who are sentenced to post-release probation supervision are a heterogeneous population. Of this group, 42 percent were convicted of violent offenses, 24 percent property offenses, 19 percent drug offenses, 10 percent motor vehicle offenses, and 5 percent other offenses (author's calculations from Massachusetts Sentencing Commission 2000b, Table 28).

It is clear that sentencing plays a large part in how the process of release unfolds. Currently, only if there is scope for the parole board to act and the board chooses to approve discretionary release does post-release parole supervision happen. At the same time, a large proportion of inmates are under the supervision of the Probation Department following release. (Some inmates are even on probation and parole simultaneously. Because no agency keeps track of this information, nobody knows how many. Of those released from Suffolk County HOC in January 2001, six of the 18 paroled inmates were on probation, too.) The remainder walk out the door without anyone checking up on them or offering support.

Prisoner Reentry and Other Agencies

While judges and the parole board play central roles, there are a number of other entities concerned with the reentry into the community. All correctional facilities have some programming for inmates and many have initiatives specifically to prepare inmates for release. There are some obstacles often faced by institutions, including the difficulty of providing a secure facility, uncertainty about the timing of release, and restrictions on movement placed by sentencing law. Nonetheless, both the state and the counties provide a variety of voluntary and mandatory initiatives whose purpose is to increase the chance that offenders succeed once they are released. However, few correctional institutions take full advantage of the time inmates have available to improve their prospects in conventional society, therefore missing critical opportunities to improve prospects for successful reintegration to society. At the same time, a variety of governmental agencies reach out to the ex-inmate population to provide employment and other services. At the same time, there are non-profit and other initiatives that seek to assist ex-inmates with the transition, with varying degrees of scale and of success. In some locations, agencies are working together in innovative ways to provide incentives to released inmates to reduce criminal recidivism, but space constraints do not allow a detailed discussion of these efforts in Massachusetts or elsewhere.

One important entity for the current discussion of Massachusetts is the Office of Community Corrections (OCC) was established in 1996 in the Administrative Office of the Trial Court to facilitate cross-agency collaboration in the management of offenders in the community. The efforts and money of the OCC have certainly pushed forward the provision of supervision and services to offenders living in the community. These are welcome improvements. The OCC's philosophy is that offenders progress through decreasing levels of surveillance and program requirements. This gradual reduction in oversight has the potential to help a number of offenders gain their footing. However, there are cautionary notes about the prospect of OCC to solve all of the problems associated with the release of large numbers of prisoners. (To be fair, this was not the goal of the OCC.) First, the issue of multiple agencies being responsible for inmates is not resolved by creating a new agency. Inmates at OCC facilities are under the legal authority of various agencies, notably the courts, corrections and the parole board. Shifting between institutions with different lines of authority can be deleterious to the provision of services and programming (LoBuglio 2001). It can be difficult to align incentives across agencies, and offenders may be able to locate holes in the system if the level of coordination is insufficient. Second, a number of categories of offenders cannot be sentenced to a community corrections center, due to exclusions specified in the enabling legislation or to mandatory sentencing laws. As we have seen before, due to a concern for public safety, some of those who pose the greatest risk to public safety are left out of these promising initiatives.

Conclusion

The point of transition from prison to the community provides an opportunity to improve public safety. Even a modest reduction in recidivism would yield substantial reductions in criminal victimization and in criminal justice expense. Yet, recent reforms have not only not taken advantage of this opportunity, but have often times made it harder to manage inmate release. Often, as the Massachusetts analysis shows, those most in need of supervision are the least likely to receive it. Mandatory sentencing laws and restrictions on community placement are some reforms responsible for this circumstance.

At one time, the multiple goals associated with managing inmate reentry through discretionary release decisions, choices of supervision mode, and offers of support services were juggled by parole agencies. Now, the responsibility is more diffuse. Although some agencies and partnerships have been quite innovative in dealing with inmate reentry, these efforts are by no means systematic. Two dramatic gaps in our knowledge provide the best evidence that inmate reentry has been overlooked in criminal justice policy. First, there is little research on the best practices of post-incarceration supervision (e.g., length of time, monitoring intensity, role of technical violations). Second, it is difficult and time consuming even to assemble to most basic information on those being released from prison. These indicate that we have not been doing a good job in this arena. They also indicate that improvements in policy and practice may well have high returns.

Endnotes

1. This is a rough calculation. According to estimates from the U.S. Census Bureau (www.census.gov) the population is approximately 285 million, of whom 25.7 percent are under age 18 and 12.4 percent are over 64. Dividing 600,000 inmates by the population age 18 through 64 yields the 1 in 300 figure.

2. California is a notable exception, having eliminated discretionary parole for all inmates except lifers and established mandatory parole for all others.

3. The statistics collected and reported by the federal government only include inmates held in state prisons. As a result, a far higher proportion of inmates in Massachusetts are excluded than in other states. To make comparisons yet more difficult, sometimes there are changes in the rules that determine where particular sentences are to be served. For example, the proportion of inmates held in county Houses of Correction rather than in state prisons has increased substantially over time. This means that looking at state figures alone is misleading.

4. Because the Houses of Correction are run by 13 different sheriffs, data collection efforts are not coordinated. These estimates come from Clausen (2000), and were derived from Department of Correction publications on inmate counts and new commitments.

5. Chapter 432 of the Acts of 1993, "An Act to Promote the Effective Management of the Criminal Justice System through Truth-in-Sentencing."

6. It should be noted that some of the move toward more determinate sentences happened before the Truth in Sentencing law. In 1993, at the time of the Truth in Sentencing legislation, for example, 37 percent of all sentences for males committed to the state Department of Correction were either split or "Concord" (reformatory) sentences, down from 46 percent in 1984 (Massachusetts Sentencing Commission 2000a, Table 2.)

7. The practice of the Massachusetts Parole Board may be changing, however. Under new leadership, the board has developed a reentry program. One change that has already occurred is how the board conducts hearings. As of November, 2000, the board began conducting all hearings for parole eligible offenders in person. This means that Parole Board members travel to county and state correctional facilities to hear inmates present their cases. It is too soon to tell if this change will impact either the rate at which discretionary release is granted or the rate at which inmates seek parole hearings, as statistics are not yet available. But early reports indicate an increase in the proportion of hearings that result in approval of discretionary release. The board is also considering implementing a program of graduated sanctions. While currently in the early stages, the reentry initiative has the potential to change important elements of parole supervision. Nevertheless, these reforms will not change the fundamental problem that those most in need of post-incarceration supervision may not receive it because of current sentencing laws.

8. Although the federal Bureau of Justice Statistics collects data intended to cover those under probation supervision, Massachusetts does not report this number. (Author's communication with BJS and Massachusetts DOC research staff.)

References

Beck, Allen J. *State and Federal Prisoners Returning to the Community: Findings from the Bureau of Justice Statistics,* presented at the First Reentry Courts Initiative Cluster Meeting, Washington, D.C. (April 13, 2000).

Beck, Allen J. and Bernard Shipley. *Recidivism of Prisoners Released in 1983,* Bureau of Justice Statistics Special Report, U.S. Department of Justice, NCJ 116261 (April 1989).

Burke, Peggy B. *Abolishing Parole: Why the Emperor has No Clothes,* American Probation and Parole Association (1995).

Clausen, Matthew N. *Prisoner Reintegration in Massachusetts,* Masters' thesis, John F. Kennedy School of Government, Harvard University (2000).

Community Resources for Justice. *Returning Inmates: Closing the Public Safety Gap.* Boston, Mass., monograph (2001).

Ditton, Pamela M. and Doris James Wilson. *Truth in Sentencing in State Prisons,* Bureau of Justice Statistics Special Report, NCJ 170032 (January, 1999).

Hughes, Timothy A., Doris James Wilson, and Allen J. Beck. *Trends in State Parole, 1990–2000,* Bureau of Justice Statistics Special Report, U.S. Department of Justice, NCJ 184735 (October 2001).

Keough, Robert. *Prisons and Sentencing in Massachusetts: Waging a More Effective Fight Against Crime,* Boston, MA: Massachusetts Institute for a New Commonwealth (1999).

Kleiman, Mark A. R. "Community Corrections as the Front Line in Crime Control," *UCLA Law Review,* vol. 46 (1999) pp. 1909–1925.

Langan, Patrick A. and David J. Levin. *Recidivism of Prisoners Released in 1994,* Bureau of Justice Statistics Special Report, U.S. Department of Justice, NCJ 193427 (June 2002).

LoBuglio, Stefan. "Time to Reframe Politics and Practices in Correctional Education," in *The Annual Review of Adults Learning and Literacy, Volume II,* National Center for the Study of Adult Learning and Literacy (2001).

Massachusetts Department of Correction. *The Background Characteristics and Recidivism Rates of Releases from Massachusetts Correctional Institutions during 1995* (May 2000).

Massachusetts Parole Board. *10-year Trends, 1990–1999* (1999).

Massachusetts Sentencing Commission. *Survey of Sentencing Practices: Truth in Sentencing Reform in Massachusetts* (October 2000a).

Massachusetts Sentencing Commission. *Survey of Sentencing Practices, FY 1999* (January 2000b).

Nelson, Marta, Perry Deess, and Charlotte Allen. *First Month Out: Post-Incarceration Experiences in New York City,* Vera Institute of Justice, monograph (1999).

Petersilia, Joan. *When Prisoners Return to the Community: Political, Economic, and Social Consequences,* Research in Brief—Sentencing & Corrections: Issues for the 21st Century, Washington, DC: U.S. Department of Justice, National Institute of Justice (November 2000).

Petersilia, Joan. "Parole and Prisoner Reentry in the United States," in Michael Tonry & Joan Petersilia (eds.), *Prisons (Crime and Justice: A Review of Research* vol. 26), Chicago, Ill.: University of Chicago Press (1999).

Petersilia, Joan. "Probation and Parole," in Michael Tonry (ed.), *Handbook on Crime and Punishment,* Oxford University Press (1998) pp. 563–588.

Petersilia, Joan and Elizabeth Piper Deschenes. "What Punishes? Inmates Rank the Severity of Prison vs. Intermediate Sanctions," *Federal Probation,* vol. 58, no. 1, (March 1994) pp. 3–8.

Piehl, Anne Morrison. *From Cell to Street: A Plan to Supervise Inmates after Release,* Boston, MA: Massachusetts Institute for a New Commonwealth (January 2002).

Travis, Jeremy. *But They All Come Back: Rethinking Prisoner Reentry.* Research in Brief—Sentencing & Corrections: Issues for the 21st Century, Washington, D.C.: U.S. Department of Justice, National Institute of Justice (May 2000).

Travis, Jeremy, Amy L. Solomon, and Michelle Waul. *From Prison to Home: The Dimensions and Consequences of Prisoner Reentry,* Washington, D.C.: Urban Institute (2001).

Note: *This article is based on From Cell to Street: A Plan to Supervise Inmates After Release, which was funded by a grant to the Massachusetts Institute for a New Commonwealth (MassINC) from the Gardiner Howland Shaw Foundation. Points of view or opinions stated in this document do not necessarily represent the official position or policy of MassINC or the Shaw Foundation. The full report published by MassINC is available at www.massinc.org.*

Anne Morrison Piehl, Ph.D. is with the John F. Kennedy School of Government at Harvard University.

Rethinking the Death Penalty

Are the growing doubts justified?

BY KENNETH JOST

Most Americans still favor the death penalty, but support has declined in the past five years. Critics point to documented attacks on the reliability and fairness of court procedures in capital cases. They claim too many death sentences are reversed on appeal and that flaws in the system, including inadequate defense counsels, create an unacceptable risk of executing an innocent person. Supporters of capital punishment say legal safeguards are adequate and that no innocent person has been put to death in recent years. The changing climate can be seen in the enactment of state laws to limit the death penalty and in cases before the Supreme Court, which is set to decide whether it is unconstitutional to execute mentally retarded offenders.

THE ISSUES

Daryl Atkins never did well in school. He never lived on his own or held a job. He scored 59 on a standard intelligence test—below the benchmark IQ level of 70 commonly used to define mental retardation.

Atkins' mental deficiencies did not, however, prevent a jury in southeastern Virginia from sentencing him to death for the 1996 robbery-abduction-killing of a U.S. airman.

The Virginia Supreme Court was also unmoved. "We are not willing to commute Atkins' sentence of death to life imprisonment merely because of his IQ score," the court wrote in a 5-2 decision in September 2000.[1]

One year later, however, the U.S. Supreme Court agreed to use Atkins' case to reconsider an issue it had decided 12 years earlier: whether it is constitutional to execute someone who is mentally retarded. In 1989 the court had held that sentencing a mentally retarded offender to death does not violate his Eighth Amendment right not to be subjected to "cruel and unusual punishments."[2]

Atkins' lawyers say things have changed since then. "The Eighth Amendment does not have a static meaning," the lawyers wrote in a petition asking the high court to hear the case. They noted that nearly half of the states with capital punishment now specifically bar execution of mentally retarded offenders.

Mental retardation advocacy groups agree. "The death penalty is supposed to be reserved for the most culpable of people," says Doreen Croser, executive director of the American Association on Mental Retardation. "By definition, a person with mental retardation doesn't meet that standard."

Some law enforcement advocates disagree. "The assessment of the retarded in criminal justice, as in all other aspects of life, ought to be on an individualized basis," says Barry Latzer, a professor at the John Jay College of Criminal Justice, City University of New York.

Atkins' case is one of the most recent manifestations of a broad reexamination of capital punishment in the United States over the last several years. While polls still show a solid majority of Americans favor use of the death penalty, critics have made headway with arguments about the fairness and reliability of the system for meting out death sentences. DNA profiling, or so-called genetic finger-printing, has been used in scores of cases in the United States since 1987 to exonerate wrongfully convicted defendants—including many on death row or serving long sentences.[3]

"Over the last few years there has been a lot of movement on the death penalty issue around the country, spurred largely by revelations about innocent people freed from death row but also by some unfairness in the process—poor representation, disparities of economics and even geography," says Richard Dieter, executive director of the Washington-based Death Penalty Information Center.

"There's a healthy skepticism about the death penalty and its reliability," Dieter adds. "That's a different tone than existed five or 10 years ago, where the emphasis was to speed up the death penalty and even to expand it."

Death penalty supporters acknowledge the gains opponents have made, but they believe the erosion in sup-

A Quarter-Century of Capital Punishment

More than 700 men and women have been executed in the United States in the 25 years since the Supreme Court allowed the reintroduction of capital punishment in 1976. Executions have been carried out in 32 of the 38 states with the death penalty, with more than 80 percent of them taking place in the South. Overall, executions are down this year. In fact, in the top three death penalty states — Texas, Virginia, and Florida — only 15 people have been executed so far in 2001, compared with 54 last year.

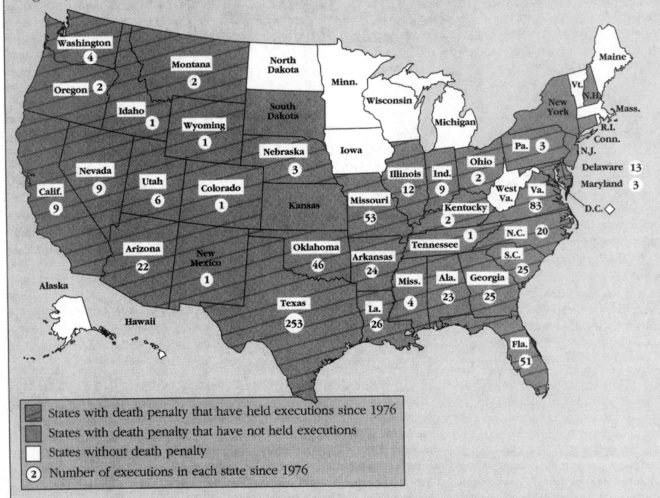

Washington **4**
Oregon **2**
Montana **2**
North Dakota
Minn.
Maine
Idaho **1**
Wyoming **1**
South Dakota
Wisconsin
Michigan
Vt.
N.H.
Nevada **9**
Utah **6**
Colorado **1**
Nebraska **3**
Iowa
Illinois **12**
Ind. **9**
Ohio **2**
New York
Mass.
R.I.
Conn.
N.J.
Pa. **3**
Calif. **9**
Kansas
Missouri **53**
West Va.
Va. **83**
Delaware **13**
Maryland **3**
D.C. ◇
Kentucky **2**
1
N.C. **20**
Arizona **22**
New Mexico **1**
Oklahoma **46**
Arkansas **24**
Tennessee
S.C. **25**
Alaska
Miss. **4**
Ala. **23**
Georgia **25**
Hawaii
Texas **253**
La. **26**
Fla. **51**

Legend:
- States with death penalty that have held executions since 1976
- States with death penalty that have not held executions
- States without death penalty
- **2** Number of executions in each state since 1976

Note: A total of 741 executions were carried out in the U.S. since 1977 through Nov. 12, 2001, including two federal executions in 2001, both at the U.S. penitentiary in Terre Haute, Ind.: Timothy McVeigh for the 1995 bombing of the Murrah federal building in Oklahoma City that killed 168 people and Texas drug kingpin Juan Raul Garza for three murders. They were the first federal executions since 1963.

Source: Death Penalty Information Center

port was ending before the Sept. 11 terrorist attacks and the issue has been relegated to a back burner since then.

"The opposition had gained some momentum, but I think a lot of the steam has gone out of that," says Kent Scheidegger, legal director of the Sacramento, Calif.-based Crimi-

nal Justice Legal Foundation, which supports capital punishment. "They got a lot of very good press with some very dubious studies. [But] some reality was beginning to set in even before Sept. 11. Since then, I haven't seen much interest."

Death penalty critics scored some of their gains by arguing that the le-

gal system, as it now operates, risks allowing an innocent person to be executed. The issue moved onto a front burner in July 1997 when Dieter's group published a report claiming that 69 "innocent" persons had been freed from death rows since the reinstitution of capital punishment in the United States in 1976. "The

Number of Executions Declining

If this year's execution rate continues as expected, 2001 will mark the first time since the death penalty was reinstated in 1976 that executions have declined for two consecutive years. While a majority of Americans support capital punishment, questions about the fairness and reliability of the judicial system have contributed to the decline.

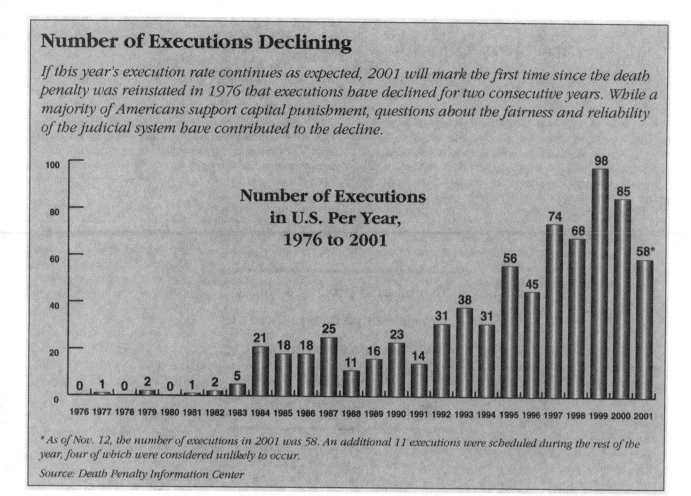

Number of Executions in U.S. Per Year, 1976 to 2001

* As of Nov. 12, the number of executions in 2001 was 58. An additional 11 executions were scheduled during the rest of the year, four of which were considered unlikely to occur.

Source: Death Penalty Information Center

risk that innocent people will be caught up in the web of the death penalty is rising," the report said.[4] Today, Dieter puts the number at 98.

But death penalty supporters note that the count includes cases in which a defendant won a reversal of his conviction or sentence because of legal error, not an actual finding of factual innocence. In addition, death penalty supporters say—and Dieter acknowledges—that critics have failed to document a single instance in which an incontrovertibly innocent person was put to death in the United States in the 20th century.

"A thorough review finds that the risk of executing the innocent has been significantly overstated by death penalty opponents," says Dudley Sharp, resource director of the Houston-based victim advocacy group Justice for All. "The risk is extraordinarily low."

Nonetheless, critics emphasize the seemingly frequent reversals of capital sentences or convictions as evidence of flaws in the trial and appellate procedures in death penalty cases. "The death penalty system is not functioning in a rational or effective measure [when] judged by the standards we would apply to any other process in the private or public sector," says James Liebman, a law professor at Columbia University in New York City and lead author of a major study of appellate court decisions in death penalty cases over the last 25 years *(See box.)*

Death penalty supporters counter that the number of reversals demonstrates the careful scrutiny that death penalty cases receive not only before and during trials but also afterward. "The American death penalty has, by far, the greatest due-process protections of any criminal sanction in the world," Sharp says.

Concerned about potential errors in Illinois' death penalty system, Gov. George Ryan, a Republican, last January temporarily halted executions in his state. Similarly, Rep. Jesse L. Jackson Jr., D-Ill., introduced a bill in Congress last March imposing a moratorium on federal executions and calling on states to follow suit. No hearings have been held.

In recent years, many state legislatures have considered other proposals tinkering with the death penalty system. In 2001, five more states prohibited the execution of mentally retarded offenders, although Texas Gov. Rick Perry vetoed such a bill.

State courts are also re-examining a variety of death penalty issues. In the first such ruling in the nation, the Georgia Supreme Court in early October outlawed electrocution.[5] The decision left Alabama and Nebraska as the only states still using electrocution as the sole method of execution; Georgia had already passed a law shifting to lethal injection if a court prohibited use of the electric chair.

Study Cites Flaws in Death Penalty System

Death penalty critics got new ammunition last year with a highly publicized academic study concluding that courts are twice as likely to reverse as to uphold death sentences on appeal. But death penalty supporters began attacking the study as soon as it was published and continue to describe it as methodologically flawed and ideologically biased.

The nine-year study by Columbia University Law School researchers bore a somewhat academic title: "A Broken System: Error Rates in Capital Cases, 1973–1995."[1] From the opening paragraphs, however, the authors bluntly described the death penalty system as marred by "serious error" in "epidemic proportions."

The study, based on an examination of some 4,700 death penalty cases reviewed by state or federal courts over a 23-year period, found that sentences were reversed in 68 percent of the cases. Only 18 percent of defendants were sentenced to death on retrial, the researchers found. The overwhelming majority—75 percent—received a lesser sentence, and 7 percent were found not guilty.

The most frequent reasons for reversals, the study found, were "egregiously incompetent defense lawyers" who failed to look for evidence favorable to the defendant or "police or prosecutors who did discover that kind of evidence but suppressed it."

> ## "Capital trials produce so many mistakes that it takes three judicial inspections to catch them — leaving grave doubt whether we do catch them all."

James Liebman, the Columbia professor who led the study, likens the courts' handling of capital cases to a "seriously flawed" manufacturing process. "Any given death sentence is much more likely—twice as likely—to get overturned, sent back and have to be redone or scrapped entirely than every one that is approved by the system's own inspectors," Liebman says.

"That's a system that appears to be costing a lot of money, producing a lot of faulty products, requiring a huge inspection system and in the end producing cases with not the results that are intended," he continues. "You not only waste a lot of time and money and frustrate the expectations of those who support the system, but you also run the huge risk that some of the errors that are being made will not be caught."

The study drew attention immediately, thanks in part to a front-page story in *The New York Times.*[2] It also promptly drew sharp attacks from death penalty supporters. In a three-page riposte, the Criminal Justice Legal Foundation termed the study "a political document, timed to impact congressional hearings" and depicted the large number of reversals in capital cases as evidence that the system had been "successfully obstructed by opponents of capital punishment."[3]

More than a year later, critics continue to discount the significance of the reversals. Barry Latzer, a professor at John Jay College of Criminal Justice, City University of New York, says the study merely demonstrates the "hypersensitivity of appellate courts" in reviewing death penalty cases. "When you have an appellate reversal, it has nothing to do with innocence or guilt," Latzer says. "An appellate reversal is about procedural errors at trial."

In addition, Latzer and a colleague—Assistant Professor James Cauthen—argued strenuously in a leading journal on judicial affairs that Liebman's study was misleading because it failed to separate cases in which appellate courts reversed a death sentence and those in which convictions themselves were reversed. "Once the distinction between guilt and sentence is taken into account," Latzer and Cauthen wrote, "only about 27 percent of capital convictions—not two-thirds—are set aside."[4]

In fact, the debate over the study got off on the wrong foot in part because of an error in the lead paragraph of the *Times'* story, which described the study as showing reversals of "convictions" in two-thirds of death penalty cases studied. Liebman says he called the error to the *Times'* attention, which published a correction the next day.

The continuing debate between Liebman, who worked for the anti-death penalty NAACP Legal Defense and Educational Fund before joining the Columbia faculty, and Latzer, who was an assistant district attorney in Brooklyn for two years, is both ideological and statistical.

Liebman says Latzer's estimate for the rate of conviction reversals in death cases—27 percent—is low because of a flawed methodology in analyzing a sample of state appellate decisions. While his initial study did not separate sentence and conviction reversals, Liebman says a study to be published soon will show that guilt reversals are more numerous than sentence reversals.

Whatever the exact number, Latzer and Cauthen say that counting sentence reversals along with conviction reversals overstates the charge of "systemic failure." "Judges and jurors disagree about the appropriateness of death sentences," they write.

Relying in the same publication, Liebman says that minimizing the importance of erroneous death sentences is "out of line with American criminal and constitutional law."

[1]James S. Liebman, Jeffrey Fagan and Valerie West, "A Broken System: Error Rates in Capital Cases, 1973–1995," June 12, 2000. The study was published originally on the Internet; it is on several Web sites, including that of the anti-death penalty Justice Project (www.thejusticeproject.org).

[2]Fox Butterfield, "Death Sentences Being Overturned in 2 of 3 Appeals," *The New York Times,* June 12, 2000, p. A1.

[3]Criminal Justice Legal Foundation, "Death Penalty 'Error' Study Has Errors of Its Own," June 19, 2000.

[4]Barry Latzer and James N. G. Cauthen, "Capital Appeals Revisited," *Judicature,* Vol. 84, No. 2 (September/October 2000), pp. 64–69. Liebman, Fagan and West replied in the same issue; a second exchange appeared in *Judicature,* Vol. 84, No. 3 (November/December 2000). The entire exchange is posted on the John Jay College's Web site: www.lib.jjay.cuny.edu/docs/liebman.htm.

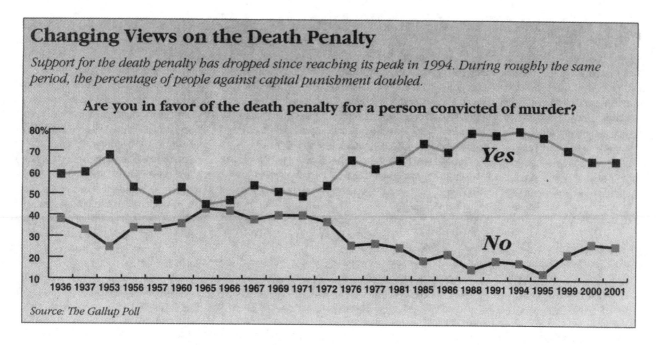

Changing Views on the Death Penalty

Support for the death penalty has dropped since reaching its peak in 1994. During roughly the same period, the percentage of people against capital punishment doubled.

Are you in favor of the death penalty for a person convicted of murder?

Yes

No

Source: *The Gallup Poll*

Meanwhile, the number of executions is declining somewhat after having reached a peak of 98 in 1999. As of Nov. 12, 58 persons have been executed in the U.S. in 2001—including Timothy McVeigh, the Oklahoma City bomber, who became the first federal prisoner to be put to death since 1963. Currently there are some 3,700 prisoners on death rows across the country.

Many of the issues surrounding the death penalty have been argued for decades, with opposing advocates and experts unable to persuade the other side. Here are some of the questions being debated in the current re-examination of capital punishment.

Is public support for the death penalty declining?

In her 20 years on the Supreme Court, Justice Sandra Day O'Connor has voted to reject most broad attacks on the death penalty and to make it harder for death row inmates to challenge their convictions or sentences in federal courts. But when O'Connor spoke to the Minnesota Women Lawyers group in Minneapolis last summer, she voiced some seemingly uncharacteristic

doubts about the death penalty in the United States.

"Minnesota doesn't have it," O'Connor said, "and you must breathe a sigh of relief every day." She warned that the death penalty system "may well be allowing some innocent defendants to be executed" and called for establishing "minimum standards" and "adequate compensation" for appointed counsel in death cases.[6]

Opponents seized on O'Connor's criticism to buttress their claims that public and official support for capital punishment has been declining in the past few years. "The climate seems to have taken a rather dramatic turn as of a few years ago," says Herbert Haines, a professor of anthropology and sociology at the State University of New York (SUNY) in Cortland and the sympathetic author of a history of the recent anti-death penalty movement. "It suddenly became politically and socially acceptable to have some degree of misgivings about the death penalty."

Supporters of capital punishment acknowledge that support has sagged recently. "There is no doubt that public support for executions has declined," says Sharp of Justice for All. But he and others stress that polls still register support for the death penalty from a substantial ma-

jority of the pubic: 67 percent in the most recent Gallup Poll on the issue. Support is "still quite high," says Latzer of John Jay College.

Supporters and opponents point to several possible explanations for the slippage, including the drop in the nation's crime rate.[7] But death penalty supporters claim the shift is due to biased media coverage.

"The media has simply reported what the anti-death penalty movement says with little or no critical review," Sharp says. "This is an extraordinary obstacle for getting an objective presentation to the public."

Both sides agree that the so-called innocence issue has played a major part in changing public attitudes toward the death penalty. "[Now] it's a debate about the management and effectiveness of this system based upon what actually happens in the system, rather than being a debate about morality in an abstract way, which is the way the debate had been before," says Columbia's Liebman.

Opponents see evidence of weakening public support for capital punishment both in polls and in the slowed pace of executions over the past two years, as well as the flurry of congressional and state proposals to overhaul death penalty proce-

Should the Mentally Retarded Be Executed?

While psychologists disagree over whether convicted murderer Daryl Renard Atkins is mentally retarded or merely slow and unmotivated, lawyers disagree over whether putting him to death would be unconstitutional.

Sometime next year, the U.S. Supreme Court is expected to decide the second question. A constitutional ban on executing the mentally retarded—which the court refused to impose in 1989—would significantly raise the stakes on an issue that already is difficult for lawyers, judges and jurors alike.

Death penalty supporters warn that a constitutional ban on executing mentally retarded offenders will encourage fabricated defenses on an issue with inevitably imprecise standards for judges or jurors to apply. Advocates for the mentally retarded insist that the condition has a clear and accepted definition, and that courts can easily weed out any false claims of mental impairment.

However the court rules on Atkins' constitutional plea, the case demonstrates how mental retardation claims can easily engender sharp evidentiary disputes between prosecutors and defense lawyers. Competing experts offered diametrically opposed opinions when Atkins was tried in York County in southeastern Virginia for the 1996 murder of U.S. airman Eric Michael Nesbitt. Atkins was 18 at the time, Nesbitt 21.

One other indicator of the scope of likely disagreements: Death penalty critics say at least 35 mentally retarded offenders have been put to death in the past 25 years.[1] Proponents of capital punishment call the count exaggerated and insist there are few, if any, retarded offenders awaiting execution today.

In Atkins' 1998 trial, evidence showed that he and a co-defendant, William Jones, abducted Nesbitt outside a store, forced him to withdraw $200 from an automated teller machine, and then shot him eight times. Jones claimed—and Atkins denied—that Atkins did the shooting. (Jones pleaded guilty in exchange for reduced charges.)

The jury convicted Atkins of capital murder and after a separate hearing sentenced him to death. The sentence was reversed because the jury form did not include the option of life imprisonment, but Atkins was again given the death penalty after a new sentencing hearing in 1999.

The jurors in the second proceeding heard testimony from two forensic psychologists: Evan Nelson for the defense and Stanton Samenow for the prosecution. Nelson, who administered a standard intelligence test to Atkins and examined his school records and other psychological data, concluded that Atkins was mentally retarded. Samenow, who interviewed Atkins twice but did not administer an IQ test, disagreed.

In his testimony, Nelson said that Atkins was "mildly" mentally retarded based on an IQ score of 59 and on what he called Atkins' "limited capacity for adaptive behavior." Nelson emphasized Atkins' record of "academic failure." Atkins consistently scored in the bottom fifth in standardized tests, failed the second and 10th grades and never graduated from high school.

By contrast, Samenow described Atkins as "of average intelligence." Samenow said that Atkins correctly identified the previous two U.S. presidents and the state's current governor and also appeared capable of carrying out such day-to-day activities as laundry and cooking. "There was no lack of ability to adapt and to take care of basic needs, certainly," Samenow concluded.

The two psychologists agreed, however, that Atkins knew that shooting Nesbitt was wrong and that Atkins fit the "general criteria" of an antisocial personality disorder. The prosecution introduced evidence that Atkins had prior convictions for robbing and maiming.

In upholding the death sentence, the Virginia Supreme Court said that the mental retardation issue was "a factual one" for the jury to decide.[2] But the majority in the 5-2 decision signaled agreement with Samenow's conclusion by saying that defense witness Nelson had failed to identify any "deficits" other than Atkins' low IQ score and academic failure. The dissenting justices said it was "clear" that Atkins was mentally retarded and called Samenow's testimony "incredulous."

Atkins' lawyers are now urging the Supreme Court to declare that executing a mentally retarded offender is unconstitutional under the Eighth Amendment. "It is time for this court to access whether American society has changed significantly over the past decade to the point that the execution of the mentally retarded now violates American standards of decency," they wrote in a petition with the high court.

Lawyers for the Virginia attorney general's office disagree. "There simply is no national consensus against execution of the mentally retarded," the lawyers wrote in their brief before the state Supreme Court last year. Eighteen states prohibit execution of the retarded.

The court is likely to hear arguments in February, with a decision sometime before July. Even if the court adopts a constitutional rule against executing the mentally retarded, it most likely would send Atkins' case back to Virginia courts for further proceedings under the new standard.

---

1. See Death Penalty Information Center, "Mental Retardation and the Death Penalty," www.deathpenaltyinfo.org.
2. *Atkins v. Commonwealth*, 534 S.E.2d 312 (Va. 2000).

---

dures. Among the reforms being sought are enforceable standards for defense counsel in death penalty trials and assured DNA testing for death row inmates who challenge their convictions. "The public strongly supports these reforms," says Peter Loge, director of the criminal justice reform campaign of the Washington-based Justice Project.

Death penalty supporters do not oppose those proposals in principle, but they disagree on details. "I know of no one opposing DNA testing," Sharp says. But, he adds, "Testing only makes sense in those cases where such testing is determinative of guilt or innocence." Similarly, Sharp says standards for defense counsel are "appropriate," depending on what those standards are.

Whatever the outcome of legislative debates, however, some prosecutors see little change in attitudes among jurors. "We haven't seen any change in support for the death penalty here, and I think most states fall in that category," says Robert McCulloch, St. Louis district attorney and chairman of the National District Attorneys' Association's committee on capital litigation.

"Nothing has changed in the 20 years I've been doing this," McCulloch adds. "We get some [jurors] who say that if they convict someone for murder, they will automatically vote for death, and others who say, 'No matter what, I won't vote for death.' But those numbers haven't changed much over the past 20 years."

Is capital punishment administered fairly?

The American Bar Association (ABA) has no official position on capital punishment. But for the past four years, the 600,000-member group has favored a moratorium on executions until states comply with a set of policies intended to ensure that death penalty cases are "administered fairly and impartially" and to "minimize the risk that innocent persons may be executed."[8]

In promoting the moratorium at the ABA's annual meeting in August, outgoing President Martha Barnett termed the existing death penalty system "absolutely unacceptable." In a letter to Congress, the Tallahassee, Fla., lawyer urged lawmakers to pass two bills—the Innocence Protection Act and the National Death Penalty Moratorium Act—as "immediate steps" to improve the fairness of the system.

Death penalty opponents say the fairness issues are helping shift public opinion in ways that the broad attacks on capital punishment failed to do. "It's not... that people are discovering that the death penalty is morally wrong," Dieter says, "but more a practical assessment that... innocent lives may be lost, that there is much that remains arbitrary and unfair about the death penalty."

Supporters of the death penalty sharply dispute the accusations of unfairness. "Capital trials are... among the fairest trials in the world," Latzer says. "The procedural protections are heightened. All of the parties—the lawyers, the prosecutors, the judges—are all aware of the stakes. The prosecutors are the most experienced, and the defense lawyers are increasingly being certified to handle those cases."

However, critics say a variety of factors demonstrate the unfairness of the system. Death penalty defenders dispute each of the points.

For one thing, Dieter notes that death sentences are "much more likely" to be imposed in murder cases with white victims than in those with African-American victims. Sharp acknowledges the statistic, but explains that whites are much more likely than blacks to be victims of the kinds of murders punishable by death—murders with aggravating factors such as robbery or carjacking or killings of police officers.

Death penalty opponents also emphasize the stark geographical disparities in the use of capital punishment. They note that 80 percent of the executions since 1976 have taken place in one region of the country—the South—with more than half from just three states: Texas, Virginia and Florida. In addition, Dieter says that 40 percent of the federal cases in which U.S. attorneys have sought the death penalty have come from just five of the country's 94 federal districts.[9]

Supporters blame geographic disparities on delaying tactics of death penalty opponents themselves. "Opponents want no enforcement of capital punishments," Sharp of Justice for All says, "and it is their efforts that continue to encourage any disparity which exists between states."

Critics also say the death penalty is more likely to be imposed on indigent defendants with court-appointed lawyers. "If you can afford good quality representation, you're much less likely to get the death penalty,"

Dieter says. But Sharp says there is "no systemic evidence that wealthier capital murderers are less likely to be executed than poorer [ones]."

Some death penalty supporters do acknowledge a problem in uneven legal representation. Latzer, for one, calls for "more money for defense counsel" in capital cases. Death penalty critics note that court-appointed lawyers are paid well under $100 an hour in most jurisdictions.[10]

To critics, the various fairness issues point to the need for a nationwide moratorium on executions. "The evidence has accumulated to a degree that we should stop what we're doing," Dieter says. The number of people freed from death rows, he says, amount to "a national alert that we're taking too many risks. We should stop and find out whether this system is irredeemably broken or whether it can be fixed."

Death penalty supporters, however, note that under the current system there is already a long time—an average of 12 years—between conviction and execution. "On average, every death row inmate already has a nearly 12-year moratorium on their individual case during appeals," Sharp says.

Questioning the true motive behind the moratorium proposals, he says, "The nationwide effort for a moratorium on executions is a prelude to doing away with the death penalty altogether."

Is it "cruel and unusual" punishment to execute mentally retarded criminals?

When the Supreme Court considered the issue in 1989, only two jurisdictions in the United States—Georgia and the federal government—specifically exempted mentally retarded individuals from the death penalty. With no "national consensus" on the issue, the court concluded—by a 5-4 vote—that execution of a mentally retarded offender was not "cruel and unusual" punishment prohibited by the Eighth Amendment.[11]

Today, nearly half of the states that allow capital punishment—18 out of 38—prohibit execution of the mentally retarded. On that basis, an array of mental health, civil liberties and human rights groups are urging the court to adopt a constitutional rule in line with what they see as the national consensus against the practice.

"We as a society, through our laws, through our organizations, have expressed an abhorrence of the execution of those with a low IQ, those with mental retardation; and therefore it's unconstitutional," says Dieter of the Death Penalty Information Center.

"We said it was cruel and unusual punishment [in arguments in the 1989 Supreme Court case], and they said they would look to the states for some consensus on the issue," says Croser of the mental retardation advocacy group. "Since that time, we've been pretty successful" in getting states to ban capital punishment for mentally retarded offenders.

Supporters of capital punishment are ambivalent about the issue. Some acknowledge the arguments against executing someone who is mentally retarded. "As a matter of policy, I would have no problem with a general rule that says we're not going to execute someone who is in fact retarded," says Scheidegger of the Criminal Justice Legal Foundation.

At the same time, most death penalty supporters appear to oppose a court-made constitutional rule against the practice. "Based on current law and legal opinion, execution

of the mentally retarded is not cruel and unusual punishment," Sharp says. Prosecutor McCulloch in St. Louis agrees: "I don't think it would qualify today as cruel and unusual under the Eighth Amendment," he says, "but I think generally it's not going to be acceptable."

Mental retardation—commonly defined by an IQ below 70—differs from two other conditions that sometimes become issues in criminal trials: competency and insanity. Competency refers to the ability to understand trial proceedings or consult with counsel; courts are not supposed to try a defendant who is not competent in that sense. Legal insanity denotes the inability to distinguish between right and wrong at the time of an offense; a defendant may be found "not guilty by reason of insanity" or "guilty but insane" and then committed to a mental institution for treatment rather than sentenced to prison. The Supreme Court in 1986 ruled that the Constitution prohibits the execution of someone who is insane.[12]

Mental health advocacy groups say no retarded person should be put to death because they lack the mental capacity to be treated as fully culpable of their crimes. "We're talking about people with intellectual capacity in the bottom 2 percent of the population," Croser says.

However, many death penalty supporters oppose a blanket exemption for the mentally retarded. Eliminating consideration of the death

penalty without examining a defendant's "individual moral culpability," Latzer says, "is a miscarriage of justice. That is a guarantee of unequal treatment."

Sharp also favors case-by-case determinations. "The current system is the best," he says. "Determine competency before trial. Establish if the defendant knew right from wrong, if the defendant can constructively participate in his own defense. And establish if he understands the nature of his punishment. And review those issues, again, on appeal."

But Dieter says case-by-case decisions put an unfair burden on a mentally retarded defendant. "It's difficult for [a jury] to decide a separate question" about whether a mentally retarded defendant should be subject to the death penalty, he says. "Their sympathies are going to be with the victim. Their feelings are going to overwhelm any feeling that there should be mercy for the defendant."

With five more states this year banning the execution of mentally retarded offenders, supporters of a ban feel momentum is on their side. "Mental retardation is an issue that has legs," Haines of SUNY-Cortland says.

Death penalty supporters acknowledge the point. Asked whether there is now a national consensus against the death penalty for mentally retarded defendants, Scheidegger replies: "It's borderline." To the same question, Croser answers without hesitation, "Absolutely."

From *CQ Researcher*, November 16, 2001, pp. 947–954. © 2001 by CQ Press, a Division of Congresstional Quarterly, Inc. Reprinted by permission.

Appendix I

AE: Criminal Justice 03/04– CHARTS AND GRAPHS

Below, we have provided the page numbers and titles for the individual charts and graphs that can be found within the articles in this volume. We hope you find this resource useful.

4–5	Criminal Justice System Caseflow
23	Internet Fraud Complaints
25	Many Firms Suffered Attacks
26	Many Firms Keep Mum About Attacks
29	Attacks Against DOD Computers
35, 36	Schemers and Scams: A Brief History of Bad Business
37	The Incredible Shrinking Fraudster
38	The SEC's Impressive Margins
39	The Odds Against Doing Time
39	Who Did What
39	A Look at Self-Policing
43	Confidence Ratings for Criminal Justice System Agencies, by Race
44	Repeat Offending After Arrest for Domestic Violence by Perceived Fairness of Arrest Process
74	Prosecutors' Responses to Scenarios Involving Children and Abuse
100	Annual Average Number of Complaints Against Officers, Before and After Intervention
165	Percentage of Arrests by Race Under Georgia's SB440 Law for 1994–2002
180	State Parole Population and Admissions to Parole, 1980–2000
181	Six-Month Growth Rates for Prisons, 1995–2001
181	State Prison/Releases
182	Method of Release from State Prison, for Selected Years, 1980–2000
182	Time Served in Prison and Jail for First Releases From State Prison, by Method of Release, 1990 and 1999
183	Releases From State Prison, by Most Serious Offense, 1985–1999
184	Success Rates for Parolees by Method of Release, 1990–1999
185	Percent Successful Among Parole Discharges in California and All Other States, 1995–1999
187	Recidivism Rates of Prisoners Released in 1994, BJS Data From 15 States
188	Terms of Release From the Massachusetts Department of Correction, 1999
189	Terms of Release by Security Level of the Correctional Institution
190	Type of Release From Suffolk County House of Correction, January 2001
196	A Quarter-Century of Capital Punishment
197	Number of Executions Declining
199	Changing Views on the Death Penalty
204	**Crime Clock, 2001, and Crime in the United States, 2001**
205	**Index of Crime, United States, 1981–2001**
206	Murder
208	Forcible Rape
208	Robbery
209	Aggravated Assault
210	Burglary
212	Larceny-Theft
213	Motor Vehicle Theft

Appendix II

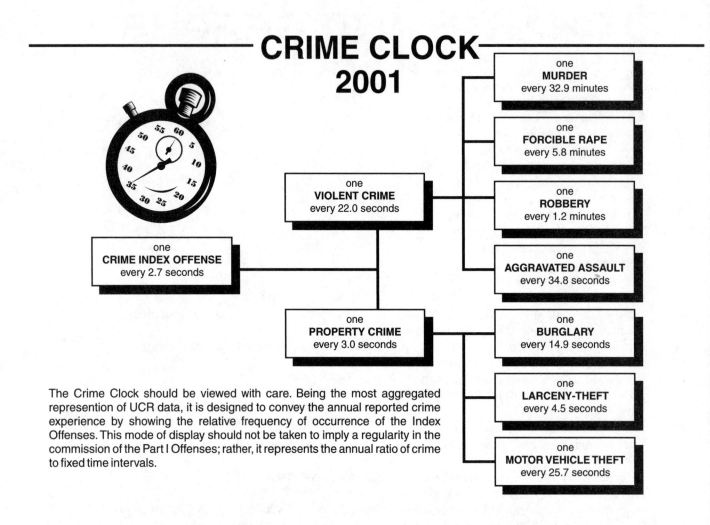

CRIME CLOCK 2001

one
CRIME INDEX OFFENSE
every 2.7 seconds

one
VIOLENT CRIME
every 22.0 seconds

one
PROPERTY CRIME
every 3.0 seconds

one
MURDER
every 32.9 minutes

one
FORCIBLE RAPE
every 5.8 minutes

one
ROBBERY
every 1.2 minutes

one
AGGRAVATED ASSAULT
every 34.8 seconds

one
BURGLARY
every 14.9 seconds

one
LARCENY-THEFT
every 4.5 seconds

one
MOTOR VEHICLE THEFT
every 25.7 seconds

The Crime Clock should be viewed with care. Being the most aggregated represention of UCR data, it is designed to convey the annual reported crime experience by showing the relative frequency of occurrence of the Index Offenses. This mode of display should not be taken to imply a regularity in the commission of the Part I Offenses; rather, it represents the annual ratio of crime to fixed time intervals.

Crime in the United States, 2001

DEFINITION

The Uniform Crime Reporting (UCR) Program's Crime Index is composed of selected offenses used to gauge fluctuations in the volume and rate of crime reported to law enforcement....

Year	Number of offenses	Rate per 100,000 inhabitants
2000	11,608,070	4,124.8
2001	11,849,006	4,160.5
Percent change	+2.1	+0.9

The estimated number of Crime Index offenses for 2001 was 11,849,006. This number reflects an increase of 2.1 percent from the 2000 estimate, the first increase since 1991.

In 2001, violent crime comprised 12.1 percent and property crime accounted for 87.9 percent of the Crime Index total. The property crime of larceny-theft, which comprised 59.7 percent of the Crime Index, was the most frequently occurring of all Index crimes, with an estimated 7,076,171 offenses. The violent crime of murder, which accounted for 0.1 percent of the Crime Index, occurred least frequently with an estimated total of 15,980 offenses.

Index of Crime[1], United States, 1982-2001

Population[2]	Crime Index total	Modified Crime Index total[3]	Violent crime[4]	Property crime[4]	Murder and nonnegligent man-slaughter	Forcible rape	Robbery	Aggra-vated assault	Burglary	Larceny-theft	Motor vehicle theft	Arson[3]
					Number of Offenses							
Population by year:												
1982-231,664,458	12,974,400		1,322,390	11,652,000	21,010	78,770	553,130	669,480	3,447,100	7,142,500	1,062,400	
1983-233,791,994	12,108,630		1,258,087	10,850,543	19,308	78,918	506,567	653,294	3,129,851	6,712,759	1,007,933	
1984-235,824,902	11,881,755		1,273,282	10,608,473	18,692	84,233	485,008	685,349	2,984,434	6,591,874	1,032,165	
1985-237,923,795	12,430,357		1,327,767	11,102,590	18,976	87,671	497,874	723,246	3,073,348	6,926,380	1,102,862	
1986-240,132,887	13,211,869		1,489,169	11,722,700	20,613	91,459	542,775	834,322	3,241,410	7,257,153	1,224,137	
1987-242,288,918	13,508,708		1,483,999	12,024,709	20,096	91,111	517,704	855,088	3,236,184	7,499,851	1,288,674	
1988-244,498,982	13,923,086		1,566,221	12,356,865	20,675	92,486	542,968	910,092	3,218,077	7,705,872	1,432,916	
1989-246,819,230	14,251,449		1,646,037	12,605,412	21,500	94,504	578,326	951,707	3,168,170	7,872,442	1,564,800	
1990-249,464,396	14,475,613		1,820,127	12,655,486	23,438	102,555	639,271	1,054,863	3,073,909	7,945,670	1,635,907	
1991-252,153,092	14,872,883		1,911,767	12,961,116	24,703	106,593	687,732	1,092,739	3,157,150	8,142,228	1,661,738	
1992-255,029,699	14,438,191		1,932,274	12,505,917	23,760	109,062	672,478	1,126,974	2,979,884	7,915,199	1,610,834	
1993-257,782,608	14,144,794		1,926,017	12,218,777	24,526	106,014	659,870	1,135,607	2,834,808	7,820,909	1,563,060	
1994-260,327,021	13,989,543		1,857,670	12,131,873	23,326	102,216	618,949	1,113,179	2,712,774	7,879,812	1,539,287	
1995-262,803,276	13,862,727		1,798,792	12,063,935	21,606	97,470	580,509	1,099,207	2,593,784	7,997,710	1,472,441	
1996-265,228,572	13,493,863		1,688,540	11,805,323	19,645	96,252	535,594	1,037,049	2,506,400	7,904,685	1,394,238	
1997-267,783,607	13,194,571		1,636,096	11,558,475	18,208	96,153	498,534	1,023,201	2,460,526	7,743,670	1,354,189	
1998-270,248,003	12,485,714		1,533,887	10,951,827	16,974	93,144	447,186	976,583	2,332,735	7,376,311	1,242,781	
1999-272,690,813	11,634,378		1,426,044	10,208,334	15,522	89,411	409,371	911,740	2,100,739	6,955,520	1,152,075	
2000-281,421,906[5]	11,608,070		1,425,486	10,182,584	15,586	90,178	408,016	911,706	2,050,992	6,971,590	1,160,002	
2001-284,796,887	11,849,006		1,436,611	10,412,395	15,980	90,491	422,921	907,219	2,109,767	7,076,171	1,226,457	
Percent change, number of offenses:												
2001/2000	+2.1		+0.8	+2.3	+2.5	+0.3	+3.7	-0.5	+2.9	+1.5	+5.7	
2001/1997	-10.2		-12.2	-9.9	-12.2	-5.9	-15.2	-11.3	-14.3	-8.6	-9.4	
2001/1992	-17.9		-25.7	-16.7	-32.7	-17.0	-37.1	-19.5	-29.2	-10.6	-23.9	
					Rate per 100,000 Inhabitants							
Year:												
1982	5,600.5		570.8	5,029.7	9.1	34.0	238.8	289.0	1,488.0	3,083.1	458.6	
1983	5,179.2		538.1	4,641.1	8.3	33.8	216.7	279.4	1,338.7	2,871.3	431.1	
1984	5,038.4		539.9	4,498.5	7.9	35.7	205.7	290.6	1,265.5	2,795.2	437.7	
1985	5,224.5		558.1	4,666.4	8.0	36.8	209.3	304.0	1,291.7	2,911.2	463.5	
1986	5,501.9		620.1	4,881.8	8.6	38.1	226.0	347.4	1,349.8	3,022.1	509.8	
1987	5,575.5		612.5	4,963.0	8.3	37.6	213.7	352.9	1,335.7	3,095.4	531.9	
1988	5,694.5		640.6	5,054.0	8.5	37.8	222.1	372.2	1,316.2	3,151.7	586.1	
1989	5,774.0		666.9	5,107.1	8.7	38.3	234.3	385.6	1,283.6	3,189.6	634.0	
1990	5,802.7		729.6	5,073.1	9.4	41.1	256.3	422.9	1,232.2	3,185.1	655.8	
1991	5,898.4		758.2	5,140.2	9.8	42.3	272.7	433.4	1,252.1	3,229.1	659.0	
1992	5,661.4		757.7	4,903.7	9.3	42.8	263.7	441.9	1,168.4	3,103.6	631.6	
1993	5,487.1		747.1	4,740.0	9.5	41.1	256.0	440.5	1,099.7	3,033.9	606.3	
1994	5,373.8		713.6	4,660.2	9.0	39.3	237.8	427.6	1,042.1	3,026.9	591.3	
1995	5,274.9		684.5	4,590.5	8.2	37.1	220.9	418.3	987.0	3,043.2	560.3	
1996	5,087.6		636.6	4,451.0	7.4	36.3	201.9	391.0	945.0	2,980.3	525.7	
1997	4,927.3		611.0	4,316.3	6.8	35.9	186.2	382.1	918.8	2,891.8	505.7	
1998	4,620.1		567.6	4,052.5	6.3	34.5	165.5	361.4	863.2	2,729.5	459.9	
1999	4,266.5		523.0	3,743.6	5.7	32.8	150.1	334.3	770.4	2,550.7	422.5	
2000[5]	4,124.8		506.5	3,618.3	5.5	32.0	145.0	324.0	728.8	2,477.3	412.2	
2001	4,160.5		504.4	3,656.1	5.6	31.8	148.5	318.5	740.8	2,484.6	430.6	
Percent change, rate per 100,000 inhabitants:												
2001/2000	+0.9		-0.4	+1.0	+1.3	-0.8	+2.4	-1.7	+1.6	+0.3	+4.5	
2001/1997	-15.6		-17.4	-15.3	-17.5	-11.5	-20.2	-16.6	-19.4	-14.1	-14.8	
2001/1992	-26.5		-33.4	-25.4	-39.8	-25.7	-43.7	-27.9	-36.6	-19.9	-31.8	

[1] The murder and nonnegligent homicides that occurred as a result of the events of September 11, 2001, were not included in this table. See special report, Section V.

[2] Populations are Bureau of the Census provisional estimates as of July 1 for each year except 1990 and 2000 which are decennial census counts.

[3] Although arson data are included in the trend and clearance tables, sufficient data are not available to estimate totals for this offense.

[4] Violent crimes are offenses of murder, forcible rape, robbery, and aggravated assault. Property crimes are offenses of burglary, larceny-theft, and motor vehicle theft.

[5] The 2000 crime figures have been adjusted. See Crime Trends, Appendix I, for details.

An estimated monetary value of $17.1 billion in stolen property was reported in 2001. Thefts of motor vehicles accounted for the greatest monetary loss…

An estimated 32.4 percent of property reported stolen in 2001 was recovered.

The Crime Index rate per 100,000 inhabitants in 2001 was 4,160.5, a 0.9-percent increase from the 2000 rate.

The United States is divided into four regions: the Northeast, the Midwest, the South, and the West. In 2001, data collected regarding the Nation's four regions reflect the following:

The Northeast The Northeast comprised 18.9 percent of the Nation's population in 2001 and posted 13.7 percent of the Crime Index offenses reported to the UCR Program. The Northeast was the only region to experience decreases in the number of offenses and the rate per 100,000 inhabitants in 2001.

The Midwest The Midwest, which accounted for 22.7 percent of the U.S. population, recorded 21.7 percent of the Nation's Crime Index offenses in 2001.

The South The South, the Nation's most populous region in 2001, comprised 35.8 percent of the total population and experienced 40.9 percent of the total Crime Index offenses.

The West The West, which constituted 22.6 percent of the population, accounted for 23.7 percent of the Nation's Crime Index offenses.

Population Groups Trends and Rates

In 2001, the Nation's cities collectively experienced an increase of 2.0 percent in the total number of crimes reported and had a rate of 5,124.8 Index crimes per 100,000 inhabitants. Additionally, suburban counties and rural counties experienced increases in total crimes reported—2.4 percent and 1.9 percent, respectively.

Within city groupings, the largest increase of reported crime, 4.1 percent, was in cities with populations of 250,000 to 499,999. The smallest change in volume from 2000, a 0.5 percent increase, occurred in cities with populations of 1 million and over. In 2001, cities with populations spanning 500,000 to 999,999 had a rate of 7,328.0 Crime Index offenses per 100,000 inhabitants, the highest among the Nation's cities. Cities with populations of 10,000 to 24,999 had the lowest rate of offenses per 100,000 inhabitants—3,875.4.

Clearances

In 2001, 19.6 percent of Crime Index offenses were cleared overall. Law enforcement nationwide cleared 16.2 percent of property crimes and 46.2 percent of violent crimes.

Among the Crime Index offenses in 2001, murder was the offense cleared most often—62.4 percent. Burglary offenses experienced the lowest percentage of clearances—12.7 percent.

Arrests

Total Arrests The estimated total of Crime Index offense arrests for 2001 was 2,245,597, approximately 16.4 percent of the U.S. total estimated arrests. Of that total, approximately 27.9 percent were arrests made for violent crimes and 72.1 percent were arrests for property crimes. Larceny-theft arrests accounted for 71.7 percent of all property crime arrests. Aggravated assaults made up the greatest portion, 76.2 percent, of violent crime arrests.

Special Note Regarding the Events of September 11, 2001

Due to the unique nature and the statistical implications inherent in the events of September 11, 2001, the crimes committed in those attacks are not included in the UCR Program's offense rate, trend, or clearance data.

Crime Index Offenses Reported

MURDER

DEFINITION

Murder and nonnegligent manslaughter, as defined in the Uniform Crime Reporting Program, is the willful (nonnegligent) killing of one human being by another.

The classification of this offense, as for all other Crime Index offenses, is based solely on police investigation as opposed to the determination of a court, medical examiner, coroner, jury, or other judicial body. Not included in the count for this offense classification are deaths caused by negligence, suicide, or accident; justifiable homicides; and attempts to murder or assaults to murder, which are scored as aggravated assaults.

Year	Number of offenses	Rate per 100,000 inhabitants
2000	15,586	5.5
2001	15,980	5.6
Percent change	+2.5	+1.3

Approximately 15,980 persons were murder victims in 2001. This estimate indicated a 2.5-percent increase over the 2000 approximation, and it was the second consecutive annual increase in the number of murders occurring nationwide. However, the 2001 estimate represented a 12.2-percent decrease from the 1997 estimate and a 32.7-percent drop from the estimate recorded for 1992. The 2001 estimate yielded a rate of 5.6 murders for every 100,000 U.S. inhabitants. That rate is 1.3 percent higher than the rate estimated for 2000.

In 2001, data collected from the Nation's four regions reflect the following:

The Northeast The Northeast, with 18.9 percent of the Nation's population, accounted for 14.3 percent of the murders during 2001. With an estimated 2,278 murders, the Northeastern States registered a 5.6-percent rise in murder volume from the previous year's figure. The rate per 100,000 inhabitants showed a 4.4-percent increase in the murder rate for the region—4.2 murders per 100,000 persons.

Murder by Month[1]
Percent distribution, 1997–2001

Month	1997	1998	1999	2000	2001
January	8.7	9.1	8.8	8.4	8.0
February	7.3	7.3	7.1	7.3	6.1
March	8.5	8.3	7.6	7.6	7.2
April	7.6	7.7	7.7	7.7	8.0
May	7.9	8.4	8.3	8.5	8.2
June	8.7	8.4	8.1	8.5	8.4
July	9.0	8.7	9.1	9.3	9.5
August	8.7	9.2	9.1	9.4	9.1
September	8.2	8.3	8.7	8.3	8.7
October	8.6	8.3	8.4	8.7	9.3
November	8.2	7.6	8.2	7.7	8.4
December	8.6	8.8	8.8	8.7	9.2

[1] The murder and nonnegligent homicides that occurred as a result of the events of September 11, 2001, were not included in any murder tables.

The Midwest The Midwest, which represented 22.7 percent of the U.S. population in 2001, accounted for 21.3 percent of the Nation's murders. The region had an estimated 3,405 murders, an increase of 3.4 percent from the 2000 number. The Midwestern States experienced 5.3 murders per 100,000 inhabitants, an increase of 2.9 percent over the murder rate recorded for 2000.

The South The Southern Region of the Nation accounted for 35.8 percent of the population and 42.4 percent of the murders committed in 2001. The Southern States experienced an estimated 6,780 murders, which represented a 1.5-percent drop for this region from the previous year's volume. The region posted a murder rate of 6.7 per 100,000 inhabitants, a 3.0-percent decline from the 2000 rate. The South was the only region to report a decline in both murder volume and rate.

The West This region accounted for 22.6 percent of the population and 22.0 percent of murders in 2001. An estimated 3,517 murders occurred in the Western States during 2001, representing an 8.0-percent increase in murder from the 2000 volume. The West experienced a 5.9-percent rise in the murder rate from the previous year's figure, with 5.5 murders per 100,000 people.

Murder Victims[1]
by Race and Sex, 2001

Race	Total	Sex of victim		
		Male	*Female*	*Unknown*
White	6,750	4,785	1,962	3
Black	6,446	5,350	1,095	1
Other race	368	245	123	0
Unknown race	188	123	34	31
Total[2]	13,752	10,503	3,214	35

[1] The murder and nonnegligent homicides that occurred as a result of the events of September 11, 2001, were not included in any murder tables. See special report, Section V.

[2] Total number of murder victims for whom supplemental homicide data was received.

Community Types

Metropolitan Statistical Areas, or MSAs, are those community types made up of a central city of at least 50,000 inhabitants, the county containing that city, and adjacent areas with strong economic or cultural ties to the central city. MSAs accounted for approximately 80 percent of the U.S. population in 2001, and they experienced 87.0 percent of total estimated murders. Murder occurred at a rate of 6.1 per 100,000 inhabitants of MSAs for 2001. Those cities outside of metropolitan areas, which accounted for 8 percent of the Nation's population, reported an estimated 3.5 murders per 100,000 people and 5.0 percent of the murder volume. The Nation's rural counties, with 12 percent of the population, reported 8.0 percent of the total murders and 3.7 murders per 100,000 people.

Population Groups Trends and Rates

Collectively, the Nation's cities experienced a 3.5-percent increase in the number of murders over the previous year's estimate.

Victims Based upon the 2001 SHR [Supplementary Homicide Report] data, the victims of homicide were most often male (76.6 percent) and adult (89.6 percent). By race, 49.8 percent of murder

victims were white, and 47.5 percent were black. The remaining victims, 2.7 percent, were of other races (Asian or Pacific Islander and American Indian or Alaskan Native). Of the total murder victims where age and sex were known, 9.1 percent of males and 14.8 percent of females were under 18 years of age.

Of the homicides for which supplemental data were received, the victim-offender relationship was unknown for 44.6 percent of the victims. Approximately 42.3 percent of the victims knew their assailants (29.2 percent were acquainted with their killers and 13.1 percent were related to them). Another 13.1 percent of murder victims were known to have been murdered by a stranger. The 2001 SHR data indicated that nearly a third of female victims were slain by a husband or boyfriend, 32.2 percent. Male homicide victims were killed by a wife or girlfriend in 2.8 percent of the incidents.

Offenders Reviewing the supplemental data for which age, sex, and race of offenders were known revealed that 90.3 percent of murder offenders were male, and 91.7 percent were over the age of 18. Considering those offenders for which race was known, 50.3 percent of murder offenders were black and 47.2 percent were white. Persons of other races comprised 2.5 percent of offenders.

Supplemental data for 2001 indicated that of those incidents with one victim and one offender, 93.6 percent of black homicide victims were killed by a black offender, and 85.4 percent of white victims were slain by white offenders.

Weapons Reviewing those incidents in which the murder weapon was known demonstrated that 69.5 percent involved the use of a firearm. Within the firearm category, handguns were used in 77.9 percent of homicides, shotguns were used in 5.7 percent, and rifles in 4.5 percent. Other or unknown firearms accounted for 12.0 percent. Knives or cutting instruments were employed in 14.3 percent of homicides for which the weapon was known. Personal weapons such as hands, fists, or feet, etc. were used in 7.4 percent of murders. Blunt objects were the weapon used in 5.3 percent of murders. Other dangerous weapons (such as poison, explosives, etc.) accounted for the remainder.

Clearances

For UCR purposes, a crime is cleared when it is solved either by arrest or by exceptional means. Murder, the most serious offense, was cleared more often than any other Index offense, 62.4 percent.

Murder was also the offense that had the lowest percentage of clearances involving only juveniles, 5.0 percent. By population groups, cities with 25,000–49,999 inhabitants recorded the highest percentage of murders cleared at 77.9 percent. Cities with 250,000 inhabitants or more cleared 56.5 percent of murders, the lowest percentage among population groups. Law enforcement agencies cleared 66.9 percent of murders in suburban counties; 77.5 percent of murders were cleared in rural counties.

Arrests

In 2001, total arrests for murder decreased 2.6 percent when compared with the previous year's data. Male arrests for murder fell 2.0 percent in 2001 when compared to the previous year's figure. Female arrests in 2001 fell 6.8 percent from the prior year.

Arrests of juveniles for murder fell 2.2 percent during 2001. By race, the number of arrestees was nearly evenly split between black arrestees and white arrestees at 48.7 percent and 48.4 percent, respectively.

FORCIBLE RAPE

DEFINITION

Forcible rape, as defined in the Uniform Crime Reporting Program, is the carnal knowledge of a female forcibly and against her will. Assaults or attempts to commit rape by force or threat of force are also included; however, statutory rape (without force) and other sex offenses are excluded.

Year	Number of offenses	Rate per 100,000 inhabitants
2000	90,178	32.0
2001	90,491	31.8
Percent change	+0.3	–0.8

The UCR Program has traditionally defined rape victims as females. Approximately 90,491 forcible rapes of females were recorded during 2001. Based on that volume, 62.2 of every 100,000 females were victims of forcible rape in 2001 compared to 62.7 in the previous year. These figures indicated a slight percentage increase in the number of rapes (0.3 percent), but a decrease in the rate of female rapes (0.8 percent).

The 2001 female forcible rape rate of 62.2 continued a downward trend. In 1999, there were an estimated 64.1 rapes for every 100,000 females in the Nation; in 1997, there were 70.3 victims for each 100,000 females; for 1992, the estimate was 83.7.

In 2001, data collected regarding the Nation's four regions reflect the following:

The Northeast The Northeast Region reported the lowest percentage of the Nation's female rapes at 13.4 percent and the lowest forcible rape rate at 44.0 per 100,000 females. The Northeastern figures showed increases of 1.6 percent in the number of rapes and 1.2 percent in the rate of rapes over the prior year's numbers.

Forcible Rape by Month
Percent distribution, 1997–2001

Month	1997	1998	1999	2000	2001
January	7.9	7.9	8.1	8.0	7.6
February	7.0	7.4	7.3	7.5	7.2
March	8.0	8.6	8.2	8.5	8.4
April	8.2	8.2	8.2	8.0	8.3
May	9.1	8.8	8.6	9.0	8.8
June	9.5	8.7	8.8	9.1	8.7
July	9.7	9.6	9.6	9.5	9.7
August	9.4	9.3	9.5	9.3	9.4
September	8.8	8.8	8.3	8.4	8.5
October	8.2	7.9	8.3	8.3	8.4
November	7.4	7.6	7.9	7.5	7.6
December	6.7	7.1	7.2	6.9	7.4

The Midwest The Midwestern States reported 25.1 percent of the forcible rapes occurring in the Nation in 2001, an increase for the region of 1.5 percent from the prior year's report. A regional rate of 68.6 rape incidents for 100,000 females showed a 1.0-percent increase from the 2000 rate.

The South Regionally, the highest percentage of female rapes, 37.8 percent, occurred in the South. The data indicated a modest decline of 0.6 percent in the number of forcible rape occurrences from the 2000 figure. The estimated rate of 65.8 rapes per 100,000 females calculated to a 2.2-percent decline in the South's female rape rate from the 2000 rate.

The West The West experienced 23.7 percent of the Nation's rape offenses. The incidence of female forcible rape in the Western States showed a slight decline of 0.1 percent from the 2000 estimate, and the rape rate of 65.2 per 100,000 females indicated a decrease of 2.1 percent when compared to the prior year's rate.

Community Types

In estimating the data by community types, cities outside metropolitan areas reported the highest rate of female rapes in 2001, 67.7 incidents per 100,000 female inhabitants. This estimate was a decrease from the 69.0 rate recorded in 2000. The Nation's Metropolitan Statistical Areas reported a nominal decrease in the female rape rate, down to 64.4 from the 65.0 recorded the prior year. Rural counties reported the lowest rate of forcible rapes of females in the Nation; however, the rate of 43.8 did indicate a minimal increase from the 2000 rate of 43.4 per 100,000 females.

Clearances

For UCR purposes, an offense is cleared when at least one person is arrested and charged or when circumstances beyond the control of law enforcement preclude an arrest for a crime that has been solved, e.g., the victim refuses to cooperate with the prosecution.

Nationally, 44.3 percent of rapes were cleared during 2001 versus 46.1 percent cleared in 2000. Regionally, law enforcement in the Northeast cleared 50.1 percent; in the Midwest, 39.3 percent; in the South, 46.0 percent; and in the West, 43.5 percent of female rapes during 2001.

Arrests

In 2001, law enforcement arrested an estimated 27,270 persons for forcible rape. Forcible rape arrests for 2001 were 2.3 percent below the 2000 number. Approximately 45.4 percent of persons arrested for forcible rape in 2001 were under the age of 25, 62.7 percent of arrestees were white, and 98.8 percent were males.

ROBBERY

DEFINITION

The Uniform Crime Reporting Program defines robbery as the taking or attempting to take anything of value from the care, custody, or control of a person or persons by force or threat of force or violence and/or by putting the victim in fear.

Year	Number of offenses	Rate per 100,000 inhabitants
2000	408,016	145.0
2001	422,921	148.5
Percent change	+3.7	+2.4

The 422,921 robberies estimated for 2001 marked the first increase in this offense nationwide since 1991. This estimate indicated a 3.7- percent increase from the 2000 figure.

Robbery accounted for 29.4 percent of all violent crimes occurring in the United States, and 3.6 percent of all Crime Index offenses.

Robbery by Weapon In 2001, robbers used firearms in 42.0 percent of the reported offenses. Thirty-nine percent of robberies involved strong-arming the victim. Offenders used knives or cutting instruments in 8.7 percent of the offenses, and the remaining 10.4 percent of offenses involved other weapons.

Robbery by Month
Percent distribution, 1997–2001

Month	1997	1998	1999	2000	2001
January	9.2	9.5	8.9	8.6	8.2
February	7.6	7.5	7.3	7.1	6.5
March	7.9	8.0	7.7	7.7	7.6
April	7.6	7.6	7.6	7.5	7.4
May	8.2	7.9	8.1	8.1	8.1
June	8.0	7.7	8.1	7.9	8.1
July	8.6	8.5	8.7	8.7	8.7
August	8.8	8.7	8.8	9.0	8.7
September	8.5	8.5	8.3	8.5	8.5
October	8.8	9.0	8.8	9.1	9.7
November	8.2	8.3	8.6	8.7	9.1
December	8.6	8.8	9.2	9.0	9.5

Dollar Loss Robbers stole more than $532 million from their victims in 2001. The average loss for each instance of robbery nationwide was $1,258. The number of banks robbed during 2001 increased 19.4 percent over the number reported for 2000.

Robbery by Type Robberies of persons on streets and highways accounted for 44.3 percent of robberies during 2001.

In 2001, data collected regarding the Nation's four regions reflect the following:

The Northeast The Northeast, which contained 18.9 percent of the population, experienced 19.1 percent of the Nation's robberies during 2001. The number of robberies declined in the region by 3.6 percent, and the rate per 100,000 inhabitants declined 4.0 percent from the previous year's rate. That region reported the greatest percentage of strong-arm robberies, 46.9 percent, in 2001.

The Midwest Claiming 22.7 percent of the population in 2001, the Midwest accounted for 19.6 percent of total robberies. The number of robberies occurring in the region increased 1.8 percent from the 2000 number, and the rate per 100,000 inhabitants increased 1.3 percent.

The South With 35.8 percent of the population, the Southern States reported 38.4 percent of total robberies. The volume of robbery offenses within the region increased 6.3 percent from the prior year's volume, and the rate per 100,000 inhabitants increased 4.6 percent over the 2000 rate. That region also reported the highest percentage of robberies involving firearms, 46.9 percent.

The West In 2001, approximately 22.6 percent of the U.S. population resided in the Western States. That region reported 22.9 percent of all robbery offenses. From 2000, the number of robbery offenses increased 7.6 percent in 2001, and the rate per 100,000 in population rose 5.5 percent.

Clearances

Law enforcement agencies cleared 24.9 percent of all robberies nationwide through arrest or exceptional means in 2001. Clearance rates ranged from the 41.0 percent reported by law enforcement agencies in rural counties to 18.5 percent recorded by those in cities from 500,000 to 999,999 in population.

Regionally, the Northeast had the highest clearance rate for robbery at 30.2 percent. The South registered a clearance rate of 24.7 percent. The clearance rate for the Western States was 24.4 percent, followed by the Midwest at 21.2 percent.

Robbery
Percent distribution by region, 2001

Type	United States Total	North-eastern States	Mid-western States	Southern States	Western States
Total[1]	100.0	100.0	100.0	100.0	100.0
Street/highway	44.3	59.0	48.8	39.2	42.2
Commercial house	14.4	9.1	10.7	14.7	18.7
Gas or service station	2.9	3.5	3.4	2.5	2.8
Convenience store	6.6	5.9	4.7	7.8	5.9
Residence	12.6	8.9	10.1	16.6	9.6
Bank	2.4	2.1	2.6	2.0	3.1
Miscellaneous	16.9	11.6	19.7	17.2	17.7

[1] Because of rounding, the percentages may not add to total.

Arrests

Law enforcement officers arrested an estimated 108,400 persons for robbery in 2001, an increase of 2.1 percent nationwide over those for 2000. Arrests of adults (18 years and older) rose 3.9 percent. However, arrests for juveniles (under age 18) decreased 3.5 percent, with arrests of those under 15 years of age falling 11.0 percent.

Arrests of males rose 2.0 percent over 2000 data and those of females increased 2.9 percent. Juvenile arrests declined for youths of both sexes, decreasing 3.5 percent for males and 4.0 percent for females.

In 2001, a total of 62.0 percent of the persons arrested for robbery were under 25 years of age. The majority of the arrestees, 89.9 percent, were males. By race, 53.8 percent of arrestees were black, 44.5 percent were white, and 1.7 percent were other races.

AGGRAVATED ASSAULT

DEFINITION

According to the Uniform Crime Reporting Program, an aggravated assault is an unlawful attack by one person upon another for the purpose of inflicting severe or aggravated bodily injury. This type of assault is usually accompanied by the use of a weapon or by means likely to produce death or great bodily harm. Attempts are included since it is not necessary that an injury result when a gun, knife, or other weapon is used which could and probably would result in serious personal injury if the crime were successfully completed.

Year	Number of offenses	Rate per 100,000 inhabitants
2000	911,706	324.0
2001	907,219	318.5
Percent change	–0.5	–1.7

With an estimated 907,219 offenses nationally, aggravated assaults accounted for 63.1 percent of the violent crimes in 2001.

Appendix II

The number of aggravated assault offenses in 2001 was the lowest since 1987.

There were 318.5 reported victims of aggravated assault per 100,000 inhabitants in 2001.

Three of the four weapon categories showed increases in usage when comparing 2001 figures to those from 2000, with personal weapons (hands, fists, feet, etc.) showing the only decrease, 2.3 percent. The increases included firearms, 1.4 percent; other weapons, 0.6 percent; and knives or other cutting instruments, 0.1 percent.

Aggravated Assault by Month
Percent distribution, 1997–2001

Month	1997	1998	1999	2000	2001
January	7.5	7.9	7.9	7.6	7.5
February	7.0	7.0	7.0	7.4	7.0
March	8.3	8.1	8.0	8.5	8.4
April	8.2	8.3	8.3	8.4	8.6
May	9.3	9.1	9.1	9.3	9.1
June	9.0	8.9	8.8	8.6	8.6
July	9.5	9.4	9.5	9.0	9.0
August	9.4	9.4	9.2	8.9	8.7
September	8.8	8.7	8.5	8.6	8.8
October	8.4	8.3	8.6	8.7	8.8
November	7.5	7.4	7.7	7.5	7.8
December	7.2	7.4	7.5	7.5	7.7

In 2001, 42.7 percent of the aggravated assault volume occurred in the South, the Nation's most populous region. The Western Region followed with 23.6 percent, the Midwest Region with 18.8 percent, and the Northeast Region with 15.0 percent.

Regionally, the aggravated assault rates ranged from 253.2 per 100,000 inhabitants in the Northeast to 380.0 per 100,000 in the South. The rates were down in all but one region. The Northeast, West, and South recorded rate decreases of 3.0, 2.7, and 2.0, respectively; however, the rate in the Midwest increased 1.0 percent.

Community Types

In 2001, the Nation's Metropolitan Statistical Areas (MSAs) experienced a rate of 343.6 aggravated assaults per 100,000 inhabitants. Cities outside MSAs had a rate of 295.0 aggravated assaults per 100,000 inhabitants, and rural counties had a rate of 168.4 aggravated assaults.

Population Groups Trends

By population group, the largest decrease in aggravated assaults, 2.9 percent, was reported in cities with 25,000 to 49,999 inhabitants, followed by cities of under 10,000 in population with a 1.4-percent decline from 2000 data. Cities with 50,000 to 99,999 inhabitants showed a 1.1-percent drop, cities with populations of 250,000 and over had a 0.8-percent decline, and cities with a population of 10,000 to 24,999 experienced a 0.4-percent fall. An increase of 0.2 percent occurred in cities with populations of 100,000 to 249,999 in 2001. Rural counties showed an increase of less than one percent (0.5), and suburban counties experienced a 1.1-percent decline in aggravated assaults.

Clearances

Overall, law enforcement agencies nationwide cleared 56.1 percent of reported aggravated assaults in 2001. Law enforcement

Aggravated Assault, Types of Weapons Used
Percent distribution by region, 2001

Region	Total all weapons[1]	Firearms	Knives or cutting instruments	Other weapons (clubs, blunt objects, etc.)	Personal weapons
Total	100.0	18.3	17.8	36.0	27.9
Northeastern States	100.0	13.9	18.4	33.7	34.0
Midwestern States	100.0	19.4	17.2	35.3	28.1
Southern States	100.0	20.0	19.5	38.7	21.9
Western States	100.0	16.8	15.2	32.7	35.3

[1] Because of rounding, the percentages may not add to total.

in cities with less than 10,000 in population reported the highest percentage of clearances for aggravated assaults, 65.7 percent. Those in rural and suburban counties recorded clearance percentages of 64.9 and 61.7, respectively.

Aggravated assaults involving personal weapons such as hands, fists, or feet were cleared 63.8 percent of the time. Aggravated assaults using a knife or cutting instrument were cleared 61.9 percent of the time. Incidents that involved firearms were cleared 41.1 percent of the time. Aggravated assaults using other weapons were cleared 55.3 percent of the time.

Geographically, the Northeastern States had the highest percentage of aggravated assaults cleared by arrest—64.4 percent. The Western States followed with 57.8 percent, the Southern States with 53.7 percent, and the Midwestern States with 52.2 percent of aggravated assaults cleared by arrest.

Arrests

Approximately 477,809 persons were arrested for aggravated assault in 2001. Of reported arrests, 79.9 percent were of males and the remaining 20.1 percent were of females. Sixty-four percent of arrestees for aggravated assault were white, 33.7 percent were black, and the remaining 2.3 percent were of all other races.

Total aggravated assault arrests were down 0.1 percent in 2001 from the 2000 figure.

BURGLARY

DEFINITION

The Uniform Crime Reporting Program defines burglary as the unlawful entry of a structure to commit a felony or theft. The use of force to gain entry is not required to classify an offense as burglary. Burglary in this Program is categorized into three subclassifications: forcible entry, unlawful entry where no force is used, and attempted forcible entry.

Year	Number of offenses	Rate per 1000,000 inhabitants
2000	2,050,992	728.8
2001	2,109,767	740.8
Percent change	+2.9	+1.6

The number of estimated burglaries for the Nation in 2001 rose 2.9 percent over those reported the previous year.

The national burglary rate of 740.8 per 100,000 inhabitants for 2001 represented a 1.6-percent increase from the previous year's

210

rate. However, this rate was significantly lower than the totals from 5 and 10 years ago.

The majority of burglaries, 65.2 percent, were residential. Most residential burglaries, 61.0 percent, occurred during the day, and most nonresidential burglaries, 58.0 percent, occurred at night. Burglaries totaled an estimated $3.3 billion for an average loss per burglary of $1,545. Residential burglaries averaged $1,381, and nonresidential burglaries averaged $1,615 in 2001.

The United States is divided into four regions: the Northeast, the Midwest, the South, and the West.

Burglary by Month
Percent distribution, 1997–2001

Month	1997	1998	1999	2000	2001
January	8.4	8.9	8.3	8.1	7.8
February	7.2	7.5	7.2	7.2	6.6
March	7.9	8.2	7.9	8.0	7.6
April	7.8	8.0	7.7	7.8	7.7
May	8.3	8.3	8.2	8.5	8.3
June	8.2	8.2	8.4	8.4	8.2
July	9.1	9.0	9.0	9.2	9.0
August	9.0	9.0	9.1	9.2	9.1
September	8.7	8.4	8.7	8.6	8.6
October	8.8	8.4	8.6	8.7	9.3
November	8.2	7.9	8.4	8.3	8.8
December	8.6	8.2	8.5	8.1	8.9

The Northeast The fewest burglaries occurred in the Northeastern States, 12.0 percent. The Northeast was the only region of the country to experience a decrease in burglary over the previous year's volume with a drop of 1.2 percent. The Northeast was also the only region to report a decrease in the burglary rate, 470.0 per 100,000 in population, down 1.6 percent from the 2000 rate.

The Midwest The Midwestern States accounted for 20.8 percent of burglaries in 2001. The burglary total represented a 2.6-percent increase over the previous year's total. The burglary rate of 677.7 per 100,000 persons denoted a 2.1-percent increase in the region's rate since 2000.

The South Proportionately, most burglaries were reported in the Southern States, 44.7 percent. The increase in the number of estimated burglaries from 2000 was 4.1 percent in these states collectively. The burglary rate for the region, 926.8 per 100,000 inhabitants, increased by 2.5 percent from the 2000 rate.

The West Western States accounted for 22.5 percent of the estimated burglaries for 2001. This total represented a 2.9-percent increase over the 2000 level. States in this region reported a slight upward trend in the burglary rate, 736.4 per 100,000, an increase of 0.9 percent over the rate from the previous year's rate.

Community Types

Metropolitan Statistical Areas (MSAs), which made up approximately 80 percent of the total U.S. population in 2001, recorded a rate of 768.8 burglaries per 100,000 persons. For cities outside MSAs, which comprised approximately 8.0 percent of the Nation's population, the rate was 764.3 burglaries per 100,000 inhabitants, and in rural counties, which accounted for approximately 12 percent of the U.S. population during 2001, the rate was 540.1. MSAs comprised 82.9 percent of the estimated burglary volume; other cities made up 8.2 percent; and rural counties, 8.8 percent.

Cities as a whole showed a 2.7-percent increase in burglaries in 2001 over burglaries reported in 2000.

Clearances

In the Nation in 2001, 12.7 percent of burglary offenses were cleared. The highest percentage of reported clearances involved unlawful entry, 14.1 percent, followed by forcible entry, 12.3 percent, and attempted forcible entry, 10.7 percent.

Law enforcement in the Northeast Region cleared 16.7 percent of burglary offenses. Those in the South cleared 12.7 percent of total burglaries; in the West, 12.1 percent; and in the Midwest, 11.1 percent.

Among the Nation's population groups, cities with populations under 10,000 revealed the highest proportion of burglary offenses cleared at 16.4 percent. Those cities with populations of 500,000 to 999,999 cleared the fewest of their burglary offenses, 8.3 percent. Total clearances for all cities was 12.3 percent.

When an offender under the age of 18 is cited to appear in juvenile court or before other juvenile authorities, the UCR Program records that incident as cleared by arrest, even though a physical arrest may not have occurred. In addition, according to Program definitions, clearances involving both adult and juvenile offenders are classified as adult clearances. In 2001, 18.5 percent of all burglary clearances involved only juveniles.

Arrests

The estimated number of arrests nationwide for burglary for 2001 was 291,444, an arrest rate of 103.3 per 100,000 inhabitants. Law enforcement agencies in the West recorded the highest rate of burglary arrests, 124.9 per 100,000. Those in the Southern States had an arrest rate of 108.9 per 100,000 persons, followed by the Northeast, 82.2, and the Midwest, 78.0. Among the population groups, arrest rates ranged from a high of 131.1 recorded for cities of 100,000 to 249,999 to a low of 84.9 reported by suburban counties.

Overall, arrests for burglary increased 0.4 percent when compared to the previous year's figure. However, the number of burglary arrests nationwide was considerably lower than the number from 5 and 10 years ago.

By age of arrestees, 31.0 percent of burglary arrestees were juveniles, and 11.7 percent of the total arrestees were under age 15. By gender, males comprised the majority of burglary arrestees, 86.4 percent, in 2001. Of these arrests, 31.6 percent were males under age 18. For females, 13.6 percent were arrested for burglary and of those, 27.4 percent were juveniles.

By race, 69.4 percent of burglary arrestees were white, 28.5 percent were black, and other races accounted for the remaining 2.1 percent. Whites made up 68.1 percent, blacks 29.9 percent, and other races comprised 2.0 percent of adult arrestees. For individuals under age 18 arrested for burglary, 72.3 percent were white, 25.2 percent were black, and 2.5 percent were of all other races.

LARCENY-THEFT

<table>
<tr><td colspan="3" align="center">DEFINITION</td></tr>
<tr><td colspan="3">Larceny-theft is the unlawful taking, carrying, leading, or riding away of property from the possession or constructive possession of another. It includes crimes such as shoplifting, pocket-picking, purse-snatching, thefts from motor vehicles, thefts of motor vehicle parts and accessories, bicycle thefts, etc., in which no use of force, violence, or fraud occurs.</td></tr>
<tr><td>Year</td><td>Number of offenses</td><td>Rate per 100,000 inhabitants</td></tr>
<tr><td>2000</td><td>6,971,590</td><td>2,477.3</td></tr>
<tr><td>2001</td><td>7,076,171</td><td>2,484.6</td></tr>
<tr><td>Percent change</td><td>+1.5</td><td>+0.3</td></tr>
</table>

In 2001, the estimated number of larceny-theft offenses in the Nation exceeded 7 million and cost the Nation an estimated $5.2 billion in losses.

The estimated 7,076,171 larceny-theft offenses reported to law enforcement in the Nation translated into a larceny every 4.5 seconds and accounted for 59.7 percent of all Crime Index offenses and 68.0 percent of all property crimes. The 2001 estimate was up 1.5 percent from the 2000 estimate of 6,971,590 offenses.

In 2001, the Nation experienced a rate of larceny-thefts of 2,484.6 per 100,000 population. This figure was a slight increase of 0.3 percent over the 2000 estimated rate but a 14.1-percent decrease in comparison to the 1997 rate and a 19.9-percent decrease when compared to the 1992 rate.

In 2001, data collected regarding the Nation's four regions reflect the following: The South, the most populous region, had 40.7 percent of all larceny offenses. The West had 22.9 percent of the total, the Midwest, 22.8 percent, and the Northeast, 13.6 percent of all larcenies.

When 2001 regional volumes are compared to the 2000 figures, the lone decrease in volume occurred in the Northeast, with a 1.4-percent drop. Of the regions posting increases, the volume of larceny-thefts in the West rose 4.8 percent. In the Midwest, the volume of larceny-theft offenses increased 1.1 percent, and in the South, the volume was up 0.9 percent.

Community Types

By community types, Metropolitan Statistical Areas had a rate of 2,647.0 larceny offenses per 100,000 inhabitants. Cities outside MSAs had a rate of 3,087.7, and rural counties experienced a rate of 1,014.0 per 100,000 population.

Distribution

Thefts from motor vehicles accounted for 25.8 percent and shoplifting 13.8 percent of all larcenies in 2001. Thefts from buildings made up 13.3 percent of the total; 10.2 percent of larcenies were thefts of motor vehicle accessories.

An estimated $5.2 billion in property was lost because of larceny-theft in 2001, an increase from the 2000 estimate of $5.1 billion. The average dollar value per offense was $730, an increase from the $727 in 2000.

In 2001, thefts from buildings was the larceny-theft offense with the highest average loss, $1,037. For thefts from motor vehicles, the average value loss was $719, and for thefts of motor vehicle accessories, $451. Purse-snatchings had an average value loss of $331, and thefts of bicycles an average loss of $318. Pocket-

picking resulted in an average value loss of $305, and in thefts from coin-operated machines, the loss was $286. The category with the lowest average loss, $182, was shoplifting. For the all other category, the average dollar loss was $1,024.

Larceny-theft by Month
Percent distribution, 1997–2001

Month	1997	1998	1999	2000	2001
January	8.0	8.4	7.8	7.6	7.7
February	7.2	7.5	7.2	7.3	6.8
March	8.0	8.2	8.0	8.2	7.9
April	8.0	8.1	8.0	7.9	8.0
May	8.4	8.4	8.4	8.6	8.6
June	8.6	8.6	8.7	8.8	8.6
July	9.2	9.0	9.1	9.2	9.0
August	9.1	9.0	9.2	9.2	9.1
September	8.5	8.4	8.5	8.5	8.4
October	8.8	8.5	8.7	8.8	9.1
November	7.9	7.8	8.1	8.0	8.3
December	8.3	8.2	8.3	7.9	8.6

Clearances

Of the larceny-thefts reported to law enforcement in 2001, 17.6 percent were cleared by arrest or exceptional means. By population group, cities with 10,000 to 24,999 inhabitants had the highest number of clearances among the Nation's cities, 22.5 percent, and cities with 500,000 to 999,999 inhabitants cleared the least of their larceny-theft offenses, 11.6 percent. Law enforcement in rural counties cleared 17.8 percent of larceny-thefts, and law enforcement in suburban counties cleared 16.0 percent.

Nearly 22 percent (21.9) of all larceny-theft clearances were of juveniles (persons under 18 years of age).

Larceny-theft
Percent distribution by region, 2001

Type	United States Total	North-eastern States	Mid-western States	Southern States	Western States
Total[1]	100.0	100.0	100.0	100.0	100.0
Pocket-picking	0.5	1.1	0.3	0.4	0.4
Purse-snatching	0.5	1.0	0.4	0.4	0.6
Shoplifting	13.8	15.0	12.8	13.3	14.7
From motor vehicles (except accessories)	25.8	21.1	23.9	24.8	31.2
Motor vehicle accessories	10.2	7.9	10.7	10.1	11.2
Bicycles	4.1	5.9	4.5	3.4	4.2
From buildings	13.3	16.8	14.8	11.4	13.7
From coin-operated machines	0.7	0.6	0.6	0.8	0.7
All others	31.0	30.6	31.9	35.4	23.3

[1] Because of rounding, the percentages may not add to total.

Arrests

The number of estimated arrests for larceny-thefts in the Nation in 2001 was 1,160,821, or 8.5 percent of the 13.7 million total estimated arrests for the United States. Larceny arrests accounted for 71.7 percent of the 1.6 million estimated arrests for all property crimes, and 51.7 percent of the estimated 2.2 million arrests for all Crime Index offenses in 2001.

Larceny-theft arrests in 2001 were down 1.9 percent from the 2000 figure. Larceny-theft arrests of juveniles declined 6.3 percent from the 2000 figure. Adult arrests for larceny-thefts showed a slight increase, 0.2 percent, from the 2000 number.

In 2001, juvenile arrests accounted for 29.6 percent of all larceny-theft arrests, and adult arrests comprised 70.4 percent. Of the juveniles arrested for larceny-theft, 68.9 percent were white, 27.8 percent were black, 2.0 percent were Asian or Pacific Islander, and 1.4 percent were American Indian or Alaskan Native.

Males accounted for 63.5 percent of the total arrests for larceny-theft, and females accounted for 36.5 percent of the arrests. By race, 66.1 percent of arrestees for larceny-theft in 2001 were white, 31.2 percent were black, 1.5 percent were Asian or Pacific Islander, and the remaining 1.2 percent were American Indian or Alaskan Native.

MOTOR VEHICLE THEFT

DEFINITION

Defined as the theft or attempted theft of a motor vehicle, this offense category includes the stealing of automobiles, trucks, buses, motorcycles, motorscooters, snowmobiles, etc. The definition excludes the taking of a motor vehicle for temporary use by those persons having lawful access.

Year	Number of offenses	Rate per 100,000 inhabitants
2000	1,160,002	412.2
2001	1,226,457	430.6
Percent change	+5.7	+4.5

The estimated 1,226,457 motor vehicle thefts in the Nation in 2001 represent a 5.7-percent increase from the previous year's estimate. When compared to 5 and 10 years ago, the level of motor vehicle theft was down 9.4 percent from the 1997 level and declined 23.9 percent from the 1992 level.

The average value of motor vehicles reported stolen in 2001 was $6,646. With the estimated total value of all motor vehicles stolen at $8.2 billion, approximately 62.0 percent of that amount was recovered.

In 2001, data collected regarding the Nation's four regions reflect the following:

The Northeast The Northeastern States accounted for 14.0 percent of all motor vehicle thefts in 2001. The region experienced a slight drop, 0.6 percent, in the estimated volume of motor vehicle thefts from the 2000 estimate. The Northeast, with a rate of 318.8 motor vehicle thefts per 100,000 persons, was the only region of the Nation that experienced a decline in the motor vehicle theft rate with a 1.0-percent drop.

The Midwest The Midwestern States reported 20.0 percent of the total estimated motor vehicle thefts. The total number of vehicle thefts in 2001 was a 3.4-percent increase from the previous year's number.

The South The Southern States reported the highest percentage of motor vehicle thefts among the Nation's four regions with 35.5 percent of the total estimate. This region saw a 4.0-percent increase

from the 2000 estimate. The rate of 427.6 thefts per 100,000 in population was a 2.4-percent increase over the previous year's rate.

The West The Western States accounted for 30.5 percent of the Nation's motor vehicle thefts. This region had the largest rise in the volume of vehicle thefts—12.9 percent—over the 2000 total.

Motor Vehicle Theft by Month
Percent distribution, 1997–2001

Month	1997	1998	1999	2000	2001
January	9.0	9.1	8.5	8.1	8.1
February	7.6	7.9	7.3	7.4	6.9
March	8.2	8.5	7.9	8.0	7.7
April	7.9	7.9	7.7	7.6	7.6
May	8.2	8.3	8.0	8.2	8.0
June	8.1	8.1	8.2	8.3	8.2
July	8.7	8.7	8.8	8.9	9.0
August	8.7	8.8	9.0	9.1	8.8
September	8.3	8.3	8.5	8.5	8.5
October	8.6	8.4	8.8	8.7	9.3
November	8.2	7.9	8.5	8.5	8.8
December	8.3	8.1	8.8	8.6	9.2

Community and Population Types

Metropolitan Statistical Areas (MSAs) had a rate of 499.1 motor vehicle thefts per 100,000 persons and accounted for 92.6 percent of all motor vehicle theft offenses; cities outside MSAs, a rate of 205.5 vehicles stolen and 3.8 percent of offenses; and rural counties had a rate of 127.3 motor vehicle thefts per 100,000 persons and accounted for 3.6 percent of all stolen vehicle offenses.

The highest rate of motor vehicle thefts, 1,072.4 per 100,000 inhabitants, was in cities with populations of 250,000 to 499,999.

Clearances

Nationally, clearances of motor vehicle thefts in 2001 totaled 13.6 percent. Clearances were highest in the Midwest and South at 15.6 percent. Motor vehicle thefts were cleared at 13.9 percent in the Northeast and 10.8 percent in the West.

Motor Vehicle Theft
Percent distribution by region, 2001

Region	Total[1]	Autos	Trucks and buses	Other vehicles
Total	100.0	73.7	18.9	7.3
Northeastern States	100.0	87.9	6.0	6.1
Midwestern States	100.0	77.7	15.2	7.1
Southern States	100.0	70.9	20.1	8.9
Western States	100.0	70.1	23.8	6.1

[1] Because of rounding, the percentages may not add to total.

In the Nation, 14.1 percent of automobile thefts were cleared, 11.6 percent of truck and bus thefts were cleared, and 13.1 percent of thefts of other vehicle types were cleared. Law enforcement in rural counties recorded the highest number of clearances for automobiles stolen, 32.1 percent, as well as for stolen trucks and buses, 28.3 percent. Cities 250,000 to 499,999 in population had the highest number of clearances in the other vehicles category at 21.0 percent.

Arrests

An estimated 147,451 persons were arrested for motor vehicle theft in the Nation in 2001.

Regionally, the Western States reported the highest rate of arrests per 100,000 persons at 70.2. The Midwestern States had a rate of 64.0, followed by the Southern States at 41.5 and the Northeastern States at 35.3.

By gender, males comprised 83.6 percent of all arrestees for motor vehicle theft. By race, whites accounted for 57.5 percent of motor vehicle theft arrestees, and blacks made up 39.8 percent. Asian or Pacific Islander, at 1.8 percent, and American Indian or Alaskan Native, at 0.9 percent, accounted for the remainder of arrestees.

Although the number of arrests were up 2.7 percent over the previous year's figure, motor vehicle theft arrests were down 11.8 percent from the 1997 number and down 30.3 percent from the 1992 number. Nationally, adult arrestees for motor vehicle theft in 2001 increased 5.2 percent from the 2000 total.

---

*Editor's note: Data in this document have been edited. The complete text for the *Crime in the United States, 2001*, report may be accessed at: http://www.fbi.gov/ucr/cius_01/01crime1.pdf.

Glossary

A

Abet To encourage another to commit a crime.

Accessory One who harbors, assists, or protects another person, although he or she knows that person has committed or will commit a crime.

Accomplice One who knowingly and voluntarily aids another in committing a criminal offense.

Acquit To free a person legally from an accusation of criminal guilt.

Adjudicatory hearing The fact-finding process wherein the court determines whether or not there is sufficient evidence to sustain the allegations in a petition.

Administrative law Regulates many daily business activities, and violations of such regulations generally result in warnings or fines, depending upon their adjudged severity.

Admissible Capable of being admitted; in a trial, such evidence as the judge allows to be introduced into the proceeding.

Affirmance A pronouncement by a higher court that the case in question was rightly decided by the lower court from which the case was appealed.

Affirmation Positive declaration or assertion that the witness will tell the truth; not made under oath.

Aggravated assault The unlawful attack by one person upon another for the purpose of inflicting severe or aggravated bodily injury.

Alias Any name by which one is known other than his or her true name.

Alibi A type of defense in a criminal prosecution that proves the accused could not have committed the crime with which he or she is charged, since evidence offered shows the accused was in another place at the time the crime was committed.

Allegation An assertion of what a party to an action expects to prove.

American Bar Association (ABA) A professional association, comprising attorneys who have been admitted to the bar in any of the 50 states, and a registered lobby.

American Civil Liberties Union (ACLU) Founded in 1920 with the purpose of defending the individual's rights as guaranteed by the U.S. Constitution.

Amnesty A class or group pardon.

Annulment The act, by competent authority, of canceling, making void, or depriving of all force.

Antisocial personality disorder Refers to individuals who are basically unsocialized and whose behavior pattern brings them repeatedly into conflict with society.

Appeal A case carried to a higher court to ask that the decision of the lower court, in which the case originated, be altered or overruled completely.

Appellate court A court that has jurisdiction to hear cases on appeal; not a trial court.

Arbitrator The person chosen by parties in a controversy to settle their differences; private judges.

Arraignment The appearance before the court of a person charged with a crime. He or she is advised of the charges, bail is set, and a plea of "guilty" or "not guilty" is entered.

Arrest The legal detainment of a person to answer for criminal charges or civil demands.

Autopsy A postmortem examination of a human body to determine the cause of death.

B

Bail Property (usually money) deposited with a court in exchange for the release of a person in custody to ensure later appearance.

Bail bond An obligation signed by the accused and his or her sureties that ensures his or her presence in court.

Bailiff An officer of the court who is responsible for keeping order in the court and protecting the security of jury deliberations and court property.

Behavior theory An approach to understanding human activity that holds that behavior is determined by consequences it produces for the individual.

Bench warrant An order by the court for the apprehension and arrest of a defendant or other person who has failed to appear when so ordered.

Bill of Rights The first 10 amendments to the U.S. Constitution that state certain fundamental rights and privileges that are guaranteed to the people against infringement by the government.

Biocriminology A relatively new branch of criminology that attempts to explain criminal behavior by referring to biological factors which predispose some individuals to commit criminal acts. *See also Criminal biology.*

Blue laws Laws in some jurisdictions prohibiting sales of merchandise, athletic contests, and the sale of alcoholic beverages on Sundays.

Booking A law-enforcement or correctional process officially recording an entry-into-detention after arrest and identifying the person, place, time, reason for the arrest, and the arresting authority.

Breathalizer A commercial device to test the breath of a suspected drinker and to determine that person's blood-alcohol content.

Brief A summary of the law relating to a case, prepared by the attorneys for both parties and given to the judge.

Burden of proof Duty of establishing the existence of fact in a trial.

C

Calendar A list of cases to be heard in a trial court, on a specific day, and containing the title of the case, the lawyers involved, and the index number.

Capital crime Any crime that may be punishable by death or imprisonment for life.

Capital punishment The legal imposition of a sentence of death upon a convicted offender.

Glossary

Career criminal   A person having a past record of multiple arrests or convictions for crimes of varying degrees of seriousness. Such criminals are often described as chronic, habitual, repeat, serious, high-rate, or professional offenders.

Case   At the level of police or prosecutorial investigation, a set of circumstances under investigation involving one or more persons.

Case law   Judicial precedent generated as a by-product of the decisions that courts have made to resolve unique disputes. Case law concerns concrete facts, as distinguished from statutes and constitutions, which are written in the abstract.

Change of venue   The removal of a trial from one jurisdiction to another in order to avoid local prejudice.

Charge   In criminal law, the accusation made against a person. It also refers to the judge's instruction to the jury on legal points.

Circumstantial evidence   Indirect evidence; evidence from which a fact can be reasonably inferred, although not directly proven.

Civil law   That body of laws that regulates arrangements between individuals, such as contracts and claims to property.

Clemency   The doctrine under which executive or legislative action reduces the severity of or waives legal punishment of one or more individuals, or an individual exempted from prosecution for certain actions.

Code   A compilation, compendium, or revision of laws, arranged into chapters, having a table of contents and index, and promulgated by legislative authority. *See also Penal code.*

Coercion   The use of force to compel performance of an action; the application of sanctions or the use of force by government to compel observance of law or public policy.

Common law   Judge-made law to assist courts through decision making with traditions, customs, and usage of previous court decisions.

Commutation   A reduction of a sentence originally prescribed by a court.

Complainant   The victim of a crime who brings the facts to the attention of the authorities.

Complaint   Any accusation that a person committed a crime that has originated or been received by a law enforcement agency or court.

Confession   A statement by a person who admits violation of the law.

Confiscation   Government seizure of private property without compensation to the owner.

Conspiracy   An agreement between two or more persons to plan for the purpose of committing a crime or any unlawful act or a lawful act by unlawful or criminal means.

Contempt of court   Intentionally obstructing a court in the administration of justice, acting in a way calculated to lessen its authority or dignity, or failing to obey its lawful order.

Continuance   Postponement or adjournment of a trial granted by the judge, either to a later date or indefinitely.

Contraband   Goods, the possession of which is illegal.

Conviction   A finding by the jury (or by the trial judge in cases tried without a jury) that the accused is guilty of a crime.

Corporal punishment   Physical punishment.

Corpus delicti (Lat.)   The objective proof that a crime has been committed as distinguished from an accidental death, injury, or loss.

Corrections   Area of criminal justice dealing with convicted offenders in jails, prisons, on probation, or parole.

Corroborating evidence   Supplementary evidence that tends to strengthen or confirm other evidence given previously.

Crime   An act injurious to the public, which is prohibited and punishable by law.

Crime Index   A set of numbers indicating the volume, fluctuation, and distribution of crimes reported to local law enforcement agencies for the United States as a whole.

Crime of passion   An unpremeditated murder or assault committed under circumstances of great anger, jealousy, or other emotional stress.

Criminal biology   The scientific study of the relation of hereditary physical traits to criminal character, that is, to innate tendencies to commit crime in general or crimes of any particular type. *See also Biocriminology.*

Criminal insanity   Lack of mental capacity to do or refrain from doing a criminal act; inability to distinguish right from wrong.

Criminal intent   The intent to commit an act, the results of which are a crime or violation of the law.

Criminalistics   Crime laboratory procedures.

Criminology   The scientific study of crime, criminals, corrections, and the operation of the system of criminal justice.

Cross examination   The questioning of a witness by the party who did not produce the witness.

Culpable   At fault or responsible, but not necessarily criminal.

D

Defamation   Intentional causing, or attempting to cause, damage to the reputation of another by communicating false or distorted information about his or her actions, motives, or character.

Defendant   The person who is being prosecuted.

Deliberation   The action of a jury to determine the guilt or innocence, or the sentence, of a defendant.

Demurrer   Plea for dismissal of a suit on the grounds that, even if true, the statements of the opposition are insufficient to sustain the claim.

Deposition   Sworn testimony obtained outside, rather than in, court.

Deterrence   A theory that swift and sure punishment will discourage others from similar illegal acts.

Dilatory   Law term that describes activity for the purpose of causing a delay or to gain time or postpone a decision.

Direct evidence   Testimony or other proof that expressly or straightforwardly proves the existence of fact.

Direct examination   The first questioning of witnesses by the party who calls them.

Directed verdict   An order or verdict pronounced by a judge during the trial of a criminal case in which the evidence presented by the prosecution clearly fails to show the guilt of the accused.

District attorney   A locally elected state official who represents the state in bringing indictments and prosecuting criminal cases.

DNA fingerprinting   The use of biological residue found at the scene of a crime for genetic comparisons in aiding the identification of criminal suspects.

Docket   The formal record of court proceedings.

Double jeopardy To be prosecuted twice for the same offense.

Due process model A philosophy of criminal justice based on the assumption that an individual is presumed innocent until proven guilty.

Due process of law A clause in the Fifth and Fourteenth Amendments ensuring that laws are reasonable and that they are applied in a fair and equal manner.

E

Embracery An attempt to influence a jury, or a member thereof, in their verdict by any improper means.

Entrapment Inducing an individual to commit a crime he or she did not contemplate, for the sole purpose of instituting a criminal prosecution against the offender.

Evidence All the means used to prove or disprove the fact at issue. *See also Corpus delicti.*

Ex post facto (Lat.) After the fact. An *ex post facto law is a criminal law that makes an act unlawful although it was committed prior to the passage of that law. See also Grandfather clause.*

Exception A formal objection to the action of the court during a trial. The indication is that the excepting party will seek to reverse the court's actions at some future proceeding.

Exclusionary rule Legal prohibitions against government prosecution using evidence illegally obtained.

Expert evidence Testimony by one qualified to speak authoritatively on technical matters because of her or his special training or skill.

Extradition The surrender by one state to another of an individual accused of a crime.

F

False arrest Any unlawful physical restraint of another's freedom of movement; unlawful arrest.

Felony A criminal offense punishable by death or imprisonment in a penitentiary.

Forensic Relating to the court. Forensic medicine would refer to legal medicine that applies anatomy, pathology, toxicology, chemistry, and other fields of science in expert testimony in court cases or hearings.

G

Grand jury A group of 12 to 23 citizens of a county who examine evidence against the person suspected of a crime and hand down an indictment if there is sufficient evidence. *See also Petit jury.*

Grandfather clause A clause attempting to preserve the rights of firms in operation before enactment of a law by exempting these firms from certain provisions of that law. *See also Ex post facto.*

H

Habeas corpus (Lat.) A legal device to challenge the detention of a person taken into custody. An individual in custody may demand an evidentiary hearing before a judge to examine the legality of the detention.

Hearsay Evidence that a witness has learned through others.

Homicide The killing of a human being; may be murder, negligent or nonnegligent manslaughter, or excusable or justifiable homicide.

Hung jury A jury which, after long deliberation, is so irreconcilably divided in opinion that it is unable to reach a unanimous verdict.

I

Impanel The process of selecting the jury that is to try a case.

Imprisonment A sentence imposed upon the conviction of a crime; the deprivation of liberty in a penal institution; incarceration.

In camera (Lat.) A case heard when the doors of the court are closed and only persons concerned in the case are admitted.

Indemnification Compensation for loss or damage sustained because of improper or illegal action by a public authority.

Indictment The document prepared by a prosecutor and approved by the grand jury that charges a certain person with a specific crime or crimes for which that person is later to be tried in court.

Injunction An order by a court prohibiting a defendant from committing an act, or commanding an act be done.

Inquest A legal inquiry to establish some question of fact; specifically, an inquiry by a coroner and jury into a person's death where accident, foul play, or violence is suspected as the cause.

Instanter A subpoena issued for the appearance of a hostile witness or person who has failed to appear in answer to a previous subpoena and authorizing a law enforcement officer to bring that person to the court.

Interpol (International Criminal Police Commission) A clearing house for international exchanges of information, consisting of a consortium of 126 countries.

J

Jeopardy The danger of conviction and punishment that a defendant faces in a criminal trial.

Judge An officer who presides over and administers the law in a court of justice.

Judicial notice The rule that a court will accept certain things as common knowledge without proof.

Judicial process The procedures taken by a court in deciding cases or resolving legal controversies.

Jurisdiction The territory, subject matter, or persons over which lawful authority may be exercised by a court or other justice agency, as determined by statute or constitution.

Jury A certain number of persons who are sworn to examine the evidence and determine the truth on the basis of that evidence. *See also Hung jury.*

Justice of the peace A subordinate magistrate, usually without formal legal training, empowered to try petty civil and criminal cases and, in some states, to conduct preliminary hearings for persons accused of a crime, and to fix bail for appearance in court.

Juvenile delinquent A boy or girl who has not reached the age of criminal liability (varies from state to state) and who commits an act that would be a misdemeanor or felony if he or she were an adult. Delinquents are tried in Juvenile Court and confined to separate facilities.

L

Law Enforcement Agency   A federal, state, or local criminal justice agency or identifiable subunit whose principal functions are the prevention, detection, and investigation of crime and the apprehension of alleged offenders.

Libel and slander   Printed and spoken defamation of character, respectively, of a person or an institution. In a slander action, it is usually necessary to prove specific damages caused by spoken words, but in a case of libel, the damage is assumed to have occurred by publication.

Lie detector   An instrument that measures certain physiological reactions of the human body from which a trained operator may determine whether the subject is telling the truth or lying; polygraph; psychological stress evaluator.

Litigation   A judicial controversy; a contest in a court of justice for the purpose of enforcing a right; any controversy that must be decided upon evidence.

M

Mala fides (Lat.)   Bad faith, as opposed to *bona fides, or good faith.*

Mala in se (Lat.)   Evil in itself. Acts that are made crimes because they are, by their nature, evil and morally wrong.

Mala prohibita (Lat.)   Evil because they are prohibited. Acts that are not wrong in themselves but which, to protect the general welfare, are made crimes by statute.

Malfeasance   The act of a public officer in committing a crime relating to his official duties or powers, such as accepting or demanding a bribe.

Malice   An evil intent to vex, annoy, or injure another; intentional evil.

Mandatory sentences   A statutory requirement that a certain penalty shall be set and carried out in all cases upon conviction for a specified offense or series of offenses.

Martial law   Refers to control of civilian populations by a military commander.

Mediation   Nonbinding third-party intervention in the collective bargaining process.

Mens rea (Lat.)   Criminal intent.

Miranda rights   Set of rights that a person accused or suspected of having committed a specific offense has during interrogation and of which he or she must be informed prior to questioning, as stated by the Supreme Court in deciding *Miranda v. Arizona in 1966 and related cases.*

Misdemeanor   Any crime not a felony. Usually, a crime punishable by a fine or imprisonment in the county or other local jail.

Misprison   Failing to reveal a crime.

Mistrial   A trial discontinued before reaching a verdict because of some procedural defect or impediment.

Modus operandi   A characteristic pattern of behavior repeated in a series of offenses that coincides with the pattern evidenced by a particular person or group of persons.

Motion   An oral or written request made to a court at any time before, during, or after court proceedings, asking the court to make a specified finding, decision, or order.

Motive   The reason for committing a crime.

Municipal court   A minor court authorized by municipal charter or state law to enforce local ordinances and exercise the criminal and civil jurisdiction of the peace.

N

Narc   A widely used slang term for any local or federal law enforcement officer whose duties are focused on preventing or controlling traffic in and the use of illegal drugs.

Negligent   Culpably careless; acting without the due care required by the circumstances.

Neolombrosians   Criminologists who emphasize psychopathological states as causes of crime.

No bill   A phrase used by a grand jury when it fails to indict.

Nolle prosequi (Lat.)   A prosecutor's decision not to initiate or continue prosecution.

Nolo contendre (Lat., lit.)   A pleading, usually used by a defendant in a criminal case, that literally means "I will not contest."

Notary public   A public officer authorized to authenticate and certify documents such as deeds, contracts, and affidavits with his or her signature and seal.

Null   Of no legal or binding force.

O

Obiter dictum (Lat.)   A belief or opinion included by a judge in his or her decision in a case.

Objection   The act of taking exception to some statement or procedure in a trial. Used to call the court's attention to some improper evidence or procedure.

Opinion evidence   A witness's belief or opinion about a fact in dispute, as distinguished from personal knowledge of the fact.

Ordinance   A law enacted by the city or municipal government.

Organized crime   An organized, continuing criminal conspiracy that engages in crime as a business (e.g., loan sharking, illegal gambling, prostitution, extortion, etc.).

Original jurisdiction   The authority of a court to hear and determine a lawsuit when it is initiated.

Overt act   An open or physical act done to further a plan, conspiracy, or intent, as opposed to a thought or mere intention.

P

Paralegals   Employees, also known as legal assistants, of law firms, who assist attorneys in the delivery of legal services.

Pardon   There are two kinds of pardons of offenses (1) the absolute pardon, which fully restores to the individual all rights and privileges of a citizen, setting aside a conviction and penalty, and (2) the conditional pardon, which requires a condition to be met before the pardon is officially granted.

Parole   A conditional, supervised release from prison prior to expiration of sentence.

Penal code   Criminal codes, the purpose of which is to define what acts shall be punished as crimes.

Penology   The study of punishment and corrections.

Peremptory challenge   In the selection of jurors, challenges made by either side to certain jurors without assigning any reason, and which the court must allow.

Perjury   The legal offense of deliberately testifying falsely under oath about a material fact.

Perpetrator   The chief actor in the commission of a crime, that is, the person who directly commits the criminal act.

Petit jury   The ordinary jury composed of 12 persons who hear criminal cases and determines guilt or innocence of the accused. *See also Grand jury.*

Plaintiff   A person who initiates a court action.

Plea bargaining   A negotiation between the defense attorney and the prosecutor in which the defendant receives a reduced penalty in return for a plea of "guilty."

Police power   The authority to legislate for the protection of the health, morals, safety, and welfare of the people.

Postmortem   After death. Commonly applied to an examination of a dead body. *See also Autopsy.*

Precedent   Decision by a court that may serve as an example or authority for similar cases in the future.

Preliminary hearing   The proceeding in front of a lower court to determine if there is sufficient evidence for submitting a felony case to the grand jury.

Premeditation   A design to commit a crime or commit some other act before it is done.

Presumption of fact   An inference as to the truth or falsity of any proposition or fact, made in the absence of actual certainty of its truth or falsity or until such certainty can be attained.

Presumption of innocence   The defendant is presumed to be innocent and the burden is on the state to prove his or her guilt beyond a reasonable doubt.

Presumption of law   A rule of law that courts and judges must draw a particular inference from a particular fact or evidence, unless the inference can be disproved.

Probable cause   A set of facts and circumstances that would induce a reasonably intelligent and prudent person to believe that a particular person had committed a specific crime; reasonable grounds to make or believe an accusation.

Probation   A penalty placing a convicted person under the supervision of a probation officer for a stated time, instead of being confined.

Prosecutor   One who initiates a criminal prosecution against an accused; one who acts as a trial attorney for the government as the representative of the people.

Public defender   An attorney appointed by a court to represent individuals in criminal proceedings who do not have the resources to hire their own defense council.

R

Rap sheet   Popularized acronym for record of arrest and prosecution.

Reasonable doubt   That state of mind of jurors when they do not feel a moral certainty about the truth of the charge and when the evidence does not exclude every other reasonable hypothesis except that the defendant is guilty as charged.

Rebutting evidence   When the defense has produced new evidence that the prosecution has not dealt with, the court, at its discretion, may allow the prosecution to give evidence in reply to rebut or contradict it.

Recidivism   The repetition of criminal behavior.

Repeal   The abrogation of a law by the enacting body, either by express declaration or implication by the passage of a later act whose provisions contradict those of the earlier law.

Reprieve   The temporary postponement of the execution of a sentence.

Restitution   A court requirement that an alleged or convicted offender must pay money or provide services to the victim of the crime or provide services to the community.

Restraining order   An order, issued by a court of competent jurisdiction, forbidding a named person, or a class of persons, from doing specified acts.

Retribution   A concept that implies that payment of a debt to society and thus the expiation of one's offense. It was codified in the biblical injunction, "an eye for an eye, a tooth for a tooth."

S

Sanction   A legal penalty assessed for the violation of law. The term also includes social methods of obtaining compliance, such as peer pressure and public opinion.

Search warrant   A written order, issued by judicial authority in the name of the state, directing a law enforcement officer to search for personal property and, if found, to bring it before the court.

Selective enforcement   The deploying of police personnel in ways to cope most effectively with existing or anticipated problems.

Self-incrimination   In constitutional terms, the process of becoming involved in or charged with a crime by one's own testimony.

Sentence   The penalty imposed by a court on a person convicted of a crime, the court judgment specifying the penalty, and any disposition of a defendant resulting from a conviction, including the court decision to suspend execution of a sentence.

Small claims court   A special court that provides expeditious, informal, and inexpensive adjudication of small contractual claims. In most jurisdictions, attorneys are not permitted for cases, and claims are limited to a specific amount.

Stare decisis (Lat.)   To abide by decided cases. The doctrine that once a court has laid down a principle of laws as applicable to certain facts, it will apply it to all future cases when the facts are substantially the same.

State's attorney   An officer, usually locally elected within a county, who represents the state in securing indictments and in prosecuting criminal cases.

State's evidence   Testimony by a participant in the commission of a crime that incriminates others involved, given under the promise of immunity.

Status offense   An act that is declared by statute to be an offense, but only when committed or engaged in by a juvenile, and that can be adjudicated only by a juvenile court.

Statute   A law enacted by, or with the authority of, a legislature.

Statute of limitations   A term applied to numerous statutes that set limits on the length of time after which rights cannot be enforced in a legal action or offenses cannot be punished.

Stay   A halting of a judicial proceeding by a court order.

Sting operation   The typical sting involves using various undercover methods to control crime.

Subpoena   A court order requiring a witness to attend and testify as a witness in a court proceeding.

Subpoena *duces tecum*   A court order requiring a witness to bring all books, documents, and papers that might affect the outcome of the proceedings.

Glossary

Summons A written order issued by a judicial officer requiring a person accused of a criminal offense to appear in a designated court at a specified time to answer the charge(s).

Superior court A court of record or general trial court, superior to a justice of the peace or magistrate's court. In some states, an intermediate court between the general trial court and the highest appellate court.

Supreme court, state Usually the highest court in the state judicial system.

Supreme Court, U.S. Heads the judicial branch of the American government and is the nation's highest law court.

Suspect An adult or juvenile considered by a criminal agency to be one who may have committed a specific criminal offense but who has not yet been arrested or charged.

T

Testimony Evidence given by a competent witness, under oath, as distinguished from evidence from writings and other sources.

Tort A breach of a duty to an individual that results in damage to him or her, for which one may be sued in civil court for damages. Crime, in contrast, may be called a breach of duty to the public. Some actions may constitute both torts and crimes.

U

Uniform Crime Reports (U.C.R.) Annual statistical tabulation of "crimes known to the police" and "crimes cleared by arrest," published by the Federal Bureau of Investigation.

United States Claims Court Established in 1982, it serves as the court of original and exclusive jurisdiction over claims brought against the federal government, except for tort claims, which are heard by district courts.

United States district courts Trial courts with original jurisdiction over diversity-of-citizenship cases and cases arising under U.S. criminal, bankruptcy, admiralty, patent, copyright, and postal laws.

V

Venue The locality in which a suit may be tried.

Verdict The decision of a court.

Vice squad A special detail of police agents, charged with raiding and closing houses of prostitution and gambling resorts.

Victim and Witness Protection Act of 1984 The federal VWP Act and state laws protect crime victims and witnesses against physical and verbal intimidation where such intimidation is designed to discourage reporting of crimes and participation in criminal trials.

Victimology The study of the psychological and dynamic interrelationships between victims and offenders, with a view toward crime prevention.

Vigilante An individual or member of a group who undertakes to enforce the law and/or maintain morals without legal authority.

Voir dire (Fr.) The examination or questioning of prospective jurors in order to determine his or her qualifications to serve as a juror.

W

Warrant A court order directing a police officer to arrest a named person or search a specific premise.

White-collar crime Nonviolent crime for financial gain committed by means of deception by persons who use their special occupational skills and opportunities.

Witness Anyone called to testify by either side in a trial. More broadly, a witness is anyone who has observed an event.

Work release (furlough programs) Change in prisoners' status to minimum custody with permission to work outside prison.

World Court Formally known as the International Court of Justice, it deals with disputes involving international law.

SOURCES

The Dictionary of Criminal Justice, Fourth Edition, © 1994 by George E. Rush. Published by McGraw-Hill/Duchkin, Guilford, CT 06437.

Index

A

abuse of force, 109
academic approach, 108–109
Afghanistan, 10
aftercare, 7
Al Qaeda, 11, 12, 13, 14
alienation, police suicide and, 113
American Bar Association (ABA), death penalty and, 201
American Civil Liberties Union (ACLU), 137–138
American Institute of Certified Public Accountants (AICPA), 37, 38–39
anger, coping after terrorism and, 59
antistalking statutes, 76–81
anxiety, police suicide and, 113
appeals, of conviction, 3
Armed Islamic Group (GIA), 9, 12
arraignment, 3
arrestees, DNA testing and, 137, 138
asset forfeiture, drug laws and, 178
Atkins, Daryl, 195, 200
Atta, Mohamed, 9, 13–14
authoritarian types, on juries, 117

B

bail restrictions, stalking and, 80
Bank of Credit & Commerce International (BCCI), 36
Bankers Trust, 36–37
Barings Bank, 36
Barnett, Jonathan David, 162
Beamer, Todd, 14
belonging, sense of, and gangs, 155
bench trial, 3
Best Buy Co., 23
bikers, 154
bin Laden, Osama, 9, 11, 12
"black-hat" hackers, 21
blindfolding, 118
Bloods, 156, 157
Boesky, Ivan, 35, 40
Bowden, Eric, 24
Brevard Correctional Institution, Florida, 150–151
broken windows theory, 103
Broward County, Florida, mental health courts in, 120, 121
BugNet, 24, 26–27
Building Blocks for Youth, 161, 166

C

California: parole in, 185; Proposition 21 in, 151–152
calls-for-service, 103
Canada, terrorism and, 12, 15
Canberra, Australia, 45–46
capital punishment: appeal of, 3; rethinking, 195–202

Cauthen, James, 198
celebrity, attitudes toward criminal justice and, 47–48
Cendant, 36
chaplains, police suicide and, 113
Charen, Mona, 92
Chase National Bank, 35
Chicago, Illinois, gangs in, 154
children: domestic violence and, 70–75; in justice system, 6–7
Children's Defense Fund, 63
China, 48
CIA (Central Intelligence Agency), 8, 9, 11, 12, 13
citizen review panels, 108
clergy, police suicide and, 113
Clinton, Bill, 12; on fighting crime, 102–103
CODIS system, 136
Columbia/HCA, 36
Community Oriented Policing Services (COPS), Office of, 102–103, 153
community policing, 17, 102–105; terrorism and, 85, 86, 88
community relations, with police, 108
competency, death penalty and, 202
Comprehensive Strategy for Serious, Violent, and Chronic Juvenile Offenders, 144
CompStat, 84, 87
computer crime, 19–27, 28–33, 104
computer scripts, 21
computer viruses, 21, 25, 28, 33
computer worms, 21, 25
computer-intrusion programs, 19
computers, use of, in photo-spread lineups, 135
confidentiality, computer crime and, 31
Constitution, U.S., and DNA testing, 137
Cornfeld, Bernie, 35
Cottages in the Pines, 121
Council for Responsible Genetics, 136
"crackers," 21
credibility, of witnesses, 134
credit card fraud, cyber-crime and, 19, 20, 22–23, 33
Credit Suisse First Boston (CSFB), 34
crime analysis, terrorism and, 84
criminal targeting, 102, 104, 105
Crips, 156, 157
critical thinking, about statistics, 63–65
Culp, Scott, 24
cybercrime. See computer crime
cyberstalking, 79–80

D

Dallas, Texas, treatment of children in domestic violence cases in, 72
Darrow, Clarence, 116
death penalty. See capital punishment
decentralization, of U.S. police forces, 16–17
decriminalization, of drugs, 175

Defense Department: biological samples and, 137; underreporting of computer crime and, 29, 30
depression: coping after terrorism and, 59; police suicide and, 113
DeWine, Mike, 121
Diallo, Amadou, 92
Diamond, Shari Seidman, 116, 118, 119
Dieter, Richard, 195, 197, 201, 202
Dilulio, John, 149
discretion, 6
distress, physical symptoms of, and coping after terrorism, 60
diversion from prosecution, 3
diversion-oriented courts, 120–122
DNA testing, 132; databases, 136–138; death penalty and, 195, 200
domestic violence, children and, 70–75
Dream Yard, 152
Drexel Burnham Lambert, 35, 40
driving while black (DWB), 104
drugs: interview with Anthony Papa on, 172–178; police corruption and, 108
Druid Heights Community Development Corp., due process and, 2
D'Souza, Dinesh, 92
Dunlap, Al, 34, 36

E

Early Identification System (EIS), for problem police officers, 98
Eighth Amendment, execution of mentally retarded and, 195, 201–202
electrical cartel, white-collar crime and, 35
embassy bombings, 11, 12
errors, by eyewitnesses, 132–133
Estes, Billie Sol, 35
ethics, in criminal justice, 106–109
ethnic gangs, 154
Europe, crime in, versus United States, 16–18
event analysis, terrorism and, 86
excitement, gangs and, 155
expert witnesses, 200; psychologists as, 134
"exploit scripts," 24
eyewitness testimony, 132–135

F

Farquharson, Atiba, 149–150
fear, coping after terrorism and, 59
Federal Bureau of Investigation (FBI), 8, 9, 11, 13; computer crime and, 32
Feinberg, Kenneth, 54–57
fingerprints, versus DNA, 136
Finkelstein, Howard, 120
Foley, Linda, 117, 119
Folk Nation, 156–157
Forbes, Walter, 36
Forty Little Thieves, 153
Forty Thieves, 153
Four Corner Hustlers, 156

Index

Four Nations, 156–157
Fourth Amendment, 87, 138
franchising, gangs and, 156
Frankel, Martin, 36
Freeh, Louis, 11

G

gangs, 153–159
Gangster Disciples, 156, 157
Gates, Bill, 26
General Accounting Office (GAO), 108
genetic discrimination, 136
Georgia, Senate Bill 440 in, 160–164, 165–169
Gibbery, Salvatore, 111
goodtime credits, 5
Goord, Glen, 174–175
grand juries, 3
"gray-hat" hackers, 21
Griffin, Ilona, 163
guilt, coping after terrorism and, 59

H

hackers, 21
Harris, David, 91
health-care product scams, 20
Healy, Timothy, 22
Hell's Angels, 154
helplessness, police suicide and, 111–112
Hendrickson, Chris, 152
Hickey, Eric, 51
Hispanic gangs, 154
Homeland Defense, 9, 10
homicide rate, in United States versus Europe, 18
hopelessness, police suicide and, 113
housing projects, crime rate and, 18
Houston County, Georgia, treatment of children in domestic violence cases in, 71, 73
Human Genome Project, 136

I

ICN Pharmaceuticals, 34
identity theft, 19, 20, 22–23, 33
Immigration and Naturalization Service (INS), released prisoners and, 191
India, gangs in, 154
Indianapolis, Indiana, gangs in, 155, 157
indictment, 3
information, issuance of, 3
innocent persons, death penalty and, 196–197, 198, 199
insanity defense, 202
Integrated Criminal Apprehension Program, 86
internal affairs, review of police misconduct by, 108
Internet access services fraud, 20
Internet auction fraud, 20
Internet Fraud Complaint Center (IFCC), 22, 33
investigation: as police strategy, 85; proactive, 86–87

investment scams, 20
Investors Overseas Service, 35
Irish immigrants, gangs and, 153
Islamic extremism, 10
isolation: coping after terrorism and, 60; police suicide and, 111, 113
Italian Mafia, 154

J

James, Frank, 154
James, Jessie, 154
jihad, 10
juries, 123–131
jury consulting, 116–119
jury trials, 10
Justice Department, computer crime and, 28
juvenile justice system, 6–7; sentencing guidelines and, 142–148; trying juveniles as adults and, 149–152, 160–164, 165–169

K

Kalven, Harry, Jr., 118
Kansas, overturning of antistalking law in, 78
Keating, Charles, 35
Keller, Robert, 162, 164
King, Rodney, 107
King County, Washington, mental health courts in, 120, 121
Kirscher, Barry E., 150
Kressel, Dorit F., 116, 117, 119
Kressel, Neil J., 116, 117, 119
Krueger, Ivar, 35

L

Latzer, Barry, 195, 198, 199, 202
Leeson, Nick, 36
legalization, of drugs, 175
Levin, Michael, 92, 93
Levitt, Arthur, 49
liberation theology, 173–174
Liebman, James, 197, 198
lifetime protection orders, stalking and, 80
Lincoln Savings & Loan, 35
lineups, 133, 135
Lloyd, Timothy, 21
loneliness, coping after terrorism and, 59
Long, Susan, 38
Lott, John, 16

M

MacDonald, Heather, 91–92
Mafia, 154
mandatory sentencing, parole and, 188
Mapp v. Ohio, 87
Maryland v. Wilson, 87
Massachusetts: case study of prisoner reentry in, 187–194; overturning of antistalking law in, 78
Maxie, Taylor, Jr., 152
McDaniel, Janice, 162

media: police corruption and, 107; public attitudes toward criminal justice and, 47–48
memory, of eyewitnesses, 132–133
mental health courts, 120–122
mentally retarded, execution of, 195, 200, 201–202
Mexico State v. Cohen, 87
Miami-Dade County, Florida, responding to problem police officers in, 97, 98
Michigan, overturning of antistalking law in, 78
Microsoft, 24
Milken, Michael, 35, 40
Miller, Zell, 166, 168
Minneapolis, Minnesota, responding to problem police officers in, 97, 99
modem hijacking, 20
money laundering, by Al Qaeda, 14
Mossad, 14
motorcycle gangs, 154
Moussaoui, Zacharias, 8, 9
Mozer, Paul, 36
multilevel marketing schemes, 20
Multnomah County, Oregon, treatment of children in domestic violence cases in, 71, 73
murder rate, in United States versus Europe, 18

N

National Association of Securities Dealers (NASD), 37, 38
National Institute of Justice, studies of, on police ethics, 108–109
National White Collar Crime Center, 33
Nelson, Evan, 200
New Breed, 155
New Jersey, racial profiling in, 92, 93
New Mexico v. Mann, 87
New Orleans, Louisiana, responding to problem police officers in, 97, 98, 99
New York City, New York, racial profiling in, 92–93
911 model, 103
noncriminal justice agencies, participation of, in criminal justice system, 2
Nosair, El Sayyid, 10, 12
numbness, coping after terrorism and, 58
nurture, gangs and, 155

O

O'Connor, Sandra Day, 199
Office of Community Corrections (OCC), in Massachusetts, 192
Office of Juvenile Justice and Delinquency Prevention (OJJDP), 144
online investment scams, 20
online vandalism, 21
Operation Weed and Seed, 153
OPTIONS, 121
Oregon, overturning of antistalking law in, 78
outlaw motorcycle gangs, 154
Owens, Richard, 40

P

panic, coping after terrorism and, 60
Panic, Milan, 34
Papa, Anthony, interview with, 172–178
parens patriae, doctrine of, 142, 143
parole, 5; inmate reentry in Massachusetts and, 187–194; trends in, 179–186
parole boards,180–181, 182, 183, 184–185, 188–189, 190
pastoral counseling, police suicide and, 113
patrolling: as police strategy, 85; target-oriented, 86
Penrod, Steven D., 116–117
People Nation, 157
pirates, 154
pleas, 3
police corruption, 106–109
Police Foundation, 109
police officers: responding to problem, 95–101; suicide and, 110–113; terrorism and, 84–90
Ponzi, Charles, 35
positive loitering, 17
post-traumatic stress disorder (PTSD), police suicide and, 110, 111
prisoner reentry, case study of, in Massachusetts, 187–194
prisoners, 4–5
privacy, threats to, 136
private sector, participation of, in criminal justice system, 2
proactive investigations, terrorism and, 86–87
probable cause, 3
problem-solving, 103
Professional Performance Enhancement Program (PPEP), problem police officers and, 97, 99
Progressive Sanctions Guidelines, for juvenile offenders in Texas, 144, 145
Proposition 21, in California, 151–152
protection orders, lifetime, and stalking, 80
pyramid schemes, computer, 20

R

race: attitudes toward criminal justice and, 42–43; death penalty and, 201; sentencing juveniles as adults and, 160–164, 165–169
racial profiling, 91–94, 102, 104–105, 138
rape victims, remaking of self and, 66–69
recidivism, 6
resentment, coping after terrorism and, 59
residential facilities, mental health, 121
reversals, death penalty and, 196–197, 198, 199
Rhode Island, overturning of antistalking law in, 78
Rich, Marc, 35
Riptech, Inc., 19, 21
Rockefeller Drug Laws, interview with Anthony Papa on, 172–178
Ross, Billie, 160, 162, 168
Ross, Glenwood, 160, 162, 168, 169
Ross, Glenwood, III, 160–161, 162, 168, 169

rotten apple theory, 106
Russian Mafia, 154
Ryan, George, 197

S

Saks, Michael, 116
Salomon Brothers, 36
Salt Lake County, Utah, treatment of children in domestic violence cases in, 71, 73
Samenow, Stanton, 200
Sampson, Robert J., 45
San Bernardino, California, mental health courts in, 120
San Diego, California, treatment of children in domestic violence cases in, 71, 72–73
SARA (Scanning, Analyzing, Response and Assessment), 84, 86, 158
School Safety and Juvenile Justice Reform Act, of Georgia, 165–166
"script kiddies," 21, 24
scripts, 21
Secure Socket Layer (SSL) protocol, 23
Securities and Exchange Commission (SEC), 34, 35, 39, 40
self-esteem, suicide and, 112
Senate Bill 440, in Georgia, 160–164, 165–169
sentencing: guidelines for, and juvenile justice, 142–148; length of, and crime, 17–18; options, 3–4; public attitudes toward, 45. *See also* mandatory sentencing; truth-in-sentencing
September 11, 2001, terrorist attacks, 8–15; victim compensation for, 54–57
Serial Murders and Their Victims (Hickey), 51
serial-murder profilers, 50–51
Shabazz-Diaab, Kameelah, 167
Sharp, Dudley, 197, 199, 201, 202
shock, coping after terrorism and, 58
sickle cell anemia, genetic discrimination and, 136
Sims, Glenn, 164, 165–166, 168–169
six-packs, 133
software companies, cyber-crime and, 24–27
Sotheby's, 36
special units, 17
spirituality, police suicide and, 110–113
Stack and Sway: The New Science of Jury Consulting (Kressel and Kressel), 116
stalking, 76–81
statistics, 63–65; importance of, and computer crime, 28–30
status offenses, 6
stress, police suicide and, 111
structure, gangs and, 155
suicide, police, and spirituality, 110–113
Sunbeam, 34, 36
Supreme Court, U.S., execution of mentally retarded and, 195, 200, 201–202
suspects, criminal, and due process, 2–3

T

"Take Away Guns" (TAG), 47

target-oriented patrolling, terrorism and, 86
Tate, Lionel, 149
Taylor, Jared, 91
Taylor-Thompson, Kim, 163–164
technology, as crime fighting tool, 102–105
teen courts, 146
terrorism, 8–15; coping after, 58–62; police strategies and, 84–90; victim compensation and, 54–57
Texas: overturning of antistalking law in, 78; Progressive Sanctions Guidelines for juvenile offenders in, 144, 145
tort reform, victim compensation funds and, 56
TRAC, 38
traffic stops: problem police officers and, 100; racial profiling and, 92–93; terrorism and, 85, 87
training, ethics, 108
transfer, juvenile justice and, 142
Traubman, Al, 36
travel scams, 20
Tremain, Johnny, 152
truth-in-sentencing, parole and, 182, 188, 189–190
Tyler, Tom R., 45

U

Uniform Crime Reporting (UCR) Program, 32
USS Cole, bombing of, 13

V

vacation scams, 20
Vesco, Robert, 35
victim compensation, for terrorist attacks, 54–57
victims: public attitudes toward, 43–44; rape, and remaking of self, 66–69
Violent Offender Incarceration and Truth-in-Sentencing (VOITIS), 182

W

Walker, A'Sheerah, 167
War on Drugs, interview with Anthony Papa on, 172–178
Waste Management, 36
weapon focus, of eyewitnesses, 132–133
Web cramming, 20
welfare, crime rate and, 18
Wheatley, Michael, 16
white-collar crime, 34–41
"white-hat" hackers, 21
Whitney, Richard, 35
Whren v. United States, 87
Wiggin, Albert, 35
Williams, Kim, 165–166, 168–169
World Trade Center bombing, 8, 10
Wynn, Aaron, 120

Z

Zeisel, Hans, 118
Zoot Suit Riots, 154

Test Your Knowledge Form

We encourage you to photocopy and use this page as a tool to assess how the articles in *Annual Editions* expand on the information in your textbook. By reflecting on the articles you will gain enhanced text information. You can also access this useful form on a product's book support Web site at *http://www.dushkin.com/online/*.

NAME: DATE:

TITLE AND NUMBER OF ARTICLE:

BRIEFLY STATE THE MAIN IDEA OF THIS ARTICLE:

LIST THREE IMPORTANT FACTS THAT THE AUTHOR USES TO SUPPORT THE MAIN IDEA:

WHAT INFORMATION OR IDEAS DISCUSSED IN THIS ARTICLE ARE ALSO DISCUSSED IN YOUR TEXTBOOK OR OTHER READINGS THAT YOU HAVE DONE? LIST THE TEXTBOOK CHAPTERS AND PAGE NUMBERS:

LIST ANY EXAMPLES OF BIAS OR FAULTY REASONING THAT YOU FOUND IN THE ARTICLE:

LIST ANY NEW TERMS/CONCEPTS THAT WERE DISCUSSED IN THE ARTICLE, AND WRITE A SHORT DEFINITION:

We Want Your Advice

ANNUAL EDITIONS revisions depend on two major opinion sources: one is our Advisory Board, listed in the front of this volume, which works with us in scanning the thousands of articles published in the public press each year; the other is you—the person actually using the book. Please help us and the users of the next edition by completing the prepaid article rating form on this page and returning it to us. Thank you for your help!

ANNUAL EDITIONS: Criminal Justice 03/04

ARTICLE RATING FORM

Here is an opportunity for you to have direct input into the next revision of this volume.
We would like you to rate each of the articles listed below, using the following scale:

1. **Excellent: should definitely be retained**
2. **Above average: should probably be retained**
3. **Below average: should probably be deleted**
4. **Poor: should definitely be deleted**

Your ratings will play a vital part in the next revision.
Please mail this prepaid form to us as soon as possible.
Thanks for your help!

RATING	ARTICLE	RATING	ARTICLE
	1. What Is the Sequence of Events in the Criminal Justice System?		33. Inmate Reentry and Post-Release Supervision: The Case of Massachusetts
	2. The Road to September 11		34. Rethinking the Death Penalty
	3. Crime Without Punishment		
	4. Cyber-Crimes		
	5. Making Computer Crime Count		
	6. Enough Is Enough		
	7. Trust and Confidence in Criminal Justice		
	8. So You Want to Be a Serial-Murderer Profiler ...		
	9. What Is a Life Worth?		
	10. Coping After Terrorism		
	11. Telling the Truth About Damned Lies and Statistics		
	12. Violence and the Remaking of a Self		
	13. Prosecutors, Kids, and Domestic Violence Cases		
	14. Strengthening Antistalking Statutes		
	15. The Changing Roles and Strategies of the Police in Time of Terror		
	16. Racial Profiling and Its Apologists		
	17. Early Warning Systems: Responding to the Problem Police Officer		
	18. Crime Story: The Digital Age		
	19. Ethics and Criminal Justice: Some Observations on Police Misconduct		
	20. Spirituality and Police Suicide: A Double-Edged Sword		
	21. Jury Consulting on Trial		
	22. Opting in to Mental Health Courts		
	23. Anatomy of a Verdict		
	24. Looking Askance at Eyewitness Testimony		
	25. The Creeping Expansion of DNA Data Banking		
	26. Sentencing Guidelines and the Transformation of Juvenile Justice in the 21st Century		
	27. Hard-Time Kids		
	28. Gangs in Middle America: Are They a Threat?		
	29. Trouble With the Law		
	30. Doubting the System		
	31. Kicking Out the Demons by Humanizing the Experience—An Interview With Anthony Papa		
	32. Trends in State Parole		

(Continued on next page)

**NO POSTAGE
NECESSARY
IF MAILED
IN THE
UNITED STATES**

BUSINESS REPLY MAIL
FIRST-CLASS MAIL PERMIT NO. 84 GUILFORD CT

POSTAGE WILL BE PAID BY ADDRESSEE

**McGraw-Hill/Dushkin
530 Old Whitfield Street
Guilford, Ct 06437-9989**

ABOUT YOU

Name   Date

Are you a teacher? ❐   A student? ❐
Your school's name

Department

Address   City   State   Zip

School telephone #

YOUR COMMENTS ARE IMPORTANT TO US!

Please fill in the following information:
For which course did you use this book?

Did you use a text with this ANNUAL EDITION?   ❐ yes ❐ no
What was the title of the text?

What are your general reactions to the *Annual Editions* concept?

Have you read any pertinent articles recently that you think should be included in the next edition? Explain.

Are there any articles that you feel should be replaced in the next edition? Why?

Are there any World Wide Web sites that you feel should be included in the next edition? Please annotate.

May we contact you for editorial input?   ❐ yes ❐ no
May we quote your comments? ❐ yes ❐ no